Entrepreneurship in Western Europe

A Contextual Perspective

Entrepreneurship in Western Europe

A Contextual Perspective

Léo-Paul Dana
Montpellier Business School, France

World Scientific

NEW JERSEY • LONDON • SINGAPORE • BEIJING • SHANGHAI • HONG KONG • TAIPEI • CHENNAI • TOKYO

Published by

World Scientific Publishing Europe Ltd.

57 Shelton Street, Covent Garden, London WC2H 9HE

Head office: 5 Toh Tuck Link, Singapore 596224

USA office: 27 Warren Street, Suite 401-402, Hackensack, NJ 07601

Library of Congress Cataloging-in-Publication Data
Names: Dana, Léo-Paul, author.
Title: Entrepreneurship in Western Europe : a contextual perspective /
Léo-Paul Dana (Montpellier Business School, France).
Description: New Jersey : World Scientific, [2017] | Includes bibliographical references.
Identifiers: LCCN 2017005933 | ISBN 9781783267934 (hc : alk. paper)
Subjects: LCSH: Entrepreneurship--Europe, Western--History.
Classification: LCC HB615 .D2933 2017 | DDC 338/.04094--dc23
LC record available at https://lccn.loc.gov/2017005933

British Library Cataloguing-in-Publication Data
A catalogue record for this book is available from the British Library.

Desk Editor: Kalpana Bharanikumar

Typeset by Stallion Press
Email: enquiries@stallionpress.com

Printed in Singapore

Dedicated to

Naomï Josephine Dana

&

Jake Dana

Foreword

This book by Léo-Paul Dana invites the reader on an enticing journey across Western Europe to discover the fundamental elements of socio-economic life, their evolution and their capacity to ensure populations' well being over time. He did it with the talent of a humanist economist, fascinated by the history of peoples and the specific cultures of countries that, together, shape the context. That context is particularly rich and diverse in Europe, a place of brilliant civilisation for more than two thousand years. In spite of the European unification process, still in progress, profound diversity does subsist and will probably and hopefully continue. Intersections of cultures can create explosions of remarkable innovations, according to F. Johansson, who called this phenomenon the Medici Effect.[1]

Yet, the analysis of the very diverse European context is not the only interesting contribution of this book principally dedicated to entrepreneurship, referring to the economic undertaking of entrepreneurs. Entrepreneurship is really the decisive factor of economic and social evolution through real value creation — be it of quantitative or qualitative order.[2] A productive firm is not just an abstract black box transforming inputs into outputs through different models of

[1] F. Johansson (2004), *The Medici Effect; Breakthrough Insights at the Intersection of Ideas, Concepts & Cultures*, Boston: Harvard Business School Press.

[2] See S. Urban, and A. Zucchella (2011), "Building the Future Through Real Value Creation and Innovation: Achieving Competitiveness in a Chaotic World," *International Journal of Entrepreneurship and Small Business* **13**(2), pp. 126–149.

processing; it is also, and probably first, a human community working together to create demanded products and services. *A Study of Economics as if People Mattered* is the subtitle of the E. F. Schumacher's famous book, *Small is Beautiful* (1973), and J. Pear added *Small is Still Beautiful* (2001).

Of course every biological or organisational life has small beginnings. Then the struggle for life soon interferes, be it through a process of "natural" selection (Darwin, 1859)[3] or through decisions taken by individual men (be they entrepreneurs, or managers, or conductors, or innovators, etc.). In fact, firms, small or large, are institutions created by men to serve the purposes of men. "If it can be admitted that to some extent firms operate automatically in accordance with the principles governing the mechanism constructed, [...] the importance of human decisions and motives, of ethics and public policy [...] needs great attention,"[4] This assertion raises the question of the respective importance of context and entrepreneurial free will. As illustrated by Professor Dana, this free-will is a critical factor of socio-economic development and explains that no hypothetical general laws may precisely predict social future. Still, managers of a firm may lay down certain rules, which are determined by some ideal interrelationships of parts of the firm (concerning quasi-automatic operations or routine decisions), but structural or breaking choices are induced in the brain of individuals. That does not mean that the context is not important: it facilitates or handicaps entrepreneurial initiatives, but the link between context and entrepreneurship is not a strict deterministic one. The variety of European ventures, as this book shows, is marked by uncertainty and complexity, that means that the future is not a given and that the unforeseeable is always possible.[5] One of the key actors of change and progress is the entrepreneur.

[3] C. Darwin (1859), *On the Origin of Species*, London: John Murray.

[4] E. Penrose (1971), *The Growth of Firms, Middle East Oil and Other Essays*, London: Frank Cass & Co., p. 6.

[5] I. Prigogine (2000), "Is the Future a Given?" in M. Ricciardelli, S. Urban, and K. Nanopoulos, Eds., *Globalization and Multicultural Societies; Some Views from Europe*, Notre Dame, Indiana: University of Notre Dame Press, p. 9.

Probably the first author who paid attention to the figure of the entrepreneur was Richard Cantillon, a French banker with Irish origins, who published in 1755 an *Essai sur la Nature du Commerce en Général* in which he delivered an overall view about economic activity. He was especially interested in the role of men in the process of wealth creation. He considered the entrepreneur as an agent playing a major role in the regulation of supply and demand, acting between capitalists (owner or lender) on the one side and workers on the other. The entrepreneur is the man who is responsible for economic transactions by engaging in pure arbitrage, buying at a certain price and *selling at varying prices*. Thus he is risk taking, but as an arbitragist, he is not necessarily an innovator.[6]

This was not exactly the idea of Jean-Baptiste Say (1767–1832), involved in textile industry before becoming a famous economist teaching industrial economics at a prestigious college for engineers and at the *College de France*, both in Paris. He was a contemporary of Ricardo and Malthus but did not share their rather pessimistic and deterministic analysis. Say demonstrated with his so-called *théorie des debouchés* (theory of outlets) that production creates its demand — through self-supported channels of circulation. The more a system is able to produce, the more it will be distributed. The products' supply creates automatically the products' demand through linked distribution of income (for the contributors to the production process) and revenue collected by the state. Hence, clearly socio-economic development is dependent on entrepreneurial dynamism. The creator of wealth is the entrepreneur i.e., a manager placed between idea and action, with specific characteristics like courage, risk acceptance, faith in chance and co-ordination abilities.

Later, the main contribution to entrepreneurship theory came from the Austrian school, in contrast with the black holes (according to Daneke[7]) in entrepreneurship analysis during the dominance of

[6] See A. Zucchella and P. Scabini (2007), *International Entrepreneurship: Theoretical Foundations and Practices*, New York: Palgrave/Macmillan, pp. 58–79.

[7] G. A. Daneke (1998), "Beyond Schumpeter: Nonlinear Economics and Evolution of the US Information System," *Journal of Socio-Economics* 27(1), pp. 97–115.

the orthodox classical and neo-classical theory period. Von Mises, Hayek, Kirzner dedicated a large place to "human action" — but the most famous equilibrium-breaker was obviously Joseph Schumpeter, still referenced by many authors. He defined entrepreneurship as new combinations including the doing of new things or the doing of things that are already being done in a new way.

This synthetic and clear definition covers a large range of entrepreneurial possibilities: the creation of small businesses, the development of medium sized or large firms, the creation of new products, services, business models or organisational arrangements, the implementation of ideas or scientific discoveries into innovations, the transformation of social or societal routines, the acceptance of values (like respect of human dignity, fundamental rights, sustainable development considerations), etc.

The thinking of Schumpeter has been relayed and discussed by François Perroux[8] who advocated the role of entrepreneur as a "motive force" in different contexts, small or large enterprises, private or public organisations. In consideration of general interdependence and the dynamics of development, the entrepreneur spirit and handling is of major importance. Since the beginning of the industrial era, capitalism has been modified by the deliberate action of actors and not by the workings of an inexorable blind mechanism. The entrepreneur is one of the most creative actors.

Different kinds of entrepreneurs do exist: those who create their personal business with their traditional handicrafts skills, others who begin their entrepreneurial activity in a garage (startup creators with new scientific knowledge or specific expertise), others with their enthusiasm for achieving something useful, others with their sense of responsibility regarding collectivity, others just in order to survive because of the reluctance of the labour market to give them a chance, still others supported by a large firm (intrapreneurship), etc. All these cases do underline the inherent characteristic of human

[8] F. Perroux (1965), *La Pensée Économique de Joseph Schumpeter: Les Dynamiques du Capitalisme*, Geneva: Droz. See Also: F. Perroux (1983), *A New Concept of Development: Basic Tenets*, London: Croom Helm/Unesco.

beings to be creative, to break away from established patterns and to compose something new. Entrepreneurship is a way to give real life to new ideas of change. It is the human condition to continuously innovate to adjust the evolving social context.

Finally, the implicit question inspired by Léo-Paul Dana is the following: Does a Western European entrepreneurship model exist? The answer is not easy to deliver, for at least two reasons: First, Europe is a very diversified cultural and political area; it is not a homogeneous set making visible a clear relation between context and entrepreneurship practices. Second, entrepreneurship is not a simple concept; it is a phenomenon with multiple facets. Nevertheless, some common aspects may be deciphered.

One trend has been analysed by the author and his McGill University colleagues, calling it symbiotic entrepreneurship.[9] Indeed, Europe today is rich with interdependence,[10] rather than independence.

Networking of knowledge, techniques, human and institutional relations became a general phenomenon in modern life, paving the way for an open social system.[11] This may change in different manners the evolution of the relations between the enterprise and its context. Entrepreneurial dynamics are concerned generally speaking, but in different ways depending on spatial, structural as well as time acceleration or behavioural differences.

The Global Entrepreneurship Monitor (GEM) grouping participating economies worldwide, distinguishes three levels of production systems: factor-driven (dominated by agriculture and extraction business), efficiency-driven (with increased reliance on economies of scale, with capital-intensive large organisations more dominant), and

---

[9] L. Dana, H. Etemad, and R. W. Wright (2008), "Toward a Paradigm of Symbiotic Entrepreneurship," *International Journal of Entrepreneurship and Small Business* 5(2), pp. 109–126.

[10] See S. Urban and S. Vendemini (1992), *European Strategic Alliances: Cooperative Corporate Strategies in the New Europe*, Oxford: B. Blackwell.

[11] See G. M. Golinelli (2010), *Viable Systems Approach (VSA): Governing Business Dynamics*, Milan: CEDAM.

innovation-driven (businesses are more knowledge intensive, and the service sector expands strongly). In efficiency-driven economies, the supply chain niches are opened up for small and medium sized enterprises. In an innovation-driven economy, a great potential for innovative entrepreneurial activity does exist. This later category of entrepreneurial development is nowadays, characteristic of Europe, especially in the fields of electronics, data processing, biotechnologies, sustainable development promoting technologies, defence and security techniques, health care, surgery research and applications, and agribusiness.

Nonetheless, a shadow is silhouetted on Western European entrepreneurship dynamics, despite the forces of historical and cultural dominance: that is the aging population, especially in some countries like Germany, Italy, and Spain. Active entrepreneurship is linked to faith in the future, creative enthusiasm, acceptance of risk and responsibility, positive motivation in a turbulent and uncertain world, and leadership willingness. These attributes are more often present in younger populations. The challenge for European countries is therefore to develop new entrepreneurial forces, eventually in integrating immigrants' entrepreneurship vocation and belief. This would be a wonderful message in favour of tolerance, peace and diversity richness in conformity with European enlightenment civilisation.

Léo-Paul Dana demonstrates in every chapter of this book that people count. Human quality is the decisive factor of progress. We are grateful to the author for this message, anchored in the past, and key to having confidence in a worthwhile future.

Sabine Urban
Professor Emeritus
University of Strasbourg
HuManiS Research Centre
France

Preface

I owe many thanks to the patient team at Imperial College Press in London and at World Scientific in Singapore. It had been agreed that the manuscript for this book would be delivered in 2011. However, I lost my home and also my office at the University of Canterbury with the Christchurch earthquakes. My mother died of earthquake injuries; I was no longer able to walk as my spine was severely damaged. I required complicated surgery at the spinal column and many months of rehabilitation, slowly learning to walk as does a child. By the time I was well enough to complete the book, much of what I had written was outdated and required rewriting. It also took time to organise for new photographs. I express much gratitude to the publisher for considerable patience. At last, here is the book … enjoy!

Léo-Paul Dana
Professor, Montpellier Business School
Marie Curie Fellow, Princeton University

About the Author

Léo-Paul Dana, a graduate of McGill University and of HEC Montreal, is Professor at Montpellier Business School and a member of the Entrepreneurship & Innovation chair, which is part of LabEx Entrepreneurship (University of Montpellier, France). This "laboratory of excellence" is funded by the French government in recognition of high-level research initiatives in the human and natural sciences (Labex Entreprendre, ANR-10-Labex-11-01). He has published extensively in a variety of leading journals including the *British Food Journal*, *Cornell Quarterly*, *Entrepreneurship & Regional Development*, *Entrepreneurship: Theory & Practice*, *International Small Business Journal*, *Journal of Small Business Management*, the *Journal of World Business*, and *Small Business Economics*.

Acknowledgements

Early versions of every chapter were sent to members of the Board of Advisors for review. The author expresses kind gratitude to each of the following who provided constructive feedback.

Board of Advisors

- Pekka AIKIO, Past President, Sámi Parliament, Finland
- Ulla AIKIO-PUOSKARI, Oulu University, Oulu, Finland
- Simo ALARUIKKA, Enontekiön Kunta, Enontekiö, Finland
- Pia ARENIUS, Université de Lausanne, Lausanne, Switzerland
- Selena AURELI, University of Bologna, Bologna, Italy
- Rico J. BALDEGGER, Director, School of Management Fribourg, Fribourg, Switzerland
- Irène BERNHARD, University West, Trollhättan, Sweden
- Carmine BIANCHI, University of Palermo, Palermo, Italy
- Piervito BIANCHI, University of Foggia, Foggia, Italy
- Alexander BIRDTHISTLE, Munster, Ireland
- Jean BONNET, Université de Caen, Caen, France
- Walter BORNETT, Executive Director, Austrian Institute for SME Research, Vienna, Austria
- Tatiana BOUZDINE-CHAMEEVA, Kedge Business School, Bordeaux, France
- Udo BRIXY, Institute for Employment Research, Nuremberg, Germany

- Guido CAPALDO, Università degli Studi di Napoli Frederico II, Naples, Italy
- Mark C. CASSON, Director, Centre for Institutions and Economic History, Henley Business School, University of Reading, Reading, UK
- Alicia CODURAS, Instituto de Empresa, Madrid, Spain
- Julio Orlando de CASTRO, IE Business School, Madrid, Spain
- Petra de GROOT, Vrije Universiteit Amsterdam, Amsterdam, The Netherlands
- Christopher DE MARCO, L'école de Management Audencia, Nantes, France
- Susanne DURST, Universität Liechtenstein, Vaduz, Liechtenstein
- Martijn DRIESSEN, University of Groningen, The Netherlands
- Susanne DURST, University of Skövde, Sweden
- Ingi Rúnar EÐVARÐSSON, University of Iceland, Reykjavík, Iceland
- Maria ELO, Turku School of Economics, Turku, Finland
- Marlene ENGLER, Liechtenstein Marketing, Vaduz, Liechtenstein
- Ulfar ERLINGSSON, Reykjavík University, Iceland
- Alain FAYOLLE, EM Lyon, France
- Susanna FELLMAN, University of Gothenburg, Sweden
- João J. FERREIRA, University of Beira Interior, Covilhã, Portugal
- Filipe FIGUEIREDO, Lisbon, Portugal
- Mário FRANCO, University of Beira Interior, Covilhã, Portugal
- Alexander FUST, Universität St. Gallen, Switzerland
- William B. GARTNER, Copenhagen Business School, Denmark
- Oliver GASSMANN, Director, Universität St. Gallen, Switzerland
- Paul GEUVERS, Open University, Heerlen, The Netherlands
- Elisa GIACOSA, University of Turin, Italy
- Philippe GIULIANI, Montpellier Business School, France
- Rüdiger GOLDSCHMIDT, Universität Stuttgart, Germany
- Dietmar GRICHNIK, Heinrich Heine University, Düsseldorf, Germany
- John GRIN, University of Amsterdam, The Netherlands
- Gilles GUIEU, Aix-Marseille Université, Marseille, France
- Antonia Madrid GUIJARRO, Universidad Politécnica de Cartagena, Spain

- Rainer HARMS, University of Twent, The Netherlands
- Kirsi HELENIUS, City Archives, Turku, Finland
- Antoine HRON, Luxinnovation, Luxembourg
- Frank JANSSEN, Louvain School of Management, Louvain, Belgium
- Brian T. JONES, Leeds Beckett University, Leeds, UK
- Peter JONES, Professor Emeritus, University of Gloucestershire, Cheltenham, UK
- Gerd JUNNE, University of Amsterdam, Amsterdam, The Netherlands
- Rachida JUSTO, Vice Dean of Research, Instituto de Empresa, Madrid, Spain
- Hannu KANGASNIEMI, Sámi Parliament, Inari, Finland
- Hugo KANTIS, Universidad Nacional de General Sarmiento, Buenos Aires, Argentina
- Christian KARITNIG, Fachhochschule Vorarlberg University of Applied Sciences, Dornbirn, Austria
- Charlie KARLSSON, Professor Emeritus, Jönköping University, Jönköping, Sweden
- Alexander KESSLER, Senior Researcher, Austrian Institute for SME Research, Vienna, Austria
- Pertti KETTUNEN, Professor Emeritus, University of Jyväskylä, Jyväskylä, Finland
- Datis KHAJEHEIAN, Aalborg University, Aalborg, Denmark
- Lars KOLVEREID, Nord University, Bodø, Norway
- Kim KLYVER, University of Southern Denmark, Kolding, Denmark
- Sascha KRAUS, University of Liechtenstein, Vaduz, Liechtenstein
- Thomas LACROIX, Université de Poitiers, Poitiers, France
- Anja LECKEL, RWTH Aachen University, Aachen, Germany
- Joao Carlos Correia LEITAO, Universidade da Beira Interior, Covilhã, Portugal
- Jan LEPOUTRE, ESSEC Business School, Cergy-Pontoise, France
- Georg LICHT, Centre for European Economic Research, Mannheim, Germany
- Michel MARCHESNAY, Professor Emeritus, Université de Montpellier, Montpellier, France

- Carlos Jerez MARROQUIN, Universitat de València, Valencia, Spain
- Michela C. MASON, Università degli Studi di Udine, Udine, Italy
- Enno MASUREL, Vrije Universiteit Amsterdam, Amsterdam, The Netherlands
- Alberto MATTIACCI, Facoltà di Economia, Università di Siena, Siena, Italy
- Gerard McELWEE, University of Huddersfield, Huddersfield, UK
- Dave McEVOY, Professor Emeritus, Liverpool John Moores University, Liverpool, UK
- Asko MIETTINEN, Tampere University of Technology, Tampere, Finland
- Maria MINNITI, Babson College, Wellesley, Massachusetts, USA
- Tuulikki MOISIO, UPM, Valkeakoski, Finland
- Susan MUELLER, Universität St.Gallen, St.Gallen, Switzerland
- Josef MUGLER, Institut für Betriebswirtschaftslehre der Klein- und Mittelbetriebe, Wirtschaftsuniversität Wien, Vienna, Austria
- Ludger MÜLLER-WILLE, McGill University, Montreal, Canada
- Emer Ní BHRADAIGH, Dublin City University, Dublin, Ireland
- Seija A. NIEMI, University of Turku, Turku, Finland
- Eva-Lena Lindster NORBERG, Umeå University, Umeå, Sweden
- Jean Jacques OBRECHT, Professor Emeritus, Université de Strasbourg, Strasbourg, France
- Catarina Reis OLIVEIRA, Director, Observatory for Migration, Lisbon, Portugal
- Robin PALMER, Professor Emeritus, Rhodes University, Grahamstown, South Africa
- Francesco PASTORE, Seconda Università di Napoli, Naples, Italy
- Elisabeth T. PEREIRA, Universidade de Aveiro, Aveiro, Portugal
- Mike PETERS, University of Innsbruck, Innsbruck, Austria
- Orlando PETIZ, Minho University, Braga, Portugal
- J. Hanns PICHLER, Vienna University of Economics and Business, Vienna, Austria
- José Carlos PINHO, University of Minho, Braga, Portugal

- Cristina PONSIGLIONE, Università degli Studi di Napoli Frederico II, Naples, Italy
- Jan POSTEMA, Open University, Heerlen, The Netherlands
- Peter PREISENDOERFER, Institute for Sociology, Universität Mainz, Mainz, Germany
- Ruth RAMA, Spanish Council for Scientific Research, Madrid, Spain
- Jan RATH, University of Amsterdam, Amsterdam, The Netherlands
- Liisa REMES, University of Jyväskylä, Jyväskylä, Finland
- Shahamak REZAEI, Roskilde University, Roskilde, Denmark
- Harald RHOMBERG, Municipal Archives, Dornbirn, Austria
- Ruth RIOS-MORALES, Zurich University of Applied Sciences, Winterthur, Switzerland
- Carel ROESSINGH, Vrije Universiteit Amsterdam, The Netherlands
- Dietmar ROESSL, Vienna University of Economics and Business Administration, Vienna, Austria
- Susanne SANDBERG, Linnéuniversitet, Kalmar, Sweden
- Ursula SCHINZEL, United Business Institutes, Wiltz, Luxembourg
- Jan-Florian SCHLAPFNER, Department of Economic and Social Geography, University of Cologne, Cologne, Germany
- Karl-Heinz SCHMIDT, Universität Gesamthochschule, Paderborn, Germany
- Jürgen SCHMUDE, University of Munich, Munich, Germany
- Thomas SCHOTT, University of Southern Denmark, Odense, Denmark
- Felix SCHÜßLER, University of Liechtenstein, Vaduz, Liechtenstein
- Pau SERRA del POZO, Diputació de Barcelona, Barcelona, Spain
- Per SERVAIS, University of Southern Denmark, Odense, Denmark
- Janne SEURUJÄRVI, Director, Inari Municipal Business Company, Ivalo, Finland
- Filippo SGROI, University of Palermo, Palermo, Italy
- Ana Paula SILVA, Manchester Business School, Manchester, UK
- Stiina SIRKIÄ-RANTALA, Secretary to Mayor, City of Valkeakoski, Finland

- Robert SMITH, University of the West of Scotland, Dumfries, UK
- Martine SPENCE, University of Ottawa, Ottawa, Canada
- Philip STEINBERG, University of Wuppertal, Wuppertal, Germany
- Rolf STERNBERG, University of Hannover, Hannover, Germany
- Andreas STROBL, Universität Innsbruck, Innsbruck, Austria
- Jan ULIJN, Professor Emeritus, Technische Universiteit Eindhoven, Eindhoven, The Netherlands
- Sabine URBAN, Professor Emeritus, Université de Strasbourg, Strasbourg, France
- Marijke van der VEEN, Dutch Institute for Knowledge Intensive Entrepreneurship, Enschede, The Netherlands
- Frank van HELMOND, Open University, Heerlen, The Netherlands
- Daan van SOEST, University of Tilburg, Tilburg, The Netherlands
- Lex van TEEFFELEN, University of Applied Sciences, Utrecht, The Netherlands
- Jan VANG, Aalborg University, Aalborg, Denmark
- Andreas WEH, Fachhochschule Vorarlberg University of Applied Sciences, Dornbirn, Austria
- Isabell WELPE, Ludwig-Maximilians University, Munich, Germany
- Friederike WELTER, University of Siegen, Siegen, Germany
- Karl WENNBERG, Stockholm School of Economics, Stockholm, Sweden
- Colin C. WILLIAMS, Professor of Public Policy and Associate Dean (Research), Sheffield University Management School, Sheffield, UK
- Lorenzo ZANNI, Rector Delegate for Technology Transfer, University of Siena, Siena, Italy

Contents

Chapter 1

Introduction

Irish economist Richard Cantillon (1680–1734) defined the French word *entrepreneur* as a person taking the risk to work for oneself (Cantillon, 1755). This includes the vendor at an impromptu stall and the organ grinder (Exhibit 1.1).

An aristocrat industrialist, and French economist, Jean-Baptiste Say (1767–1832) defined the entrepreneur as the agent who "unites all means of production and who finds in the value of the products ... the re-establishment of the entire capital he employs, and the value of the wages, the interest, and the rent which he pays, as well as the profits belonging to himself" (1816, pp. 28–29). Fraser (1937) associated entrepreneurs with the management of a business unit, profit taking, business innovation and uncertainty bearing. Belshaw argued, "an entrepreneur is someone who takes the initiative in administering resources. He is probably not an entrepreneur unless he does undertake ordinary management tasks" (1955, p. 147). Casson elaborated, "an entrepreneur is someone who specializes in taking judgemental decisions about the coordination of scarce resources" (1982, p. 10).

Gartner (1989) defined entrepreneurship as the creation of new organisations. The Gartner (1990) Delphi study linked entrepreneurship to individuals with unique personality characteristics and abilities.

Others focused on innovation. Schumpeter wrote, "The carrying out of new combinations we call 'enterprise'; the individuals whose function it is to carry them out we call 'entrepreneurs'" (1934,

Exhibit 1.1 Vendors and organ grinder; photo © 2017 Léo-Paul Dana.

p. 74). Scase and Goffee explained, "They are seen as risk-takers and innovators who reject the relative security of employment in large organisations to create wealth and accumulate wealth" (1987, p. 1). Given that Schumpeterian innovators are relatively few, this book accepts the notion that small and medium-sized enterprises (SMEs) comprise the more common flagship of entrepreneurship — as described by Cantillon (1755) — in the broadest sense.

Based on the classical definition of the word entrepreneurship, which can be traced to the German *Unternehmung* (literally: undertaking) and to the French *entreprendre* (literally: between taking), in this book, the word entrepreneur refers to "an individual who earns his livelihood by exercising some control over the means of production and produces more than he can consume in order to sell (or exchange) it for ... income" (Dana, 1995a, pp. 57–58). Therefore, in this volume, the word entrepreneur includes the self-employed, as well as the founder or current owner of a business entity, usually a small or medium firm and sometimes a large one.

There are also different definitions of SMEs. In Australia, small firms have fewer than 20 employees, except small manufacturers, which have up to 99. In Canada, a small service firm has up to 49 employees, while a small manufacturer may have up to 499. In Japan, a firm with up to 250 employees is deemed to be small. In the United States, a small business may have up to 500 employees.

Prior to standardisation, different countries within Europe had diverse definitions: In Italy, a microenterprise could have up to 100 employees while a small enterprise had 101–300 employees. In the Netherlands, a business with nine or fewer employees was a small enterprise, while 10 or more constituted a medium-sized firm. In Portugal, a medium enterprise required 100 or more employees, while in Spain it was at least 500. In Sweden the term SME applied to firms with fewer than 200 employees.

Until 1996, the European Union defined an SME as having fewer than 500 employees. In April 1996, the European Commission adopted the following definitions:

- SMEs are independent firms with fewer than 250 employees and have either an annual turnover not exceeding ECU[1] 40 million, or a balance sheet total not exceeding ECU 27 million.
- The small enterprise has fewer than 50 employees and has either an annual turnover not exceeding ECU 7 million or an annual balance-sheet total not exceeding ECU 5 million and conforms to criterion of independence.

[1] The European Currency Unit (ECU) was the predecessor of the euro.

- Independent enterprises are those which are not owned, as to 25% or more of the capital or the voting rights are held by one enterprise, or jointly by several enterprises, falling outside the definition of an SME or a small enterprise, whichever may apply.[2]

Among several later definitions, SMEs were defined as independent firms (i.e., other companies' share of ownership could not exceed 25%), with fewer than 250 employees, and annual sales not exceeding 20,000,000 euro.

Since January 1, 2005, an enterprise is officially considered to be any entity engaged in an economic activity, irrespective of its legal form. This includes, the self-employed as well as family businesses, partnerships and associations that are regularly engaged in an economic activity. European Commission definitions have been as follows:

- Microenterprises are firms with up to nine full-time-equivalent employees — including owner–managers — and whose annual turnover or annual balance sheet is below 2,000,000 euro.
- Small businesses have between 11 and 49 employees inclusively, and sales of up to 10,000,000 euro.
- Medium-sized enterprises have 50, and up to 250 employees, with sales not exceeding 50,000,000 euro and an annual balance sheet not exceeding 43,000,000 euro.

The Context

"Entrepreneurship was born in Europe" (Fayolle, Kyrö, and Ulijn, 2005, p. 4). In fact, the concept of the entrepreneur first appeared in 1437, in a French dictionary (Landström, 1999). Pioneers of entrepreneurship theory include Cantillon (1755) and Mill (1848), both Europeans. Entrepreneurship as a social science came to America later, with great minds like Ely and Hess (1893, p. 95). From a pedagogical perspective, Groen, Ulijn, and Fayolle (2006)

[2] *Source*: European Commission Recommendation 96/280/EC.

suggested that entrepreneurship has been so far very much an American concept; nevertheless, entrepreneurship in Europe has been gaining importance, as is the small business sector. According to Mugler (1998), the renaissance of the small business sector in Europe has been a spill-over of the sector's revival initiated in the United States.

Reynolds (1997) noted that the expansion of markets has not been associated with an expanded role for larger firms; instead, smaller firms are filling niche roles (Buckley, 1997; Malaise, 1988). Fotopoulos and Spence (1998) suggested that small firms use survival strategies and overcome barriers to entry, and Kemp and Lutz (2006) found that microfirms perceive lower barriers to entry than medium-sized and large businesses. In fact, society needs SMEs to undertake functions that multinationals do not do because of the opportunity cost involved. SMEs often excel in niche markets. The European Charter for Small Enterprises, adopted by the General Affairs Council, recognised small firms as the backbone of the European economy.

The purpose of this book is to provide an introduction to entrepreneurship in countries of Western Europe. As discussed by Kaynak and Jallat, this "will necessitate consideration of the broader social, cultural, and legal-political systems" (2004, p. 5). *History will be emphasised* because, "Progress, far from consisting in change, depends on retentiveness. When change is absolute there remains no being to improve and no direction is set for possible improvement ... Those who cannot remember the past are condemned to repeat it" (Santayana, 1905, Volume 1, p. 284).

Bamford (1987) suggested that SMEs are strongly shaped by historical factors. History shapes countries — and countries shape the environment for entrepreneurship. The Armistice signed November 11, 1918 brought a truce to the Great War (World War I), but it was the Treaty of Versailles of 1919 that fixed new borders. World War II and events in the Balkans further changed the map of Europe. Political entities are born; they grow and shrink, but they do not always correspond to nations — people sharing a culture, language, and entrepreneurial outlook.

Over the years, economic power has shifted across Europe. Sombart noted, "One of the most important facts in the growth of modern economic life is the removal of the centre of economic activity from the nations of Southern Europe — the Italians, Spaniards, and Portuguese, with whom must be reckoned some South German lands — to those of the North-West — the Dutch, the French, the English and the North Germans" (1913, p. 11).

Indeed, Europe has a very rich history, including important wars as well as prosperous times of peace. In Paris, the *Arc de Triomphe* (Exhibit 1.2) is a reminder of Napoleon's victories. In some countries, including France, the 11th of November is a legal holiday, ever since 1919 (see Exhibit 1.3).

In 1944, Belgium, the Netherlands and Luxembourg entered the Benelux customs union. In 1951, Belgium, France, the Federal Republic of Germany, Italy, Luxembourg and the Netherlands signed the Treaty of Paris creating the European Coal and Steel Community.

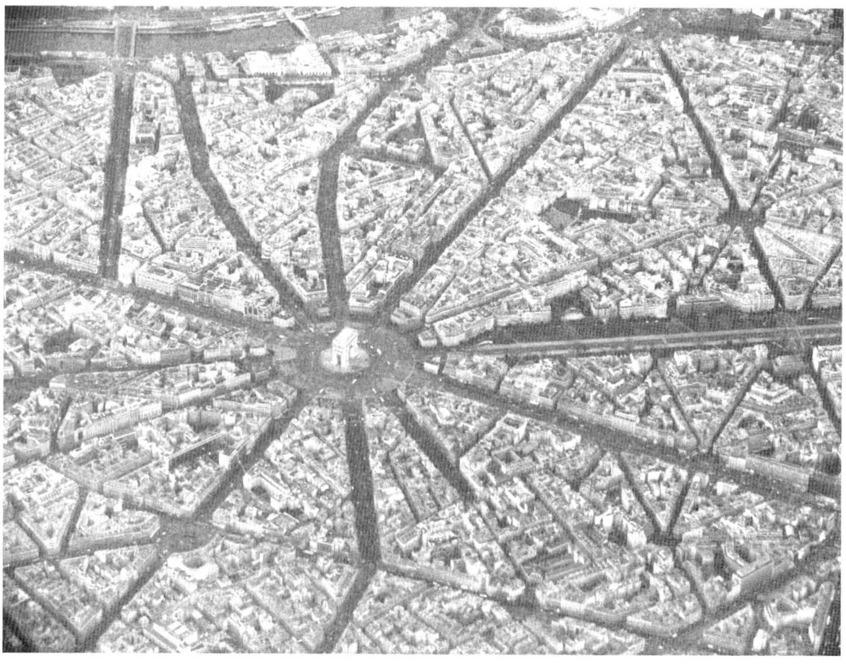

Exhibit 1.2 The *Arc de Triomphe* at sunrise; photo © 2017 Léo-Paul Dana.

Exhibit 1.3 Remembering the fallen; photo © 2017 Léo-Paul Dana.

Although a Scandinavian customs union proposed in 1947 was rejected, in 1952, the Nordic Council was established by Denmark, Iceland, Norway and Sweden, for cooperation between these countries and in 1954 its members agreed to a common labour market; in 1955, Finland joined. The 1957 Treaty of Rome came into effect on January 1, 1958, establishing the European Common Market (later the European Economic Community), uniting Belgium, France, the Federal Republic of Germany, Italy, Luxembourg and the Netherlands.

In 1959, the Stockholm convention established the European Free Trade Association (EFTA), allowing Austria, Iceland, Norway, Sweden, and Switzerland to maintain different external tariffs while eliminating internal tariffs on industrial products originating within the free trade area. Finland joined EFTA in 1961.

In 1973, the European Economic Community welcomed the Kingdom of Denmark, the Republic of Ireland and the United Kingdom of Great Britain and Northern Ireland. Greece joined in 1981, followed by Portugal and Spain in 1986. In 1989, the Council of Ministers of the European Economic Community adopted the decision to make SMEs a priority. This included the creation of a favourable environment with limited regulation, the encouragement of new venture creation and the establishment of R&D priorities.

In 1991, the Maastricht Treaty laid the foundation for an Economic and Monetary Union (EMU). In 1993, the Single European Act created a European Union allowing free movement of goods, services, capital and labour. At the time there were 17 million privately owned enterprises in the non-primary sector of the European Union, of which 93.3% were microfirms, 6.2% were small, 0.5% were medium, and 0.1% were large (Mulhern, 1995).

Potts argued that the concept of a single European market was supported by, "to be accurate, big business more than small business" (2000, p. 322). In 1995, the European Union grew with the entry of three former members of EFTA, namely Austria, Finland, and Sweden.

Until the 20th century, there were huge discrepancies in infrastructure and technology across Europe. In Portugal, telecommunications development relied on the Anglo Portuguese Telephone Company (see Chapter 18 in this volume). In France, the government funded the *Postes Telegraphes Telephones* (PTT), which facilitated business. Exhibit 1.4 features the PTT of Vétheuil, a village in the area of which Claude Oscar Monet (1840–1926) painted 26 scenes.

Recent years have witnessed the spread of technology. Another trend across Europe has been for former colonisers to give various levels of autonomy including independence to territories overseas. In 2009, Denmark granted Greenland (see Exhibit 1.5) the right to have self-rule.

Exhibit 1.4 PTT in Vétheuil; photo © 2017 Léo-Paul Dana.

At the macro-economic level, Europe has been experiencing convergence; technology, for instance, is becoming increasingly similar in different countries. At the micro-level, however, Europeans from different regions are maintaining cultural uniqueness. In the words of McCall, "There are many more nations in the world than there are states for them" (1980, pp. 538–539). As observed by Berlinski, "Unsurprisingly, it is difficult to cobble nation-states together into a grand transnational entity" (2005, p. A-17).

Entrepreneurship is also maintaining its regional characteristics, but co-operation, networking, and clustering into industrial agglomerations (Baptista and Swann, 1998; Glassman and Voelzkow, 2001) has gained importance. Formerly independent entrepreneurs are increasingly collaborating for mutual benefit, resulting in symbiotic business networks linking small and large firms (Wright and Dana,

Exhibit 1.5 Nuuk, Greenland; photo © 2017 Léo-Paul Dana.

2003), as well as symbiotic entrepreneurship (Dana, Etemad, and Wright, 2008).

Diversity

Does enterprise develop the same way amongst all people? Farmer and Richman explained, "the sociological or cultural environment of a country has an impact on the ways in which industrial enterprises and their personnel carry out their functions" (1965, p. 109). They then discussed "the *dominant* human attitudes, values, and beliefs in a given society or country and the way they tend to influence the motivation, behavior, and performance of individuals working in productive enterprises" (Farmer and Richman, 1965, p. 109). For example, "In the first half of 1976, the total days lost by strikes per 1,000 workers was ... 177 in France, but the German rate was only 19" (Putman, 1977, pp. 158–159).

Farmer and Richman elaborated, "Prevailing religious beliefs and cultural values, in conjunction with parental behavior, child-rearing practices, and the formal system of education in a particular country, usually have a direct and very significant bearing on the dominant view toward work and achievement" (1965, pp. 156–157). Farmer and Richman also addressed the issue that, "Since there may be various subcultures in a particular country, research in this area can be very complex" (1965, pp. 109–110). Discussing subculture, Jennings reported about an interviewer who explained to him that, "The Bavarians shoot slower than the Prussians" (1974, p. 413).

Hofstede (1980) examined cultural differences, and based on research with INSEAD Executive Development students, Laurent concluded, "Deep seated managerial assumptions are strongly shaped by national cultures and appear quite insensitive to the more transient culture of organizations" (1983, p. 75). Huntington (1993, 1996) and later Marsh (2004) argued that globalisation neither standardised societies, nor produced a homogeneous world culture. Jenniskens, Ulijn, and Tywuschik (2011) showed that the level of entrepreneurship is contingent upon the cultural environment in which it takes place — and cultural values vary greatly across Europe.

Séraphin, Stoll, and Carteron wrote that France has "one of the highest fertility rates in Europe" (2016, p. 92). Its neighbour, "Germany has one of the lowest birth rates in the world" (Shaboian and Motala, 2016, p. 106).

Audretsch and Fritch (1994) found that education increased entrepreneurship in Germany. Garofoli (1994) reported the same for Italy and Guesnier (1994) for France. In contrast, Hart and Gudgin (1994) and Rotefoss and Kolvereid (2005) found the opposite in Ireland and Norway respectively.

At a Spanish bullfight the bullfighter is hero for killing the bull. In France, the bull is considered the hero (see Chapter 7 in this volume) and a bull of the year is elected.

As Europe is heterogeneous, one country is not necessarily culturally homogenous. Baldegger *et al.* (2016) observed that fear of failing is very low in the German-speaking regions of Switzerland, while in French-speaking Switzerland there are significantly more people with entrepreneurial intentions but higher fear of failure.

Adding to the excitement is constant change. Bergh (2011) wrote that Sweden went from having a per capita income of half that in the United Kingdom during the 1800s, to becoming the fourth richest country in the world.

Yet, some truths do not change. Western Europe has never been a monolith market. Hanson wrote, "Iceland's salted and spiced herring find a ready market in Sweden; the dried cod go to Spain" (1928, p. 50). Differences remain as Europe today consists of diverse markets of different sizes and importance, and unlike preferences. In some regions, wine is favoured over beer, while the opposite is true elsewhere. In Alsace, both are produced; Gewürztraminer wine is among the favourites here, made from an aromatic grape (see Exhibit 1.6).

Even the making of wine varies from one country to another. Ribéreau-Gayon explained, "Vinification describes the first phase of winemaking. It comprises all technical aspects from grape maturity and harvest to the end of alcoholic and sometimes malolactic fermentation. The second phase of winemaking 'wine maturation, stabilization and treatments' is completed when the wine is bottled ... This distinction of two phases is certainly the result of commercial practices. Traditionally in France, a vine grower farmed the vineyard and transformed grapes into an unfinished wine. The wine merchant transferred the bulk wine to his cellars, finished the wine and marketed the product, preferentially before bottling ... In countries with a more recent viticultural history, generally English speaking, the vine grower is responsible for winemaking and wine sales. For this reason, the Anglo-Saxon tradition speaks of winemaking, which covers all operations from harvest reception to bottling" (2000, p. 10).

Entrepreneurship exists around the world; yet, it is far from standardised. Entrepreneurship means different things to different people. In recent years, there has been increasing interest in comparing entrepreneurs from different cultures. Scheinberg and MacMillan (1988) found significant differences across cultures in motivations to launch a new business.

Exhibit 1.6 Gewürztraminer grapes; photo © 2017 Léo-Paul Dana.

Dana (1995a) concluded that entrepreneurship was not simply a function of opportunity recognition in isolation, but coloured by cultural perception of opportunity. As noted by Aldrich (1999), the environment constitutes the initial conditions facing the entrepreneur.

People from different ethnic backgrounds have been exposed to dissimilar cultural values, and this is reflected in their respective entrepreneurship models. Various cultural aspects, such as the social value ascribed to the entrepreneur, attitudes toward the risk of failure, and the presence of exemplary entrepreneurial models are cultural factors that have an impact on the formation of the entrepreneurial calling (McGrath, MacMillan, and Scheinberg, 1992; Wennekers and Thurik, 2001). Hofstede *et al.* found, "Countries in which people are less satisfied with life as a whole have a higher level of entrepreneurship" (2004, p. 195).

Among important explanatory variables is the role of the state. Spencer, Murtha, and Lenway (2005) described Finland as having a social corporatist institutional structure with the state playing a facilitative role; in contrast, they described Germany as a country as having a State corporatist structure, in which, "Networks among organized social actors may equilibrate state centralism" (2005, p. 326). They grouped Belgium, France and Italy as having political and managerial leaders who "tend to cooperate rather than act as adversaries" (Spencer, Murtha, and Lenway, 2005, p. 326).

Europe is rich with different styles of entrepreneurship. Savitt (1998) suggested understanding the differences before attempting to find similarities. As noted by Ulijn and Fayolle (2004), people from one European country tend to value self-employment over employment, while the opposite is true in another country. Along the same lines, Obrecht (2005) argued that the cultural environment affects entrepreneurial capabilities.

Different Policy Models

Up to the late 1970s, government policies, in Europe, tended to encourage mergers of existing firms into larger units (Strinati, 1982).

In 1974, for example, the state firm Aeroporti di Roma was formed, absorbing about 60 SMEs. Scase (1980) noted that the trend, in Europe, was to evolve away from small independent businesses, as governments believed instead that a measure to facilitate economic growth would be to encourage a close partnership between the existing large firms in the private sector and state agencies. More recently, the trend has been for the state to recognise the usefulness of entrepreneurs, and an environment fostering entrepreneurship.

As demonstrated by Rainnie and Scott (1986), entrepreneurship became increasingly recognised as a means of improving output and as discussed by Scase and Goffee (1987), the policy of some governments gradually shifted from discouraging to encouraging independent business. Entrepreneurship has been recognised as being in the national interest, making important contributions to economic expansion and job creation.

Nevertheless, while governments have raced to promote entrepreneurship and innovation, there has been a lack of consensus about the means to attain this objective (Dana, 1987). Among the environmental factors that powerfully condition the ease and scope of entrepreneurial activity, are government, laws, regulations and procedures (Staley and Morse, 1971). Furthermore, government policy reflects the attitude of legislators. In some countries the role of government is to assure a market is free such that Adam Smith's hand can assure the common good. At the opposite extreme, the government sees itself as competing with others to be an active coach. Along a broad continuum, one can identify two ideal types of models to which government policies belong:

Model I, Regulation for Protection: Rules are established to protect existing business — even if this hinders entrepreneurial behaviour. This is the model adopted by many countries such as France, where regulation has been instituted to protect firms, as well as consumers.

Model II, Protection from Regulation: A policy of minimal intervention and minimal regulation allows entrepreneurs to dedicate more resources to their enterprises, protecting them from the burden of excessive paperwork requirements and the constraints of heavy regulations.

The nature of intervention by a government — through regulations, paperwork requirements, subsidies, and trade agreements — affects entrepreneurial opportunities, entrepreneurship and innovation. Peterson and Peterson (1981) showed that government paperwork requirements could be a burden on the managerial time of owner–managers. In contrast, the state may foster entrepreneurship, by creating an inviting environment for enterprise.

This Book

The objective of this book is to briefly introduce facts in order to provoke thought, analysis and discussion — but how does one bring together descriptions of 21 nations in one book, introductory in nature? It has been necessary to be concise rather than pretend to be comprehensive. It is not assumed that the reader shall be interested in every detail; rather, leads are provided for individuals to pursue references of empirical investigations and historical works that could be useful as additional readings. This volume cites almost 800 works, many of which are inspiring for future research.

The following chapters shall provide brief overviews of entrepreneurship across Western Europe. It shall be evident that entrepreneurship is *not* homogeneous across Western Europe. Rather, entrepreneurship reflects history, and culture, both affecting the perception of entrepreneurial opportunities. As Pascal (1701) explained, that which is truth on one side of the Pyrenees is not so, on the other. His sister quoted his exact words, "Vérité en deçà des Pyrénées, erreur au-delà" (Perier, 1842, p. 61).

Chapter 2
Andorra

Introduction

Nestled in the Pyrenees, between France and Spain,[1] the Principality of Andorra covers 468 square kilometres, an area less than that of Chicago. Catalan is the official language here. The nation's capital is Andorra la Vella. There are two heads of state: the Bishop of Urgel and the President of France. The country's airport is at Seo de Urgel. Tourism is the nation's principal industry. Taxes are low and the country has a budget surplus.

Historical Overview

Tradition tells us that Charlemagne (circa 742–814) granted Andorra a charter of independence in exchange for help fighting the Moors. In 1278, the French Count of Foix and the Spanish Bishop of Urgel were made co-princes of land. The rights vested in the House of Foix eventually passed by marriage to the French crown. Beginning in 1868, the General Council of the Valleys has been responsible for administration of the principality.

In April 1933, a group of young men forced the council to allow men 25 years old or older to vote. Fernsworth wrote about Andorra at the time: "It is a land of unwritten law, where custom and usage,

[1] See relevant chapters in this volume.

handed down for centuries from father to son, are more binding than written word" (1933, p. 493).

In 1934, a new motorway linked Andorra with France, but snow often blocked the road. Blizzards are common in Andorra and heavy snowfall days have been theme of academic inquiry (Esteban *et al.*, 2005).

Women were granted the right to vote here, in 1970. A new democratic constitution came into effect in 1993, empowering Andorra to conduct its own foreign affairs. Admitted to the United Nations on July 28, 1993, Andorra joined the Council of Europe in 1994.

Low taxation has attracted immigrants and this has caused concern about the rapid development of urbanisation and the limited space in mountain valley floors. The need for housing has prompted the construction of buildings in zones potentially exposed to debris flow hazard. Hürlimann *et al.* (2006) studied debris flow hazard assessment in Andorra.

The Environment for Entrepreneurship

Andorrans were for centuries self-sufficient, cultivating crops (including tobacco) and raising cattle as well as sheep. Fernsworth (1933) noted that Andorra rented pastureland to French and Spanish sheep-owners and that Andorran shepherds cared for Spanish sheep. Complementing fishing, Andorrans would hunt a variety of chamois, the izard (a small goat-like antelope, *Rupicapra pyrenaica*) for food; these mammals are now on the Red List of threatened species.

Fernsworth wrote, "the Council General granted a monopoly for the contrabanding of sulphur and matches ... The smuggling across borders of sheep, horses, and mules is still practiced ..." (1933, p. 501). Manufacturing traditionally focused on cigarettes and cloth, and more recently the making of furniture. The government also obtained money from automobile licences, postage stamps and the electric utility.

Andorra still provides an environment of very low taxation. Anisette and brandy are distilled locally and tobacco is still the most

Exhibit 2.1 Imported produce; photo © 2017 Léo-Paul Dana.

important crop along with potatoes. Corn, grain and grapes are also grown here, but most food is imported (see Exhibit 2.1). Tourism has become very important, representing most of the nation's GDP. A popular Andorran ski resort, near the French border, is Pas de la Casa (Exhibit 2.2).

Local law protects domestic enterprises, through ownership requirements. It takes a residency of 10 years in Andorra before one can be a sole trader here. This provides opportunities for Andorran entrepreneurs to form joint ventures with foreigners. Local trading companies most often take the form of a *Societat Limitadad*, with a minimum of two shareholders.

Andorra's status as a free port has contributed to exports. Moskowitz provided the first systematic study on the internationalisation of SMEs in Andorra noting, "Until recently, the internationalization of Andorra's SMEs was of a 'passive' nature … internationalization

Exhibit 2.2 On the border with France; photo © 2017 Léo-Paul Dana.

came to Andorra, in large measure, because of favourable taxation policies ... An important part of this type of internationalization was Andorra's participation ... in shadow economic activity" (2008, p. 31). He elaborated, "Food is mostly imported into Andorra" (2008, p. 34).

Toward the Future

Andorra is among few principalities surviving today — a remnant of feudal Europe surviving into the future, with opportunities for entrepreneurs. As noted by Moskowitz, "The next few years will determine whether Andorra is prepared to compete actively in the global economy" (2008, p. 31).

Chapter 3

Austria

Introduction

The Republic of Austria covers 83,879 square kilometres, bordering the Czech Republic,[1] Germany, Hungary, Italy, Liechtenstein, Slovakia, Slovenia, and Switzerland.[2] Formerly imperial capital of the Austro-Hungarian Empire, Vienna (Exhibit 3.1) is capital of the federal republic.

According to McMillan, Salzburg-born "Mozart earned his living as an entrepreneur in the marketplace" (2002, p. 26). Bolton and Thompson described Mozart as "both a genius and an entrepreneur" (2004, p. 229). Among notable Austrian industrialists was textile magnate Josef Marx Alois Luger; Exhibit 3.2 shows his residence in Dornbirn — for centuries, an important textile centre. Weitensfelder (2001) provided a rich history of the industrialisation of this province during Luger's lifetime. Luger needed no factory because weavers used their respective homes to make textiles. Also Austrian, economist Joseph Alois Schumpeter (1883–1950), Austrian Minister of Finance, banker and Harvard professor, was a precursor of entrepreneurship research (Schumpeter, 1912); yet, Haberfellner (2003) argued Austria was a highly regulated corporatist country with limited entrepreneurship. Comparing Austria with France, Ulijn

[1] For discussions of entrepreneurship in the Czech Republic, Hungary, Slovakia, and Slovenia, see Dana (2010).
[2] See relevant chapters in this volume.

Exhibit 3.1 Urania Bridge, Vienna; photo © 2017 Léo-Paul Dana.

and Fayolle wrote that in contrast to French people who tend to value self-employment over employment, Austrians "prefer the employment and not the self-employment status" (2004, p. 211).

Miles, Feulner, and O'Grady (2005) observed that although there are still some complex and slow bureaucratic procedures, the role of the state in the economy has been decreasing. The influence of the Church is also less prominent than it was in former times.

Historical Overview

Count Rudolf (1218–1291) of Habsburg (sometimes anglicised to Hapsburg) became German king in 1273, and within five years conquered Austria — *Österreich* (literally Eastern Kingdom) — which his descendants would rule for many generations. During the 16th century, the Habsburg dynasty acquired Bohemia, Spain, and parts of Hungary and Italy as well. Ehmer (1997) provided an account of 18th century artisans in Vienna. Meanwhile, western Austria prospered with the textile industry. Entrepreneurs Burger and Rhomberg launched the industrialisation of Vorarlberg with cotton spinning. Exhibit 3.3 features one of their properties dating back to 1795.

Exhibit 3.2 Luger's home; photo © 2017 Léo-Paul Dana.

In 1804, the Habsburgs adopted the title of emperor. In 1867, a dual monarchy was created, including Hungary in addition to Austria. In 1878, the Ottoman provinces of Bosnia and Herzegovina became a protectorate of the Empire, annexed in 1908 (see Dana,

Exhibit 3.3 Burger & Rhomberg offices; photo © 2017 Léo-Paul Dana.

1999a, 2010). Meanwhile textiles created much prosperity for Austrians (see Exhibit 3.4).

The world's first regular international air connection was established in April 1918, with an airmail route between Vienna and Kiev. Service was soon expanded. On November 12, 1918, following the collapse of the Austro-Hungarian Empire, Austria was proclaimed a republic, within today's borders. Bachinger (1987) described the economic situation of the Austrian relict of the Habsburg monarchy. An energy crisis coupled with a food shortage, while the debasement of the currency accompanied an unstable political situation. However, the weak currency favoured exports, and Austria experienced remarkable economic growth until the Great Depression. Chater (1929) provided an account of interwar Austria.

Exhibit 3.4 Formerly a clothing and fashion store, featuring *art nouveau* architecture; photo © 2017 Léo-Paul Dana.

The republic was short-lived as Austria was annexed into the German Reich in 1938. During World War II, the Nazis took over all industry of significant size in Austria. Following the war, a provisional government was set up on April 27, 1945. As noted by Dana (1992a) one in three Austrians worked on a farm in 1945. In 1948, the European Recovery Programme began pumping investments and new life in Austria. In his discussion of prices and salaries, Long noted "the average in Vienna last summer being 730 schillings ($28) a month" (1951, p. 752). Austrian economic policy envisaged a reconstruction based on large firms and reconstruction took place at an amazing pace; a discussion appears in Bowie (1959).

Until 1955, Austria was administered as four zones, occupied by France, the United Kingdom, the United States, and the Union of Soviet Socialist Republics. Austria recovered full independence that year and got admitted into the United Nations on December 14, 1955 (Clute, 1962). Also in 1955, Austria regained sovereignty over its airspace. In 1957, Austrian Airlines (AUA) was created, and in March 1958 the new airline began operations with flights between Vienna and London, using four chartered Vickers Viscount 779 turbo-props. AUA became a member of the International Air Transport Association (IATA) in April 1958. In March 1960, AUA inaugurated the larger Vickers Viscount 837, replacing the smaller Viscount 779. Exhibit 3.5 shows the Viscount 837 with registration

Exhibit 3.5 Viscount 837; photo courtesy of Austrian Airlines.

OE-LAF; this particular aeroplane crashed while approaching Moscow, in September 1960. In 1964, Innsbruck hosted the Winter Olympics.

In 1972, Austrian statesman Kurt Waldheim (1918–2007) became Secretary-General of the United Nations (see Exhibit 3.6), a position he kept until 1981. From 1986 to 1992, he was the President

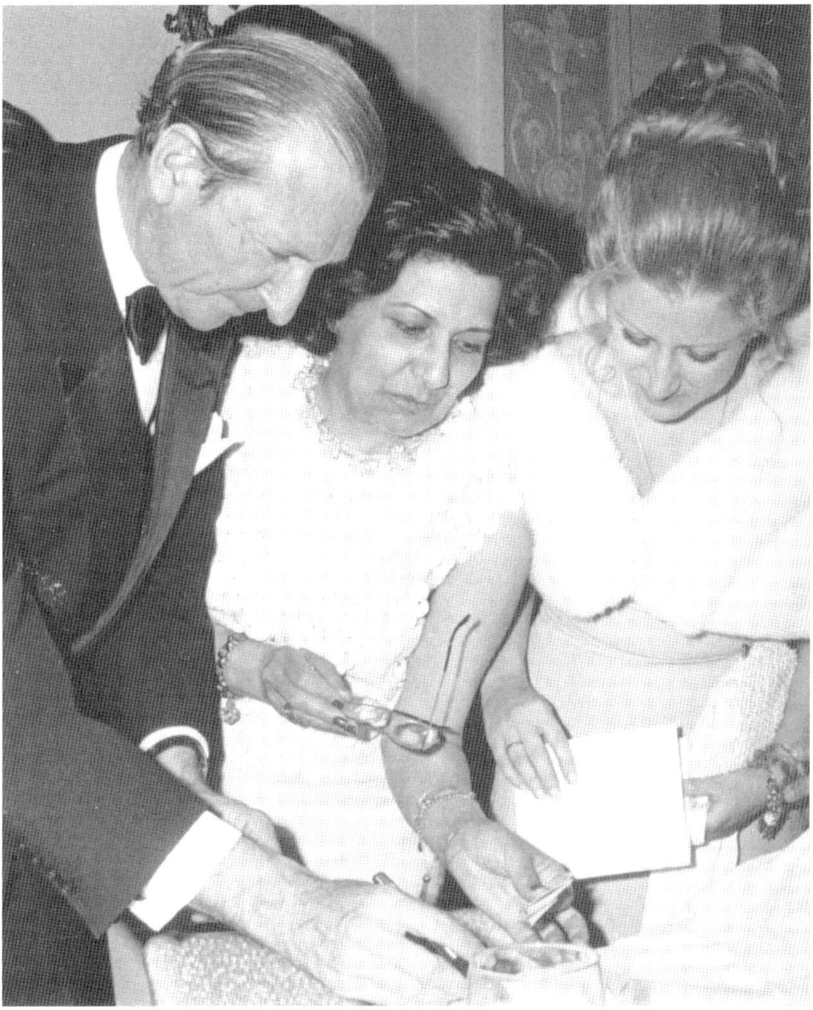

Exhibit 3.6 Kurt Waldheim during official visit to Canada; photo courtesy of Clemy Dana.

of Austria. The self-employment rate, especially in agriculture, fell sharply between the 1980s and the 1990s (Haberfellner, 2003). Austria had low self-employment and start-up rates (Austrian Institute for SME Research, 1996). Yet, start-ups were found to have high survival rates (Wanzenböck, 1998), so the government established initiatives to increase the relevance of entrepreneurship. This included campaigns promoting self-employment in the media, the establishment of university chairs and programmes of emphasis for entrepreneurship at schools, business plan competitions, a reduction of bureaucratic procedures, and support programmes for start-ups. While the number of start-ups was between 14,000 and 15,000 during the period from 1993 to 1995, during the late 1990s, start-up rates and rates of self-employment began rising significantly.

In 2002, approximately 28,000 new enterprises were founded in Austria; a third of these reflected the net growth in the number of companies, while the other two thirds were substitutes for other, closing companies (Getzner, Haber, and Schwarz, 2004, p. 16). Yet, Van Stel (2005) observed that business ownership in Austria fell between 1972 and 2002. According to the Austrian Federal Economic Chamber, self-employment outside the agricultural sector was 7.9% of the workforce in 2003 (Wirtschaftskammern Österreichs, 2003, p. 25). That year, Austria's per capita GDP was 26,900 euro, placing it in fourth place among the 25 member-states of the European Union (after Luxembourg, Ireland and Denmark). The unemployment rate in Austria during 2003 was 4.5%, the second lowest after Cyprus within the EU25; this was relatively low when compared to the average of the EU25 with 9%, or the United States with 6% (Wirtschaftskammern Österreichs, 2004, p. 17). In 2004, there were nearly 30,000 new firms in Austria, (Wirtschaftskammer Österreich, 2005) setting a new trend. Yet, economic growth in 2004 was only 1.8%, while the total growth of the EU25 was 2.1% (Wirtschaftskammern Österreichs, 2004, p. 13). This may be a result of the weak economy of Germany (Landler, 2005) — the most important export market for Austria. Worth noting, however, the number of textile factories (see Exhibit 3.7) and food-processing firms has been decreasing in Austria.

Exhibit 3.7 J. M. Fussenegger Textil GMBH — a successful manufacturer; photo © 2017 Léo-Paul Dana.

According to the first longitudinal studies analysing the development of start-ups during the years 1996 and later (Frank *et al.*, 2002, p. 33; Schwarz and Grieshuber, 2003, p. 19), survival rates did not suffer from the higher number of start-ups; the higher quantity of start-ups did not cause a lower quality of the start-ups when measured by survival rates. Austria scored 71.6 in the 2010 Index of Economic Freedom, placing it among the top 30 in the world.

For the decade from 2004 to 2013, Mandl (2004) noted that 51,500 Austrian SMEs with approximately 440,000 employees would be up for succession or transfer, representing nearly 25% of all Austrian firms. Most business successions were carried out within a family; the prime motive is generational change, but analysis suggested about 9% of these enterprises were not qualified for transfer, due to negative equity capital.

As of 2010, serious unrest in the Arab world led to mass migration to Austria, among other members of Europe. Rezaei, Goli, and Dana (2014) studied illegal entrepreneurship of migrants in Austria.

The Environment for Entrepreneurship

The Austrian Industrial Code defines business as any independent, continuous activity carried out for profit, excluding learned and artistic professions and other exceptions. As noted by Peters, Märk, and Kraus (2011), most Austrian SMEs are family businesses (see Exhibit 3.8), some in the same family for many generations (Exhibit 3.9).

Exhibit 3.8 Many bakeries are family firms; photo © 2017 Léo-Paul Dana.

Exhibit 3.9 The Red House — built in 1639 by Michael Danner and Verena Rhomberg — served as a private residence, and later as an inn, before being renovated in 1954 by August Rhomberg; photo © 2017 Léo-Paul Dana.

Austria is highly supportive of its entrepreneurs, with a highly developed infrastructure, including a high concentration of accountants, banks, and legal advisors. Although trade licenses may be perceived as barriers to entry, Austria provides financial and practical support to growing businesses. Not surprisingly, SMEs constitute the backbone of the economy, in large and small towns alike.

More than 210,000 enterprises employ over 1.5 million people. According to the Federal Ministry of Economy and Labour, 99.5%

Exhibit 3.10 Alpine terrain; photo © 2017 Léo-Paul Dana.

of the enterprises in Austria are SMEs, as per the European Union definition, including firms with up to 249 employees. These firms employ 65% of the Austrian labour force and produce 58% of total income. Furthermore, they provide about 80% of Austria's income tax revenues, and about 70% of the total revenue of sales tax.

Due to the physical terrain of the Alps (Exhibit 3.10), much land is difficult to cultivate, and farms in Austria tend to be much smaller than those in Germany and tiny when compared to American farms. High elevations translate to short growing seasons due to cold climate (see Exhibit 3.11).

Austrian SMEs are remarkable, considering that a long lasting economic malaise did not result in job losses in the SME sector; instead, the number of jobs provided by SMEs increased by about 8% between 1995 and 2003 (Pichler and Bornett, 2005). Compared with other countries in Europe, Austria has a particularly high proportion of small (10–49 employees) and medium-sized (50–249 employees)

Exhibit 3.11 Double windows are appreciated during winters; photo © 2017 Léo-Paul Dana.

enterprises, while the share of microenterprises (up to nine employees) and large enterprises (more than 249 employees) is comparatively low (Pichler and Bornett, 2005, p. 123). With regards to the number of enterprises, commerce was the leading sector in 2003 with 29% of all enterprises, followed by economic services and tourism (each with 18%) and manufacturing (12%); due to a superior average size of enterprises, the latter sector provides the highest share of jobs (24%), followed by commerce (24%) and economic services (14%).[3]

Within the SME sector about 473,000 people work in companies with 50–249 employees. Approximately 530,000 persons are employed

[3] *Source*: Pichler and Bornett, 2005, p. 126.

in enterprises with 10–49 employees and about 500,000 persons in the so-called smallest-enterprises with less than 10 employees. Between 1995 and 2003 the number of SMEs rose by 11.6%. The highest increase was noted by the smallest-companies. The growth in the production and service sector was mainly the result of SMEs (*Bundesministerium für Wirtschaft und Arbeit*, 2005, p. 69f).

In general, Austria offers a SME-friendly environment. Several public institutions support the establishment and expansion of new ventures. These include the Austria Wirtschaftsservice GmbH, the economic departments of every provincial government and the Austrian Federal Economic Chamber[4] with its subsidiaries in each federal region. Well-networked, such institutions offer support with business planning and assistance with risk evaluation. Moreover, they conduct market research and provide the results in exchange for a nominal fee. In addition, the state provides grants and loans to entrepreneurs. Also worth mentioning are various organisations, such as the *Industriellenvereinigung* (Federation of Austrian Industries), that lobby to enforce the interests of the entrepreneurs at a political level.

Arguing that Austria was highly regulated, Haberfellner (2003) noted the decision by the Federal Economic Chamber to implement a quota on the number of Eastern European entrepreneurs operating in Austria. A considerable number of immigrants from Turkey and from the former Yugoslav republics have become self-employed in Austria, largely in the retail and catering sectors — both of which have low barriers to entry. Kurtoglu (2007) reported on immigrant entrepreneurs in Austria. As noted by Rath (2011), to help immigrant entrepreneurs the Vienna Economic Chamber provides information in several languages, including Turkish.

Subcontracting is important for SMEs in Austria. Austria's Ministry of Economy and Labour has helped establish the Association of Austrian Subcontractors, which in turn facilitates matchmaking; the result is a *symbiotic interdependence* among partners in international alliances.

---

[4] Membership in this Chamber is compulsory for all Austrian companies.

Several institutions, along with the Austrian Ministry of Economy and Labour, have been quite creative with regards to the internationalisation of Austrian SMEs. This includes project guarantees, financing guarantees, and export risk guarantees available to small-scale exporters.

The Federal Economic Chamber has an *Exportakademie*, which offers courses in internationalisation and foreign languages. The Chamber also has Economic Promotion Institutes that provide training and consultancy to entrepreneurs, as well as subsidies for advertising and participating in trade fairs abroad. In addition, the Chamber has established a fund to help cover eventual losses of entrepreneurs who opt to internationalise their operations, with the objective of strengthening competitiveness in foreign markets.

While savings banks (see Exhibit 3.12) specialise in smaller transactions, the *Österreichische Kontrollbank* administers export guarantee schemes against economic and political risks. SMEs are entitled to loans at special conditions; these are administered by the Austrian Export-Fonds GmbH. *Exportfinanzierungsverfahren* is a special export financing scheme. Export intensity in 2002 was 35.6% of GDP, ranking Austria among the upper third, in an international comparison (Wirtschaftskammern Österreichs, 2003, p. 7).

In a longitudinal survey of 634 Austrian new ventures founded in 1999, Kraus and Schwarz (2007) and Kraus, Harms, and Schwarz (2008) found that although pre-start-ups planning and formalisation led to greater employment growth, only about one third of all companies (and about a fifth of sole proprietors) had prepared a business plan for their start-up.

In their Global Entrepreneurship Monitor (GEM) report, Apfelthaler *et al.* (2008), noted that Austrian culture was risk averse, making employment relatively attractive when compared to entrepreneurship. Fink and Teodorowicz (2008) discussed trust-based cooperation as a driver for the internationalisation of Austrian SMEs, as did Fink, Harms, and Kraus (2008) in their study of cooperative internationalisation of SMEs. Between 2007 and 2014, Austria witnessed a rise in early stage entrepreneurial activity from 2.4% in 2007 to 8.7% in 2014 (Schmalzer *et al.*, 2015).

Exhibit 3.12 Savings bank; photo © 2017 Léo-Paul Dana.

Traditional constraints on entrepreneurship have been the tax-system, the bureaucracy, and (compared to other European countries) high labour costs (Wirtschaftskammern Österreichs, 2003, p. 27f). Schmalzer *et al.* (2015) noted more persisting constraints, including cultural and social norms that prevent individuals from taking risk, possibly due to the fact that the educational system may be lacking in teaching entrepreneurial thinking and business and management basics. They also observed that bureaucracy, high taxes and tariffs, inhibit business growth. Income tax reform was introduced in 2016; it is hoped this may reduce effectively high labour costs. Investments are being funnelled into research centres, business parks and business incubators.

Toward the Future

In former times, labour intensive manufacturing was commonplace in Austria (see Exhibit 3.13). Liberalisation of trade encouraged an increase in specialisation, and low-technology labour-intensive production is being transferred abroad, often to Eastern Europe (see Dana, 2010), in favour of value-adding opportunities. As a result, the services sector has been growing considerably, while the number of Austrian SMEs in textiles has been decreasing. Yet, Turkish entrepreneurs *often with networks in Turkey* are heavily involved in Austria's garment sector. Such trends are likely to continue, reflecting differences in labour costs.

Situated in the heart of Europe, Austria's geographical situation, its closeness to Eastern Europe and the possibilities of *cost-efficient outsourcing opportunities can be very advantageous for Austrian entrepreneurs.* High technical standards in Austria, an excellent infrastructure and the quality of the dual education system are additional assets; the education process includes on-the-job practical learning and the vocational training school. While Austria is a suitable business location for service and engineering enterprises, high labour and living costs make Austria less attractive for labour-intensive firms requiring unskilled labour.

Entrepreneurs, in Austria, appear to be increasingly focused or specialised. A trend has been the reduction of start-up sizes, measured by employees. There has been significant growth in the number of one-person-firms. A study of the Tyrol province showed that in 2004, 41.4% of the members of the regional economic chamber (membership

Exhibit 3.13 Made in Austria; photo © 2017 Léo-Paul Dana.

in the economic chamber is compulsory for all Austrian companies) were one-person-firms (Beyer, Hämmerle, and Garbislander, 2005).

Schmalzer *et al.* (2015), noted that Austria was experiencing adverse economic conditions characterised by low growth rates and increasing unemployment; sole proprietorships were on the rise, but growth expectations of entrepreneurs reflected these realities. The authors suggested that Austria would have to put a special emphasis on reforms in the tax system, social security contributions for sole proprietorships and small growing firms as well as paperwork reduction.

The government intends to become more customer-orientated when dealing with entrepreneurs. Plans are to reduce bureaucracy and thus to avoid entry barriers while attracting entrepreneurs. Meanwhile, the educational system is adapting to the changing requirements of the economy.

Chapter 4

Belgium

Introduction

The Kingdom of Belgium covers 30,528 square kilometres, bordering France, Germany, Luxembourg, and the Netherlands.[1] Belgium is a multicultural, federal state, consisting of three linguistic communities (Dutch, French, and German) and three regions: (i) bilingual Brussels; (ii) Flanders, the Flemish region, and (iii) Wallonia, the Walloon region, which includes French and German speakers. While the Flemish people are Germanic, the Walloons trace their origins to Romanised Celts. Brussels (Exhibits 4.1 and 4.2) is an important business centre and the national capital, as well as capital of the European Union. The oldest citizen of Brussels, the Manneken-Pis (Exhibit 4.3) is considered to be the protector of Brussels.

Belgium was the first on the continent to experience the industrial revolution (Kossman-Putto and Kossman, 1996). In 2015, it ranked number one in government entrepreneurship programmes (Kelley, Singer, and Harrington, 2016). It leads in innovation, with close cooperation between researchers and industry. Funded by the Flemish government, the *Vlaams Instituut voor Biotechnologie* (VIB) focuses on translating research into agricultural, industrial and pharmaceutical applications; the result is an ecosystem with important spin-offs. Also in Flanders, the Interuniversity Microelectronics

[1] See relevant chapters in this volume.

Exhibit 4.1 Grand' Place; photo © 2017 Léo-Paul Dana.

Exhibit 4.2 Guildhalls; photo © 2017 Léo-Paul Dana.

Centre (IMEC) focuses on nanoelectronics. In Wallonia, the state has implemented its *quatre fois quatre pour entreprendre* initiative; this includes creating awareness of entrepreneurship, fostering new venture creation, providing assistance to enterprises, and improving corporate governance.

Exhibit 4.3 Manneken-Pis; photo © 2017 Léo-Paul Dana.

Historical Overview

Brussels is a historic city, with a city hall dating back to the 15th century (see Exhibit 4.4). In 1519, the area that is now Belgium came under Spanish rule, and in 1555 Philip II (1527-1598) ascended to the throne, ushering in an era of Spanish Inquisitions. For Antwerp, the economic heart of Flanders, prosperity came to an end in 1585 when Antwerp surrendered to the Spanish army, and wealthy citizens moved north to the Netherlands.

Sombart wrote, "Antwerp lost no small part of its former glory by reason of the departure of the Jews, and in the 17th century especially it was realized how much they contributed to bring about material prosperity" (1913, p. 19). Today, 1,800 Jews cut diamonds in Antwerp, the transit centre for 80% of the world's diamonds (Exhibit 4.5). Brussels also has an important Jewish community; Exhibit 4.6 shows the *Grande Synagogue* of Brussels.

During the late 17th century, guilds in Brussels were very affluent and hence powerful, creating barriers to entry. Exhibit 4.7 features the bakers' guildhall of 1697. Exhibit 4.8 illustrates the brewers' guildhall of 1698.

The southern Netherlands remained under Spanish rule until 1700. In 1713, the region fell under Austrian rule and Antwerp prospered

Exhibit 4.4 City hall; photo © 2017 Léo-Paul Dana.

Exhibit 4.5 Antwerp; photo © 2017 Léo-Paul Dana.

once again, as the economic and commercial centre of Flanders. In 1794, this land was annexed to France and the Belgian textile industry prospered, possibly because Napoléon I (1769–1821) had banned the imports of English cloth. The merger with France did not last long, however. In 1815, the Congress of Vienna incorporated Belgian lands into the Kingdom of the United Netherlands, with William I (1772–1843) on the throne.

Belgium became a country after it decreed its independence from the Netherlands in 1830; by national congress, the following year, Prince Leopold of Saxe-Coburg (1790–1865) was elected king. In 1839, the Treaty of London established peace with the Netherlands. In 1847, King Leopold assisted with the inauguration of the *Galeries Royales St. Hubert* (Exhibit 4.9). Leopold II (1835–1909) succeeded his father in 1865.

Exhibit 4.6 *Grande Synagogue*; photo © 2017 Léo-Paul Dana.

Soon after the invention of the telephone, American Bell Telephone licensed Western Electric to manufacture telephone equipment. Western Electric built its first European factory in Antwerp in 1882. Antwerp thus became an important centre for the

Exhibit 4.7 Bakers' guildhall; photo © 2017 Léo-Paul Dana.

manufacture of telephones. Exhibit 4.10 features a 1929 model made in Antwerp. Chater (1925) provided an overview of Antwerp as an international diamond centre.

Formerly a personal possession of the king, the Belgian Congo was taken over by the kingdom, in 1907. The Congo Free State became a colony in 1908. When King Leopold died, in 1909, his nephew Albert Leopold Meinrad (1875–1934) succeeded him, becoming King Albert I. During the Great War (World War I), Germany ignored Belgium's neutrality. Following the German invasion of Belgium in August 1914, Albert I stayed with his soldiers and became a war hero. His wife, Elisabeth of Bavaria (1876–1965), worked in a hospital for soldiers.

Chater (1925) gave an account of Belgium after World War I. In 1926, Prince Léopold (1901–1983) — later Léopold III — married

Exhibit 4.8 Brewers' guildhall; photo © 2017 Léo-Paul Dana.

Princess Astrid of Sweden (1905–1935). King Albert was killed in a 1934 mountain climbing accident. Between the World Wars, Brussels was considered "a typical buffer state between the Great Powers represented by France on the one hand and Germany on the other" (Stamp, 1939, p. 360). Chandler (1938) described Belgium shortly before World War II. In early 1940, $1 traded at 29.45 Belgian francs (see Exhibit 4.11). The Nazis invaded in 1940 and Leopold III was interned. Klemmer (1948) noted that Belgium served as a battleground for some of the fiercest fighting of World War II, and that during Nazi occupation Belgians lived on fewer than 1,300 calories a day. He was impressed with the fast recovery of the economy: "Meat was derationed on February 1, 1948, leaving only coal, sugar, fats, and cereals still subject to control. Belgian industry, always dynamic, is operating at more than 100 percent of the pre-war level" (1948, p. 575).

The 1950s brought new life. In 1951, King Leopold III abdicated in favour of his son Baudouin (1930–1993). Marden (1955) focused

Exhibit 4.9 *Galeries Royales St. Hubert*; photo © 2017 Léo-Paul Dana.

on post-war Bruges, describing this town as the heart of Flanders. In the province of Namur, SMEs like Wilmotte Frères created jobs manufacturing inland motor freighters such as that built in 1956 and featured in Exhibit 4.12. In 1958, Brussels hosted the 1958 Universal

Exhibit 4.10 Made in Antwerp; photo © 2017 Léo-Paul Dana.

Exhibition (see Walker, 1958), a feature of which was the Atomium (Exhibit 4.13). On December 15, 1960, King Baudouin married Fabiola de Mora y Aragon (1928–2014), a daughter of the Count of Mora. She was known to have rejected numerous other wedding proposals. Pang noted, "there was a decrease in self-employment in the post-war period from 1947 to 1980. This might be explained by the new welfare state with its safety net and economic expansion, which guaranteed nearly full employment until the early 1970s. With the recession it is argued that households, mainstream and

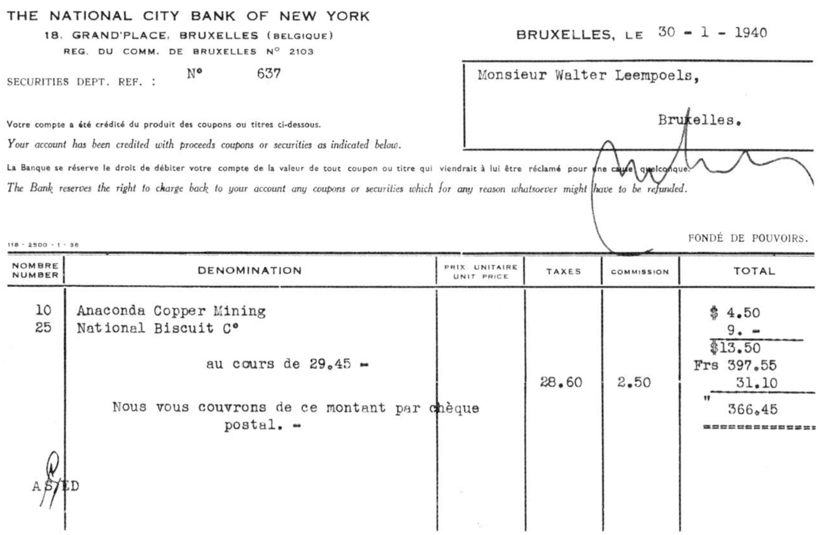

THE NATIONAL CITY BANK OF NEW YORK
18. GRAND'PLACE, BRUXELLES (BELGIQUE)
REG. DU COMM. DE BRUXELLES N° 2103

BRUXELLES, LE 30 - 1 - 1940

SECURITIES DEPT. REF. : N° 637

Monsieur Walter Leempoels,
Bruxelles.

Votre compte a été crédité du produit des coupons ou titres ci-dessous.
Your account has been credited with proceeds coupons or securities as indicated below.

La Banque se réserve le droit de débiter votre compte de la valeur de tout coupon ou titre qui viendrait à lui être réclamé pour une cause quelconque.
The Bank reserves the right to charge back to your account any coupons or securities which for any reason whatsoever might have to be refunded.

FONDÉ DE POUVOIRS.

118 - 2500 - 1 - 36

NOMBRE NUMBER	DENOMINATION	PRIX UNITAIRE UNIT PRICE	TAXES	COMMISSION	TOTAL
10	Anaconda Copper Mining				$ 4.50
25	National Biscuit C°				9. -
					$13.50
	au cours de 29.45 -				Frs 397.55
			28.60	2.50	31.10
	Nous vous couvrons de ce montant par chèque postal. -				" 366.45

A S/ED

Exhibit 4.11 Bank document; photo © 2017 Léo-Paul Dana.

Exhibit 4.12 Made in Belgium; photo © 2017 Léo-Paul Dana.

Exhibit 4.13 Atomium at Expo 1958; photo © 2017 Léo-Paul Dana.

immigrant alike, were driven into self-employment as a survival strategy" (2003, p. 208).

Cerruti wrote, "Belgium is *not* inhabited by Belgians but by Flemings and Walloons, and it is more a broken marriage than a nation" (1979, p. 395). On May 5, 1993, Belgium officially became a federal state. In July 1993, King Baudouin died leaving no children; his brother Albert, Prince of Liège (1934–) became Albert II.

During the late 20th century, the City of Ghent launched a business incubator for the social economy (see Meulemans, 2000). In November 2001, Belgium's national airline, SABENA (*Société anonyme belge d'exploitation de la navigation aérienne*) was liquidated. The subsequent economic downturn had a profound effect on SMEs (see Exhibit 4.14). Yet, underground activities flourished (Rezaei, Goli, and Dana, 2013a).

Following the abdication of King Albert II, his son Prince Philippe (1960–) was crowned the new monarch of Belgium on July

Exhibit 4.14 Feeling recession; photo © 2017 Léo-Paul Dana.

21, 2013. Belgium experienced substantial improvements in opportunity perception between 2013 and 2015 (Kelley, Singer, and Herrington, 2016).

The Environment for Entrepreneurship

De Clercq *et al.* wrote, "Until some years ago, entrepreneurs had a very bad image and the image as a whole was very bad" (2004, p. 72). In 2001, Belgium ranked as the least entrepreneurial country out of the 29 participants in the Global Entrepreneurship Monitor (GEM) research project. Entrepreneurial activity declined by 35% from 2001 to 2002. Simultaneously, the proportion of female entrepreneurs to male entrepreneurs dropped dramatically. De Clercq *et al.* observed, "In 2002, across all GEM countries, men were about 50% more likely to be involved in entrepreneurial activity than women. In Belgium, men were about three times more likely to be involved than women ... Further, there was a strong notion that starting a business is not a socially accepted option for Belgian women" (2002, p. 25, 26). The study also reported, "Entrepreneurs lack communication skills" (De Clercq *et al.*, 2002, p. 39).

The situation brightened and the following GEM study showed an increase in entrepreneurial activity. De Clercq, Manigart, Crijns, Clarysse, Verzele, and Zegers noted, "Belgium seems to be somewhat more entrepreneurial than France, Finland, Italy, and the Netherlands ... The Walloon figure is somewhat higher than the Belgian average" (2004, p. 3). Findings showed that 75% of all Belgian entrepreneurs, and almost 85% of all Walloon entrepreneurs were men. The authors suggested, "The picture is even more worrying when analyzing the type of companies that men and women start. As many men as women start a company out of necessity in Wallonia ... In Belgium as a whole, there are even slightly more women entrepreneurs who start a company out of necessity than men. This further implies that the discrepancy between male and female entrepreneurs is even higher for opportunity entrepreneurship" (De Clercq *et al.*, 2004, p. 48). With regards to job creation, the study revealed, "Only 5% of the Belgian starters created more than 20 jobs. The results for Wallonia show that none of the starters has so far created more than 20 jobs" (De Clercq *et al.*, 2004, pp. 28–29).

Given the limited growth potential of a small domestic market, internationalisation is important for Belgium. The 2004 GEM report stated, "a substantial part of the Belgian and Walloon entrepreneurs have chosen to enter the international arena. Further our results suggest that the Belgian starters, on average, have a high international orientation in their business activities ... However, given the overall low level of people choosing for a career as entrepreneur in Belgium, relatively few Belgian adults (1.5%) are involved in international start-up activity compared to many other EU countries. Further, we find that new ventures do not necessarily follow the classical pattern from less risky to more risky modes of foreign entry. Although export and import appear to be an important entry mode, in many cases foreign entry also involves more substantial commitments ..." (De Clercq *et al.*, 2004, p. 4). The same authors elaborated, "We find that 69% of the Belgian nascent entrepreneurs were planning to enter a foreign market ... Overall, our results show that the Belgian starters, on average, have a high international orientation in terms of the location of their customers" (De Clercq *et al.*, 2004, pp. 35–40). Degadt (2008) focused on the internationalisation of Belgian SMEs.

Lepoutre *et al.* (2009) noted that most entrepreneurship occurs between the ages of 25 and 35 and that women were under-represented; they emphasised the importance of improving people's perception entrepreneurship and recommended that entrepreneurship should be taught beginning at primary school. Lepoutre *et al.* (2009) noted that opportunities could be increased by encouraging clustering and intensive cooperation.

Bosma, Holvoet, and Crijns observed "that whereas perceived opportunities in Belgium and Flanders are in par with those of the benchmark economies, the other indicators show a less positive picture. Perceived skills to start a business are — similar to France — reported by one in every three persons. The other benchmark economies score somewhat higher on this indicator. In none of the other benchmark countries, we see such a high fear of failure. Almost five in 10 individuals actually state that fear of failure would prevent them from starting a business" (2014, p. 9).

Bosma, Holvoet, and Crijns also noted, "Belgium and Flanders, like most benchmark economies, witness an increase in job-growth expectation early-stage entrepreneurship. The rates have declined in Spain and leveled in France in the same time period. Flanders scores among the lowest among the benchmark countries at about one percent — twice as low as the Netherlands and the United Kingdom. Modest expectations and/or modest ambitions may also be caused by a perception of (nascent) entrepreneurs that regulations hinder hiring employees. At the same time, we cannot rule out that Belgian entrepreneurs may exhibit more realistic expectations concerning job creation than individuals in other countries who may be overly optimistic" (2014, p. 17).

With regards to internationalisation, Bosma, Holvoet, and Crijns wrote, "International orientation is relatively high in Belgium and Flanders. Of course this should be placed in the context of small countries and the existence of obvious partners in neighboring economies. Still, the international orientation of the average Belgian early-stage entrepreneurs is high (the high level in the period 2008–2010 may be an outlier; there are no obvious explanations for this particular finding). It signals that even though there appears to be fewer early-stage entrepreneurs in comparison to other countries, the international orientation is adequate ... Belgian and Flemish early-stage entrepreneurs are among the most prone to exhibit an international orientation. Part of this result is probably driven by the small and open economy that characterizes both Belgium as a whole and Flanders as one of its regions" (2014, p. 18–23).

Kelly, Singer, and Harrington commented on the low rate of discontinuance in Belgium, coupled with low Total Early-stage Entrepreneurial Activity (TEA) and established business rates; they stated, "This suggests a small foundation of businesses that can be discontinued. Issues such as complicated regulatory systems that increase the bureaucracy of starting and exiting businesses may produce barriers to entry, as well as barriers to exit, reducing people's willingness to venture into starting a business" (2016, p. 21).

Kelley, Singer, and Herrington (2016) mentioned that few people in Belgium are launching new firms, but those who are likely to, state that theirs is innovative. The authors pointed out, "Sweden and Belgium report the highest level of information and communications technology (ICT) entrepreneurs" (Kelley, Singer, and Herrington, 2016, p. 27).

SMEs continue to reflect the language of their regions — but not exclusively. Stores also reflect the language of their owner and/or market; see Exhibits 4.15 and 4.16.

Exhibit 4.15 Bilingual in Antwerp; photo © 2017 Léo-Paul Dana.

Exhibit 4.16 French in Brussels; photo © 2017 Léo-Paul Dana.

Toward the Future

Historically, guilds served as barriers to entry. Nowadays, groups (see Exhibit 4.17) result in barriers to entry for independent start-ups. Persons considering entrepreneurship might benefit from tapping into existing resources, including the Small Business Association of Self-employed Entrepreneurs (UNIZO), and the Flemish Institute for Enterprises (VIZO).

Bosma, Holvoet, and Crijns (2014) indicated the entrepreneurship supports most frequently cited by 15 experts: government entrepreneurship programmes, cited 13 times; government policy, cited 10 times; and (entrepreneurial) education, cited six times. The most cited restrictions were: government policy, cited 26 times; and

Exhibit 4.17 Groups are fashionable; photo © 2017 Léo-Paul Dana.

cultural and social norms, cited 10 times. The most cited suggestions for improvement in the future: government policy, cited 18 times; and (entrepreneurial) education, cited nine times. The authors noted, "In contrast to last year, Entrepreneurial Finance is less often mentioned as a critical factor. A thorough consultation with the experts, e.g., in the form of a dialogue and by linking to the GEM results on entrepreneurial perceptions and entrepreneurial activity, may help to further probe the particular bottlenecks in Belgium and Flanders and make suggestions to improve the entrepreneurial climate" (2004, p. 23).

They also offer a further suggestion for future research: "When it comes to self-perceptions to starting a business in Belgium and Flanders, perceived opportunities to start a business are at a high level — certainly in Flanders. At the same time, however, the perceived skills and knowledge required to start a business are relatively low and the fear of failure associated with starting a business is also relatively high. This may signal that many people accept (perhaps wisely) that starting a business is suited better for others. On the other hand, it may also indicate some untapped entrepreneurial potential that does not surface in the presence of attractive job alternatives. More in-depth research is needed to help determine the precise nature of the observed pattern" (Bosma, Holvoet, and Crijns, 2014, p. 23).

Chapter 5

Denmark

Introduction

The Kingdom of Denmark includes the peninsula of Jutland and the island of Zealand along with 405 smaller ones, in all covering 43,094 square kilometres, sharing a border with Germany.[1] Since 2000, the Øresund Link bridge tunnel connects Denmark to Sweden. Denmark's capital is Copenhagen (on Zealand), since 1903 home to the Little Mermaid (see Exhibit 5.1) — literary creation of Hans Christian Andersen (1805–1875). Among entrepreneurs of Denmark were J. C. Jacobsen (1811–1887), founder of Carlsberg, with the first Bavarian lager brewery in Denmark and the first brew completed in 1847; Peter Mærsk Møller (1836–1927) and his son, Arnold Peter Møller (1876–1965) whose enterprise evolved into the AP Møller–Mærsk group; and Ole Kirk Christiansen (1891–1958) inventor of Lego (Exhibit 5.2). Denmark ranked number one in the 2016 Happiness Index, with per capita GNP among the world's highest.

Historical Overview

In prehistoric times, Denmark was home to several local cultures. The first king of Denmark was Gorm, who ruled until his death in approximately 958. In 986, Viking leader Eric the Red (circa 950–1003)

---

[1] See relevant chapter in this volume.

Exhibit 5.1 The Little Mermaid; photo © 2017 Léo-Paul Dana.

Exhibit 5.2 Lego; photo © 2017 Léo-Paul Dana.

colonised Greenland. In 1013, Danish ruler Sweyn Forkbeard (circa 960–1014) attempted to take over England; in 1014, his son Canute the Great (circa 995–1035) succeeded. Canute the Great added Norway to his father's acquisitions and established a Scandinavian empire.

Beginning in the 11th century, internal feuding weakened Denmark, but the nation recovered with the election of a strong monarch, Valdemar the Great (1157–1182). During the 12th century, the site of Copenhagen was a fishing village (Hildebrand, 1932). Valdemar II the Victorious (1170–1241), who reigned from 1202 to 1241, built a Danish Empire that included much of Germany. In 1397, Queen Margrethe (1353–1412) of Denmark formed the Kalmar Union with Norway (including Iceland) and Sweden (including Finland). This lasted until 1523, when Sweden broke away. In 1536, Denmark adopted Lutheranism, which entailed a shift toward a Protestant work ethic and entrepreneurial values.

In 1574, at Helsingør, construction of Kronborg Castle commenced; it was used to collect taxes from passing merchant ships. In 1599, enterprising King Christian IV (1577–1648) decided to build Frederiksborg; when it had a major fire, entrepreneur Jacob C. Jacobsen contributed most of the funds to repair it (Exhibit 5.3). In 1606, Christian IV launched Rosenborg Castle (see photo in Light, Rezaei, and Dana 2013). To benefit from their international trade networks, in 1622, Christian IV invited Jews to settle in Denmark to improve the economy. There was particular interest in Sephardic Jews, the first of whom arrived from Amsterdam and Hamburg. They were educated and affluent and were given different rights than Ashkenazi Jews from Germanic lands. Sephardic Jews were allowed to travel and trade throughout Denmark; those who leant money to the Danish royal family were called "Royal Jews." King Christian V (1646–1699) only allowed Ashkenazi Jews to operate as tobacco spinners if they built houses made of stone in Christianshavn, but not in central Copenhagen.

The year 1722 marked the inauguration of Fredensborg — literally Peace Castle — named so by King Frederik IV (1671–1730) to commemorate the end of the Great Northern War. This baroque style palace is featured in Exhibit 5.4. In 1747, the Moravian Brethren built the *Herrnhut Huset* (Exhibit 5.5) mission in Godthåb. Legislation was introduced, in 1782, "for the benefit of the Greenlanders. Skilled hunters were not to be taken into the service of the Trading Company and private intercourse between the population and the personnel stationed in Greenland were to be kept to

Exhibit 5.3 Frederiksborg; photo © 2017 Léo-Paul Dana.

Exhibit 5.4 Fredensborg; photo © 2017 Léo-Paul Dana.

Exhibit 5.5 Brethren Mission in Greenland; photo © 2017 Léo-Paul Dana.

a minimum in order to protect the Greenlanders from harmful influences ... The directive provided for uniform prices on retail wares and the purchase of products from Greenland, a system that is still in effect today ... necessities were to be sold at cost, but luxury items, such as sugar and coffee, were to be offered at very high prices" (Fleisher, 2003, p. 36).

In 1775, entrepreneur Frantz Heinrich Müller (1738–1820) launched the Royal Danish Porcelain Manufactory, in partnership with Queen Dowager Juliane Marie (1729–1796). This evolved into today's Royal Copenhagen.

According to the census of 1787 census, 212 adult males in Copenhagen indicated their profession as "Jew." This meant that they were entrepreneurs, involved in money lending, tobacco spinning and small-scale trading. Others described themselves as brokers, commission agents, merchants, or manufacturers of leather products, paper, soap or tobacco. The census of 1801 confirmed the clustering of Jews in only a few activities. These people were not allowed to own real estate, and they were not allowed to become craftsmen, due to prohibition from guilds.

Denmark remained united with Norway, which had control of Iceland. However, because Denmark sided with France during the Napoleonic Wars, Norway was lost according to the peace settlement of 1815.

In 1819, 14-year old Hans Christian Andersen moved to Copenhagen. He later became an author whose fairy tales were translated to over 100 languages.

In 1820, in Copenhagen, Hans Christian Ørsted (1777–1851) discovered electromagnetism. Among the first amusement parks in the world, Tivoli Gardens opened in 1843. Hildebrand referred to this as "a mid-city Coney Island, sometimes gaudy with its carousels and acres of colored lights" (1932, p. 248). Still intact is a windmill (see Exhibit 5.6) built in 1847, at Kastellet. Absolutism was abolished in 1849, as Denmark became a constitutional monarchy. Hans Christian Ørsted's brother, Anders Sandøe Ørsted (1778–1860) served as Danish prime minister from 1853 to 1854.

Until 1857, Copenhagen thrived on Sound dues — a toll of passing ships; however, the levy was abolished that year (Hildebrand, 1932). Denmark fought Prussia for the control of Schleswig-Holstein, but in 1864 almost a quarter of Danish territory was lost to the Germans who required resident Danes to serve in their army.

Exhibit 5.6 Windmill at Kastellet; photo © 2017 Léo-Paul Dana.

This prompted mass emigration of Danes. In 1874, Copenhagen celebrated the opening of the Royal Danish Theatre (Exhibit 5.7). In the countryside, until the 1870s, farmers "grew wheat and timothy, barley and apples, or raised a few pigs, poultry, or horses, each farmer according to his whim ... The crops of Germany, grain from

Exhibit 5.7 Royal Danish Theatre; photo © 2017 Léo-Paul Dana.

the States, and cattle from Argentina wrecked Denmark's markets, and within a few years the country experienced the greatest transformation of its agriculture in the history of cultivation" (Hildebrand, 1932, p. 247). During the 19th century, Denmark witnessed an enriching agricultural revolution.

Meanwhile, in 1863, the eldest daughter of King Christian IX (1818–1906), namely Princess Alexandra of Denmark (1844–1925), married Albert Edward, Prince of Wales (1841–1910). She became Queen of the United Kingdom of Great Britain and Ireland and the British Dominions and Empress of India, when her husband became King Edward VII, in 1901 (Exhibit 5.8).

In 1904, Captain Peter Mærsk Møller and his son Arnold Peter Møller purchased a second-hand tramp steamer. Their family-owned shipping business would eventually expand with a fleet of 800 vessels and diversify into an airline, banking, data processing and supermarkets, developing the AP Møller–Mærsk Group into the largest corporation in Denmark, with sales approaching 20% of the nation's GDP.

Exhibit 5.8 Edward VII & Alexandra; photo © 2017 Léo-Paul Dana.

Copenhagen's central train station (Exhibit 5.9) dates back to 1908. Also in 1908, architect Anton Rosen (1859–1928) designed the nearby Palace Hotel (Exhibit 5.10), which was completed in 1910. Meanwhile the head office for Kjøbenhavns Telefon Aktieselskab (predecessor of today's TDC) opened in 1909 (Exhibit 5.11).

Just opposite the Palace Hotel is Copenhagen's city hall (Exhibit 5.12) described by Hildebrand as "stalwart and impressive ... It is a conglomerate mass of rust-red brick, granite, limestone, and terra cotta — a strange blending of ancient Danish and Italian touches. Its tiers of windows, for example, are each of a different design; there are additional casual oriels that would be at home in Nuremburg, and battlements on the roof suggest the peak line of a modern New York skyscraper ... Along its roof are figures of the town's ancient watchmen, flanked by polar bears. An ornate

Exhibit 5.9 Copenhagen Station; photo © 2017 Léo-Paul Dana.

Exhibit 5.10 Palace Hotel, Copenhagen; photo © 2017 Léo-Paul Dana.

Exhibit 5.11 21 Nørregade, Copenhagen; photo © 2017 Léo-Paul Dana.

pigeon-cote houses the birds that flutter about ... A lofty tower, 342 feet high, which seems to have no bearing whatsoever upon its accompanying building, is proclaimed 'highest of its kind' in northern Europe ..." (1932, p. 222).

Copenhagen's central post office (Exhibit 5.13) was completed shortly before the start of the Great War (World War I); during the war, Denmark maintained its neutrality. In 1915, Danish women were allowed to vote.

In 1917, Denmark sold its Caribbean colony, the Danish West Indies, to the United States. This consisted of the islands of St. Croix, St. John, and St. Thomas, now collectively known as the U.S. Virgin Islands. In 1920, Denmark recognised the independence of Iceland, but the Danish monarch remained king of Iceland until 1944.

Exhibit 5.12 City hall; photo © 2017 Léo-Paul Dana.

During the early 1920s, climate change brought cod to Greenland's waters and a commercial cod fishing industry resulted in a cash economy that began to phase out the existing barter economy. Cod salting houses replaced blubber houses. Fleischer wrote, "Now it was possible to acquire luxuries such as Danish clothes instead of traditional hide clothing… Now they danced the tango and foxtrot to the tones of a new musical apparatus, the gramophone" (2003, p. 55). By the end of the 1920s, industrial exports accounted for 20% of Denmark's total export earnings.

In 1932, Ole Kirk Christiansen started making toys. The firm he created was Lego. His son took over the business and made the product globally available. Nowadays, hourly production of Lego can exceed 2.5 million bricks per hour.

Hildebrand (1932) referred to Denmark as a farming kingdom, and observed, "Lacking the coal and iron of Germany, the great

Exhibit 5.13 Post office; photo © 2017 Léo-Paul Dana.

forests of the Baltic countries, or the colonies of the Netherlands, except for icy Greenland, Denmark has developed the world's most highly specialized agriculture" (p. 247). Lindquist likewise referred to Denmark as "Farming Kingdom" (1940, p. 3).

After the Nazis overran Denmark, in 1940, the British occupied Denmark's Faeroe Islands to prevent these falling to the Nazis. In 1941, Faeroese boats supplied 75% of Britain's demand for fish (Bradford, 1970).

During the Nazi occupation of Denmark, Greenland was *de facto* independent, run by a central government office, in Godthåb. A Greenland defence pact was signed in 1941, allowing the United States the right to establish and operate bases in Greenland. In 1942, "Bluie West 8" was established at Kangerlussuaq in the west of Greenland, and "Bluie West I" at Narsarsuaq, in the south. Narsarsuaq was Greenland's largest community during World War II. Throughout the war, Greenland traded with Canada and the United States. On May 5, 1945, Germans in Denmark surrendered.

After the war, the United States offered $100,000,000 in gold to purchase Greenland. Although Denmark was impoverished by the war, Greenland was not sold. Instead, recovery was expedited by Marshall Plan aid.

Hutchison wrote, "In 1947, when one strictly rationed egg was a blessing in England, Denmark sent more than $100,000,000 worth of eggs, butter, bacon, and other products to Great Britain" (1949, p. 147).

When, in 1949, the sterling was devalued relative to the dollar, Great Britain was Denmark's most important export market and the Danish crown remained pegged to the sterling. The Danish currency remained unchanged at 19.34 crown per pound until 1967.

Galenson (1952) introduced the term Danish model. This refers to the absence of strict laws in Denmark, coupled with the relatively peaceful relationships between capital and labour.

Decolonisation also took place peacefully. Fleischer provided an excerpt of a 1952 speech by Danish King Frederik IX (1899–1972), "Now after the war, work in Greenland has entered a new phase. We are working to bring the society of Greenland into line with the new conditions for business and social and cultural development in today's Greenland. For everyone in Denmark, it is a cause close to our hearts to find a way to bring this about and to forge closer and closer ties between Denmark and Greenland, not as a colony but as an equal member of Danish society" (2003, pp. 62–63). In 1953, Greenland ceased being a Danish colony and became a province of the Kingdom. At the time, Godthåb had 1,200 inhabitants (Fleisher, 2003).

The Basic Law of June 5, 1953 became the basis of a new constitution. This required the Danish monarch to be a member of the Evangelical-Lutheran Church. In 1970, Finland turned down a Danish initiative for a Nordic common market. Shortly after Denmark joined the European Economic Community, Graves wrote, "Denmark's 135,000 farmers have more than doubled production in the past 20 years" (1974, pp. 270). Since then, Denmark has become increasingly similar to other countries of the European Union, and has been losing its autonomy and uniqueness as a society of great welfare of its inhabitants.

In 1984, Denmark began extracting natural gas from the North Sea. In 1987, foreign investors acquired control of Denmark's largest paint and lacquer company Sadolin & Holmblad. This caused grave concern. Given that Danish firms were relatively small by international standards, other enterprises joined forces with each other and with institutional investors, and supported restructuring in order to remain under local ownership. When Dæhnfeldt was sold to a British company, most other firms in the Danish seed sector joined forces to create Dan-seed.

Van Stell (2005) observed that business ownership rates in Denmark fell between 1972 and 2002. Yet, Kelley, Singer and Harrington reported, "Denmark shows the highest percentage of entrepreneurs with innovative products and services. This country also has low TEA rates. This suggests that although there are fewer entrepreneurs in Denmark, the higher proportion of innovativeness is an important quality dimension" (2012, p. 20). Meanwhile, Schøtt (2010a) remarked that Denmark had become more individualistic than is typical among developed countries.

In 2012, eight Danish banks were downgraded. In 2013, Denmark ranked in first place in the World Global Sustainable Competitive Index (Ellis and Rømer, 2016).

An immigration crisis followed. Rezaei, Goli, and Dana (2013b) studied underground activities of migrants in Denmark. Terjesen,

Siri, and Ainsley Lloyd (2015) observed that Denmark was among the top four countries whose institutions support female high-growth entrepreneurs.

The Environment for Entrepreneurship

The environment for enterprise changed drastically after serfdom in Denmark was removed in 1788. Peasants were formally emancipated and commerce then flourished. The environment for self-employment in the farming sector changed again during the late 1880s (Hildebrand, 1932). With the introduction of democracy, Denmark witnessed an agricultural revolution that greatly enriched the nation. Across Denmark, small-scale farmers saw the advantage of cooperation and the first cooperative dairy was established in 1882. The separator, invented by Gustaf de Laval (1845–1913), further advanced Denmark's dairy industry (see Sweden chapter below). By 1882, Denmark also had a cooperative slaughterhouse, where bacon and ham could be prepared for export to the United Kingdom. Agricultural exports brought foreign exchange to Denmark.

In 1920, the Axelborg Building (Exhibit 5.14) was built for the Danish Cooperative Bank and the Workers' Cooperative Housing Society (International Labour Organisation, 1925). The Axelborg was the second largest secular building in Copenhagen at the time (Vestergaard, 2014). That year, Desmond wrote, "Denmark has obtained a significance throughout the world out of all proportion to its size, due, primarily, to the fact that it practically leads the world in agriculture ..." (1920, p. 1575). He explained, "The value of the butter for export amounts to nearly 40 per cent of the total value of Danish exports" (Desmond, 1920, p. 1577).

Desmond elaborated, "there are over 1,500 cooperatives... there are formidable cooperatives societies for manure, fodder, corn and seed, machinery, cement and coal" (1920, p. 1600). Egan concurred, "Denmark is, above all, a land of cooperation ... It may seem strange that the royalist court of Europe should exist in a country which is largely constructively socialist. It seems even stranger to us that the

Exhibit 5.14 Axelborg Building; photo © 2017 Léo-Paul Dana.

farmers in Denmark, who are the most influential part of the population, should take to socialist methods" (1922, p. 129). Cooperatives are still important in Denmark. Members' liability may be limited or unlimited.

During the late 1950s the environment changed again when Denmark formulated and began to implement a policy aimed at improving the conditions with which industry had to cope. For example, schemes were designed to encourage investment. Results were soon visible. The number of unemployed in Denmark fell from 75,000 in 1958 to 25,000 in 1962. Many small firms focused on engineering and food production, usually labour-intensive.

Due to the small size of its domestic market, Denmark's manufacturers have long been highly export driven. In 1960, Denmark was among the founding members of the European Free Trade

Association (EFTA), along with Austria, Norway, Portugal, Sweden, Switzerland, and the United Kingdom. This promoted closer economic cooperation and free trade. By 1965, Denmark's industrial exports approached the level of agriculture. Although the government paid increasing subsidies to farmers, the number of people working in agriculture fell from half a million in 1950 to 2,50,000 in 1970. When, in January 1973, Denmark became a member of the European Economic Community (and thereby today's European Union), this led to further facilities for trade. Servais, Rasmussen, Nielsen, and Madsen noted two patterns of internationalisation among firms in Denmark, "The first group consists of larger and older firms, which have conducted a array of activities abroad. ... The second group consists of smaller and younger firms, which ... typically leapfrogged" (2008, p. 173).

The Ministry of Economic and Business Affairs launched several action plans to enhance Denmark's environment for entrepreneurship. Prior to 2005 the focus was on volume, after which policy shifted to a growth-oriented policy. Incentives included the: 2002 Competitive Power Package; 2003 Action Plan for Entrepreneurs; 2003 A Society with Room for the Free Initiative; 2005 Action Plan on Venture Capital; and 2005 Law on Promotion of Trade. The Globalisation Strategy followed these.

Today, various initiatives promote entrepreneurship in Denmark. The nation has adopted a wide range of schemes, providing relevant training and counselling as well as facilitating access to finance and credit. Denmark has traditional and technical universities, as well as institutions with a particular focus, e.g., the Danish Technological Institute (DTI). Growth Houses have been introduced to encourage and facilitate the fast growth of firms. Incubators enable students to test and develop their ideas with experienced entrepreneurs.

Schøtt (2010b) observed that government policies have become increasingly more supportive of entrepreneurship. The Danish Foundation for Entrepreneurship promotes entrepreneurship education and culture. Schøtt noted an increase in the social desirability of entrepreneurship, with an increase in people feeling that, "In Denmark, the creation of new ventures is considered an appropriate way to become rich ... In Denmark, most people consider becoming an entrepreneur as a desirable career choice" (Schøtt, 2010a, p. 30).

Toward the Future

Ellis and Rømer summed up the current situation, "With a nation of 5 million people, limited resources and Nordic values such as equality, trust, low power distance, inclusion and respect for nature, along with Protestant work ethic and cooperative traditions, Denmark has over the past two centuries built a strong foundation for both social entrepreneurship and corporate responsibility ... Even though Denmark is ranked by the IMF among the ten wealthiest nations in the world, the Danish welfare model is under severe pressure" (2016, p. 71–72).

As long as Denmark continues to have a well-educated and flexible work force, the nation shall have a high standard of living. Denmark promotes comprehensive entrepreneurship education. Schools increasingly teach the practical aspects of entrepreneurship as well as management skills; intensive training includes how to place an order, how to write a business letter, negotiation and even how to prepare a window display for a shop. Among others, the International Danish Entrepreneurship Academy, (IDEA), works to increase the number of competent entrepreneurs with a higher education.

As noted by Schøtt, "Training creates human capital, especially entrepreneurial competences in the minds of the trained persons. This training-based human capital brings a comparative advantage in the way that trained persons get higher income than untrained persons. Furthermore, entrepreneurs invest their training-based human capital in the creation of social capital in the way that trained entrepreneurs create networks that are especially large and resourceful in that the market sphere and the professional sphere in their

Exhibit 5.15 Copenhagen; photo © 2017 Léo-Paul Dana.

networks, are especially salient. This training-based social capital brings comparative advantages in the way that salience of the market sphere enhances innovation and in the way that large networks enhance exporting as well as growth-expectation" (2010, p. 155).

As its name implies, Copenhagen continues to be a merchants' haven. Its harbour has become so clean that people swim here all year long. It is the largest city in Scandinavia and on track to become the first carbon-neutral capital in the world; see Exhibit 5.15.

Chapter 6

Finland

Introduction

The Republic of Finland covers 304,593 square kilometres of land, and encompasses 33,551 square kilometres of inland waters. It shares borders with Norway, Russia, and Sweden.[1] Graves noted, "A third of Finnish territory, the portion known as Lapland, lies almost entirely above the Arctic Circle," (1968, p. 590). Finland is multicultural, including descendants of a Swedish-speaking elite, as well as indigenous Sámi people.

Famous Finnish entrepreneurs include Rudolf Walden (1878–1946) who in 1920 founded Yhtyneet Paperitehtaat Oy, a business that would develop into United Paper Mills, later UPM. With his son, Juuso (1907–1972), he practised paternalistic management, making mill-towns, including Valkeakoski (Exhibit 6.1), models of the industry. Well-known in the creative sector is Sámi entrepreneur Ulla Pirttijärvi (1971–), joik singer (Exhibit 6.2) and reindeer herder.

In 2004, Transparency International identified Finland as having the least corruption, falling to number two in 2015. Miles, Feulner, and O'Grady (2005) found that Finland had little regulation, low barriers, a low level of restriction on financing, a low level of intervention on prices, a very high level of protection with respect to property rights, and a very low level of informal market activity.

---

[1] See relevant chapters in this volume; for a discussion of entrepreneurship in Russia, see Dana (2010).

Exhibit 6.1 Tervasaari Paper Mill belonging to UPM–Kymmene Corporation; photo © 2017 Léo-Paul Dana.

Finland was number one in the World Economic Forum's Global Competitiveness Report, falling to fourth place for 2014–2015. Labour costs are high and Finland is far from first place in entrepreneurial activity. Arenius *et al.* (2001) reported that Finns had little motivation to be entrepreneurs. The Global Entrepreneurship Monitor (GEM) was central in reducing administrative barriers to entrepreneurial activity; it also promoted entrepreneurship education.

Routamaa and Mäki-Tarkka stated, "the micro enterprises are of vital importance for the Finnish economy" (2005, p. 114). They noted, "relatively low motivation of Finns to start their own businesses, shortage of entrepreneurial skills, and fear of failure hinder entrepreneurial activities. ... Young people seem to prefer paid work instead of entrepreneurship. ... Also the tradition of entrepreneurship and natural business transfer from one generation to another is more or less missing[2] from our entrepreneurship culture" (2005, p. 114).

An exception to this lies with a small minority — the Sámi people, who have a long tradition of passing reindeer (*Rangifer tarandus*)

[2] Family Business Network (FBN) Finland arranges seminars to promote succession.

Exhibit 6.2 Entrepreneur Ulla Pirttijärvi; photo © 2017 Léo-Paul Dana.

to their offspring, thereby maintaining a spirit of self-employment. Müller-Wille and Pelto observed occupational clustering was segmented along ethnic lines, "The Finns are mostly employed in administration, construction, and services whereas most of the Lapps still follow their traditional occupations — fishing, trapping,

Exhibit 6.3 Salmon; photo © 2017 Léo-Paul Dana.

small farming, and reindeer herding" (1971, p. 142). Both Sámi and non-Sámi participate in the reindeer economy (Dana and Light, 2011) and in fishing (Exhibit 6.3).

Generalising for mainstream society in Finland, Fayolle, Kyrö, and Ulijn wrote, that in Finnish mainstream society, "Entrepreneurship effort is accepted, but success is not" (2005, p. 23). In Sámi society, self-employment is well looked upon and success is desirable. *While reindeer, in Finland, are individually owned, their care is a communal activity shared among entrepreneurs.* Sharing of work within the family is usually with no remuneration other than in kind; each entrepreneur is interdependent with others, in a network of symbiotic interaction. While Sámi are pulled to reindeer husbandry as a means of self-employment, economic need also pushes them to work elsewhere (Dana and Riseth, 2011).

Stenholm *et al.* observed, "Despite of high level of perceived capabilities and high recognition of business opportunities, actual engagement in entrepreneurship remains low. Only 8% of the adult population intends to become an entrepreneur in the next three years" (2015, p. 18). While most Finnish companies are SMEs, most people work for the large companies or in the public sector.

Historical Overview

From 1155 until 1809, Finland was part of Sweden. Swedish remains an official language, spoken by an important ethnic Swede minority in Finland. The Swedish embassy is prominent in Helsinki (Exhibit 6.4). Roma (gypsies) arrived during the 16th century (Hunnisett and Pennanen, 1991).

Between the 13th century and 1809, Turku (Exhibit 6.5) was the most important city of Finland. A consequence of the Finnish War (1808–1809), Finland became an autonomous duchy within the Russian Empire. In 1812, the capital of the Grand Duchy of Finland was transferred from Turku to Helsinki (*Helsingfors* in Swedish). A statue of Tsar Alexander II (1818–1881) stands in front of Government Palace (Exhibit 6.6) in Helsinki.

Exhibit 6.4 Embassy of Sweden in Helsinki; photo © 2017 Léo-Paul Dana.

Exhibit 6.5 Turku; photo © 2017 Léo-Paul Dana.

Exhibit 6.6 Senate Square, Helsinki; photo © 2017 Léo-Paul Dana.

The industrial revolution gained momentum in 1871 when chemist Edward Julius Granberg (1823–1884) established a pulp and paper operation with partners Carl Oskar Willgren (1832–1882) and Carl Johan Helin (1844–1902); this was located on Myllysaari (literally Mill Island), facing the strong, never-freezing rapids of Valkeakoski. Gristmills had been in operation here since the Middle Ages. In 1873, a paper mill belonging to E. J. Granberg & Co. began manufacturing bag paper, beater paper, mackle paper, sugarloaf paper, wallpaper and writing paper; until the Russian Revolution, the firm was profitable with most of its exports destined for Russia.

The 20th century brought new opportunities. In 1903, the vessel *S/S* Nautilus was built at Hietalahti for marine research. The ship had a laboratory aboard with aquariums. The new century also brought with it a new look. In 1903, in Turku, a 1832 house designed by Pehr Johan Gylich (1786–1875) was transformed into *art nouveau* style by architect Fritjof Strandell (1865–1925); the new owner, entrepreneur Wallina Valtin from Stockholm transformed this into a luxury hotel, the Hamburger Börs. During the Great War (World War I), the name was changed to Grand Hotel Börs, later reverting to the name Hamburger Börs (Exhibit 6.7). Sculpted by Ville Vallgren (1855–1940) in 1906, the *art nouveau* fountain statue Havis Amanda (Exhibit 6.8) was erected at Helsinki's Market Square, in 1908. Also in *art nouveau* style, Finn architect Eliel Saarinen (1873–1950) designed Helsinki's train station (Exhibit 6.9), built in 1914.

Beginning in 1916, *S/S* Nautilus served as a war hospital for the army of Nicholas II; today the vessel is known as *M/S* Nikolai II (Exhibit 6.10). Finland declared its independence from Russia, on December 6, 1917. Finland thus became the "farthest north republic" (Olson, 1938, p. 499).

Glassey described Finnish mercantile activity at the open-air markets, noting that self-employed vendors were chiefly women, "While the Finns are fishing, their wives bring the catch to the market" (1925, p. 608). Niskanen (2001) studied the role of women in the Finnish economy, finding that between the 1920s and 1950s, women on farms worked longer hours than did men.

Exhibit 6.7 The Hamburger Börs; photo © 2017 Léo-Paul Dana.

Soviet forces attacked Finland in 1939 creating demand for military supplies. In 1940, Jylhävaara Oy began its versatile engineering operations at a red brick building that from 1873 to 1938 had served as Myllysaari Paper Mill (Exhibit 6.11) in Valkeakoski; Jylhävaara produced grenades and other military supplies, later focusing on components for the pulp and paper industry.

Finland fought alongside Germany against the Union of Soviet Socialist Republics until an armistice in September 1944 prompted the surrender of territory and the relocation of many Finns, including the Skolt Sámi (Ingold, 1976). Rovaniemi, the capital of Finland's

Exhibit 6.8 Havis Amanda; photo © 2017 Léo-Paul Dana.

Exhibit 6.9 Helsinki station; photo © 2017 Léo-Paul Dana.

Exhibit 6.10 M/S Nikolai II; photo © 2017 Léo-Paul Dana.

Exhibit 6.11 Jylhävaara workshop 1941–1969; photo © 2017 Léo-Paul Dana.

Lapland province, was devastated when the Nazis retreated from Finland in late 1944.

Bradley (1947) provided an account of post-war Finland. In 1955, the country was admitted to the United Nations. In 1961, Finland joined the European Free Trade Association (EFTA).

During the mid-1980s, high domestic demand led to output growth. Low interest rates during the late 1980s maintained high consumer demand. However, the boom overheated, house prices jumped and Finland found itself with a serious trade deficit. Interest rates were hiked and by 1990, local consumption was almost stagnant, trade with the Union of Soviet Socialist Republics was dwindling, and unemployment was on the rise. The worst recession in several decades started in 1990 (Mahlamäki-Kultanen, 2005). Unemployment doubled in less than a year. In 1992, Finland experienced its deepest slump since World War II. Domestic demand tumbled again in 1993, before the economy began to recover in 1994.

Beginning in 1994, improved competitiveness helped exports, resulting in a current account surplus and a drop in interest rates, stimulating investments, housing starts, and employment. On October 16, 1994, 56.9% of voters opted for the nation's entry into the European Union, and Finland became a full member on January 1, 1995.

On February 6, 1995, Finland set up a venture capital investment company to assist entrepreneurial activities. Nonetheless, economic growth slowed in 1995. In 1996, the Foundation of Private Entrepreneurs established a fund for young entrepreneurs; an annual competition was co-organised with the Federation of Finnish Enterprises.

Stenholm, Pukkinen, Heinonen, and Kovalainen (2009) ranked Finland 7th among 18 innovation-driven countries in early-stage entrepreneurship. Of 104 ranked in the 2009 Legatum Prosperity Index, Finland was on the very top; it fell to 9th place in 2015. Stenholm, Suomalainen, Kovalainen, Heinonen, and Pukkinen observed, "Finland scores better than its peers in the overall governmental support for entrepreneurship ... the regulatory environment is perceived more suitable for entrepreneurship than in other EU member states. This is supported by the Ease of Doing Business index's results" (2015, p. 13).

Indigenous Sámi Entrepreneurship in Finland

Indigenous peoples have been referred to as the Fourth World (Manuel and Posluns, 1974). Paine explained, "The Saami ... are not immigrant groups but autochthonous" (1984, p. 212). He used the term Fourth World "to refer to (a) ethnicity within a minority context, but (b) a minority context different from that of immigrant groups" (Paine, 1984, p. 213). Although the Sámi are a minority in Finland, they form a majority in Ohcejohka/Utsjoki. Paine (1985) emphasised they were once free, but disqualified by foreign forces.

The Finnish State Commission included as Sámi individuals who spoke the Lapp language, and who had at least one parent who spoke Lapp as a native language (Ohlson, 1960); since 1996, Finland considers an individual to be Sámi if: (i) the person considers himself/herself to be Sámi, and has learned Sámi as mother tongue; (ii) the person considers himself/herself to be Sámi, and Sámi was the first language of at least one parent or grandparent; or (iii) the parents or grandparents was recorded as a Lapp in 1932 or earlier. Yet, the Sámi are not homogeneous (Lehtola, 2002).

The Sámi were formerly referred to as Lapps. During the 19th century, Clarke wrote, "The Laplanders ... constitute the only remaining branch of the ancient inhabitants of Finland" (1824a, pp. 328–329). Ruong (1937) provided a rich literature review of studies about these people.

With reindeer pastures comprising about 40% of Fennoscandia (Turi, 2002), the Sámi people developed a subsistence economy, including the domestication of reindeer (see Exhibit 6.12). Reindeer provided transport, milk, and meat. Olson described reindeer

Exhibit 6.12 Reindeer; photo © 2017 Léo-Paul Dana.

transport, "In descending a very steep grade, the reindeer is hitched behind the sleigh" (1938, p. 512). As noted by Ingold, "The reindeer, although independent by nature, is amongst the easiest of animals to tame. It is of gentle disposition ... and appreciative of the comforts that association with man can provide" (1980, p. 97).

Traditionally, "indigenous land use was based on locally available resources" (Müller-Wille, 1987, p. 352). Until the 1940s, the Sámi people relied on local sources, for their energy requirements. Given the centrality of reindeer, to Sámi life, Collinder (1949) asserted the existence of thousands of words describing reindeer herding. In 1962, the Sámi of Utsjoki were the first in Finland to use snowmobiles in their herding. Before that, "the costs for equipment to work in reindeer herding were essentially zero ... Full participation in mechanized reindeer herding, on the other hand, means cash outlays for the snowmobile" (Pelto and Müller-Wille, 1972/1973, p. 136). Paine (1994) portrayed Sámi pastoralists in the 1960s. Müller-Wille wrote, "one can refer to the modification of the reindeer economy in northern Fennoscandia with the use of the snowmobile and the motorcycle between 1962 and 1968; this meant a considerable financial outlay for the Lapp reindeer herder and led to a reindeer meat industry oriented to a market economy" (1978, p. 110). Thus, traditional subsistence herding yielded to a cash sector.

Pelto and Müller-Wille observed, "The use of reindeer sleds for any sort of transportation was almost completely obsolete by 1967, and even economically marginal households throughout northern Lapland found means to purchase machines during the late 60s (1972/1973, p. 119).

Today, in Finland, a local reindeer association managed either by Finnish herders or by Sámi people is called *paliskunta*. This is essentially a system of associational management, among self-employed reindeer owners. As explained by Beach, "A *paliskunta* is a type of economic cooperative with a communal treasury to which members pay according to their reindeer herdings" (1990, p. 277). Lee *et al.* (2000) noted that northern Finland contains 57 of these reindeer herding units. Unlike entrepreneurs who compete against one another in other cultural contexts, the success of each Sámi reindeer herder has traditionally been, and continues to be, dependent on the mutual cooperation of reindeer herders.

Sámi complain about changes brought about by European Union policies (Dana and Dana, 2007; Dana and Remes, 2005). Legislation is changing the nature of this sector. Clarke described the way by which reindeer were traditionally slaughtered, "attended with the least pain to the animal, and the greatest profit to its possessor. They thrust a sharp-pointed knife into the back part of the head, between the horns; so as to divide the spinal marrow from the brain. The beast instantly drops, and expires without a groan or struggle, as if it fainted" (1824b, p. 173). No part of an animal was wasted. Today, European Union legislation causes inefficiencies along with a move away from environmentally friendly sustainability. Jernsletten and Klokov explained, "The slaughter houses have strict regulations connected to the activity. They have to conform to the EU-directives. ... This is creating troubles for reindeer owners trying to establish a small scale production ... many of the regulations are unnecessary and only create extra costs" (2002, p. 105). Jääskö observed, "the commercialisation and centralization of meat processing (including slaughtering) causes a decrease in numbers of people practising a reindeer economy as well as a decrease in opportunities for other local people to benefit from raw materials from reindeer" (1999, pp. 37–38).

Direct dependence on nature and on the traditional family business has been reduced. In his study of northern Finland, Burgess (1999) found that although nobody lives exclusively from fishing, this provides a supplementary source of income and food. A problem, however, is that substantial commercial fishing has over-fished some waters. Some Sámi people must now buy fish and meat. Haetta observed, "Mechanization and the market economy have replaced self-sufficiency" (1996, p. 3). Farmers have claimed land traditionally used by the Sámi people, reducing the area (see Exhibit 6.13) available for reindeer.

Yet, reindeer herding remains important. Although "Twenty females are the minimum for a practical herd" (Shor and Shor, 1954, p. 269), Lee *et al.* (2000) found that among 7,000 reindeer owners in

Exhibit 6.13 No longer pasture; photo © 2017 Léo-Paul Dana.

Finland, two-thirds own fewer than 25. They explained, "Reindeer herding is an important source of income for the Saami, bringing in between half and three-quarters of their gross earnings. However, this income has to be supplemented by agricultural and forestry work, as well as cash-earning jobs ... Although many Saami herders have additional employment, reindeer herding is still regarded as being of high cultural importance" (2000, pp. 101–103). In the words of Daes, "They do not accept the assumption that humanity will benefit from the construction of a world culture of consumerism" (2003, p. 67).

The Environment for Entrepreneurship

Routamaa and Mäki-Tarkka wrote of the economy revolving around "forestry, metal, engineering, telecommunication and electronic industries" (2005, p. 113). As 35,000 entrepreneurs ceased operations during the recession of the 1990s, Employment and Economic Development Centres were created, and began in 1997, to assist SMEs. "With special reference to rural young entrepreneurship, a more active role for existing enterprises in terms of developing practical training in their home district was suggested in order to reduce migration from scattered settlements" (Routamaa and Mäki-Tarkka, 2005, p. 123). Using a large data set from Finland, Johansson (2000) analysed the choice between being self-employed or employed. Findings suggest that, "the predicted earnings differential between self-employed and paid employment has a positive influence on the probability of being self-employed in Finland" (Johansson, 2000, p. 45). Johansson elaborated, "the group of self-employed is a very heterogeneous group, ranging from successful entrepreneurs with many employees to the local pizza-maker or baby-sitter" (2000, p. 53). Yet, it can be said that the economy of Finland, formerly dominated by forestry, is now dominated by the high-tech sector.

As noted by Wolf-Knuts (2001), the Swedish minority in Finland was formerly very active as self-employed farmers and fishermen. As the nature of agriculture has changed, the new generation tends to choose a different sector, but self-employment is still a favoured option.

While self-employment and reindeer ownership is common among Sámi women, Arenius, Autio, and Kovalainen (2004) showed that in Finland's mainstream society, men are more active than women in terms of start up and in terms of new business activity.

Routamaa and Mäki-Tarkka (2005) discussed the Finnish Polytechnics Incubators Network, a brainstorming community that promotes entrepreneurship. Today, entrepreneurship in Finland is facilitated by a variety of institutions and schemes. At the time of writing this book, the Entrepreneurship Policy Programme consists of five sub-sectors: (i) entrepreneurship education, training and advisory services; (ii) launch, growth and internationalisation of firms; (iii) taxation; (iv) regional entrepreneurship; and (v) relevant legislation. In eastern Finland, the Small Business Centre (established by the Helsinki School of Economics and Business Administration, in 1980) provides a variety of educational offerings, including a Degree for Rural Entrepreneurs. Among the research interests of the centre is the internationalisation of SMEs. There are 27 polytechnics operating in Finland, and each has an incubator (or equivalent).

The Inari Municipal Business Company has as its objective to facilitate work and subsistence in Inari for the inhabitants of this municipality. The municipality assists entrepreneurs and other economic implementing bodies with its services, cooperative network and partners to increase the economic well-being within the municipality. Another success story in Finland is Oulu, formerly an industrial city with a heavy reliance on chemicals, pulp, and paper. Today it is home to high-tech entrepreneurs (Susiluoto, 2003).

Facilitating finance, Finnvera Plc provides microloans (up to 16,800 euro) to microenterprises with up to five employees. Interest rates are low and even lower for women entrepreneurs. Networks of coethnic immigrants are also facilitating entrepreneurship (Elo, 2015; Jafarov, 2015).

Of course, not all entrepreneurial activity is legal. According to Lehti and Aromaa, "In addition to eastern prostitution, the Russians and Estonians, the Thai community in Finland also runs organised prostitution on a considerable scale with regard to the small size of the community ... The centres of the community and its social meeting places are massage parlours, some of which also sell sex services. In addition to the Thai women permanently living in the country, the parlours also employ "girl relatives", who visit Finland as tourists, work a three-month-period and return to Thailand" (2002, p. 69).

Luostarinen and Gabrielsson (2004) and Nummela (2004) focused on the internationalisation of Finnish entrepreneurs. Wahlbeck (2007) studied Turkish entrepreneurs in Finland. Peltoniemi (2009) explored entrepreneurship within creative industries in Finland.

Stenholm *et al.* (2009) noted that every sixth new business is related to the creative sector in Finland and observed that although approximately half of the country's adult population has recognised business opportunities and most of these perceived they have necessary skills,

Exhibit 6.14 Closed in 2015; photo © 2017 Léo-Paul Dana.

only 8% of the adult population had actual intentions to launch a business within three years. This was the fifth lowest among counties participating in the Global Entrepreneurship Monitor.

Kelley, Singer, and Herrington (2016) noted that between 2013 and 2015 fear of failure went down in Finland. They reported notable upward trends in both TEA and established business ownership in Finland (Kelley, Singer, and Herrington, 2016, p. 21). Nevertheless, the financial crises of the new millennium did bring new challenges. Adapting to the changing environment, Royal Restaurants closed their upscale Sundmans (Exhibit 6.14) restaurants in Helsinki, to focus on more casual places based in shopping malls.

Toward the Future

The future appears to be bright for entrepreneurship in Finland. Enablers of entrepreneurship here include good infrastructure and education. Stenholm, Suomalainen, Kovalainen, Heinonen and Pukkinen obsrved, "In general Finland has a well-developed support system for entrepreneurship: Finnish governmental policies, regulation, financing, physical infrastructure, and internal market dynamics are supportive for entrepreneurship" (2015, p. 9).

Entrepreneurship has become a top priority on the government's agenda, with entrepreneurship promotion programmes including regional business programmes, as well as national ones. As well, entrepreneurship is highly emphasised in the educational system. In addition to polytechnics, that offer undergraduate degrees, Finland has nine universities that teach enterprise, and most of these have specific degrees in entrepreneurship. The Turku School of Economics, the University of Kuopio and the University of Vaasa all have small business promotion centres. A network of 22 technology and science parks promotes *entrepreneurship through symbiotic networking*.

Among challenges facing Finland is to renew its major industrial sectors given the global competition of the future. Although Stenholm *et al.* (2015) suggested that the key elements of the entrepreneurial ecosystem — including education, finance and infrastructure — are fine, a country with a small domestic market is very dependent on its export sectors and on global development, as well as on its ability to renew itself.

Future research will be able to determine the level of success of recently introduced new pilot and development projects. Another issue of interest is the "disconnect in Finland, where over two-thirds of the population see positive representations around entrepreneurship and nearly 85% believe entrepreneurs have high status; yet very few Finns (33%) would consider starting a business a good career" (Kelley, Singer, and Herrington, 2016, p. 15).

Chapter 7

France

Introduction

Neighbouring Andorra, Belgium, Germany, Italy, Luxembourg, Monaco, Spain and Switzerland,[1] the French Republic covers 543,965 square kilometres, with distinctive regional, cultural, and linguistic differences. In much of France, the French word for cherry, *cerise*, is normally pronounced with two distinct syllables audible. In Normandy, it is often pronounced quickly as if it were a one-syllable word. In the southwest, it can be stretched as if it had three syllables, pronouncing clearly even the silent *e* at the end — as if it were *ce rise eux*.

Dana (1996) investigated a sample of 296 owner-managers in Alsace, finding that motivations for self-employment varied along religious lines; for a historical study of entrepreneurial families in Alsace, see Hau and Stoskopf (2005). The Basques were discussed by Laxalt (1968) and by Dana (1995b), the latter suggesting that entrepreneurs in the Basque Country are culturally predisposed toward self-employment; for a discussion of Basque entrepreneurs in the United States, see Laxalt (1966). The Bordelais is the focus of Davenport (1980); Brittany the focus of Walker (1965); Languedoc of Edwards (1951); the Loire of MacLeish (1966); Provence of Bryson (1995); and the Pyrenees of Laxalt (1974). Laxalt (1968) focused on self-employed sheepherders in the Pyrenees. Dana (2005)

[1] See relevant chapters in this volume.

gave an account of a typical small business in the Pyrenees. Self-employed goat herders and shepherds form the heart of the local economy in Aregno, on the island of Corsica; Range noted that while this island was annexed by France in 1769, some residents "remain defiantly un-French" (2003, p. 57). Meanwhile, Toulouse is home to a global aerospace industry.

The word millionaire was first used in France. Among the great entrepreneurs of France were Félix Potin (1820–1871), Alexandre-Gustave Eiffel (1832–1923), Armand Peugeot (1849–1915), Louis Renault (1877–1944), and André-Gustave Citroën (1878–1935). Born into a farming family, Félix Potin was attracted to commerce and following apprenticeship in various shops, opened his own when he was 24. This developed into a retail empire (Exhibit 7.1). Alexandre-Gustave Eiffel set up a new venture in 1867, and became well known for a variety of projects, among these the wrought iron tower (Exhibit 7.2) that he designed for the *Exposition Universelle* (Universal Exhibition) of 1889, and the elevator that he built in Lisbon (Conger, 1948). Armand Peugeot was born into a Lutheran family, who beginning in the 17th century, led an industrial empire that manufactured farm equipment, hand tools and kitchenware, while pioneering elements of social welfare. He diversified into bicycles and innovated with the world's first steam-powered tricycle, displayed at the 1889 Exhibition. At the time of Armand's death, Peugeot was the largest automobile maker in France. Louis Renault's first car was the Voiturette, produced in 1898. The following year Louis and his brothers Fernand and Marcel created Renault Frères (Renault Brothers), which would become the largest automaker in France. Son of a Jewish diamond merchant, André-Gustave Citroën was the entrepreneur who introduced Fordist methods of mass production to French (and European) car manufacturing. Citroën's 2CV model (Exhibit 7.3) was launched in 1949 and produced until 1990.

Ulijn and Fayolle (2004) found that France had a higher rate of self-employment than Germany or the Netherlands, "The low cost of setting up a business in France ... might explain partly the higher percentage of self-employed" (Ulijn and Fayolle, 2004, p. 211).

Exhibit 7.1 Potin's former head office; photo © 2017 Léo-Paul Dana.

Exhibit 7.2 Eiffel Tower; photo © 2017 Léo-Paul Dana.

Exhibit 7.3 Citroën's 2CV model; photo © 2017 Léo-Paul Dana.

Today, France is considered to be a role model for its science parks and business incubators for new and growing firms. Although Volery and Servais (2001) found that France displayed one of the lowest rates of entrepreneurial activity among countries participating in the Global Entrepreneurship Monitor (GEM), and the lowest Total Entrepreneurial Activity Prevalence of all the countries in the eurozone, France is one of the world's most innovative countries when it comes to IT. French government agencies have a multitude of incentives to start new enterprises. Although most new firms fail — as is the case elsewhere — new ventures in France, created by former employees of large corporations often do well. Perhaps because the large corporations are assisting these, four-fifths are still in business, several years after their launch.

Nziali and Fayolle (2013) explained that the 2013 GEM data showed a notable paradox in France. There was a very high level of entrepreneurial intention — higher than that in comparable countries — as entrepreneurship was increasingly perceived to be a desirable career choice; yet, results suggested that there was a strong fear of failure in France, coupled with low levels of opportunity perception and entrepreneurial competences. This led these authors to conclude that France was experiencing a weak perception of feasibility, despite a strong feeling of desirability.

France is a country that is rich in history and in tradition, and national culture may explain the low level of entrepreneurial activity. Society, here, gives importance to the privileges of the elite; with the French Revolution (for a detailed account see Bertaud *et al.*, 1976), privileges of birth were eliminated, but replaced by a scholarly meritocracy. Education is valued and academics are praised. Entrepreneurs have not been as valued; neither is the move to entrepreneurship.

Historical Overview

France has a long history of innovation, as well as self-employment. During the Middle Ages, Benjamin of Tudela wrote about his travel in France: "Montpellier ... is a place well situated for commerce. It is about a parasang from the sea, and men come for business there from all quarters ... Lombardy, the dominion of Rome the Great, from all the land of Egypt ... Asia and England. People of all nations are found there doing business through the medium of the Genoese and Pisans," (Adler, 1907, p. 3).

Mumford (1938) explained that from the 16th century on, new monopolies issued in France were not town monopolies but trade monopolies. In 1642, Blaise Pascal (1623–1662) made a mechanical calculator out of brass. At the age of 13, Louis XIV (1638–1715) danced his first ballet and in 1672, he established the *Académie Royale de Danse,* the director of which recorded steps and positions that form the basis of technique today.

Born in 1695, Henri Pitot (1695–1771) was the French engineer who invented the Pitot tube, used on today's airplanes to measure airflow; complementing an old Roman aqueduct, he inspired an aqueduct system in the Languedoc (Exhibit 7.4). Coquery (1997)

Exhibit 7.4 Aqueduct in the Languedoc; photo © 2017 Léo-Paul Dana.

studied self-employed artisans of Paris in the 18th century. Women and guilds in 18th century Nantes was the focus of Musgrave (1997).

Established in 1740, a brewery in Strasbourg was appointed supplier to the Court of France — thus obtaining the title *Brasserie Royale* (Royal Brewery). It had the monopoly providing beer to the armies of Louis XV (1710–1774) and Louis XVI (1754–1793). Its owner Jean-Melchior Klein died in 1765, leaving the family business to his wife Anna-Catharina Bickelhaub. In 1766, she married Jean-Daniel Schutzenberger (1737–1798) who carried on the family tradition. During the French revolution (1789–1799) it was referred to as the "Great Brewery of the Fatherland." In 1847, this brewery was the first in Alsace to introduce the Bavarian process, replacing infusion. In 1866, Jean-Daniel's grandson Louis Schutzenberger (1802–1887) relocated the brewery to Schiltigheim. The enterprise was incorporated in 1866 but remained family-managed. The firm was the first to introduce industrial refrigeration technology in breweries. A diversification strategy and intense worldwide competition led to closing it in 2006 — until December 2012, when "Schutz" as people call it, resumed activities with a special edition

Exhibit 7.5 Schutzenberger; photo © 2017 Léo-Paul Dana.

of Christmas beer and a limited range of traditional genuine beers (see Exhibit 7.5).

Between 1774 and 1789, the debt of France tripled (Severy, 1989), much of it incurred by supporting the United States in its War of Independence. In 1789, an entrepreneur from the Cachat family began distributing mineral water from his garden; this would eventually lead to the establishment of the *Societé Anonyme des Eaux Minérales d'Evian-les-Bains,* distributors of Evian water. At that time, French chemist Antoine Augustin Parmentier (1737–1813) promoted the potato as a food source (Parmentier, 1789).

On July 14, 1789, the Bastille — symbol of royal absolutism — was toppled. With the fall of the Bourbon monarchy in 1792, France became a republic.

French economist and entrepreneur Jean-Baptiste Say (1767–1832) became well known for his *Traité d'économie politique* (Say, 1803). He was among the first to observe that the value of a widget was derived from utility rather than from the labour used to produce it.

The first French republic lasted until 1804 when Napoléon I (1769–1821) established his empire. Rose (1902) provided a detailed account of the life of Napoléon I and Castelot (1971) of his empire. In 1806, Napoléon I ordered work to begin on the *Arc de Triomphe*, which soars 49.5 metres above the 12 avenues that converge at *Place de l'Etoile*. The monarchy was restored in 1814, with an interval the following year. In 1820, a 60% duty was applied to steel imports. In 1822, duty payable on iron from England was raised to 120%.

Charles X (1757–1836), King of France and of Navarre — brother of the guillotined Louis XVI and of the post-Napoleonic King Louis XVIII (1755–1824) — was the last Bourbon monarch of France, overthrown in July 1830, and replaced by more liberal King Louis Philippe (1773–1850). Following the 1830 revolution, the *Colonne de Juillet* was erected at the *Place de la Bastille*. In 1843, the *Passage Pommeraye* (Exhibit 7.6) was inaugurated in Nantes, capital of the formerly independent Duchy of Brittany (circa 939–1532) — ruled by a duke or duchess until Brittany became a province (1532–1789) of the Kingdom of France (see Exhibit 7.7).

At the time, quinine was the only prophylactic against malaria and, given France's conquest of North Africa, French authorities offered a reward for the creation of a wine-based recipe that would result in a palatable form of quinine. Chemist and wine merchant Joseph Dubonnet (1818–1871) responded in 1846 with his invention of the wine tonic that bears his name — a *Grand Aperitif de France* (Exhibit 7.8).

Exhibit 7.6 Pommeraye shopping mall; photo © 2017 Léo-Paul Dana.

Exhibit 7.7 Brittany's Queen Anne (1477–1514); photo © 2017 Léo-Paul Dana.

Exhibit 7.8 Joseph Dubonnet's tonic; photo © 2017 Léo-Paul Dana.

In 1848, Louis Philippe abdicated and the Second Republic was established. It lasted until the Second Empire was born in 1852, under the nephew of Napoléon I, namely Louis-Napoléon Bonaparte (1808–1873) — Napoléon III. The Second Empire favoured economic growth and modernisation. In London, Queen Victoria's husband Albert (1819–1861) saw the value of showcasing Britain to the world. His efforts led to the Great Exhibition of the Works of Industry of all Nations (the Crystal Palace Exhibition), held in 1851 at Hyde Park. This prompted Napoléon III to issue an imperial decree in 1853 for a Paris fair. Hence, the *Exposition Universelle des Produits de l'Agriculture, de l'Industrie et des Beaux-arts* (Universal Exhibition of Agricultural Products, Industry and Fine Arts) took place in 1855, with 23,954 exhibitors in the industry section. Among products featured here were the lawnmower, the Singer sewing machine, the washing machine, and the first saxophone — a recent innovation by Adolphe Sax (1814–1894), who received, at this fair, a medal for his invention. It was also at this Exhibition that the

Exhibit 7.9 Salt extraction at Aigues Mortes; photo © 2017 Léo-Paul Dana.

classification of Bordeaux wines used today was first introduced. The event received over five million visitors, among them Queen Victoria. Not everything was grand during this decade. In southern France, the 1850s saw the decline of the textile industry (Soulier, 1993). However, other industries would blossom. In 1856, independent entrepreneurs joined forces to create the salt extraction firm, Renouard et Cie., at Salin D'Aigues Mortes (Exhibit 7.9), by the Mediterranean coast. In 1868, it became *La Compagnie des Salins du Midi.*

In 1867, Paris hosted another exhibition at Champs de Mars — the *Exposition Universelle d'Art et d'Industrie* (Universal Exhibition of Art and Industry). This time there were 52,200 exhibitors.

When Napoléon III was captured, in 1870, during the Franco-Prussian war, the Third Republic came into existence. Losing the war, France ceded most of Alsace and part of Lorraine to the Germans.

To assert itself as a cultural capital, France organised the 1878 Universal Exhibition in Paris. Among displays at that fair were the recently completed head of the Statue of Liberty, and a recent innovation — the phonograph. In contrast to the 1855 and 1867 fairs, where most exhibitors in the industry section were small family businesses or even smaller enterprises, there were many larger firms at the 1878 event.

At a local exhibition in 1882, in Nantes, entrepreneurs Jean-Romain Lefèvre and Pauline-Isabelle Utile were awarded the gold medal for products of their Lefèvre–Utile bakery that they had established in 1848, in Nantes (Lefèvre and Utile, 1995). In 1886, their son Louis Lefèvre–Utile created the *Petit Beurre* — a biscuit that could be eaten any time. Even today, its shape is symbolic of time. Each biscuit — seven centimetres long, symbolising the days of the week — has 24 dots, representing the hours of the day. As for the shape, the 52 teeth represent 52 weeks of the year and the four ears symbolise the seasons. In 1887, Louis Lefèvre–Utile and his brother-in-law Ernest Lefèvre founded the Lefèvre–Utile Company. The factory (Exhibit 7.10) was designed by Auguste Marie Joseph Bluysen (1868–1852). Louis commissioned top graphic designers to create promotional art (Exhibit 7.11).[2]

In 1888, Vincent van Gogh (1853–1890) arrived in Arles, in Camargue. Kammerman called this river delta of Provence, "land of cowboys and gypsies" (1956, p. 667). Here, the bull is not killed at a bull-fight, and it is the bull who is considered a hero (Exhibit 7.12).

Among innovations displayed at the 1889 *Exposition Universelle* were automobiles, cinema, electric lighting, turbines, and wireless telegraphy. Built for this fair, the Eiffel Tower — 300 metres in height — remained the world's tallest structure until surpassed in 1930 by the Chrysler Building in New York.

During the late 19th century, single mothers struggled to find employment because of the fact that they were single mothers; to obtain income, they sometimes leased their children to entrepreneurs known as *loueurs d'enfants* — renters of children — whose service involved hiring out children to people seeking inexpensive labour (Tomel, 1894). In 1895, Auguste Lumière (1862–1954) and Louis Lumière (1864–1948) introduced the concept of the commercial movie theatre with paid entry.

The *Exposition Universelle* of 1900 prompted the construction of the Paris metro. Today, the network includes 303 stations,

---

[2] At the Universal Exhibition of 1900, Lefèvre-Utile received the unique grand prize for biscuit making. In 1967, the family business and its Lefèvre-Utile brand were transferred to Danone, acquired by Kraft in 2007, and the market leading Lefèvre-Utile brand is currently made by Mondelēz International.

Exhibit 7.10 Lefèvre-Utile factory; photo © 2017 Léo-Paul Dana.

Exhibit 7.11 Lefèvre-Utile promotional art; photo © 2017 Léo-Paul Dana.

Exhibit 7.12 Bulls are the heroes; photo © 2017 Léo-Paul Dana.

Exhibit 7.13 The metro; photo © 2017 Léo-Paul Dana.

serving over 1.5 billion passengers annually, along 205 kilometres of rails (Exhibit 7.13). For this fair, steam and electric locomotives were put on display, along with various railcars, at the *Invalides*, a rail station built for this fair and nowadays serving as an intermodal hub for Paris. Also built for this event were the *Petit Palais* and the *Grand Palais* (Exhibit 7.14). This fair had an unprecedented number of commercial venues operated by entrepreneurs and enterprises, including major department stores each with its own pavilion. Meanwhile in Pau,[3] the *Palais Beaumont* (Exhibit 7.15) was built in 1900.

French entrepreneur and aircraft manufacturer Louis Charles Joseph Blériot (1872–1936) made world news in 1909. He was the first to fly across the English Channel, from Calais to Dover, in a heavier-than air aircraft.

In 1911, Louis-Charles Bréguet (1880–1955) established *La Société Anonyme des Ateliers d'Aviation Louis Bréguet*, a prominent

[3] A century later, Herve and Christophe Pando, a Pau father and son team, were the last in France to manufacture shepherd umbrellas by hand.

Exhibit 7.14 *Grand Palais* built for 1900 fair; photo © 2017 Léo-Paul Dana.

Exhibit 7.15 *Palais Beaumont*; photo © 2017 Léo-Paul Dana.

Exhibit 7.16 Bréguet 765 *Deux-Ponts*; photo © 2017 Léo-Paul Dana.

manufacturer of wide double-decker aircraft (Exhibit 7.16). In 1919, he was among the founders of the *Compagnie des Messageries Aériennes*, which — after mergers with other small firms — resulted in Air France. (Air France acquired the airline *Union de Transports Aériens* (UTA) in 1990, merged in 1992. In 1997, Air France also absorbed Air Inter. In 2003, the agreement was signed for Air France and the Dutch flag carrier KLM to become sister companies.)

Meanwhile, with World War I, Alsace was returned to France. In 1924, art deco took the place of *art nouveau*. In 1926, France had 20,000 immigrant business owners, of whom 7,500 were Armenians, Greeks and Jews (Mauco, 1932). Williams (1930) gave a descriptive account of inter-war Paris.

In October 1933, at *Le Bourget* airport (Exhibit 7.17), Air France was born from the merger of five existing enterprises: Aéropostale, Air Orient, Air Union (successor of *Compagnie des Messageries Aériennes*), the *Compagnie Internationale de Navigation Aérienne* (CIDNA), and the *Société Générale de Transport Aérien* (SGTA). At the time of writing this book, *Le Bourget* was the leading business airport in Europe.

In 1936, a Jew by the name of Léon Blum (1872–1950) became the prime minister of France. Among his social reforms, he passed legislation to introduce a 40-hour workweek and a paid vacation leave for employees.

The Nazis invaded France, and the Third Republic fell in 1940. Alsace was annexed by the Nazis and fully integrated into the Reichsland. Occupied France was administered by the Vichy regime,

Exhibit 7.17 *Le Bourget*; photo © 2017 Léo-Paul Dana.

Exhibit 7.18 Vichy; photo © 2017 Léo-Paul Dana.

a puppet government based in Vichy — widely known for its mineral water (Exhibit 7.18). Walker (1940) reported about self-employed farmers in France, during World War II, and Moore (1943) provided an overview of France during the war.

Exhibit 7.19 Alsace; photo © 2017 Léo-Paul Dana.

On D-Day, June 6, 1944, 156,000 American, British and Canadian forces landed at Normandy to liberate France from the Nazis. Casualties were high. Simpich (1945) described the liberation of Paris. As the Nazis surrendered in 1945, Alsace (Exhibit 7.19) was returned to France. By the end of the war, thousands of American boys were killed (Exhibit 7.20).

Williams (1946) provided a description of post-war France. In 1946, Léon Blum negotiated a $1.37 billion loan from the United States, for post-war reconstruction. The Fourth Republic was established and Charles de Gaulle (1890–1970) appointed Jean Monnet (1888–1979) "to put the country back on its economic feet," (Fontaine, 2000, p. 11).

In 1950, inspired by Jean Monnet, the French Foreign Minister Robert Schuman (1886–1963) made a proposal to Bonn (then capital of the Federal Republic of Germany) for France and Germany to cooperate in the coal and steel industries. Originally conceived to encourage industrial investment, French *TVA* (value added tax) was

Exhibit 7.20 Normandy; photo © 2017 Léo-Paul Dana.

introduced in 1954. Vindt (2012) noted that this was particularly advantageous for large corporations.

Industry in France was highly regulated. The production of cognac, for instance, was increasingly controlled: In 1909, the French government passed a law defining the geographic regions in which cognac could be produced. In 1936, the use of sugar in cognac was controlled and types of grapes used were limited. In 1946, regulation stipulated the type of wood used in barrels to age cognac and the state decreed that the amount of alcohol in cognac sold for public consumption would not exceed 40% by volume. A 1955 law determined the minimum age of cognacs to be used for various indications, e.g., Napoléon or Very Superior Old Pale (VSOP).

A French protectorate since 1912, Morocco became independent on March 2, 1956, followed by Tunisia on March 20, that year. The Algerian War would last until 1962.

Meanwhile, in 1960, France introduced a new currency — the new franc, equal to 100 old ones. In 1961, Charles de Gaulle inaugurated the new south terminal (Exhibit 7.21) at Orly Airport. During the 1960s, the state relaxed some its regulations (Pattisson and Lindgreen, 2004).

The 1970s witnessed modernisation in methods. In Alsace, where livestock markets had been venues for economic transactions, the last livestock market took place in 1973 (Dana, 2006). Born into

Exhibit 7.21 *Orly Sud*; photo © 2017 Léo-Paul Dana.

a Jewish family who emigrated from Egypt, to France, Roland Moreno (1945–2012) invented the computer chip smart card, for which he obtained a patent on March 25, 1974.

During the 1980s, France introduced incentives to entrepreneurs in the textile industry, and leading stores (see Exhibit 7.22) promoted French clothing. The *Fonds Industriels de Modernisation* made available low interest loans. Subsidies were created for the acquisition of equipment, and the *Agence pour le Developpement de la Production Automatique* provided assistance for modernisation of the clothing industry. To encourage exports, additional funding was made available through the *Compagnie Française d'Assurance pour le Commerce Exterieur.* Although the larger firms criticised state intervention, these were able to benefit from schemes, more so than those with fewer resources to complete an application for assistance.

Exhibit 7.22 *Le Printemps* department store; photo © 2017 Léo-Paul Dana.

Mayer (1987) observed that people were attracted to small business proprietorship, with the hope that it would help them become socially mobile. Instead of mobility, they often experienced economic hardship, and marginality, "The price of 'freedom' for small proprietors is high" (Mayer, 1987, p. 56).

The frequency of business failures in France more than doubled between 1987 and 1993, while banks were more inclined to invest in government securities rather than lend to the business sector, especially small and medium-sized firms. According to the European Observatory for Small & Medium Enterprises, small business employment growth in France from 1989 to 1993 — less than 0.5% — was among the lowest in Europe. This should be read with caution, however, as there may be considerable under-reporting; many small-scale service providers operate in the black market, to avoid paperwork and taxation (Windebank, 1991).

Vidal (1995) demonstrated that small producers were very active in the food distribution channel in France. Paché (1996) explained that despite the marketing advantages held by larger firms, small producers may have a competitive advantage when they offer niche items that suit local preferences. In 1997, the French minister for SMEs, Jean-Pierre Raffarin (1948–) pushed for 37 measures to simplify entrepreneurship in France. Yet, Fayolle (2000) found that the start-up phenomenon remained fairly marginal among students and young graduates in France despite the apparent trend for entrepreneurship in the French education system.

According to the state statistics bureau, between 1966 and 1998, butcher shops, cheese outlets and one-man grocery stores disappeared from half the villages of France. During that time, the number of family-run grocery stores fell by at least 80%.

Van Stel (2005) observed that business ownership rates in France were lower in 2002 than they had been in 1972. According to state statistics, the number of fishmongers fell from about 4,000 in 1966, to roughly 2,000 in 2006; three quarters of all cheese shops also closed down.

Lasch and Yami (2008) reviewed 254 articles from the period 1995–2005. They noted a preference for qualitative methods and wrote, "A particular strength of the French approach is also a strong focus of small and medium-sized organizations" (2008, p. 339).

In 2008, the *regime d'auto-entrepreneur* was introduced in conjunction with the Law for the Modernisation of the Economy. With the status of auto-entrepreneur, one could launch a 1-person enterprise rapidly online and could benefit from reduced paperwork requirements. A commercial activity could not exceed 80,300 euro in turnover. A service business or liberal profession also had a turnover in limit, in order to benefit from this scheme.

Séraphin, Stoll and Carteron noted, "In 2010, the French government launched a 35 billion euro investment plan to foster innovation and growth from five priority areas: higher education, research, industrial sectors (including SMEs), IT and sustainable development" (2016, p. 94). France scored 64.2 in the 2010 Index of Economic Freedom, placing it among the least free economies in

Western Europe. Le Galès (2010) reported that in June 2010, French President Nicolas Sarkozy (1955–) addressed 3,000 SME leaders in Paris reminding them of the measures he took in favour of SMEs since 2007. Nekka and Fayolle (2010) studied Muslim entrepreneurs in France.

In June 2013, a bill was introduced to limit the duration one could be an auto-entrepreneur. The bill proposed that if income of 19,000 euro would be exceeded two years in a row, then the entrepreneur would need to create a classic business.

In November 2013, in the traditional garment district of Paris, a former sweatshop was reborn as a digital innovation hub. Known today as Numa, the high-tech incubator was conceived to house more than 200 start-ups and host 45,000 people daily.

Chanut-Guieu and Guieu (2014) studied hyper-growth of five SMEs that experienced growth in excess of 20% annually for at least four years in Provence and Rhône-Alpes. The authors found that the high growth of these firms was a result of the psychological state of their respective leaders and a manifestation of a secure enterprise geographically based where the company originated.

In 2014, the unemployment rate reached a new high of 10.2% (Séraphin, Stoll, and Carteron, 2016). That year, work began on the new Halle Freyssinet, in Paris. An initiative of French entrepreneur and founder of French broadband provider Iliad, the plan was to house the world's largest digital business incubator.

Lacroix and Dumont (2015) focused on Moroccans in France. In 2016, mergers took effect among some of the 22 *régions* of metropolitan France, reducing the number to 13.

The Environment for Entrepreneurship

There are several legal forms of businesses in France. It is possible to be self-employed or to have one of the following:

(i) *societé unipersonelle* ou *responsabilité limitée* (EURL), which is a company with limited liability and non-negotiable shares belonging to *one* entrepreneur;

(ii) *societé à responsabilité limitée* (SARL), which is a company with limited liability and non-negotiable shares belonging to multiple owners;
(iii) *societé anonyme* (SA), which is a limited, incorporated company; or
(iv) *societé civile*, which is a non-commercial company.

These terms are common in France:

- ETI: *Entreprise de taille intermédiaire* (firms with 250–4,999 salaried employees).
- PMI: *Petites et moyennes industries* (small and medium, industrial firms with 10 or more salaried employees).
- PME: *Petites et moyennes entreprises* (small and medium, non-industrial firms with 10 or more salaried employees).
- TPE: *Très petites entreprises* (microenterprises with up to nine salaried employees) — this includes "Mom & Pop" retailers (Exhibit 7.23) and small scale industries (Exhibit 7.24).
- *Entreprise unipersonnelle à responsabilité limitée* (solo enterprise).
- *Etudiant-entrepreneur*: In 2014, Jean-Pierre Boissin initiated the creation of the student-entrepreneur status. This helps students to start an entrepreneurial project at specific incubators known as PEPITEs (*pôle étudiants pour l'innovation, le transfert et l'entrepreneuriat*).

The above have surpassed the achievements of large corporations, in as far as job creation and prompt adaptation to technological and regulatory changes. Entrepreneurs succeeded in innovating, while internationalising effectively and efficiently, thereby yielding high productivity per limit of investment. The *Confédération Générale des Petites et Moyennes Entreprises* represents 1.5 million SMEs, 80% of salaried employees in the private sector.

France is rich in terms of new venture creation programmes. The *régions* have become the units of regional socio-economic development in France, and these *régions* have been the stage for the

Exhibit 7.23 Traditional bakery; photo © 2017 Léo-Paul Dana.

Exhibit 7.24 Small-scale industry; photo © 2017 Léo-Paul Dana.

evolution of several regional development networks promoting small business.

The *Agence Nationale pour la Création et le Développement des Nouvelles Entreprises*, formerly referred to by the acronym ANCE, was established in 1979, to promote entrepreneurship and to observe new venture creation in each of the *régions*. Its name was since changed to *Agence pour la Création d'Entreprise* (APCE). APCE conducts research, publishes guides in English as well as in French, offers specialised training courses and provides technical assistance to entrepreneurs. In addition to orienting entrepreneurs, the regional representatives of APCE also function as advisers to local government.

A parallel network was that of the National Agency for Research Development,[4] known as the *Agence Nationale pour la Valorisation de la Recherche* (ANVAR). It had regional delegations ensuring the promotion of innovation and of technological development in particular. ANVAR played a major role offering direct assistance, including financial support, management advice, and technical assistance. Like ANCE, ANVAR was a public, regional development network, under the direction of the central government in Paris. (These are now respectively APCE and Oséo, now integrated into the Banque Publique d'Investissement (BPI).)

Yet another network, the *Agences Régionales d'Information Scientifique et Technique* (ARIST), was set up jointly by various chambers of commerce and industry and by *Chambres de Métier* (guilds and other professional associations). The objective of ARIST is to contribute to the transfer of data and intelligence among small and medium-sized firms, especially where these are weak relative to larger ones. The ARIST offices, therefore, collect data, which could be of specific utility for small and medium enterprises.

Another important regional development network is the *Centres Régionaux d'Innovation et de Transfert Technologiques* (CRITT), which co-ordinates regional talent such as to adapt technological innovation to new product development and to new production

[4] For a discussion, see Obrecht (2002).

processes. The *régions* have also given rise to other functional networks including incubators.

Furthermore, the *Conseils Régionaux* (local governments of the *régions*) have supported specific small business programmes at various universities. The latter, in turn, also contribute to the regional networks. The *Instituts Universitaires de Technologie* (IUT) network of technical universities offers one and two year programmes in management with an option in small business management. Also, a diploma of scientific and technical studies (*Diplome d'Etudes Universitaires Scientifiques et Techniques*) is available with a focus in small business. Universities across France are offering programmes in small business or entrepreneurship.

The central government has also contributed to the small business sector by relaxing regulation. Employers are no longer required to obtain government authorisation to dismiss an employee. Also helpful is that under certain conditions, an entrepreneur may be exempted for paying social security contributions for employees.

Corporate initiatives have also encouraged entrepreneurship in France. In their attempt to rationalise and become more efficient, some large corporations in France have encouraged qualified employees to quit their jobs, in order to establish independent firms, which then receive sub-contracts. Most striking is that the corporations assist their senior managers to set up the new ventures, and the new enterprise is free to provide services to other large companies, even competitors. The employee's former employer provides advice, training and networking. Forty percent of the new ventures are service firms. Major corporations involved in such schemes include: Alcatel Alsthom; the large bank, *Banque Nationale de Paris* (BNP); the power utility, *Electricité de France — Gaz de France*; Hewlett-Packard; the post office, *La Poste*; the car manufacturer, Renault; and Sanofi. Each of several years, 20,000 salaried employees have been giving up their jobs to become entrepreneurs with the assistance of their respective former employers. While most small businesses in France fail in their early stages, the success rate of the former employees leaving their jobs to become self-employed sub-contractors is 80%, even after five years.

In addition to the networks promoting and facilitating entrepreneurship in France, there are others, which assist in financing new ventures. Several foundations offer grants and/or interest-free loans. Capital may also be obtained from local financing companies — *Sociétés de Capital Risque* (SCR). Among these are the *Sociétés de Développement Régional* (SDR), known in English as Regional Development Companies.

Depending on one's field of business and geographic location, it is sometimes possible, to qualify for other financial aid. The *Prime à la Creation d'Emploi d'Initiative Locale* (EIL) is a local job creation grant, while the *Prime d'Aménagement du Territoire* (PAT) is a regional development grant. The *Prime Régionale à la Création d'Entreprise* (PRCE) is a regional grant for new companies. There is also the *Prime Régionale à l'Emploi*, a regional employment grant.

Considering the availability of the above-mentioned networks of assistance, it might appear that setting up a new venture in France is relatively simple; however, the complexity of administrative formalities must not be underestimated. Paperwork must be completed at an administrative centre known as *Centre de Formalités des Entreprises* (CFE) in the district of enterprise. Once this has been done, then the applicant waits for registration to come into effect, and this may be a slow process. To expedite the process, after having completed the initial paperwork at the appropriate CFE administrative centre, it is possible to apply for a rush registration. This is done at the *Greffe du Tribunal de Commerce*. The rush procedure allows a company to be registered within five working days. With few exceptions, individuals who have not been French residents for a minimum of three uninterrupted years may not become company directors without a Commercial License for Foreigners, known as the *Carte de Commerçant Etranger*. To be self-employed, even in the arts and crafts field, one must also abide by the requirements of company directors.

Once an enterprise is created, keeping it in business is a greater challenge. There are constant paperwork requirements, numerous taxes, and costly social security payments along with rigid bureaucratic procedures.

The combination of entrepreneurship promotion along with the disincentives discussed, results in significant volatility within the small and medium-sized enterprise sector. A paradox here is that while the government encourages new venture creation in France, bureaucratic regulation and taxation decrease the chances of a firm's survival. Thus, high mortality rates accompany the high birth rates. Jobs are created, but often temporarily — not necessarily the optimal scenario for France.

The costly access to financial markets and the lack of cooperation from the mainstream banks is also an issue. Grants are available for start-ups, but unless day-to-day banking is smooth, then periodic financial difficulties may be encountered. It would be in the mutual interest of banks and small business, if the former would improve their attitude towards the latter. In most of Europe, the most common source of capital for new ventures is the entrepreneur himself; in France, financial institutions have been the principle source of funds. The *Fonds National de Garantie à la Création d'entreprise* (National Fund for Business Loan Guarantees) known by the acronym SOFARIS may provide a bank with financial guarantees. Belletante, Levratto, and Paranque (2001) focused on the financing of SMEs in France.

It appears that conditions are such that many people are pushed into necessity self-employment, as opposed to being pulled toward opportunity entrepreneurship. Ma Mung and Lacroix noted that, "immigrant workers, especially vulnerable to unemployment, are forced to set up their own businesses in order to survive, especially in economic sectors where sub-contracting is developing" (2003, p. 187).

To overcome difficulties, small firms often find a route to success by means of collective action. Gundolf and Jaouen (2005) found that *collective actions were allowing very small French firms to benefit from exterior resources, without loosing autonomy or making heavy capital investments.*

Obrecht (2005) pointed out that the concept of *collective entrepreneurship, although new in the entrepreneurship literature, is an important feature in France, inspired by the ideology of 19th century* *co-operative movements in Europe*. It can take the form of *Coopératives d'Activités et d'Emploi* whose workers are entrepreneurs in their own right i.e., entrepreneurial individuals who enterprise together, with common resources. In France, the number of such cooperatives of entrepreneurs is increasing; they were 30 in 2005, and 72 according to latest reports. There is also an umbrella organisation *Coopérer pour Entreprendre*, which has recently expanded its activities to educational programmes addressing 16 to 18-year-old adolescents in view of promoting the spirit of initiative together with cooperative values. In the same vein, Obrecht (2016) emphasised the necessity to have innovative approaches to entrepreneurship education such as to promote participatory sustainability along values that are closer to cooperative principles.

Nziali and Fayolle (2013) clearly explained enablers and constraints in the environment for entrepreneurship in France. The foremost enabler of entrepreneurship is socialisation. The principal constraint is the lack of appropriate education to develop entrepreneurial capabilities and relevant competences.

Among the pioneers of entrepreneurship research in France is Michel Marchesnay, now Professor *Emeritus* at the Université de Montpellier. He emphasised to the author the prominent power of the central government in France, centred in Paris with civil servants selected from the *Ecole Nationale d'Administration* (ENA), with influence on the environment for entrepreneurship in France. Pointing out the dominance of *grandes familles* (prominent families with old money), he cautioned against overvaluing meritocracy, given the huge power of the upper bourgeoisie in France. He argued that France could be seen as a predominantly risk-avoiding nation of rent-seeking rentiers, with few success stories of self-made entrepreneurs. As well, he underlined the dominant rule of the *grandes écoles* and also the elitist *écoles de commerces* — that cater, according to him, to *héritiers* — heirs of business dynasties.

Toward the Future

At the time of writing, France was a candidate for the 2025 World Expo exhibition, sanctioned by the Paris-based *Bureau International des Expositions* (BIE); if successful, France would again become an international showcase hosting the world and entrepreneurs would have a grand event to look forward to.

Meanwhile, business start-ups are facilitated by a variety of networks and incubators, but the probability of survival is low. Bureaucratic procedures and regulations appear to be a burden on the limited time and resources of owner-managers. Combined with high taxes and social contributions, this leads to high unit costs, which in turn decreases the competitiveness of small firms. This current situation is not the optimal scenario for France. The creation of a more transparent regulatory framework with simplified bureaucratic procedures would be most welcome.

Recommending reform, Ducros, Guérin, and Jacquot wrote, "La création d'entreprise ne se porte pas si mal en France. Mais des réformes sont encore nécessaires" (2004, p. 18). The following have been among suggestions: more flexible labour laws; the reduction of taxes; emphasis on entrepreneurship, in the educational system; and attempts to legitimise entrepreneurship. The latter seems especially important given Fayolle's (2004) finding that, in France, at a quantitative level, entrepreneurship among students and graduates was low. The economic and legislative environment often has a negative impact, and compared to other countries, entrepreneurship is more difficult in France.

Chapter 8

Germany

Introduction

The Federal Republic of Germany (formerly also known as West Germany) covers 356,978 square kilometres, neighbouring Austria, Belgium, the Czech Republic, Denmark, France, Luxembourg, the Netherlands, Poland, and Switzerland.[1] An important German inventor/entrepreneur was Johannes Gutenberg (circa 1395–1468), the first printer/publisher in Europe to use moveable type. Examples of science-based entrepreneurs include Carl Zeiss (1816–1888), Otto Schott (1851–1935), and Ernst Abbe (1840–1905), who together pioneered modern optics. Other famous German entrepreneurs include Friedrich Engelhorn (1821–1902) founder of BASF, Gottlieb Daimler (1834–1900) who in 1885 patented one of the first successful internal-combustion engines, and Karl Friedrich Benz (1844–1929) who in 1886 received the first patent for a petrol-fuelled car. Adolf Dassler (1900–1978) created Adidas; his brother Rudolf Dassler (1896–1974) launched Puma. More recently, Berlin has become Europe's most vibrant centre for venture capital. Berlin and Munich both have important clusters with many high-tech start-ups. Germany is a champion at exporting, and many of its producers are SMEs from the *Mittelstand* — including family enterprises. There is an important interplay, here, between heavy industry and the development

[1] See relevant chapters in this volume; for a discussion of entrepreneurship in Eastern Europe, see Dana (2010).

Exhibit 8.1 Station at Wiesbaden; photo © 2017 Léo-Paul Dana.

of SMEs. The automotive industry, for example, is a platform for supplying and supporting SMEs; simultaneously, this fosters their internationalisation.

Sternberg, Vorderwülbecke, and Brixy (2015) identified government policy and a modern infrastructure (Exhibit 8.1) as enabling German entrepreneurship; constraints included: a surplus of good job opportunities contributing to opportunity cost; a lack of entrepreneurial values and social norms; and the education system.

Ulijn and Brown noted, "the percentage of self-employed people and new start-ups in Germany is comparatively low compared with Japan, the USA, France and the Netherlands" (2004, p. 4). Ulijn and Fayolle (2004) suggested that the German engineer appears to be less market oriented than the Dutch one. Groen, Ulijn, and Fayolle wrote, "To the statement: One should not start a business if there is risk to fail ... Germans would react with 'Don't even try'" (2006, p. 529). Henschel (2006) suggested that among German SMEs, risk management is carried out with little planning. Henschel and Durst (2016) showed that German SMEs are more risk averse than their counterparts in Scotland.

It is important to note that there are significant demographic and regional differences within this federal republic. Stuetzer *et al.* (2014) revealed the importance of regional characteristics, including culture and the economic context that have an effect on perception of opportunities, affecting intentions and activity.

In addition to the incentives made available by the central government, different *Bundesländer* — federal states — (often shortened to *Länder*) have state-level entrepreneurship initiatives. Each has its government. Exhibit 8.2 features Karin Stoiber (1943–), formerly First Lady of Bavaria; her husband, Dr. Edmund Stoiber (1941–), was Minister-President at the federal state level.

Exhibit 8.2 Karin Stoiber; photo © 2017 Léo-Paul Dana.

Bavaria is a large state with vast differences within it. It is home to three dialects: Bavarian, Franconian and Swabian. Jennings (1974) focused on Bavaria's regional characteristics. Home to Audi and BMW, Bavaria is an industrial powerhouse — a main contributor to the inter-state fiscal adjustment, *Länderfinanzausgleich*. Bavaria is also home to agriculture (Exhibit 8.3).

Klandt observed that a Protestant upbringing "is more likely to lead to independent business activity than a Catholic upbringing (1987, p. 31)." Benoit (2004) and Williamson (2004) argued that important differences persisted between the east and west of this country.

Benoit wrote, "it is becoming apparent that the two sides have begun to diverge — economically, politically and culturally," (2004, p. 11). Grichnik and Hisrich (2005) explained that new ventures in the eastern states of Germany — the former German Democratic Republic also known as East Germany — were being created out of economic necessity, while entrepreneurs in the west of the country

Exhibit 8.3 Bavarian farmland; photo © 2017 Léo-Paul Dana.

were likely to be motivated by wealth and independence; the authors suggested that people from former West Germany were relatively more entrepreneurial than Germans from the east of the country. Rocha and Sternberg confirmed, "there is a Länder effect on entrepreneurship" (2005, p. 287). Welter (2006) noted a lower participation of female entrepreneurs in the western states. Regional differences remain.

Historical Overview

The Germans have a rich history. Castles dot the landscape. Exhibit 8.4 features *Schloss Staufenberg* overlooking vineyards.

The guilds of medieval times established a very efficient system of local development. They established market places, warehouses and administrative systems, thus protecting pre-industrial entrepreneurship and local trading. In his discussion of German-speaking Europe, Mumford (1938) explained that even the prostitutes formed guilds; he noted that in Augsburg and Hamburg the brothels were under municipal protection.

The Hanseatic League — from the medieval German word *Hanse*, for guild or association — formed a network that provided protection of trading interests. It dominated commercial activity in northern Europe between the 13th and 15th centuries, but declined slowly with the destruction of monopolies from the 15th to the 17th century.

Friedrichs (1997) focused on German artisans of 17th century. Sombart wrote, "In the 17th century the importance of the Jews had grown to such an extent that they were regarded as indispensable to the growth of Hamburg's prosperity" (1913, p. 20). Hamburg prospered further with the arrival of Huguenots during the early 18th century. Exhibit 8.5 illustrates the 19th century *Fischauktionshalle* (fish auction hall) in Hamburg.

In 1791, the first Prussian-made steam engine was completed, and this paved the way for the industrial revolution that arrived during the 19th century (see Schmidt, 1999). There were political changes too, as several German states formed a union, in 1818.

Exhibit 8.4 *Schloss Staufenberg*; photo © 2017 Léo-Paul Dana.

In 1821, Prussia created the Institute of Trades, the objective of which was to spread knowledge of new industrial methods. In 1834, a union for free trade — the *Zollverein* — was established. To facilitate transport, the railway system was developed during the

Exhibit 8.5 Fish auction hall in Hamburg; photo © 2017 Léo-Paul Dana.

1840s; this contributed to the development of coal mining and industries that were made possible by coal power.

Having served as ambassador of Prussia to the court of Napoléon III (1808–1873), Otto Eduard Leopold Fürst von Bismarck (1815–1898) became prime minister of Prussia, where in 1863, he called for the suppression of French in all administrative documents. He embarked to establish a German Empire by unifying independent states. Taking place gradually during the 1860s, German unification was finalised by the Franco-Prussian War of 1870–1871 — orchestrated by Bismarck to attract the western German states into an alliance with the North German Confederation. Napoléon III was defeated and in 1871 the Germans proclaimed the birth of the German Empire, which included Alsace-Lorraine — the name given to the territory that was ceded by France to Germany.

Hence, in 1871, Wilhelm Friedrich Ludwig (1797–1888), sometimes anglicised to William I — who had been king of Prussia since 1861 — became emperor, Kaiser Wilhem I. In French, he was known

Exhibit 8.6 *Palais Universitaire*, Strasbourg; photo © 2017 Léo-Paul Dana.

as *le Kaiser Guillaume Ier*. He and his chancellor Otto von Bismarck planned to make Strasbourg a heart of the empire and decided to build here a university. Inaugurated by Wilhem I in 1884, the *Palais Universitaire* (Exhibit 8.6) was built in Italian neo-renaissance style. In 1872, regulation mandated the use of German in documents and minutes throughout Alsace-Lorraine.

In 1887, *Brachhausen & Riesener* was established as a company to commercialise a recent German invention, the polyphon, a mechanical music machine that played a punched, metal disc (Exhibit 8.7). Advancing technology even further, was the grooved, flat gramophone record and gramophone record player (Exhibit 8.8) — predecessor of today's turntable; this was the invention of Emil (later Emile) Berliner (1851–1929), who was born in Hannover to Jewish entrepreneur Samuel Berliner (1813–1872) and Sally Friedmann (1826–1903). Based on the principle of etching a lateral cut into a zinc disc, in 1887 the inventor obtained patents for this, in England, Germany, and the United States.

Exhibit 8.7 German polyphon; photo © 2017 Léo-Paul Dana.

In 1889, serial production began of the Emil Berliner gramophone. Having established the *Telephon-Fabrik Berliner AG* to be run by his brother Jacob (1849–1918) in Hannover, Emile Berliner established the United States Gramophone Company in 1893, and the German *Deutsche Grammophon Gesellschaft*, in Hannover, in 1898.

Exhibit 8.8 Invented by Emil Berliner; photo © 2017 Léo-Paul Dana.

In 1899, he established E. Berliner of Canada in Montreal, which — based on a Canadian patent — would hold exclusive rights to gramophones and discs in Canada. Berliner transferred US Patent rights to Eldridge R. Johnson (1867–1945), who — using the name Victor Talking Machine Company and manufacturing in Camden, New Jersey — developed the business that evolved into RCA-Victor. In 1899, the Gramophone Company purchased from artist Francis Barraud (1856–1924) copyright for "His Master's Voice" — a painting of the artist's dog Nipper. Registered to Emile Berliner on July 10, 1900, this became a widely recognised trade-mark (Exhibit 8.9). Meanwhile, Wilhelm I died in 1888 and his eldest son Friedrich (1831–1888) was emperor — Friedrich III — for 99 days until he died from cancer of the throat. Friedrich III was succeeded by his son, Wilhem II (1859–1941). In 1889, Germany became the first nation to adopt an old-age social insurance programme.

Synagogues were built for Jews, an important ethnic community with prominent entrepreneurs contributing to the economy. Existing synagogues were enlarged. An example is that at Ingwiller, enlarged in 1891 and further renovated 1903 (Exhibit 8.10).

Exhibit 8.9 Nipper; photo © 2017 Léo-Paul Dana.

Italians comprised another important ethnic minority in Germany. During the late 19th century, Italian immigrants established enterprises to import Italian goods into Germany (Wilpert, 2003).

In 1899, a factory established by Andreas Hamm (1824–1894) was incorporated and in 1906 the name was changed to *Schnellpressenfabrik AG Heidelberg*. Flatbed cylinder presses and other innovations for book printing were developed here. A highlight was the Heidelberg Original press of 1919, incorporating a cylinder inking system that replaced the earlier revolving ink technology. The automatic high-speed press offered a windmill gripper coupled with precision (Exhibit 8.11).

The 20th century would witness more changes, not all of them good. Nasmith wrote, "In the town of Zabern in Alsace in 1913 a German lieutenant cut a lame cobbler over the head with a sword because the cobbler had failed to salute" (1919, p. 41).

Germany declared war on Russia on August 1, 1914 and on Belgium and France two days later. England declared war on Germany on August 4, 1914, followed by Serbia on August 9, and

Exhibit 8.10 Ingwiller synagogue; photo © 2017 Léo-Paul Dana.

by Japan on August 23, 1914. In March 1916, Germany declared war on Portugal. By August that year, Italy and Romania were also at war with Germany. On April 6, 1917, the United States declared war on Germany. By the next day Cuba and Panama were also at

Exhibit 8.11 Heidelberg Original of 1919; photo © 2017 Léo-Paul Dana.

war with Germany. By the summer of 1917, Siam (as Thailand was then known), Liberia and China were also at war with Germany. By October 1917, Brazil was at war with Germany. In February 1918, Argentina broke diplomatic relations with Germany. By July that year, Haiti was also at war with Germany (Nasmith, 1919).

As a result of the Great War (World War I), the Weimar Republic replaced the German monarchy. Germany lost Alsace-Lorraine to France and part of Prussia to Poland. Germany's colonies, including South-West Africa (SWA) — today's Namibia (see Dana, 1993a) — and Togoland (see Dana 2007; Dana and Anderson, 2007) were taken away. Germany lost New Guinea to Australia. Samoa was lost when New Zealand forces landed at Apia. After the war, the German economy suffered from the lack of natural resources, from huge payments to the Allies — and from hyperinflation never experienced by any other industrialised nation.

Although Sombart (1922) lauded entrepreneurs, high unemployment was inevitable. Fuelled by the Great Depression in 1933, the Nazi party rose to power. In violation of the Treaty of Versailles, Germany occupied the demilitarised zone of the Rhineland, in March 1936. That summer, Germany sent troops and arms to assist Francisco Franco (1892–1975) in Spain.

In March 1938, Austria was annexed into the German Reich. That year, a Lufthansa Focke-Wulf Fw 200 Condor made a world record, flying from Berlin to New York, non-stop in 24 hours 56 minutes and 12 seconds.

In March 1939, German troops invaded Moravia and Bohemia and set up a German protectorate in Czechoslovakia. Germany's invasion of Poland in September 1939 prompted the declaration of World War II. The Nazis took neutral Denmark in April 1940, invading neutral Norway next, followed by Belgium, the Netherlands and Luxembourg in May. France surrendered in June. Alsace, a fertile plain, became part of the German province of Baden. Lorraine, an agricultural land with some of the richest iron mines in Europe, was joined to the Saarland, also an important coal-mining region.

Juillard (1947) focused on atrocities that happened in concentration camps. Whereas much literature is dedicated to events of World War II, details shall not be presented here.

As World War II came to a close, a black market developed and much trade took the form of barter as many people had little confidence in currency. Henry (1945b) provided a contemporary account. United States military script — denominated in dollars — was used only at designated posts.

As a result of the war, Germany lost the northern part of its province of East Prussia to the Eastern Bloc; the provincial capital, Königsberg was renamed Kaliningrad. Alsace and Lorraine were returned to France, and the Rhine River (Exhibit 8.12) became the border between France and Germany. For six decades, the United States kept a military presence at the Rhein-Main Air Base (Exhibit 8.13).

East Germany and West Germany were founded as separate states, in 1949. While West Germany worked toward becoming a

Exhibit 8.12 Along the Rhine; photo © 2017 Léo-Paul Dana.

showpiece of private enterprise, East Germany became the vanguard of socialism. In West Germany, "Only seven years after surrender, German factories rebuilt with U.S. Marshall Plan aid were churning out a trade surplus. ... The now-famous Wirtschaftswunder — the 'economic miracle' — propelled the Federal Republic into the role of Western Europe's most powerful economic force" (Putman, 1977, p. 151). Explanatory variables included, "a remarkable political stability; a cooperative labor movement; a social calm; the industrious German nation itself" (Putman, 1977, p. 151).

Rapid recovery, in West Germany, led to a labour shortage and series of migrations by *Gastarbeiter* (guest workers); see Herbert (1990). A wave of Italians began coming in 1955, followed by Greeks and Spanish people in 1960, Turks in 1961, and Portuguese in 1964. Later, some of these would become self-employed (see Fertala, 2003). As Putman wrote, "The Federal Republic of Germany

Exhibit 8.13 Rhein-Main Air Base; photo © 2017 Léo-Paul Dana.

has emerged as Western Europe's strongest, most prosperous nation" (1977, p. 149).

Meanwhile, East German entrepreneurs were banished as their estates were subdivided; the restructuring of land tenure eliminated the family farm, formerly a significant element of the small business sector. Of 855,000 farms in 1952, by 1990 only 3,850 remained.

On June 13, 1990, at Bernauerstraße, 300 East German border guards began tearing down the Berlin Wall. After 40 years of centralised planning, on July 1, 1990 a treaty on economic, monetary and social union came into effect, introducing to East Germany a social market economy — an economy based upon private ownership, competition, freedom to set prices and freedom of movement of capital, labour, goods, and services.

On October 3, 1990 East Germany was transformed into five new states (Brandenburg; Mecklenburg-Western Pomerania; the

Free State of Saxony; Saxony-Anhalt; and the Free State of Thuringia) of the Federal Republic of Germany, already comprised of eight states (Baden-Württemberg; the Free State of Bavaria; Hesse; Lower Saxony; North Rhine-Westphalia; Rhineland-Palatinate; Saarland; and Schleswig-Holstein) and two city-states (the Free Hanseatic City State of Bremen and the Free and Hanseatic City of Hamburg), plus West Berlin with its special status. East Berlin and West Berlin were also reunited.

In 1990, politically unified Germany represented 23% of the population of the European Economic Community; yet mind-set was not homogeneous. Transition here was like a natural experiment of the power of entrepreneurial initiative, or at least it is an excellent example how free enterprises can profoundly change a situation in a very short period of time. This merits detail, below. As the poorly performing economy of the east (1989 per capita GDP was $4,500) was grafted to the dynamic and successful one of the West (1989 per capita GDP was $19,300), most East German enterprises could not survive. Unemployment in East Germany skyrocketed immediately from almost nil in June 1990 to 200,000 following unification in July (*The Economist*, July 7, 1990, p. 48) and possibly over 2,000,000 (*The Financial Post*, October 3, 1990, p. 1) after political unification in October 1990.

For entrepreneurs, however, there were countless opportunities. Small enterprises could provide employment with relatively low inputs; they could also curb existing monopolies. Indicative of an emerging entrepreneurial class in the East, 150,000 new ventures were registered during the summer of 1990.

Entrepreneurs were about to be social agents (Barth, 1963, 1967) of change as well as pathfinders for economic growth. Those from former East Germany were not alone in embarking on unprecedented opportunities (Hinz, 1998). West German entrepreneurs were fast to begin their search for opportunities, and given the availability of more venture capital in the West as well as Western entrepreneurs' experience with a market-oriented economy, they had a competitive edge over their less experienced Eastern counterparts. Entrepreneurs from elsewhere in the European Economic Community also identified possibilities in former East Germany, but unfamiliarity with German language, culture and market needs, increased risk and decreased the expected value of various transactions.

As noted by Brixy and Kohaut, "Most of the larger businesses that had been founded prior to unification were being administered by the *Treuhandanstalt*, a special body charged with privatising these formerly stateowned enterprises" (1999, p. 155). In the course of replacing the centrally planned economy of East Germany, by one based on free market principles, 8,000 government-owned firms, formerly the backbone of East German business, were available to be privatised as of 1990. Yet, disputed property claims, poor infrastructure and low labour productivity caused big business from the West to opt against acquiring many of the state-run money-losing giants of East Germany. Western firms turned down factories, which they could have obtained for free. Sources at the Berlin Economic Development Corporation indicated to the author that 70% of existing East German firms were expected to collapse. Many firms were bought and shut down.

As defunct industry needed to be replaced, the role of entrepreneurs increased, creating new ventures and jobs for former state workers. The former East German government-owned travel agency was ordered in 1990 to reduce the number of its outlets by a third; by August 1990, 2,500 entrepreneurs had applied to set up travel agencies.

By October 1990, 1,800,000 former civil servants of the former communist regime were jobless, and another 1,500,000 East Germans were working in temporary or other non-standard jobs; this was a large pool of labour from which entrepreneurs could recruit. Aside from migrating, self-employment and entrepreneurship were the only option for many.

The East Germans had long experienced shortages of consumer goods, while demand was high. Finally, the opportunity arose to supply such demand. There was also a tremendous demand for support services such as Western accounting previously non-existent in East Germany.

There was high demand for technical, management and marketing skills. East German farmers, for example, faced a new learning curve with regards to selling their livestock on an open market. The result was imported meat on store shelves and a surplus of local cattle in the fields.

Annexe IX of the Germany Economic and Monetary Union (GEMU) Treaty indicated that to facilitate new venture creation, the government officially committed itself to provide "adequate property for private enterprise." Moreover, investors in former East Germany received a 12% grant from the federal government. Having achieved the world's largest trade surplus in 1989, the government could afford to invest much into its new states, particularly into a much-needed infrastructure (telephones, rails, roads, etc.), which would in turn enhance the environment for business. Meanwhile, for entrepreneurs in construction or providing infrastructure, there were tremendous opportunities.

Banks too, were active in encouraging entrepreneurial activity. Given that post-1972 nationalisations were declared reversible, banks also offered consultations to entrepreneurs on how to buy back a family business from the state. Financial institutions competed to lend capital to entrepreneurs. Enhancing one's balance sheet was the fact that although savings were converted from East German *Ostmarks* to Deutsche Marks at par (whereas the actual black market conversion rate for cash was 10:1), the conversion rate for debits was 2:1, effectively reducing debts by 50%.

West German entrepreneurs contributed to joint ventures with East Germans, by providing market skills. On the other hand, given that in 1988, 28% of East German exports went to Eastern Europe and 37% to the Union of Soviet Socialist Republics, East German networks introduced new export opportunities for entrepreneurs from the West. German unification resulted in unprecedented opportunities for entrepreneurship.

Producers in East Germany formerly depended on subsidised pricing, without which they could not be competitive. It was no longer the case that food subsidies would allow pigs to feast on sub-

Exhibit 8.14 Rich variety in the West; photo © 2017 Léo-Paul Dana.

sidised potatoes and even bread. Western products in the marketplace challenged East German goods, formerly protected by the Council for Mutual Assistance (COMECON). West Germany was the land of plenty (Exhibit 8.14). Who would buy an East German television set for the price of 500 kilogrammes of beef when a superior set became available from the West at a fraction of the price?

As mentioned by Welter (2006), the 1990s saw a considerable increase in gender-specific public–private and wholly private networks for women entrepreneurs in Germany. Nevertheless, Germany experienced an overall decrease in new venture creation during the late 1990s, until the trend was reversed in 2000. Between 1991 and 2009, the number of self-employed people in Germany increased by 40% (Fritsch, Kritikos, and Rusakova, 2012).

Haunschild *et al.* (2007) noted that more than 95% of enterprises in Germany were family firms. Although Germany is the home of many large international companies, Deimel, Kraus, and Reiche

(2009) emphasised that 90% of all enterprises were SMEs supplying almost 70% of all jobs in Germany.

Hundt and Sternberg (2014) analysed entrepreneurship before, during and after the Great Recession of 2008–2009. They noted that the rapid economic downturn was preceded by a period of growth and followed by an economic upswing in many regions of Germany and they showed that both space and time mattered for individual entrepreneurial behaviour.

In contrast to other countries that struggled to recover from the Great Recession, Cienski and Atkins (2010) observed that Germany had a stronger-than-expected economic revival (Exhibit 8.15), and that Germany's rising exports were benefitting Czech and Polish factories. Schäfer and Goldschmidt (2010) showed that family firms in Germany were not only protagonists in an economic sense, but also as important actors of corporate social responsibility.

Examining the rise in self-employment during the period 1990–2010, Fritsch, Kritikos, and Sorgner (2015) observed that Germany experienced a unique rise in the level of self-employment

Exhibit 8.15 Stronger than expected; photo © 2017 Léo-Paul Dana.

in the 20 years following unification. Applying the non-linear Blinder-Oaxaca decomposition technique, they found that the main factors driving these changes in the overall level of self-employment were demographic developments, the shift towards service sector employment, and a larger share of population holding a tertiary degree. While these explained most of the increase in self-employment in West Germany, their explanatory power is much lower for the stronger increase of self-employment in former East Germany.

Hadad *et al.* (2012) found that the German manufacturing sector was more efficient than that of Spain. Despite Germany's a thriving tourism industry (Exhibit 8.16), they also found that the Spanish tourism sector was more efficient than that of Germany.

In 2014 — for the first time since the 1969 budget — the central government assumed no new debt, with revenues equal to expenditures at 296.5 billion euro. According to the German Federal Statistics Office, Germany's top export destination in 2014 was France, followed by the United States and thirdly by the United Kingdom. Kelley, Singer, and Herrington observed, "over one-fourth of entrepreneurs

Exhibit 8.16 Among boutique hotels; photo © 2017 Léo-Paul Dana.

in Germany ... operate service businesses in health, education, government and social concerns" (2016, p. 27).

Wyrwich, Stuetzer, and Sternberg (2016) showed that observing entrepreneurs reduces fear of failure in others in environments where approval of entrepreneurship is high, while this effect is significantly weaker in environments having low approval. Germany scored 74.4 in the 2016 Index of Economic Freedom, placing it among the top 17 in the world.

The Environment for Entrepreneurship

Among the early reviews of entrepreneurship research in Germany was that by Szyperski and Klandt (1981). Schmidt (1992) focused on the internationalisation of the German *Mittelstand.* Klandt (1997) provided an update. Kontos (2003) found that between 1980 and 2000, the self-employment rate among immigrants in West Germany had increased by about 30%, while the rate was 1% among West Germans with local roots.

Kraus and Werner showed "that a higher tendency of integrated migrants to start a business is mostly attributable to their background in an industrialised nation, and not from the former 'Anwerberstaaten' or developing/emerging nations (2012, p. 320)." Light, Rezaei, and Dana (2013) studied entrepreneurs — mainly Iranian in origin — who exported Persian carpets from the Hamburg Free Harbour area to about 10,000 carpet traders throughout the world.

Examining the environment for entrepreneurship, Sternberg, Otten, and Tamásy observed, "Germany's relative strengths lie in the financing, the government programmes and political framework conditions and the status of the country's physical infrastructure," (2000, p. 22). They elaborated, "The financing of start-ups and of new, growing firms can be counted among the relatively well established framework conditions in Germany," (Sternberg, Otten, and Tamásy, 2000, p. 23). In their analysis, they suggested, "The number of state promotion programmes in Germany is seen as appropriate ... but the experts do criticize the lack of transparency due to the large variety of programmes," (Sternberg, Otten, and Tamásy, 2000, p. 26).

Between 1998 and 2004, the *Deutsche Forschungsgemeinschaft (DFG)* — German Research Association — funded over 20 research projects in a programme of Interdisciplinary Entrepreneurship Research. Wiessner (2001) considered entrepreneurship as an option for unemployed persons.

Networking was shown to be an important facilitator (Brüderl and Preisendörfer, 1998). Sternberg, Bergmann, and Tamásy wrote, "The personal and professional network around a potential startup founder is very likely to influence the decision to launch a business. This network is primarily regional in nature. However, startup and support frameworks vary considerably between the German regions. One reason is the federal structure, which has resulted in the development of 16 different policies for promoting startups at state level alone. A lack of co-ordination is obvious," (2001, p. 13). They explained, "given the regional differences, the same business start-up programmes and techniques would have very different outcomes in different regions" (Sternberg, Bergmann, and Tamásy, 2001, p. 13).

Lehnert (2003) noted that more new ventures were being launched in the service sector than in any other. Brüderl, Preisendörfer, and Ziegler (1992) analysed the success of new ventures in Munich and Upper Bavaria. Jansen and Weber (2003) focused on the Ruhr area.

Reviewing the situation, Klandt wrote, "In spite of all the activities over the past years, entrepreneurship research in German-speaking Europe is still lagging behind" (2004, p. 299). Shortly thereafter, however, several important studies became available. These included: Fritsch and Müller (2004); Sternberg and Wagner (2004); Wagner (2004, 2005); Wagner and Sternberg (2004, 2005); Rocha and Sternberg (2005); Sternberg (2005); Fritsch and Schmude (2006); and Brüderl, Preisendörfer, and Ziegler (2007).

Using Gartner's (1989) definition that entrepreneurship is the creation of new organisations, and Porter's (1988b) definition that a cluster is a geographically proximate group of interconnected firms and institutions in related industries, Rocha and Sternberg suggested that *clusters* added "important mechanisms to foster entrepreneurship" (2005, p. 273).

Sternberg and Lückgen (2005) confirmed that Germany's relative strengths were still in its government programmes, the political framework conditions, and the national infrastructure. This time they elaborated, "Germany receives best marks of all 30 GEM countries for their government programmes," (Sternberg and Lückgen, 2005, p. 30). They explained, "the number of state promotion programmes in Germany is seen as appropriate ... but financing of very small new firms became more and more difficult in recent years: financing experienced the worst development of all entrepreneurial framework conditions in Germany between 2001 and 2004" (Sternberg and Lückgen, 2005, p. 27).

Bergmann and Sternberg (2005) reported on Hartz IV, the reform programme focusing on the labour market and social policy in Germany at the time. They noted that the *Ich-AG* (I-Inc) proved to be very popular. (This was replaced by a similar programme *Gründungszuschuss* aiming to stimulate unemployed persons to launch new ventures.)

Schmude, Welter, and Heumann (2008) reviewed relevant literature. They wrote, "A particular strength of the German approach to researching entrepreneurship, which can be traced back directly to the historical roots, is found to be its consideration of context specificity and embeddedness, going hand-in-hand with a strong multidisciplinary tendency" (Schmude, Welter, and Heumann, 2008, p. 289).

Sternberg, Vorderwülbecke, and Brixy (2015) summarised initiatives supporting entrepreneurship in Germany. The government-owned KfW Bank offers programmes — funded by the European Recovery Programme — directed at individuals who wish to become self-employed, as well as to persons who already are. Programmes include: (i) the European Recovery Programme Start-Up Loan StartGeld, dedicated to enterprises that have been active in the market for less than three years and require little start-up capital; (ii) the European Recovery Programme Start-Up Loan Universal, dedicated to business founders, company successors, self-employed professionals and small and medium-sized enterprises which have been active in the market for less than five years and have funding requirements of up to 25 million euro; and (iii) the European Recovery Programme Capital for Start-Ups, dedicated to business founders, self-employed professionals and small enterprises which have been active in the market for less than three years and do not have enough equity. Also shaping the environment for entrepreneurship is the EXIST programme, run by the Federal Ministry of Economic Affairs, with the objective of improving the entrepreneurial environment in universities and other research institutions, in particular supporting technology-oriented and knowledge-based start-ups. This programme is restricted to founders who are university employees or students.

Herrington noted that the EXIST programme has enabled the German government to encourage university students to start-up their own business elaborated, "The country also produces considerable high quality research, but fails to exploit its commercial potential. Through "EXIST" programme, which has been running since 1998, the Federal Ministry of Economic Affairs and Energy (BMWi) aims to foster a culture of entrepreneurship among students and researchers at universities, create more innovative start-ups and to help commercialise research" (2016, p. 16). Herrington also provided background on changes with the EXIST programme:

> In 2000 the initiative added a second programme (EXIST SEED, replaced by the EXIST "Business Start-up Grant" programme in 2007) to fund students, young graduates and university staff with grants to cover one year of living costs and business coaching. Currently the EXIST programme has three schemes:
>
> - EXIST — Culture of Entrepreneurship supports universities in formulating and implementing a university-wide strategy for increasing entrepreneurial culture. The government has supported 72 projects at universities with about 104 million euro from 1998 to 2012. The funding went on developing contact points for those interested in a startup, educating and training potential entrepreneurs and networking with those with entrepreneurial interests in

> the region. Since 2010 it has run an Entrepreneur University Award for the best entrepreneurship strategy and support. The current focus is on incentivising the creation of Entrepreneurial Universities through funding, namely those that have a strategy for becoming involved in spin-offs and offer entrepreneurial support.
>
> - EXIST — Business Start-up Grant supports students, graduates and scientists in preparing innovative technology and knowledge based startup projects. The grant covers personal living expenses and coaching costs, for up to one year.
> - EXIST — Transfer of Research funds both the resource development necessary to prove the technical feasibility of startup ideas based on research and the preparation necessary to launch a business.
>
> The European Social Fund (ESF) has been cofinancing the "EXIST-SEED" and "EXIST Business Start-up Grant" programmes since 2005, and the "EXIST Culture of Entrepreneurship" programme since 2007 (2016, p. 17).

Herrington summarised the environment, "Germany outperforms its EU peers in access to finance, state aid and public procurement and insolvency but has a weak level of entrepreneurship (partly because of its aging population), with the low number of new start-ups" (2016, p. 16). He also pointed at possible improvements, "Despite the achievements of EXIST, the European Commission says policies to substantially improve the image of entrepreneurship in society starting with awareness-raising throughout the school system could be made more systematic and improved. In addition, a 2014 OECD report said teaching techniques at universities need to be improved by for example including the use of more experience-based teaching methods — like visits to companies and the developing prototypes and learning about enterprise failures" (2016, p. 18).

Toward the Future

Nothdurft once wrote, "Officially, Germany's export assistance programs are the territory of the private sector, particularly the chambers of industry and commerce, their overseas bilateral affiliates, the trade associations, and the banking system" (1992, p. 67). Today, there is a greater interest about, and awareness of, the importance of entrepreneurs and their international activities. Internationalisation of German entrepreneurship is a growing field of research. SMEs participate in the car industry and German vehicles are exported around the world. Likewise, both SMEs and large firms are involved in the production of German beers (see Exhibit 8.17) and wines (Exhibit 8.18).

In a federal country, regional differences should not be ignored. As suggested by Sternberg, Bergmann, and Tamásy, "From a federal point of view, the emphasis should be on considering the comparative strengths of the regions and their endogenous potentials and to derive benefits from regional diversities" (2001, p. 13). Sternberg (2003)

Exhibit 8.17 White, top-fermented wheat beer — a specialty of Bavaria; photo © 2017 Léo-Paul Dana.

Exhibit 8.18 German vineyards; photo © 2017 Léo-Paul Dana.

further explained that entrepreneurial activities, especially from a federal point of view, are primarily an element of *endogenous* development potential and entrepreneurial activities to promote regional development in the area of economic growth. Welter (2007) suggested that regional patterns of entrepreneurship across the East German region became increasingly distorted since the 1990s. She noted that Saxony had a high density of entrepreneurship, compared to Mecklenburg-Western Pomerania and Sachsen-Anhalt.

Ethnic minority entrepreneurship is a topic gaining significant importance, both, in an economic and a political sense. Although the Foreigner's Law of 1965 prohibited non-Europeans from being entrepreneurs unless they had a residence permit (Kanein and Renner, 1988), until the 1970s, foreign labourers migrated to Germany and found employment relatively easily; self-employment was not a necessity. Since, foreigners have been turning to self-employment in

Germany. According to Wilpert, "Entrepreneurs of Greek nationality continue to have the highest self-employment rate" (2003, p. 241). According to Leicht, Leiss, and Fehrenbach (2005), Austrians had the highest rate of self-employment in Germany in 2003, and in absolute terms self-employed Italians outnumbered all other ethnic minority entrepreneurs in Germany. Turkish entrepreneurs are also highly visible. Kontos (2007) revisited immigrant entrepreneurship in Germany, as did Leung (2007); Fertala (2007) focused on immigrant entrepreneurs in Hamburg. Pütz, Schreiber, and Welpe (2007) examined immigrant entrepreneurs in Germany, with a particular focus on gender.

On the subject of female entrepreneurs, Fehrenbach and Lauxen-Ulbrich (2006) noted that these tended to be in the sectors of consumer-oriented and personal services. Welter reported, "the German government only recently started paying attention to the topic of female entrepreneurship as an important means to raise the overall level of entrepreneurship ... In Germany ... only 6 per cent of all women qualify as entrepreneurs (2004, p. 212)." This is less than half the proportion among men. Welter (2006) noted that compared to men, women entrepreneurs frequently start small businesses that do not have any employees.

The mind-set of potential entrepreneurs appears to have evolved since the turn of the millennia, with more tolerance for risk and increased excitement about entrepreneurship. Nevertheless, a concern today and opportunity for further research is that over time, there has been a decrease in the Total Early-stage Entrepreneurial Activity (TEA) rate of persons under 25 years old (Sternberg, Vorderwülbecke, and Brixy, 2015). Future research may wish to address this.

Chapter 9
Gibraltar

Introduction

Physically an enclave at the southern tip of Spain,[1] Gibraltar (Exhibit 9.1) is a British Overseas Territory, only 32 kilometres from Africa, and overlooking the Strait of Gibraltar — the direct sea-route from the Atlantic Ocean to the Mediterranean Sea. Its area is 6.7 square kilometres including reclaimed land; some of its housing on the west side and also a portion of its airport (Exhibit 9.2) runway is on reclaimed land.

Gibraltar has a multicultural society, with Catholic and Protestant churches, synagogues, a Hindu temple and a mosque. Haller wrote, "Gibraltarians speak English, Spanish and a mixture of both, and/or a local idiom Yanito, spiced with many Hebrew and Genoese words. Ethnically, they are of British, Spanish, Italian, Portuguese, Moroccan, Maltese, Indian, and Jewish origin" (2003, p. 77). Government policy is supportive of entrepreneurship. In the absence of springs, rivers, agriculture, and other resources, policy has been among this duty-free port's most important assets.

During the 1980s, Gibraltar took steps to become a low-tax banking centre somewhat like the (also British) Cayman Islands. Bryson described Gibraltar as "Britain's precarious stronghold,"

[1] See relevant chapter in this volume.

Exhibit 9.1 The Rock of Gibraltar; photo © 2017 Léo-Paul Dana.

Exhibit 9.2 Royal Air Force base at Gibraltar; photo © 2017 Léo-Paul Dana.

(1996, p. 54), which "has come to symbolize strength and stability" (1996, p. 55).

Today, Gibraltar has a highly developed business infrastructure. This includes one of Europe's most advanced fibre-optic communications networks, coupled with a variety of incentives for start-ups and existing entrepreneurs as well as a low levels of paperwork requirements, restrictions and taxes.

Historical Overview

Ever since the Phoenicians, the Rock of Gibraltar's strategic geographic position — at the tip of the Iberian Peninsula and overlooking Africa and Europe — caused it to be the envy of many. During the years 711 and 712, Arab and Berber armies crossed the Strait of Gibraltar, from Africa to Europe, captured the peninsula and settled here, before spreading Islam into Spain, where they became known as the Moors. The emperor of Morocco founded the city of Gibraltar in 1160.

Spaniards from Granada arrived and occupied the rock from 1462 until 1704. Under Admiral Sir George Rooke, British and Dutch allies captured Gibraltar during the War of the Spanish Succession (1701–1704).

In 1706, Queen Anne (1665–1714) declared Gibraltar to be a free port (Grocott and Stockey, 2012) and self-employed merchants, from England and from the Netherlands, arrived and created new ventures in Gibraltar. By 1712, half the rents collected by the governor came from Jewish entrepreneurs (Dana, 1993b).

Formal recognition of British rule in perpetuity only happened in 1713, at which time Article X of the Treaty of Utrecht officially ceded Gibraltar to Great Britain. To appease Spain, neither Muslim Moors nor Jews were allowed to stay in Gibraltar, but this was not immediately enforced, because these mercantile minorities included entrepreneurs with important trade connections, crucial to the well-being of the British outpost. Later, in the 18th century, traders from Genoa themselves established the main town, at Catalan Bay. Haller wrote about international entrepreneurship of those times, "A treaty with the sultan of Morocco in 1729 provided for the tax-free import of goods into the colony through Moroccan Sephardic merchants," (2003, p. 78). In 1763, the Treaty of Paris confirmed British rule of Gibraltar.

Exhibit 9.3 *Shaar Hashamayim*; photo © 2017 Léo-Paul Dana.

In 1768, the *Shaar Hashamayim* synagogue (Exhibit 9.3) was built at 49 Engineer Lane. In 1783, the Treaty of Versailles reconfirmed British sovereignty.

Immigrants arrived from Morocco and in 1820 founded the *Snoga Abudarham* synagogue (Exhibit 9.4), in a building that had previously been the Freemasons Hall. Located at 19 Parliament Lane, the synagogue still functions, and Parliament Lane is still referred to as *Callejon de los Masones* — literally "street of the Freemasons."

In 1830, Gibraltar was designated a Crown Colony (Jordine, 2007). In 1946, the United Nations recognised it as such.

Gibraltar had long been the home of a colony of Barbary monkeys (Exhibit 9.5). Although these animals have no tail, they are not apes but macaques. During World War II, when civilians were evacuated from Gibraltar, all but 10 of the monkeys died due to lack of food and water (Wexler, 1979). Winston Churchill (1874–1965) ordered for the colony to be replenished with imported macaques.

A 1955 ordinance, "defined as British subjects all those listed in the Register of Gibraltarians and who either were born in the colony

Exhibit 9.4 *Snoga Abudarham;* photo © 2017 Léo-Paul Dana.

Exhibit 9.5 Barbary monkeys; photo © 2017 Léo-Paul Dana.

prior to June 30, 1925, or who were born as the legitimate offspring of a male born prior to that date. The Gibraltarian Status Ordinance of 1962 succeeded that of 1955 and regulated local affairs" (Haller, 2003, p. 77).

Gibraltar enjoyed political and economic stability under British rule, but since the 1960s, tension with Spain has escalated, as the latter has second thoughts about the Treaty of Utrecht that had given Gibraltar to the British, in perpetuity. In 1964, Spanish authorities severely curtailed traffic between the two entities.

La Fay quoted Chief Minister, Sir Joshua Hassan (1915–1997), a son of Jewish entrepreneurs, "As many as 1,500 cars a day used to enter from Spain. Now only 30 or so squeeze through. Tourism is a major factor in our economic life. It would be idle to pretend that we haven't been hurt" (1966, p. 105). In fact, in 1964, Spain barred most exports to Gibraltar.

In 1967, a referendum confirmed the British connection, 12,138 votes to 44. In 1969, a new constitution was introduced and Spain closed its border with Gibraltar. Royal Mail (see Exhibit 9.6) between Gibraltar and Spain transited via London.

The preamble of the *Gibraltar Constitution Order 1969* stipulated that Gibraltar's sovereign status would not be changed without consent of the people: "Whereas Gibraltar is part of Her Majesty's dominions and Her Majesty's Government have given assurances to the people of Gibraltar that Gibraltar will remain part of Her Majesty's dominions unless and until an Act of Parliament otherwise provides, and furthermore that Her Majesty's Government will never enter into arrangements under which the people of Gibraltar would pass under the sovereignty of another state against their freely and democratically expressed wishes ... " Gibraltarians were granted full British citizenship, in 1981. The border between Gibraltar and Spain remained closed until the Brussels Agreement reopened it, in February 1985.

Located at the southern-most point of the Iberian Peninsula, Gibraltar's Europa Point Lighthouse (Exhibit 9.7) was automated in February 1994. Its loom can be seen from 37 kilometres away. First inaugurated in 1841, the lighthouse continues to be operated by the London-based endowed charity, Corporation of Trinity House. It was the *Merchant Shipping Act 1894* that made Trinity House the General Lighting Authority for Gibraltar.

Based on participant observation in Gibraltar, Haller (2003) compared two merchant diasporas residing in Gibraltar: Sephardic Jews and Sindhi Hindus. He noted, "The Sindhi community has traditionally

Exhibit 9.6 Victorian mailbox; photo © 2017 Léo-Paul Dana.

been a merchant community. Its corporation, the Hindu Merchant Association, is influential in the Chamber of Commerce. Today, most shops deal with cheap electrical goods, but also with cameras, perfume, cigarettes, alcohol, watches, and jewellery… Gibraltarian Sindhis and

Exhibit 9.7 Europa Point Lighthouse; photo © 2017 Léo-Paul Dana.

Sephardim can be compared as ethno-religious merchant diasporas integrated into worldwide webs of ethnic, religious, economic, familial, and interpersonal relations. Both groups are probably privileged in economic terms, in that they can profit from the transport and communications infrastructure ... Sindhis and Sephardim in particular, are real Internet fanatics" (Haller, 2003, pp. 89–92).

A sovereignty referendum, in 2002, gave voters the chance to express themselves about a plan that would have shared sovereignty over Gibraltar between Spain and the United Kingdom. The result was almost unanimous support for maintaining British sovereignty.

Spain was not happy with this, but in 2004, tension was eased when the Trilateral Forum of Dialogue brought together government representatives from Gibraltar, Spain, and the United Kingdom. Approved by a referendum in November 2006, a new Constitution Order was implemented in January 2007. This renamed the House of Assembly as the Gibraltar Parliament. Spain and Gibraltar had a dispute over fishing rights in 2013.

The Environment for Entrepreneurship

Gibraltar provides a highly developed business infrastructure, including one of Europe's most advanced fibre-optic communications network, coupled with a policy of low intervention. Entrepreneurs benefit from a variety of incentives, as well as minimal paperwork requirements, few restrictions and low taxes. Given its status with the United Kingdom, Gibraltar became a member of the European Union; yet, it was excluded from the common agricultural policy and common external tariff. Gibraltar was also exempted from the requirement to levy a value added tax (VAT); this allows traders to distribute from Gibraltar competitively priced VAT-free goods and services across Europe and beyond. Furthermore, Gibraltar is classified as a developing country and is therefore entitled to preferential trade tariffs under the Generalised System of Preferences. All the above results in a special position within the Union, although the United Kingdom's 2016 decision to exit the Union may have consequences yet unknown.

The Ministry of Business and Employment engaged with the Gibraltar Chamber of Commerce and the Gibraltar federation of Small Businesses to develop the Gibraltar Business Nurturing Scheme, to support the development of start-ups. Business entities according to local law include: sole traders, partnerships (including limited liability partnerships), companies (including Protected Cell Companies — PCC), trusts and non-profit organisations.

Enterprises in Gibraltar include: (i) sole traders engaged in informal activity, such as fishing from lateen-rigged boats; (ii) formal firms (including sole traders, partnerships and companies), with locations in Gibraltar at which business is conducted; and (iii) non-residents using a Gibraltar address for their corporation, in order to benefit from local government policy. Given that paperwork requirements and other regulations are relatively easy to comply with, informal sector is less attractive than it might be otherwise.

The formal sector includes light industry such as the preparation of beverages, canning, and tobacco. Exhibit 9.8 features the manufacturing firm Gibraltar Crystal. Service industries including tourism are also very important. Splendid Bar (Exhibit 9.9), on George's Lane, caters to visitors as well as to a local clientele. The exemption of value added tax increases the appeal of local retailers, as consumers buy cameras, computers, diamonds, elegant watches, and other jewellery. Sailors stock up on cigarettes here (Exhibit 9.10).

Exhibit 9.8 Manufacturing; photo © 2017 Léo-Paul Dana.

Exhibit 9.9 Splendid Bar; photo © 2017 Léo-Paul Dana.

The Abudarham grocery (Exhibit 9.11) is a family business that has long been catering to mainstream shoppers as well as to an ethnic enclave. Workers from Morocco and commuters from Spain add to demand in this market. Population density results in a tightly clustered market, and this simplifies transportation logistics of distribution. All the above has helped contribute to the development and maintenance of healthy small business in the local formal sector.

Non-residents launch corporations in Gibraltar, to benefit from the pro-enterprise environment, using Gibraltar-based companies to collect patent royalties, copyright fees and the like. Thus, for many entrepreneurs, the physical relationship with Gibraltar is simply that their corporate books lay on a shelf here; hence the expression shelf-corporation. It is easy for non-residents to incorporate a shelf company in Gibraltar and to lease registered company offices with access to a variety of business services. Thus, without having a physical operation in Gibraltar, non-resident

Exhibit 9.10 No value added tax; photo © 2017 Léo-Paul Dana.

entrepreneurs use Gibraltar as an official business address, thereby benefitting from a variety of incentives, including the absence of capital gains tax.

The Gibraltarian pound is interchangeable, at par, with the pound sterling and a policy of low intervention makes Gibraltar attractive for offshore banking and investment. When real estate or a vessel is registered as the property of a Gibraltar-based shelf company, the shares can be transferred, reducing expenses that may be otherwise payable. Given that these assets are the property of the company and therefore when the owner dies, inheritance taxes may be avoided, given that shares of a Gibraltar-based company can be transferred without succession duties, given that the company lives on.

Exhibit 9.11 Family business; photo © 2017 Léo-Paul Dana.

Interest arising from bank deposits of non-residents is non-taxable in Gibraltar. Trusts established for non-residents are also normally exempt from income tax. As detailed by Dana (2002):

> A corporation may also receive an "Exemption Certificate" valid for 25 years of exemption from income tax and estate duty. However, such tax exemption is valid only as long as the company does not conduct any unauthorised business in Gibraltar, except with other tax-exempt companies. These companies owned by non-resident entrepreneurs need one symbolic meeting of shareholders in Gibraltar each year. At the meetings, company accounts are submitted as a formality, but these are not available for public inspection (2002, p. 40).

The existence of non-resident entrepreneurs has provided opportunities for others who provide consulting and/or support services. Registration agents in Gibraltar also provide non-resident entrepreneurs with directors, secretaries and nominee shareholders. These service firms also open bank accounts, maintain accounting books, register trademarks and do related paperwork. Various enterprises provide relevant services to non-resident entrepreneurs and to their shelf corporations.

Some offer specialised services in a specific sector, for instance, providing registration and/or insurance for maritime vessels. A ship registered in Gibraltar is considered to be a British ship and is entitled to the European Union cabotage (coastal trade) privileges. With regards to a sale, rather than sell a ship, it may be advantageous to sell the shares of a company owning it. No annual tax is payable on a yacht registered in Gibraltar. Insurance on a yacht is paid according to physical location of the vessel, for example, 1.3% of the vessel's value in northern Europe, or 1.4% in Greek waters.

In summary, Gibraltar's policy environment and tax incentives result in an environment that is attractive for entrepreneurs and other investors seeking protection from estate duties, gift taxes, and wealth taxes and estate duties. It is a positive environment for investments and for the management of assets. Entrepreneurs create shelf-corporations in Gibraltar; these serve as holding companies, with property worldwide.

Toward the Future

Government policy has, since long ago, made Gibraltar a hub of global entrepreneurial activity. With the introduction of *The Electronic Commerce Act,* the government is creating conditions to make Gibraltar an international e-business centre for the future.

Haller observed, "In contrast with cities such as Alexandria, Trieste, Tangier, Odessa and Izmir, it is still characterized by a multiethnic, multilingual and multi-religious character" (2003, p. 77). The Union Jack flies over Gibraltar (Exhibit 9.12) and from vessels registered here. Local folklore suggests the rock will remain British (see Exhibit 9.13) as long as Barbary monkeys live there (Wexler, 1979). Although Spain has referred to Gibraltar as occupied land, the environment for entrepreneurship is such that entrepreneurs in Gibraltar have reasons to support the status quo.

Exhibit 9.12 Union Jack over Moorish castle; photo © 2017 Léo-Paul Dana.

Exhibit 9.13 Royal Gibraltar Police; photo © 2017 Léo-Paul Dana.

Chapter 10

Iceland

Introduction

The westernmost country of Europe, the Republic of Iceland covers 103,000 square kilometres, including the largest volcanic island in the world. Iceland's landscape includes fumaroles emitting hot steam (Exhibit 10.1) and geysers (Exhibit 10.2), as well as snow-capped volcanoes (Exhibit 10.3). Subterranean hot water is used to heat fish hatcheries, greenhouses, homes, and swimming pools. Its capital, Reykjavík (Exhibit 10.4), is the northern-most capital of any nation.

Hansson *et al.* reported, "One out of every nine Icelanders at the age 18–64 is entrepreneurially active, or 11.3% of the population; this places Iceland in tenth place of all the GEM nations. No European country has a higher rate than Iceland ... Very few start companies out of necessity" (2002, p. 8).

Baldacchino noted that although Iceland's prohibitive labour costs made it uncompetitive in labour-intensive products, it has nevertheless "done well in spawning a clutch of diverse, successful, small firms from its major export industry (fishing), as well from a burgeoning information technology sector," (2005, p. 23). Jónsson observed, "The population is young compared to other European countries and the ratio of those aged over 65 compared to working age is one of the lowest in the OECD countries. Furthermore, the labour activity rate is 83% in total and 78% for females which is one of the highest female activity rates in the OECD" (2008, p. 23).

Exhibit 10.1 Fumarole; photo © 2017 Léo-Paul Dana.

Exhibit 10.2 Geysers; photo © 2017 Léo-Paul Dana.

Exhibit 10.3 Among 100 volcanoes; photo © 2017 Léo-Paul Dana.

Although severely hit by the 2008 financial crisis, Iceland recovered faster than others. Founded and owned by entrepreneur Skúli Mogensen (1968–), the airline WOW air is debt free.

Historical Overview

Iceland has been inhabited for over a thousand years. When a group of Norwegians settled here, they brought with them a unique breed of small horse today known as the Icelandic (Exhibit 10.5); these usually stand between 132 and 142 centimetres high, weighing between 330 and 380 kilograms. In 930, the *Althing* was established and remains the oldest parliament in the world today. In 1262, the *Althing* voted for Iceland to join Norway. Soon thereafter, Norwegian entrepreneurs began importing dry fish from Iceland.

In 1380, both Iceland and Norway came under Danish rule. Thus, Iceland became a Danish possession and it remained so even

Exhibit 10.4 Reykjavík; photo © 2017 Léo-Paul Dana.

after Norway gained independence. Aðalsteinsson and Steinþórsson wrote, "King Fridrik II of Denmark decreed in 1562 that he would purchase all the fish oil produced in Icelandic towns, and a year later, he proclaimed his ownership of the sulfur mines in the Myvatn area in northeast Iceland" (2015, p. 157).

In 1602, Denmark declared a trade monopoly over Iceland. In 1786, the Danish king allowed 167 merchants the right to establish Reykjavík as a trading centre (Levathes, 1987).

Iceland was granted limited home rule in 1874. A cooperative movement was started in Iceland, in 1882. In 1900, there was still not a single factory in the country. People lived largely depending on animal husbandry and the sea. Raising sheep (Exhibit 10.6) was still Iceland's most important occupation. Aðalsteinsson and Steinþórsson

Exhibit 10.5 The Icelandic horse; photo © 2017 Léo-Paul Dana.

Exhibit 10.6 Icelandic sheep; photo © 2017 Léo-Paul Dana.

Exhibit 10.7 Gullfoss; photo © 2017 Léo-Paul Dana.

wrote, "Iceland's modernization and economic development were triggered and then fueled by industrialization in the fisheries sector. Iceland's economic development started late in the 19th century, but it gained serious momentum after the first trawler came to Iceland in 1905" (2015, p. 155). (Large-scale industrialisation would later escalate with the Marshall Plan.)

Tómas Tómasson was the local farmer who owned Gullfoss (Exhibit 10.7), on the Hvítá River. In 1907, a foreign entrepreneur attempted to purchase the falls from him, for the generation of electricity. Legislation later restricted foreign acquisition of waterfalls in Iceland. Exhibit 10.8 features another famous waterfall in Iceland, Goðafoss.

Aðalsteinsson and Steinþórsson wrote: "transportation, the important lifeline to and from the country, was limited; a few shipping routes were served on a regular basis mainly by the Icelandic

Exhibit 10.8 Goðafoss; photo © 2017 Léo-Paul Dana.

Steamship Company, established in 1914, and the Danish shipping company DFDS. Iceland was then a very poor country but on the brink of modernization. It had a population of around 80,000 and a GDP per capita that was 50% that in Denmark, with as much as 70% of the population working in fisheries and agriculture" (2015, p. 154).

In 1918, Icelanders gained authority over decisive matters (Jónsson and Saemundsson, 2006). That same year, Iceland declared "perpetual neutrality," (Aðalsteinsson and Steinþórsson, 2015, p. 155). Denmark recognised Iceland as a separate state under the Danish crown, and "only foreign policy was controlled by the Danish Government" (Jónsson and Saemundsson, 2006, p. 220).

Hanson noted, "To-day the literacy rate is higher in Iceland than in many countries of Europe" (1928, p. 499). He observed, "Iceland's salted and spiced herring find a ready market in Sweden; the dried cod go to Spain" (Hanson, 1928, p. 500).

Hutchison (1928) mentioned herring fishing stations at Isafjördur and Siglufjördur. She reported that there were no maps "as there are no roads" (1928, p. 467).

Aðalsteinsson and Steinþórsson wrote about Norwegian legislation that affected Icelandic exports beginning in 1929: "This legislation was primarily aimed at Iceland, as Norwegian producers had imported Icelandic fish oil when there were shortages of supply in Norway. Iceland's export to Norway fell dramatically in the years 1934 and 1935" (2015, p. 158).

Jónsson and Saemundsson explained, "The social structure was basically rural, a society with a few scattered fishing ports located around the country close to the most important and rich fishing grounds. The few signs of the drift towards modernisation was prolonged because of the Spanish Civil War (1933–1939) as Spain was the main market for Iceland's primary export, salted cod. In 1930, for example, approximately 60% of exports were salted cod, with 35% of all exports being sent to Spain. In comparison, in 1936, only 3% of exports went to Spain" (2006, p. 221).

In the United States, Upjohn was seeking a replacement for Norwegian cod liver oil, not as rich in vitamins as Icelandic cod (Exhibit 10.9). In 1936, Icelandic entrepreneur Tryggvi Ólafsson received a telegram from Upjohn, subsequently requesting an annual supply of approximately 1,000 tons of cod liver oil; this prompted the establishment of LYSI Ltd in January 1938, eventually becoming a local company with global reach (Aðalsteinsson and Steinþórsson, 2015).

When the Nazis invaded Denmark, the Iceland Cabinet replaced the royal power. In 1940, Britain unilaterally decided to occupy

Exhibit 10.9 Fresh cod; photo © 2017 Léo-Paul Dana.

Iceland (Aðalsteinsson and Steinþórsson, 2015). In May 1940, Iceland "was occupied by the Allies whose first task was to build or amend the basic infrastructure; build functional airports, roads and telecommunications ... The Americans replaced the British in 1941" (Jónsson and Saemundsson, 2006, p. 223).

Aðalsteinsson and Steinþórsson observed, "The Second World War marked an important milestone; unlike most countries, the effect of the war greatly enriched Iceland" (2015, p. 155). In 1942, a large-scale system was completed piping hot water from mineral springs to Reykjavík. Clark wrote, "hot water escapes to the surface in boiling springs ... 10 miles to a pumping station ... it flows into radiators at about 175°F., keeping the city's homes and offices cozy even in blizzard weather" (1951, p. 600).

In March 1944, three young Icelandic pilots formed a new airline, Loftleiðir. The Danish monarch remained that of Iceland until the former colony became a republic with full independence in June that year.

After the war, "Marshall-aid was utilized ... to provide the basic means of economic development, e.g., to erect a fertilizer plant, a cement factory, and increasing the catching and processing capacity in the fishing sector" (Jónsson and Saemundsson, 2006, p. 223). In 1948, President Harry S. Truman (1884–1972) signed the Civil Aeronautics Board (CAB) paperwork authorising Loftleiðir to fly to Idlewild Airport (later JFK).

In 1949, the Icelandic Parliament decided to join the North Atlantic Treaty Organisation (NATO). The United States Armed Forces operated a Naval Air Station in Keflavík as a NATO base from 1951 to 2006. Exhibit 10.10 features a Douglas C-117D skytrooper that was based at Keflavík.

Jónsson and Saemundsson explained that post-war construction of a modern fishing fleet resulted "in a shift from exporting salted cod to the Mediterranean to supplying the United State's emerging fast food chains and public institutions such as hospitals, schools and prisons ... In 1940, for example, less than 14% of Icelandic goods were exported to the US, but in 1975 the percentage had increased to 29%" (2006, p. 224).

Exhibit 10.10 Navy C-117D; photo © 2017 Léo-Paul Dana.

Whereas foreign fleets had previously exploited Icelandic fishing grounds, in 1952, Iceland set the limit to four miles from its coast (Jónsson and Saemundsson, 2006). In 1958, Iceland's reliance on fishing prompted it to extend its territorial waters to 12 miles and this caused a dispute with the United Kingdom. In 1961, the United Kingdom accepted the new 12-mile limit, but the cod war broke out again 10 years later, when Iceland proposed an extension to 50 miles. While the economy of some coastal communities is largely dependent on fish, Akureyri diversified its economy during the 20th century, with a shoe factory, a tannery and a wool-processing plant (Britton, 1969).

Pioneering a low-cost strategy across the Atlantic, Loftleiðir inaugurated Canadair CL-44 (Exhibit 10.11) turbo-props, in 1964. With a capacity of 189 passengers, the Canadair CL-44 was the largest passenger airliner to cross the Atlantic. This would help develop tourism in Iceland, both in urban (Exhibit 10.12) and rural areas (Exhibit 10.13).

In 1968, Iceland made the switch to driving on the right-hand side of the road, thus conforming to its Scandinavian neighbours 900 kilometres away. Iceland joined the European Free Trade

Exhibit 10.11 CL-44; photo, courtesy of Erik Frikke, used with permission.

Exhibit 10.12 Urban Reykjavík; photo © 2017 Léo-Paul Dana.

Association (EFTA) in 1970. In 1972, the republic extended its territorial waters to 50 miles and to 200 miles in 1979 (Jónsson and Saemundsson, 2006). The overexploitation of fish stocks led to the imposition of limits on catches, and the consequence was a slowdown in economic growth as of the late 1980s.

In 1994, Iceland became a member of the European Economic Area. Beginning in 1997, government-owned banks and companies

Exhibit 10.13 Rural road; photo © 2017 Léo-Paul Dana.

were privatised. In 2002, fishing and related industries employed 12% of the labour force (Aðalsteinsson and Steinþórsson, 2015).

Hansson, Tómasdóttir, Sigurðardóttir, Elíasson, and Sæmundsson wrote, "General knowledge of how to run a company is lacking, as is knowledge of marketing goods and services abroad" (2002, p. 9). They suggested that this could "hinder the effective exploitation of these opportunities. While the entrepreneurial spirit exists, it seems likely that it is under-utilised," (Hansson *et al.*, 2002, p. 10).

Hallgrímsdóttir and Sigurdardóttir (2003) listed several start-up grants, available at the time. These included: (i) IMPRA's Start-up Fund; (ii) the National Start-up Fund; (iii) the New Business Venture Fund; and (iv) the Regional Development Fund.

Comparing data from 17 countries, Einarsson (2004) found that Iceland spent more than other countries on cultural activities. Reykjavík (Exhibit 10.14) remains the cultural centre of Iceland.

Exhibit 10.14 Pósthússtræti; photo © 2017 Léo-Paul Dana.

Jónsson and Saemundsson wrote, "In the last decade, Icelandic entrepreneurs ... have managed to identify and exploit international business opportunities in such diverse fields as aviation, retail, biotechnology, banking, and medical instruments around the world," (2006, p. 218). They elaborated, "Iceland now consistently ranks in the top 10 nations in the world in the various measures of human development index (HDI), infrastructure development (IMD International), income per capita (GNI), gender empowerment ... and life expectancy" (Jónsson and Saemundsson, 2006, p. 218).

By 2006, formerly isolated Iceland had the world's highest broadband penetration. Edvardsson (2006) found that Icelandic firms had a flat structure, were lacking strategy and formalisation, and that they relied on an unsystematic manner of sharing and utilising knowledge.

In a follow-up study of knowledge management in Icelandic SMEs, Edvardsson (2009) found that even when SMEs were aware of the importance of their knowledge, they usually followed an unplanned, unsystematic and informal approach to knowledge management. In 2007, the Icelandic Building Research Institute was merged with the Technical Institute of Iceland, resulting in an innovation centre, Nýsköpunarmiðstöð Íslands. Under the Ministry of

Industry, Nýsköpunarmiðstöð Íslands was given the responsibility to provide entrepreneurship and SME services, and technological research.

Jónsson (2008) remarked that entrepreneurial activities were constantly higher in Iceland than in the European Union countries. Following the 2008 collapse of Iceland's banking system, Iceland experienced an inflation rate of 14% and the interest rate was raised to 15.5%. The Icelandic crown depreciated by more than 35% against the euro during the first nine months of 2008. As a result of the crisis, the government assumed control of much of the banking sector.

In November 2009, interest rates were reduced to 11%. Stenholm *et al.* (2009) noted Iceland as having the highest overall entrepreneurial activity rate among the Nordic countries.

Based on a survey sent to 560 SMEs in Iceland, with a response rate of 21%, Jónsson (2010) found that boards had a variety of roles, and concluded that boards determine their own value. Iceland scored 73.7 in the 2010 Index of Economic Freedom, placing it among the top 18.

Edvardsson, Oskarsson, and Versteinsdottir (2011) studied 381 service SMEs in Iceland finding that reasons for outsourcing were not based on costs. Rather, motives for outsourcing were related to strategic aspects, including a focus on core competencies, increased external expertise, and improved customer service.

Although Iceland was badly hit when banks went bankrupt during the 2008 financial crisis, this country recovered faster than others. Mingels (2014) summed up his perception that Icelanders were traditionally farmers and fishermen until they decided to turn their country into a casino for global capital around the turn of the millennium, and that now they have returned to fishing.

The Environment for Entrepreneurship

Jónsson and Saemundsson wrote, "the modernization process in Iceland has been a move from a paternalistic guidance of a poverty ridden population towards the creation of an outward reaching and uncertain global business environment, definably risky at times, but as yet, extraordinarily successful," (2006, p. 218). They suggested that entrepreneurship in Iceland went through distinct stages: (i) Collective Agrarian Entrepreneurship (1910–1939); (ii) Government Entrepreneurship (1940–1960); (iii) Corporate Local Entrepreneurship (1960–1995); and (iv) Heroic International Entrepreneurship (1995–2005).

Today, Iceland provides a highly supportive environment with a low level of corporate tax. Jonnsson wrote, "The Science and Technology Policy Council operates under the direction of the Prime Minister and consists of ministers, scientists and business representatives. The Council formulates public policy to promote scientific research and research training in the sciences and encourage technological progress in Iceland, for the purpose of strengthening the foundations of the country's culture and boosting the competitive capacity of its economy" (2008, p. 25).

Agricultural support is higher in Iceland than in most other OECD countries; yet, Japan, Norway, South Korea, and Switzerland are even more supportive. Iceland provides two main pillars of agricultural support: (i) direct payments based on entitlements to (mainly dairy) cattle and sheep farmers, and on a smaller scale to some greenhouse producers; and (ii) market price support (for all livestock products and some horticultural products) maintained by border control measures. A state-chaired committee determines guaranteed minimum prices for milk delivered within production quotas. Thus, Icelandic producers obtain 82% more for milk than they would in the absence of state intervention.

Jónsson and Saemundsson explained, "in Iceland the farmers created an early advantage because of the early establishment of various cooperatives (Co-ops), which operated simultaneously as distribution and production collectives, and then ventured into fisheries and industrial production in the early 1950s. The farmer's ideology was generally based on the belief that it was possible to steer the ragged route to modernity by empowering the population through education and allowing the small farmer, local fisherman or craftsman to pave their own route to prosperity ... somewhat at conflict with scale arguments being made by corporations at the time. The basic idea was that the cooperatives, or the workers collectives, would protect the vulnerable small entrepreneur, or allied workers organizations, by rationalizing production and distribution through the non-profit seeking co-ops ... They regarded themselves as 'collective entrepreneurs'" (2006, p. 221). Jónsson and Saemundsson elaborated, "The shift from a local agricultural society, which was close to a subsistence level and governed by a complex redistribution system, to fisheries geared for export represents a shift from collective entrepreneurship to a more government-based entrepreneurship ... the Icelandic government came to take an active role in expanding the necessary infrastructure" (2006, p. 224).

Since 1995, support for SMEs has been a policy issue and the importance of entrepreneurship policy has gradually increased since; institutions for supporting innovation and entrepreneurship have also grown (Jónsson, 2008). These include: (i) the business venture fund NSA Ventures; (ii) the innovation centre, Nýsköpunarmiðstöð Íslands; and (iii) Rannis, the Icelandic Centre for Research. Other important players in shaping a positive environment for entrepreneurship include: the Federation of Icelandic Industries; Innovation Iceland; Klak Innovit; Reykjavík University; and the University of Iceland. Startup Reykjavík is a mentorship-driven seed stage investment programme. It provides selected projects with $18,500 in seed funding. In summary, Iceland has supportive policies coupled with a well-educated, highly skilled workforce, affordable green energy and several accelerator opportunities.

Toward the Future

Iceland's success stories have a bright future ahead. Since its creation in 1938, LYSI has become a global leader in the production of fish oils. As of 2016, it can offer fish oil certified by the Marine Stewardship Council (MSC), an international certification authority for sustainable fishing. In 2016, LYSI was aiming to obtain MSC certification for the fish liver rendering plant in Thorlakshofn, so that all its pure cod liver oil would be MSC-certified. Even global warming may have its bright side. In 2016, Prime Minister Sigmundur Davíð

Exhibit 10.15 Faxaflói Bay; photo © 2017 Léo-Paul Dana.

Gunnlaugsson suggested that global warming may help Icelandic agriculture. That said, challenges are unavoidable. Currently, whale-watching boats allow visitors to watch minke whales (*Balaenoptera acutorostrata*) swim in Faxaflói Bay (Exhibit 10.15). While watching was previously considered to be harmless, Christiansen and Lusseau (2015) highlighted substantial disruptions.

Chapter 11

Ireland

Introduction

The Republic of Ireland covers 70,283 square kilometres. It neighbours Northern Ireland, which is part of the entity officially called the United Kingdom of Great Britain and Northern Ireland.[1] The Republic of Ireland has two official languages, Irish and English.

Founded as a family business in 1944, Dunnes Stores developed into an important chain including operations outside Ireland. A more recent success story is that of Irish-born entrepreneur Patrick Collison (1988–) who was number 23 of the Forbes list, 2015 America's Richest Entrepreneurs Under 40.

With the lowest corporation tax in the European Union, Ireland is very open to and also dependent on foreign multinationals, which in the 1980s and 1990s were attracted by a low wage rate coupled with a skilled, English-speaking workforce. Foreign firms have facilitated some entrepreneurial activity. Yet, the Enterprise Strategy Group has warned of falling competitiveness, and highlighted the increased importance of developing indigenous enterprise. Those who are not concerned about growth (Exhibit 11.1) may be at risk.

[1] See relevant chapter in this volume.

Exhibit 11.1 Not focused on growth; photo © 2017 Léo-Paul Dana.

Historical Overview

Ireland was ruled by London until the first half of the 20th century. In an attempt to establish an Irish republic, on Easter Monday 1916, Irish nationalists staged the rebellion that came to be known as the 1916 Easter Rising.

One of the activists was Éamon de Valera (1882–1975), who was saved from a death sentence, thanks to his American birth and instead given a prison term. In December 1921, a treaty was signed whereby Ireland accepted dominion status subject to the right of Northern Ireland to remain under British rule. The Irish Free State thus became a dominion in 1922.

In December 1925, a border was agreed to whereby six of the counties of Ulster were in Northern Ireland, and the remaining 26 counties were in the Free State. Exhibit 11.2 features a traditional cottage in the Free State.

As of 1928, the Irish pound was at par with the Sterling. Until 1931, the State had a *laissez-faire*, non-interventionist policy for

Exhibit 11.2 Traditional cottage; photo © 2017 Léo-Paul Dana.

business. Through protectionism, in 1932, the state attempted to encourage manufacturing (see Exhibit 11.3) in Ireland.

Also in 1932, construction began on a new civic building for Cork, along Terence MacSweeney Quay (Exhibit 11.4). Already released from prison, Éamon de Valera laid the foundation stone and in 1936 he officially opened the new Cork City Hall. (He would later be inaugurated as President of Ireland.)

The Republic of Ireland was proclaimed in 1949, at which time it withdrew from the British Commonwealth. Dublin (see Exhibit 11.5) became capital of the new republic. About the new republic, Sheats wrote, "there is no industry" (1951, p. 657). In December 1955, Ireland became a member of the United Nations.

In 1969, Penneys (Exhibit 11.6) opened its first shop in Dublin, later expanding to over 250 outlets in eight countries. Until 1970, most of Ireland's exports were agricultural (Scofield, 1969). Ireland joined the European Economic Community in 1973, and pursued a policy of rapid industrialisation. For a discussion of industrial development in Ireland, see Burke (1995).

Exhibit 11.3 Industry; photo © 2017 Léo-Paul Dana.

Exhibit 11.4 Terence MacSweeney Quay; photo © 2017 Léo-Paul Dana.

Exhibit 11.5 Dublin; photo © 2017 Léo-Paul Dana.

Until 1979, the Irish pound remained at par with the sterling. Following Ireland's adherence to the European Monetary System, this was no longer the case.

Putman (1981) observed growing prosperity in Ireland. Yet, entrepreneurship did not thrive. El-Namaki (1992) noted that propensity to enterprise in Ireland decreased between 1971 and 1975, dropping further by 1981, and even lower by 1985. As unemployment peaked at 17.8% in 1986, the Industrial Development Act recognised the need to encourage the small enterprise sector.

Simultaneously, the concept of technology parks was tested. Abetti *et al.* (1987), described key factors influencing the location decision process of new entrepreneurial firms at Ireland's Plassey Technology Park, adjoining the National Institute of Higher Education of Limerick — now the University of Limerick — close to Shannon Airport where the first duty free shop in the world was established as part of the Shannon Free Area Development Company.

Exhibit 11.6 Flagship store; photo © 2017 Léo-Paul Dana.

Exhibit 11.7 Logo with Irish Setter; photo © 2017 Léo-Paul Dana.

Bus Éireann was formed in 1987 to provide bus services throughout Ireland, except Dublin City. The logo (Exhibit 11.7) features the Irish setter — a species that originated here.

Pastures are abundant in Ireland (Exhibit 11.8) and until the 1980s, cattle (Exhibit 11.9) and sheep (see Exhibit 11.10) were very important for the economy. Farms tended to be small (Exhibit 11.11).

During the following decade, Conniff (1994) noted that manufacturing surpassed farming in Ireland. Walsh and Anderson found, "Irish entrepreneurs who start a business are not as innovative in their decision-making preference as are U.S. entrepreneurs" (1995, p. 5).

Exhibit 11.8 Pasture; photo © 2017 Léo-Paul Dana.

Exhibit 11.9 Watching young calf; photo © 2017 Léo-Paul Dana.

Exhibit 11.10 Sheep; photo © 2017 Léo-Paul Dana.

Exhibit 11.11 Small-scale farming; photo © 2017 Léo-Paul Dana.

In 2002, foreign-owned enterprises accounted for 76.26% of sales (Enterprise Strategy Group, 2004). This was echoed by the low level of investment in research and development in Ireland (Enterprise Strategy Group, 2004). In March 2004, Ireland implemented smoke-free regulations to ban smoking in pubs. This raised concerns about the impact this may have on pub patrons who might move their smoking and drinking from pubs (see Exhibit 11.12) to homes. Hyland *et al.* (2008) found that smoking in the home was not greater

Exhibit 11.12 Among many pubs; photo © 2017 Léo-Paul Dana.

in smoke-free Ireland than in the United Kingdom, where there was no smoke-free law at the time.

In May 2005, the Minister for Enterprise, Trade & Employment launched a new strategy for Enterprise Ireland. With the theme of transforming Irish industry, this focused on accelerating the development and internationalisation of Irish-owned firms.

Reflecting industry changes, the Grand Canal Dock (Exhibit 11.13), in Dublin, was completely transformed — but before that, a speculative housing bubble burst, and Ireland suffered with the 2008 financial crisis. For retailers, sales were slow. Exhibit 11.14 features shops on Henry Street, in Kilrush.

Fitzsimons and O'Gorman (2009) observed a significant decline in those actively planning a new business, and an increase in exit of owner–managers and a considerable rise in entrepreneurs motivated by necessity; as well, they noticed a decrease in women entrepreneurs, increasing the gender gap in entrepreneurship. After Ireland accepted a $90 billion rescue package and the government nationalised several banks, the 2010 National Recovery Plan was implemented.

Fitzsimons and O'Gorman (2015) noted that only half the population considered starting a business as being a good career choice,

Exhibit 11.13 Grand Canal Dock; photo © 2017 Léo-Paul Dana.

Exhibit 11.14 Kilrush; photo © 2017 Léo-Paul Dana.

with just one third perceiving good opportunities to start a business. These authors found that a "relatively high number of early stage entrepreneurs (30%) report that they are motivated by necessity — that is they perceive no better alternative for employment" (Fitzsimons and O'Gorman, 2015, p. 22).

Herrington (2016) noted that Ireland's Total Early-stage Entrepreneurial Activity (TEA) rate rose from 6.5 in 2014 to 9.3 in 2015. Kelley, Singer, and Herrington (2016) observed a high rate of medium-to-high growth entrepreneurs in Ireland. In the 2016 Index of Economic Freedom, this republic ranked second in Europe and eighth in the world.

The Environment for Entrepreneurship

Up to the 1980s, Ireland's economic strategy was heavily focused on foreign direct investment and this investment is largely responsible for the Celtic Tiger phenomenon. The Telesis Report of 1982 and later the Culliton Report of 1992 led the shift to more attention being paid to indigenous enterprise. Many of the recommendations of the subsequent Task Force on Small Business were implemented and local enterprise support was provided through the establishment of County Enterprise Boards in each county, aimed at supporting small scale and microenterprises. At the other end of the scale, Enterprise Ireland supported high-potential startups and the export activities of established enterprises (Ní Bhrádaigh, 2007).

Fitzsimons and O'Gorman (2004) highlighted the shortage of seed capital, and the relatively low proportion of women entrepreneurs. The Irish Global Entrepreneurship Monitor (GEM) report stated, "the rate of participation by Irish women in entrepreneurial activity halved between 2001 and 2003" (Fitzsimons and O'Gorman, 2004, p. 2). Fitzsimons and O'Gorman elaborated, "the ratio of female to male entrepreneurs in Ireland is much lower than it is in Europe" (2004, p. 5).

The Irish GEM found that entrepreneurs tend to be well-educated men in their mid-thirties, slightly older than in other participating countries. Entrepreneurship in Ireland was opportunity driven, mostly in the service sector. "The majority of the business ideas being exploited are not characterised by significant innovation" (Fitzsimons and O'Gorman, 2004, p. 19).

Fitzsimons and O'Gorman's report included the following recommendations: "Enterprise Ireland must reduce its bureaucracy, improve the speed of its decision making and its delivery of services to clients. Enterprise Ireland should confine its VC activity to areas where there is real market failure, i.e., early stage and in the area of business angels. Enterprise Ireland must become a deeper knowledge resource for potential entrepreneurs and new companies. The resources of Enterprise Ireland should be made available to a broader group of new and potential entrepreneurs than at present ... Young companies should be given access to international marketing mentors, relevant and experienced executive directors and to entrepreneurs who have experience of starting and growing a successful business" (2004, p. 51). The Enterprise Strategy Group made the same recommendations.

In addition, it was suggested to expose all students to the possibility of an entrepreneurial career, and to equip them with relevant skills. Experts interviewed for the GEM report suggested the following: "Integration of the concept of enterprise into all levels of the education system. Increasing linkages between industry and the education system at all levels. Reviewing the education system to ensure that it is delivering appropriate skills, such as independence and innovation" (Fitzsimons and O'Gorman, 2004, p. 53). The authors of that GEM report added, "A way needs to be found to identify the most appropriate delivery mechanism to fill the management gap that currently exists among entrepreneurs. This may take the form of mentoring or training" (Fitzsimons and O'Gorman, 2004, p. 54).

As discussed by Bell *et al.* (2004), initiatives included guidance on addressing financial, human, and managerial resource gaps, assistance in developing international market research skills, encouraging technology transfer from academia to industry and the support of management development. *Facilitating the development of networks is also a common feature of programmes, and these networks are crucial to improving the international competitiveness and performance of entrepreneurs and their SMEs.*

Herrington wrote, "One of the findings of the GEM research was that women did not have as strong business networks as men. This prompted many of the local government agencies, responsible for micro-enterprise development at a local level, to set up specific networks for women entrepreneurs. The report of the Small Business Forum published in 2004 recommended to the Irish Government that a National Entrepreneurship Policy be adopted and that the latent entrepreneurial potential identified among women would be one of three specific platforms on which the policy should be built" (2016, p. 21).

Tourism is Ireland is greatly affected by the environment overseas. When the financial crisis of 2008 impacted source countries, tourism in Ireland dropped. Prior to the crisis, the population of Kinsale (Exhibit 11.15) — a historic fishing town about 15 kilometres from Old Head of Kinsale, of which Cunard's *RMS* Lusitania was torpedoed and sunk by a German U-boat in 1915 — swelled considerably during the summer. Between 2008 and 2010, visitors to

Exhibit 11.15 Kinsale; photo © 2017 Léo-Paul Dana.

Exhibit 11.16 Blennerville Windmill, Tralee; photo © 2017 Léo-Paul Dana.

Ireland dropped by 15% annually, and this was noticeable. Exhibit 11.16 features the Blennerville Windmill in Tralee (County Kerry) — with no visitors.

Fitzsimons and O'Gorman (2015) noted that entrepreneurs and key informants most frequently cited government policies as fostering entrepreneurial activity in Ireland. It was reported that most believed that the support for new and growing firms was a high government priority. Positive features of the environment also included the educational system and the portrayal of role models in the media.

At present, Ireland is highly supportive of SMEs, providing accelerated depreciation, cost-free advice, grants, interest allowance, interest subsidies, social security concessions, soft loans, tax concessions, tax relief for exports, and training. The Accelerated Export Development Programme assists SMEs to accelerate exports. Area Based Partnerships (ABPs) provide access to networks, booking service, business advice, grants, incubators, legal assistance, loan guarantees, revolving loans, secretarial service, and training. Business Innovation Centres help entrepreneurs to network and thus internationalise. The ABPs are largely about community development and the social economy.

The government is also supportive through development agencies, including Local Enterprise Offices and Enterprise Ireland. The Local Enterprise Offices have 31 dedicated teams fostering an enterprise culture and providing advice, information, training, mentoring and in some cases financial support to newly established and growing microenterprises.

At the national level, Enterprise Ireland provides a range of support to start-ups considered to have growth potential; to qualify, a venture must be headquartered and controlled in Ireland, younger than six years old, led by a management team, involved in manufacturing or internationally traded services and capable of creating 10 jobs in Ireland and realising 1 million euro in sales within three to four years of starting up, while introducing a new or innovative product or service to international markets. Business Innovation Centres also help entrepreneurs to network and internationalise. *Networking results in a symbiosis, making the group stronger that the sum of its constituents.*

The Fusion Programme of Inter*Trade*Ireland encourages cooperation between Northern Ireland and the republic. LEADER, an initiative funded by the European Union, provides grants to stimulate innovation in the rural sector. Shannon Development (formerly the Shannon Free Airport Development Company) provides grants and mentoring in the mid-west region. The state's Small Business & Local Enterprise Unit formulates policy proposals. *Údarás na Gaeltachta* (The Gaeltacht Authority) provides grants and equity in Irish-speaking areas.

Herrington wrote, "A report by a special committee in Ireland's parliament in ... 2015 found that female-led enterprise is growing in Ireland and that the gap with male entrepreneurial start-ups is narrowing and that women entrepreneurs have responded strongly to programmes established for them and directed specifically toward them" (2016, p. 23). A concern remains, with regards to motivation; whereas in the Netherlands, women are only half as likely as men to become self-employed out of necessity (Kelley, Singer, and Herrington, 2016), in Ireland, 39% of female entrepreneurs are motivated by necessity — a rate considerably higher than the 26% among male entrepreneurs in Ireland (Fitzsimons and O'Gorman, 2015).

Toward the Future

Ireland has a culture supportive of entrepreneurial spirit, and entrepreneurs are well regarded. Arnotts (Exhibit 11.17) has been respected since 1843; it remains the oldest and largest department store in the country. Thanks to multinational corporations, Ireland's exports have been very high. In fact, Ireland is the world's largest exporter of Viagra. However, there is a risk inherent in an economy being largely dependent on a small number of large multinationals, such as HP, IBM, Intel, Microsoft, and Pfizer.

Although government policy is promoting entrepreneurship, a problem is that there are perhaps too many facilities with overlapping services and a gap between services provided. "There is no cause for complacency" (Fitzsimons and O'Gorman, 2004, p. 49).

Fitzsimons and O'Gorman (2014) noted observations of constraints on entrepreneurship. Among these, were: difficulties securing finance; the lack of safety net in event of failure; the prevailing economic climate and recession; and lack of confidence among women.

Exhibit 11.17 Respected name since 1843; photo © 2017 Léo-Paul Dana.

Chapter 12

Italy

Introduction

The Italian Republic covers 301,308 square kilometres, neighbouring Austria, France, Slovenia, and Switzerland.[1] Rome (see Exhibit 12.1) is the capital of Italy. Italian territory enclaves two different states, i.e., San Marino and the Vatican.

Not long ago, large firms — including family firms such as Fiat — were praised while SMEs remained in their shadow. Kenney wrote, "Fiat ... makes buses, trolleys, the G.91 fighter plane of the North American Treaty Organization, steel, household appliances, and a myriad other things ... It does business with flair" (1961, p. 599). As recently as the 1970s, the Italian government did not foster small and medium enterprises (SMEs); however, it was lax in extracting tax[2] from owner–managers (Bagnasco and Messori, 1975). Until the mid-1980s, the concept of entrepreneurship enjoyed very little popularity in Italy. Amatori and Colli wrote, "To the most important ideologies which dominated the intellectual climate — Catholic, Marxist, Idealistic — 'entrepreneur' appeared a minor if not negative, characteristic of the national scenario. He or she was often blamed as a 'freeloader' of public resources, an exploiter of workers, a fiscal evader — essentially a social actor inclined to

[1] See relevant chapters in this volume; for a discussion of entrepreneurship in Slovenia, see Dana (2010).

[2] A generation later, Smiley wrote, "a good fifth of the tax due, it is generally reckoned, remains uncollected" (2001, p. 13).

Exhibit 12.1 *Fontana di Trevi*, Rome; photo © 2017 Léo-Paul Dana.

violate common rules of society in favor of self-interest" (2004, p. 243). Today, public funds encourage entrepreneurial spirit in Italy. Famous for its industrial districts, Italy has a tradition of cooperation (Defourny and Nyssens, 2010), and entrepreneurs are cooperating to be competitive. Legislation facilitates collaboration.

Minniti and Venurelli (2000) observed that the Italian economy was in general characterised by a large number of microfirms, which created jobs and contributed to GNP. Magatti noted that Italy had a higher concentration of microfirms than was the case in most of Western Europe but qualified this by stating, "self-employment is mainly prevalent in the most advanced and dynamic Italian regions (Emilia Romagna, Lombardy, Veneto, etc.) ..." (2003, p. 163). Indeed, entrepreneurship is not uniform.

This is a country with important regional differences, including latitudinal variations in cultural heritage, attitude and lifestyles, as well as climatic differences; even architecture varies, reflecting historical and economic factors. By identifying oneself as *Fiorentino* (Florentine), *Palermitano* (from Palermo) or *Romano* (citizen of Rome), one expresses a unique cultural identity.

Mitchell (1970) discussed Capri, and two decades later Bianchi (1990) studied Tuscany. Judge (1972) discussed Venice and Zwingle (1995) focused on artisan glassmakers in that particular city.

Porter (1990) examined the ceramics sector in Sassuolo. Bianchi compared regions in Italy, noting that the centre-north-east "despite the absence of standard prerequisites for development, was growing faster than the old industrialized regions in the north (Piedmont, Lombardy), while those regions of the south — the 'Mezzogiorno' — that received massive public investment refused to adapt" (1998, p. 94).

Magatti wrote, "In addition to self-employment (involving an activity where there are no employees involved), a major component of the Italy economy consists of millions of micro-firms ... They constitute an essential component of the Italian economy as well as Italian society. Their presence is stronger in the north and centre of Italy than in the south" (2003, p. 163).

The *Sviluppo Italia* agency for economic and entrepreneurial development helped the south develop faster than the already-advanced north. Minniti (2005) observed that the attitude toward entrepreneurship in Italy improved and noted an increasing number of small ventures being initiated by younger Italians in the south. Antonelli and Corbo noted GDP per capita varied, "Average GDP per capita is \$33,816 (2012), ranging from \$59,000 in the north and \$22,000 in the south. Medium and large enterprises are concentrated in industrial districts, mostly in the north" (2016, p. 139).

Italy's famous entrepreneurs include: Guglielmo Marconi (1874–1937) the Italian entrepreneur who invented the wireless telegraph, patented his system in England and launched a wireless telegraph company; Gaspare Campari (1828–1882) inventor of the aperitif that bears his name (Exhibit 12.2); wine merchant Alessandro Martini (1834–1905) who cofounded Martini vermouth (Exhibit 12.3); Pietro Barilla (1845–1912), founder of the Barilla foodstuffs company — still a family business (see Alberoni, 2013); and Gennaro Fabbri

Exhibit 12.2 Founded in 1860; photo © 2017 Léo-Paul Dana.

Exhibit 12.3 Produced since 1863; photo © 2017 Léo-Paul Dana.

(1860–1935) founder of the G. Fabbri liqueur distillery. It was in 1905 that Gennaro Fabbri borrowed funds from his brother to acquire a general store and convert it into a venue for the production and sale of liqueurs. Gennaro was a believer in the importance of sponsoring activities; Exhibit 12.4 illustrates a 1951 Amarena Fabbri event at the Grand Hotel Baglioni, in Florence. Later entrepreneurs include: chocolatier Michele Ferrero (1925–2015) creator of Ferrero Rocher pralines, Kinder products, Nutella and Tic Tac mints; fashion designer Giorgio Armani (1934–) who was discussed by Ellis (1984); apparel manufacturer Luciano Benetton (1935–) who founded the Benetton Group (see Exhibit 12.5) in 1965; and media tycoon Silvio Berlusconi (1936–) — see McCarry (1992).

Exhibit 12.4 Family firm sponsoring since mid-20th century; photo © 1951.

Exhibit 12.5 Family business since 1965; photo © 2017 Léo-Paul Dana.

Historical Overview

Bamford (1987) suggested that SMEs in Italy are strongly shaped by historical factors, and Italy has had a rich history, with regional events shaping various regions. During the 13th century, that which is known as Italy today was made up of multiple feuding states.

In Pisa, seven forms of coins in circulation complicated transactions, as did the use of Roman numerals. This changed when Leonardo Fibonacci (circa 1170–1245), also known as Leonardo of Pisa, wrote *Liber Abaci* — published in 1202 — meaning Book of the Abacus. This book introduced decimal (Hindu–Arabic) numerals to Europe (Fibonacci, 1854), facilitating financial calculations and hence commerce.

Throughout the Middle Ages, Florence prospered as a manufacturing and financial centre. Born in Florence, Dante Alighieri (1265–1321) ushered in the Renaissance that would begin in his home city soon after his death. Capitalism developed during the Renaissance. As a result of the revival of commerce, Tuscany prospered and a bourgeoisie class arose independent of feudal nobility. The Tuscans had a long tradition of being individualists and Tuscany produced many of the great persons of the Renaissance, with Florence its cultural, financial and political capital. William Shakespeare (1564–1616) selected Verona as the setting for three of his plays, including *Romeo and Juliet*. Exhibit 12.6 shows a stage set in Verona. Shakespeare also used Venice as a setting.

Of the Italian city-states, Venice was the most exposed to the East, and became a centre of trade and money lending. In fiction, it was home to Shakespeare's (1637) Shylock. Venice depended on international trade, but voyages entailed risk; the Catholic Church did not allow compensation for risk — interest — and so Jews were among the world's first moneylenders, providing a service that the Church forbade Christians to do. Financiers of international entrepreneurship, Jews were therefore allowed to reside in Venice, but were confined to a ghetto at night. Jewish entrepreneurs would conduct their business from benches — *banchi* in Italian, and the root of the word *banca* meaning bank.

In Florence, the Medici family created the Medici Bank, causing credit to shift from the ghetto to the legitimate activity of banks (De Roover, 1963). Instead of charging interest, this bank charged commission on foreign exchange. Its scale and diversity reduced the risk inherent in lending money.

In 1797, the last doge of Venice surrendered to Napoléon I (1769–1821), bringing to an end the 1,100-year-old Venetian Republic — once great maritime power. Exhibit 12.7 features Venice today. The vessel shown in Exhibit 12.8 belongs to a fruit and vegetable wholesaler.

The year 1831 saw the creation of an insurance company, the imperial *Regia Privilegiata Compagnia di Assicurazioni Generali Austro-Italiche*. This was the predecessor of the Generali Group (Exhibit 12.9), the largest insurance provider in Italy and one of the largest in the world (Scalero, 2011).

Exhibit 12.6 Romeo and Juliet; photo © 2017 Léo-Paul Dana.

Exhibit 12.7 Venice; photo © 2017 Léo-Paul Dana.

Exhibit 12.8 Venetian trader; photo © 2017 Léo-Paul Dana.

Exhibit 12.9 Winged lion logo; photo © 2017 Léo-Paul Dana.

In 1848, Italians began to fight Austrian rule. Giuseppe Garibaldi (1807–1882) — the son of an entrepreneur — led the movement to unite Italy. The Kingdom of Italy was proclaimed in 1861, and Victor Emmanuel II (1820–1878) became king.

At the turn of the century, the Lido was an unusable sandbar between the Adriatic and the Venetian Lagoon. Despite repeated sceptical civic resistance, entrepreneur Nicolò Spada succeeded in raising the necessary capital to drain an area, to raise land at least two metres (in order to solidify the marshy bed) and to build the Excelsior Palace — inaugurated with a high society ball in 1907 and elaborated into a beach-front hotel in 1908. Nicolò Spada travelled to Versailles to study the Louis XV style, which he used for the third floor dining room, *Salone degli Stucchi* (Exhibit 12.10) that was added in 1914.

Exhibit 12.10 Excelsior Palace; photo © 2017 Léo-Paul Dana.

Regulars at the Excelsior Palace included actor Erroll Flynn (1909–1959), Edward, the Duke of Windsor (1894–1972) and Wallis (1896–1996) — the former Mrs Simpson. When Prime Minister Winston Churchill (1874–1965) was staying along the Grand Canal, he would come to spend the day (Denby, 2002). Today, the resort is the Westin Excelsior (Exhibit 12.11).

In 1912, during the Italo-Turkish War, Italy occupied Rhodes and other Dodecanese Islands. Until the Great War (World War I), Italy was allied with the Austro-Hungarian Empire and Germany in the Triple Alliance, but when the war started Italy declared neutrality.

When promised several territories, Italy agreed to join the Triple Entente of France, Russia and the United Kingdom, thereby entering the war. Casualties were high including 60,000 Italians dead and over one million Italians wounded. War debts accelerated inflation and in 1920 an economic crisis followed; banks had recently been built (see Exhibit 12.12), but savings fell.

Exhibit 12.11 Lido Beach; photo © 2017 Léo-Paul Dana.

Exhibit 12.12 Built in 1916; photo © 2017 Léo-Paul Dana.

In 1922, King Victor Emmanuel III (1869–1947) invited Benito Mussolini (1883–1945) to form a government. Mussolini gradually dismantled the institutions of democratic government; in 1925, he made himself dictator — with the title *Il Duce*. Until 1936, Italy's colonial possessions were Tientsin in China and Eritrea, Libya and Somaliland, in Africa. That year Italy took over Abyssinia (Stamp, 1939).

During World War II, gasoline was rationed and motor vehicles were converted to use charcoal (Patric, 1940). In her account of war-time Rhodes, and the neighbouring islands also occupied by Italy since 1912, Hosmer noted occupational clustering: "The Orthodox population lives chiefly from the sea ... while the Jewish population busied itself with commerce ... The Mussulmans, aloof and conservative, live almost entirely from the land" (1941, p. 449). In July 1943, Allied troops landed in Sicily. Mussolini was overthrown and imprisoned by his former colleagues until the Nazis occupied Italy and rescued him. When the Allies advanced through Italy, Mussolini fled toward Switzerland, but was captured by Italian partisans and shot in April 1945.

On June 10, 1946, Italy became a republic, ending the reign of the House of Savoy, kings of Piedmont for nine centuries, and kings of Italy since 1861. Hume (1949, 1951) and Hutchison (1951) provided accounts of post-war Italy. In 1955, Italy agreed with Belgium, France, Germany, Luxembourg, and the Netherlands, to strive toward economic integration, and this led to the signing of the Treaty of Rome, in March 1957.

Walker (1963) discussed self-employed Italian artisans, farmers, fishermen and winemakers during the early 1960s. Typically, farms (Exhibit 12.13) and vineyards (Exhibit 12.14) were — and continue to be — small.

Amatori and Colli wrote, "During the Seventies Italy appeared on the verge of total collapse. Inflation post oil shock approached 20%, official unemployment 8%" (2004, p. 251). Large firms began subcontracting an increasing amount to SMEs and, as noted by Luciani, "the number of small firms in Italy employing fewer than 100 workers increased by 21% over the 1970s compared to just 4% in the 1960s" (1987, p. 35). He added, "the number of industrial

Exhibit 12.13 Traditional farm; photo © 2017 Léo-Paul Dana.

Exhibit 12.14 Vineyard; photo © 2017 Léo-Paul Dana.

firms in Italy rose from 650,000 in 1971 to 958,000 in 1981, as masses of Italian workers left their employers to start their own small workshops and factories" (Luciani, 1987, p. 35).

A means by which small firms could become competitive was by cooperating. Bagnasco and Messori (1975) noted that Italian firms had developed complex networks of reciprocal relationships amongst themselves. This often involves specialisation made possible by the division of labour among firms.

Describing Italy during the 1980s, Ellis noted, "There are tens of thousands of small and medium-size manufacturing companies throughout the country today, and they are the sprinters in the race against crushing recession. In many cases, employees of a company all belong to a single family" (1984, p. 193). Comparing firms in the Federal Republic of Germany with those in Italy, he pointed out that "the average Italian company has 14 workers as compared with ... West Germany's 80" (Ellis, 1984, p. 193).

Luciani also provided comparative statistics, "Firms with fewer than 100 workers employ 51% of the Italian production workforce vs. 29% in West Germany, 17% in Britain and 25% in France" (1987, p. 35). McCarry observed, "In 1986 the country's gross national product surpassed that of Britain, making it the fifth largest economy in the world, after the US, Japan, Germany and France. To a large extent Milan was the locomotive of this success. Milan alone accounts for 10 percent of Italy's GNP, has 38 percent higher per capita than the rest of Italy, and pays 25 percent of the nation's taxes" (1992, p. 94). Milan also accounts for considerable consumer spending.

On the eve of the 1990s, Bianchi noted, "In Italy 99 out of 100 enterprises (of all sectors: agriculture, industry, tertiary sector) are Small/Medium Sized Enterprises (SMEs), with less than 50 employees; 62 out of every 100 workers are employed in a SME" (1990, p. 57). He concluded that the state was not doing enough for the SME sector and that policies targeted for SMEs were making a negligible contribution to the sector in terms of technological enhancement and competitiveness. Nevertheless, *intense co-operation among SMEs* helped them compete successfully with vertically integrated large firms (Beccatini, 1990).

Grimond wrote, "Hardly any Italians can really bring themselves to believe in privatisation" (1990, p. 13). Yet, Italy launched its privatisation programme in 1993.

The new millennium ushered in a variety of incentives and tax reliefs to SMEs in Italy. Tax credits were introduced for the purchase of machinery and subsidies for employee training programmes. Yet, much employment continued to be unofficial. McDonald, Dwyer, and Wendt noted, "Small and medium-sized companies in Italy, particularly where they are owned by the management of the company, are thought to be extensively involved in black economy activities" (1994, p. 49). Cockburn reported, "Among the estimated 60,000 Chinese now living in Italy, legal and illegal immigrants have been found laboring side by side with slaves" (2003, p. 12). Santini, Rabino, and Zanni (2011) found that in Prato (Tuscany) — where many Chinese people work in the textile industry — Chinese firms follow different paths than the Italian firms, and attributed differences to the role of Chinese cultural heritage that strongly influences entrepreneurial orientation, strategic decisions and know-how improvement. The Chinese community has since grown and is estimated to be the fourth largest ethnic minority in Italy — after Romanians, Albanians and Moroccans.

Majocchi and Zucchella (2003) investigated the relationship between internationalisation and performance and suggested that the former was not determined by export intensity nor by the number of international agreements; they found that "performance tends to suffer when SMEs internationalize through FDI, a finding that suggests a 'liability of foreignness' effect at the outset of international expansion" (2003, p. 249).

Peet (2005) observed that Italian industry was highly vulnerable to Asian competition. In 2005, the Italian economy dipped into recession that resulted in the failure of many enterprises, increased unemployment rate, and reduced household incomes. In 2007, the size of the undeclared economy in Italy was larger than in any other country studied by Williams *et al.* (2015).

Meanwhile, Bianchi and Winch (2006) focused on *nanismo aziendale* — dwarfism among stunted small and micro firms that did not grow. Along a related vein, Mattiacci, Simoni, and Zanni (2008) noted that the Italian fashion industry was suffering "from an excessive fragmentation ('entrepreneurial dwarfism'), a low level of capitalization, low technological innovativeness (R&D at a system level) and limited capability to manage available marketing levers … difficult relationships with retailers, lack of balance in the product portfolios, price policies inconsistent with product quality …" (2008, pp. 342–343).

The general situation worsened with the global financial crisis. Kelley Singer and Herrington wrote, "It is notable that Italy and Greece have been hard-hit by the 2007–2008 global economic downturn" (2016, p. 29). Antonelli and Corbo elaborated, "The 2008–2009 economic crisis impacted Italy severely. By mid-2012, Italy had the second-highest level of public debt in the euro-zone. Since 2007, investments dropped by almost 30%. Italy's real household disposable income decreased, from 2007 to 2011, by around 7%, one of the largest declines among the OECD countries" (2016, p. 140).

Boesso, Favotto, Menini and Kumar observed, "Italian SMEs are strong analyzers of the market trends and how the limited dimension may be presented as an innovation's strength. However, Italian SMEs are not able to impose upon the market the largest mark-up and they always price below the MNE average" (2009, p. 45). In the 2010 Index of Economic Freedom, Italy scored 62.7, placing it among the least free economies in Western Europe.

Culasso *et al.* (2012) found that medium-sized listed family businesses were performing better than their non-family counterparts. In 2012, a special law (DL 179/2012) was introduced to define an innovative company and to assist in the creation and growth of innovative start-ups. An austerity plan implemented in 2012, to shield Italy from the debt crisis, was followed by a recession. Italy made

Exhibit 12.15 Hit hard; photo © 2017 Léo-Paul Dana.

International Herald Tribune headline news in March 2013 when Alderman reported, "Italy's travails are hitting small firms the hardest ... among Italy's estimated six million companies, businesses of all sizes have been going belly up at the rate of 1,000 a day over the last year, especially among the small and midsize companies that represent the backbone of Italy's ... economy" (2013, p. 1). Economic malaise was evident (Exhibit 12.15) as the survival of many enterprises was at risk (see Exhibit 12.16).

Muffatto *et al.* (2015) identified a growing trend in Italy: more and more people with positive perceptions to start a business were increasingly indicating the fear of failure was their main reason for giving up. The rate rose from 28% in 2001 to 45% in 2008 and 58% in 2012, before stabilising at 49.1% in 2014.

In 2015, the government was seeking ways to reduce Italy's national debt. In October that year, the state announced the partial privatisation of postal services — *Poste Italiane* (see Exhibit 12.17). In November, plans were announced to partially privatise the state rail system — *Ferrovie dello Stato* (see Exhibit 12.18).

Acs, Szerb, and Autio wrote "Italy's performance ... is alarmingly weak, ranking below Portugal, Spain, Cyprus, and Greece, a group of countries that have suffered badly throughout the global

Exhibit 12.16 Veneri Giuseppe Giorgio, butcher specialising in horse meat; photo © 2017 Léo-Paul Dana.

financial crisis that started in 2008. Indeed, Italy performs worse than many countries with socialist legacies, ..., and even Romania, Bulgaria, and Hungary. This is an alarming situation, especially given that Italy's ranking appears to be on a downward trend" (2016, p. 47). Kelley, Singer, and Herrington explained, "Europe reports the lowest average regional TEA rate. Bulgaria, Germany and Italy, in particular, exhibit among the lowest rates in the overall sample, with less than 5% of the adult working-age population starting or running new businesses" (2016, p. 18). Kelley, Singer, and Herrington also noted, "economies showing the lowest TEA rates in the sample — Italy ... also show low established business ownership" (2016, p. 20). Regardless, Zaharia *et al.* (2016) noted that social enterprises were experiencing extraordinary growth.

Exhibit 12.17 Padua (*Padova* in Italian) post office, formerly also telegraph and telephone office; photo © 2017 Léo-Paul Dana.

The Environment for Entrepreneurship

Weber wrote, "As every employer knows, the lack of *coscienziosità* of the labourers of ... Italy as compared with Germany, has been, and to a certain extent still is, one of the principal obstacles to their capitalistic development" (1930, p. 57). In Italy, family businesses[3] have been central to economic development.

Italians feel more loyal to the family than to the firm or to the state. Ellis noted, "For the average Italian the first loyalty is to family" (1984, p. 185). Luciani observed, "To prosper, many Italian firms depend on family financing" (1987, p. 34).

McCarry further explained, "Unlike those in most industrialized nations, in Italy about four-fifths of private companies are small

[3] For a discussion of family businesses in Italy, see Shor (1968).

Exhibit 12.18 Train station; photo © 2017 Léo-Paul Dana.

businesses, the vast majority family owned" (1992, p. 98). Blim (1992) showed how *kin networks* were important in generating labour and capital in the launch of small scale industry in Italy. Smiley reported, "The bonds of family, which elsewhere in Europe are getting weaker, in Italy seem pretty sturdy" (2001, p. 3). Marriage is taken seriously (see Exhibit 12.19).

Some firms are registered in the name of mothers or wives, in order to take advantage of special tax laws and programmes that favour female ownership (Minniti, 2005). This is perhaps why Capaldo (1997) found that female entrepreneurship was already widespread in Italy.

Bianchi (1998) noted that production, in Italy, tended to possess — among other characteristics — the following: labour intensiveness; flexibility; elasticity; and technologically divisibility. Examining the agglomeration of enterprises, Bianchi (1998) observed non-competitive relationships and emphasised the importance of the family.

Exhibit 12.19 Wedding in Milan.

Magatti listed reasons for the strength of self-employment and small firms in Italy, "The artisan tradition so strong in many Italian regions, the role of the family as an economic unit, the tacit pact between the *ceti medi* (middle class) and the political power since 1945, the weakness of large Italian corporations, the deep-seated inclination toward autonomous initiative and the existence of a cooperative climate in many localities, the possibility of social mobility made available by autonomous activities, the high level of unemployment and rapid industrial organization which encouraged redundant workers to find alternative employment, and strategies followed by many firms toward externalization. These important

Exhibit 12.20 Italian bank in France; photo © 2017 Léo-Paul Dana.

factors all served to reinforce this sector in Italy" (2003, p. 163). The banking and finance system followed a similar path and expanded from Italy. Exhibit 12.20 features the Strasbourg branch of the *Banca Monte dei Paschi di Siena*, which is the oldest surviving bank in the world dating back to 1472.

Minniti (2005) suggested a possible shift in the economic landscape of Italy as she found that people in the south are more likely to launch a new venture, than those in the north; this may be due to legislation that provides support to young entrepreneurs in the south (Maggioni, Sorrentino, and Williams, 1999). Further evaluating the effectiveness of this law, Del Monte and Scalera (2001) found that assisted firms had higher survival rates.

Emphasising the importance of social capital, Barzini (1987) stressed the importance to "entertain as many useful friends ... as one can, and therefore perfect the art of being obliging and 'simpatico' at all times" (p. 229). Exhibit 12.21 shows a social moment among negotiators.

Birley, Cromie, and Myers likewise emphasised the importance of social skills and networks in Italy, "The formality and reserve of

Exhibit 12.21 Being obliging, in Naples; photo © 2017 Léo-Paul Dana.

the British can be contrasted with the gregariousness of the Italians. ... people in Italy are rather individualistic and in the pursuit of individual or family goals they are masters of persuasion, intrigue, influence, politics, flattery and negotiation ... Success depends ... on the choice of a suitable 'entourage' who provide information ... Personal contacts, informants, etc., are essential to supplement business skills, craftsmanship, and resources. Italian businessmen invariably succeed by 'using the protection of powerful relatives, personal charm, a facility for flattering people, and a keen eye' " (1991, p. 60).

Adding to Brusco's (1986) study of industrial districts in Italy, and contributing to the canonical district model, Harrison (1992) focused on the cooperative climate found in Italian industrial districts. Rama, Ferguson, and Melero found the canonical district model to emphasise: "(1) spatially concentrated and sectorally specialized small and medium-sized producers; (2) intensive vertical and horizontal inter-firm linkages, consisting of market and non-market exchanges of goods, information, services and people, within a deep and localized social division of labour; (3) a common social and cultural background that connects economic actors and provides a common code of behaviour; and (4) supportive public and private institutions" (2003, p. 73). Rabellotti (1995) also studied industrial districts, comparing footwear districts in Italy and Mexico. A comprehensive collection on this subject is by Becattini *et al.* (2003), and a later contribution is by Becattini (2004).

Portes and Haller (2005) wrote about the industrial district composed of small, highly dynamic firms many of which started as informal enterprises and continue to use informally produced inputs and labour in the central region of Emilia-Romagna in northern Italy, "Small enterprises ... seek to respond quickly to market demand, specializing in particular market niches, cooperating with each other in meeting sudden surges in demand, and resisting outside manipulations to undercut prices. Workers are hired informally, but are paid reliably and are treated as apprentices who eventually may be able to set up their own firms ... This system of egalitarian flexible specialization, explicitly opposed to the regulatory dictates emanating from the central government in Rome, is anchored in tightly bound community networks ... Emilia-Romagna is the core of the Italian 'red belt' that witnessed militant organized opposition to the Fascist regime and, subsequently, to the designs of Christian Democratic governments to industrialize the nation on the basis of mass-producing companies concentrated in Turin and other northern Italian cities. Instead, the Communist regional government of Emilia-Romagna encouraged and sponsored skilled workers and artisans to develop their own firms as an alternative to deskilling and mass migration north. The successful small firms thus created were not isolated instances, but became embedded in an overarching normative framework" (2005, p. 407).

Hanna and Walsh added, "The industrial districts of the northeast and centre of Italy are an acknowledged example of successful interfirm cooperation ... Small firms have joined together to build strong market positions in traditional industries such as mechanical engineering, ceramics and knitwear. The clusters consist not only of manufacturers, but trade associations and membership service centres that provide expert assistance in areas such as training, access to capital and R&D. Competition between firms with similar competencies is intense and cooperation tends to occur at different stages of the manufacturing process ... The districts support innovation and the application of advanced technology in all firms, and while networks are promoted, they form and dissipate on demand" (2008, p. 303).

The Cluster Management Network was created to manage and promote the Venetian Innovation Cluster for Cultural and Environmental Heritage, with the objectives: (i) to stimulate the territorial development of the public-private supply chain of Cultural and Environmental Heritage; (ii) to identify and coordinate projects, at regional, national and international levels; (iii) to stimulate competitiveness; (iv) to foster coordination and synergy within this sector; and (v) to promote and nurture innovation, research and technological transfer projects.

Comparing Italy with other countries, Kantis (2005) found that entrepreneurs in Italy were more likely to have had self-employed parents, than was the case elsewhere. He found that role models were not a very important factor, in Italy, but that family influence perpetuated the tradition of being in business; he noted that this tradition was more prominent here than in East Asia, Latin America, and Spain. He also mentioned the high interrelationship existing in Italian industrial districts between the different spheres where, for example, there is great deal of overlap between business and family.

About families in the shadow economy, Ellis wrote, "Behind the familiar trademarks of Italy's official marketplace has emerged a dynamic 'shadow economy' of unreported wages and profits. Producing a cornucopia of leather goods, textiles, furniture, and other products, tens of thousands of family workshops add perhaps 15 to 20 percent to the nation's GDP" (1984, p. 187). He elaborated with the comments of an interviewee: "According to the figures, we have high unemployment in Naples ... But the figures are misleading. Many people are on the unemployment list, but not all of them are telling the truth. They are working ... for friends and cousins" (1984, p. 192).

Ellis quoted professor of economics Bruno Contini of the University of Turin: "I would estimate that the people included in the underground economy account for about 20 percent of the work force in Italy ... These economic activities are not necessarily illegal, but in most cases they do violate certain existing government regulations, both for tax evasion purposes and for the purposes of evading legislation having to do with labor protection" (1984, p. 193). Magatti confirmed, "the Italian informal economy is rather large, especially in the south where, according to some scholars, a quarter of all employment is irregular" (2003, p. 158).

Law 266 of November 22, 2002 attempted to make SMEs emerge from the underground economy by reducing their fiscal burden. However, only 632 emerged, with a total of 2,216 workers. (According to the World Bank, the informal economy represented 27% of the gross national income in Italy, in 2004.)

Magatti observed, "in the Italian social hierarchy, self-employment offers good opportunities for social mobility, which can be taken even by people without a formal education" (2003, p. 163). This is consistent with earlier findings by Dana (1992b), who concluded that in Italy the most significant training of entrepreneurs appears to be the marketplace, as opposed to academic institutions. Entrepreneurial skills are developed through practice, with concrete experience leading to observations and reflections which are used to form abstract concepts, the implications of which are eventually tested in new situations, setting the ground for more concrete experience which again becomes the basis for further learning.

As entrepreneurs learned about their changing environment, they adapted strategies accordingly. An example is that of wine producers who adopted strategies of vertical integration, improving their economic performance and avoiding the rural exodus phenomena (Tudisca *et al.*, 2014; Tudisca, Sgroi, and Testa, 2011).

Learning through networking can be an effective substitute for academic credentials. Kantis (2005) found that only one in four entrepreneurs in Italy was a university graduate, less than half the rate in the other countries. He suggested that this shows that technical knowledge circulates through broader channels than those provided by institutions of higher learning. In Italian industrial districts, networks of SMEs are channels of knowledge. These networks result in economies of scale external to each individual entrepreneur, but internal to the network.

Networks also provide entrepreneurs in Italy with access to funding resources. Kantis (2005) found that in contrast to Latin America, where the main reason offered to explain the non-use of outside sources of finance was the lack of an appropriate supply, 86% of respondents on Italy stated that there was no need for additional funding. Rocha and Sternberg (2005) discussed the networking with multinational companies that fostered entrepreneurship in Italy. According to Peet, "The problem with Italy's small firms is that too many of them are in the wrong industries, relying for too long on cheap labour for their competitive advantage" (2005, p. 7).

Corbetta, Dawson, and Valentini (2009) reported that becoming an entrepreneur in Italy is a desirable career choice but that early-stage business is constrained by several structural challenges, including little attention by government policy and a lack of effective government programmes; they noted that established business owners in Italy were typically male and younger than their counterparts in Denmark, Finland, Germany, Japan, The United Kingdom, and the United States.

Mattiacci, Simoni, and Zanni (2008) examined internationalisation of Italian entrepreneurs. According to Corbetta, Dawson, and Valentini (2009), 35% of early stage activities and 33% of established activities have up to a quarter of their customers outside the country.

In 2011, the state refinanced the Central Guarantee Fund for small enterprises. The fund was a main source of emergency financing for entrepreneurial enterprises. Simultaneously, the state-owned *Cassa Depositi e Prestiti* made available a billion euro to banks in Italy, for loans to entrepreneurial businesses. The project was extended until 2014.

De Marchi and Grandinetti (2014) observed a changing environment. They noted globalisation, immigration, increased concentration of the turnover and workforce within districts and a weakening of the fabric of relations between firms, all this prompting a collapse of the Marshall (1890) model that formerly characterised most Italian industrial districts.

Muffatto *et al.* (2015) observed the lack of a supportive entrepreneurial ecosystem in Italy. Their study revealed that Italy ranked worse than the big European countries across most aspects: education, government policies and programmes were singled out as particularly lacking and this was perceived as constraints on entrepreneurship by the majority of the experts interviewed.

More recently Antonelli and Corbo stated, "The Italian government promotes sustainable development policies, with a predominant concern for environmental aspects. Italian enterprises are subject to different environmental laws according to the specific sector, geographical area and the products or services they provide. The regulatory areas of concern include water consumption, effluents, air emissions, solid waste, noise, hazardous materials, soil contamination, energy, electromagnetic pollution, and the prevention of accidents" (2016, p. 142).

Toward the Future

Smiley wrote, "Italy today is richer, better-run and a bit less corrupt than it was ten years ago, but there is still plenty more to do" (2001, p. 3). Corbetta, Dawson, and Valentini noted, "Since 2003, the Italian level of early-stage entrepreneurial activity has been constantly below the average of the most representative innovation-driven economies. And this has happened despite the fact that starting a business is widely considered a desirable career choice in Italy, and consumers are regarded to be widely open to experiment new products or services" (2009, p. 38). There is still much to do.

Kantis (2005) explained how business activities associated with outsourcing the work of other firms were more likely to be taken advantage of in Italy than elsewhere. In Italy, one in three enterprises arose aimed at producing goods previously processed by other companies. This nation has *networks comprised of specialised SMEs*, and already much sub-contracting. Unlike the situation in London and New York, the informal SMEs of Milan do not provide low-cost services to people from around the world, working for the world economy; rather, foreign entrepreneurs in Milan often provide goods or services to larger firms in the same production sector. Italy appears to be increasingly characterised by decentralised and reticular forms of industrial production, including flexible specialisation and industrial districts. *With a sub-contracting market saturated, the future may hold increased success of clusters*, as discussed by Pereira and Fernandes (2006). The Italian clusters comprise about 90,000 firms, mostly SMEs. A proof of their efficiency is that they are responsible for around 43% of Italy's exports (Pereira and Fernandes, 2006).

There are three specific types of clusters in Italy: embryonic clusters, consolidated clusters, and mature clusters. As each of these has specific needs, it would be very useful, in the future, to have policies for each of these types. Embryonic clusters would benefit from the reduction of barriers to entry. Consolidated clusters (such as the wooden furniture cluster in Pesaro) have a different set of challenges, as these would benefit from intangible infrastructure for technology transfer. Finally, mature clusters (such as the agro-food cluster in Parma) would benefit from increased internationalisation; for a discussion on the importance of internationalisation of Italian firms, see Pereira, Fernandes, and Diz (2004).

Muffatto *et al.* (2015) observed that the average entrepreneur in Italy is male, with an upper or lower secondary level education active in the service sector (commercial activities in particular); almost twice as many men as women are involved in early-stage entrepreneurial activity. Kelley, Singer, and Herrington confirmed that Italy had "male rates over twice as high as the female rate. Low female participation in entrepreneurship therefore reduces overall rates ... Morocco, Bulgaria, Italy and Malaysia report the lowest female TEA rates in the sample, where just under 3% of the working-age female population are entrepreneurs" (2016, pp. 24–25). Future research may focus on gender issues.

Chapter 13

Liechtenstein

Introduction

The Principality of Liechtenstein covers 160 square kilometres of fertile Alpine terrain (Exhibit 13.1) between Austria and Switzerland.[1] Its capital city is Vaduz. Despite its small geographic area and the lack of abundant natural resources, this constitutional monarchy has managed to achieve notable economic importance. Liechtenstein's flag was officially adopted on June 24, 1937 and modified several times since then (Exhibit 13.2).

Prince Franz Josef II (1906–1989) is credited for building up a formerly poor country into one of the wealthiest in Europe, during his reign from 1938 to 1989. Booth noted that in 1946, nearly half of all Liechtensteiners were farmers and that by 1981 this country was "the most intensively industrialized nation on earth. Some 50 light-to-medium industries run the gamut from central-heating systems to sausage skins" (1981, p. 273).

Contributing to the facilitation of entrepreneurship, Liechtenstein's innovative policies resulted in an unusually high ratio of companies per capita. Among entrepreneurs here was Martin Hilti (1915–1997), founder of Hilti AG whose sales equalled four times the national budget.

Schuessler, Schaper, and Kraus observed that Liechtenstein had "one of the highest rates of entrepreneurship in the developed world.

[1] See relevant chapters in this volume.

Exhibit 13.1 Swiss Alps in background; photo © 2017 Léo-Paul Dana.

More than 14% of the population is self-employed or works in their own firm, and there are more than 4,000 businesses in a population of just 35,000 people, even though the country has few natural resources or advantages" (2014, p. 106).

The Princely House of Liechtenstein has an entrepreneurial arm — the LGT Group, which is the world's largest family-owned private banking and asset management group. Also prominent here is *Stiftung Fürst Liechtenstein*, a foundation with almost 20,000 hectares of agricultural and forestry land, and a vineyard among other properties. *Stiftung Fürst Liechtenstein* is also involved in energy production. The ruling family is popular; the princely crown adorns the national flag and even car license plates (Exhibit 13.3).

Exhibit 13.2 National flag (1957–1982), with banner of Princely House to the right; photo © 2017 Léo-Paul Dana.

Exhibit 13.3 Featuring princely crown; photo © 2017 Léo-Paul Dana.

Historical Overview

In 1342, Count Hartmann II (circa 1343–1416) became the ruler of the Principality of Vaduz. In 1699, Prince Johann Adam von

Exhibit 13.4 Liechtenstein is on the left and Switzerland is to the right of this railroad bridge across the Rhine River; photo © 2017 Léo-Paul Dana.

Liechtenstein (1657–1712) purchased the Barony of Schellenberg; he bought the County of Vaduz in 1712. In 1719, the Holy Roman Emperor created an imperial principality from these two. Thus was born the Principality of Liechtenstein, and it remained autonomous, although surrounded by the Austro-Hungarian Empire to the northeast and by the Swiss confederation to the west and south. Schellenberg and Vaduz remained fiefs of the Holy Roman Empire until Napoléon I (1769–1821) abolished that empire and allowed Liechtenstein to become a sovereign state in 1806 (Willoweit, 1987). During the rule of Napoléon I, the principality retained full sovereignty within the Confederation of the Rhine. Today, the Rhine River — shown in Exhibit 13.4 — forms part of the border between Liechtenstein and Switzerland.

In 1815, Liechtenstein became a member of the German Confederation. The principality signed a customs treaty with the Austro-Hungarian Empire in 1852. A new constitution, in 1862, provided for more input from the people (Raton, 1969). Liechtenstein stayed within the German Confederation until 1866, when the latter was dismantled. However, the principality never joined Bismarck's Germany; instead, it maintained excellent relations with the Habsburgs, and used the Austrian crown as its currency.

Liechtenstein was neutral during the Great War (World War I), but the collapse of the Austro-Hungarian Empire crippled the currency and this was an issue for Liechtenstein given that, until 1919, Liechtenstein was economically allied to Austria (Williams, 1927).

Exhibit 13.5 Vaduz Castle; photo © 2017 Léo-Paul Dana.

Liechtenstein's reaction was to sign diplomatic and postal union treaties with the Swiss cantons. The principality adopted a new constitution in 1921 and the Swiss franc as its currency, in 1924. It also entered a customs union with Switzerland in 1924, and that same year Prince Franz Josef II decided to shift his residence from Austria to Vaduz Castle (Schuessler, Schaper, and Kraus, 2014); the castle is featured in Exhibit 13.5. Economic recovery escalated in 1926, with quite innovative legislation; the *Personen- und Gesellschaftsrecht mit dem Gesetz über das Treuunternehmen* (*TrUG*) — Persons and Company Law with the Law on Registered Trusts — attracted foreign capital and encouraged the creation of new venture formation. Liechtenstein thus became the first nation on the continent to recognise Common Law trusts.

Prince Franz Josef II studied forestry engineering at university, graduating with distinction in 1930. During World War II he focused on keeping his principality out of the conflict. This allowed the country to develop its industrial base (Schuessler, Schaper, and Kraus, 2014). After the war, the prince encouraged cultural, economic and social progress — resulting in a modern country.

Schuessler, Schaper, and Kraus (2014) noted that in 1970, Liechtenstein had a per capita income of \$4,219. In 1978, Liechtenstein joined the Council of Europe. In 1979, the principality purchased the Gutenberg Castle (Exhibit 13.6), in former times owned by the House of Habsburgs.

Exhibit 13.6 Gutenberg Castle; photo © 2017 Léo-Paul Dana.

To prevent abuse, trust legislation was overhauled in 1980. Booth wrote about the people here, "They know little if anything of unemployment or inflation, crime or pollution ... " (1981, p. 273).

In 1989, Prince Hans-Adam II (1945–) succeeded Franz Josef II. Liechtenstein was admitted to the United Nations in 1990. The following year, the principality joined the European Free Trade Association (EFTA). After several former members of EFTA (including Austria) left EFTA to join the European Union (EU), Liechtenstein maintained a tax treaty with Austria. As of 1995, Liechtenstein's inclusion in the European Economic Area (EEA) gave local firms access to European Union markets.

In 2004, Hans-Adam II appointed Hereditary Prince Alois (1968–) to be his permanent deputy for exercising sovereign powers. In 2011, Liechtenstein became part of the Schengen Area, facilitating mobility. Schuessler, Schaper, and Kraus noted that in 2011 "estimated per capita GDP was USD 170,373" (2014, p. 109).

Agriculture (including viticulture), once the main economic sector in Liechtenstein, plays a marginal role today. Yet, vineyards continue to produce high-quality grapes for exquisite wines (see Exhibit 13.7).

Exhibit 13.7 Vines at Balzers; photo © 2017 Léo-Paul Dana.

The Environment for Entrepreneurship

Liechtenstein has been at the forefront of innovative policy shaping its environment for enterprise. Since 1924, Liechtenstein was a pioneer with regards to participating in a customs union with Switzerland; this was a time when other markets were relatively closed.

Rather than spending excessively on a strategic interventionist approach, Liechtenstein has adopted a limited environmental approach — creating very positive environment, including low tax rates. Incorporation here requires very few formalities. Company law in Liechtenstein allows new ventures to be established within 15 working days. The *Anstalt* is a unique establishment with no shareholders and no requirement to have company meetings in Liechtenstein; no annual return is required. Other legal entities include the following: (i) *Aktiengesellschaft* (AG), a company limited by (bearer or registered) shares, that may have one or more directors, but the identity of the beneficial owner(s) is not disclosed; (ii) *Gesellschaft mit beschränkter Haftung* (GmbH), a limited liability firm that can have one or more directors but shares, although it is required to submit audited financial statements to the state tax administration; (iii) *Stiftung*, a foundation with Council of Members rather than a board of directors; (iv) *Treuhandschaft*, a trust of unlimited duration, which — unlike the Anglo-Saxon Trust — permits accumulation of income in perpetuity, in the absence of any taxation or stamp duty; and (v) *Treuunternehmen*, a registered trust, not subject to any taxation or stamp duty.

In 2012, Liechtenstein enacted a Public Corporate Governance Code (Durst and Henschel, 2014). Also facilitating is the Institute for Entrepreneurship, with a specialisation in international entrepreneurship and management, at the University of Liechtenstein — accredited by Switzerland.

Toward the Future

Despite the lack of abundant natural resources, Liechtenstein has created a competitive advantage for itself by means of innovative policies that foster enterprise. As noted by Kaufmann, "Liechtenstein is keen to promote the image of an attractive business location with a very high standard of living. With a highly attractive economic, political and legal environment (tax system) the country would like to increase the attraction for investors, companies (that is, holding companies) and highly qualified human capital and to create an innovative and dynamic setting for large companies and SMEs ..." (2008, p. 386).

Liechtenstein and Switzerland have a joint customs, monetary and trade union. Companies in Liechtenstein even have a Swiss postal code (Rigtering *et al.*, 2014). Further integration may be a wise option.

Chapter 14

Luxembourg

Introduction

The Grand Duchy of Luxembourg is a constitutional monarchy covering 2,586 square kilometres, surrounded by Belgium, France, and Germany.[1] Government policies — including three official languages (see Schinzel, in press) — have contributed to making this country very attractive. A founding member of the European Union, Luxembourg is home to the European Court of Auditors, to the European Court of Justice, to the European Investment Bank and to the Secretariat of the European Parliament. By world standards, Luxembourg is a tiny nation, with a disproportionate number of financial institutions (see Exhibit 14.1). Its importance has exceeded its size, and the nation enjoys the highest per capita GDP in Europe. Ben Aoun-Peltier, Höck, Peroni and Riillo observed, "One noticeable difference between Luxembourg and other E.U. countries concerns the social perception of entrepreneurs and the entrepreneurial careers ... Luxembourgish respondents do not see an entrepreneurial career as a good choice" (2015, p. 27).

Historical Overview

Luxembourg was part of the Holy Roman Empire, until conquest by France in 1795. In 1815, the Grand Duchy of Luxembourg was

[1] See relevant chapters in this volume.

Exhibit 14.1 National Savings Bank; photo © 2017 Léo-Paul Dana.

founded, under the House of Orange-Nassau, also rulers of the Netherlands. In 1839, the Walloon-speaking area of Luxembourg was annexed by Belgium. Luxembourg's fortress was one of the few that held back Bismarck during his quest to unify German states.

Until the 1880s, Luxembourg depended on a faltering agrarian economy, but then the duchy welcomed Italians who developed the steel industry.[2] The commercial realm evolved too, and The Companies Law came into effect on August 10, 1915.

In 1921, Luxembourg was a founding member of the Benelux customs union. In May 1922, Luxembourg adopted Belgian currency and the customs barrier between the two countries was eliminated (Williams, 1924).

The *Bourse* (Luxembourg Stock Exchange) opened in 1929. During World War II, the Nazis outlawed the French language in

[2] See Conly (1970).

Luxembourg (Clark, 1948a). Luxembourg was a founding member of the European Coal and Steel Community.

In April 1983, legislation confirmed the legal status of virtually tax-free enterprises in Luxembourg. In 1985, Letzeburgesch became one of the country's three official languages, along with French and German. Following a European Union directive of July 1990, certain small and medium-sized Luxembourg companies became exempt of withholding tax, provided the ownership was within the European Union.

Van Stel (2005) observed that business ownership in Luxembourg was lower in 2002 than had been the case 30 years earlier. As the European Union harmonised many policies across its member nations, Luxembourg insisted to maintain its banking secrecy and the absence of withholding taxes on dividends from investments. In January 2003, European Union finance ministers reached an agreement with Luxembourg to impose a withholding tax on bank accounts in Luxembourg, held by non-residents.

Luxembourg scored 75.4 in the 2010 Index of Economic Freedom, placing it among the top six in Europe and among the world's 14 most free countries for which data was available. In 2016, it ranked number 19. People in Luxembourg have also been found to be happy (Schinzel, 2013).

Luxembourg joined the Global Entrepreneurship Monitor (GEM) in 2013, with a first data collection exercise that year. Ben Aoun-Peltier *et al.* (2015) noted that entrepreneurs in Luxembourg were motivated by opportunity, with only 12% driven by necessity. They specified, "Low income entrepreneurs are nearly twice more likely to be driven by necessity" (2015, p. 21).

Schinzel (2016) found human resource managers reluctant to use e-recruitment. This suggested the desire to keep traditional human resource management practices mainly unchanged in Luxembourg.

In January 2016, Jean (1921–), Grand Duke of Luxembourg from 1964 to 2000, celebrated his 95th birthday. Böhmer (1979) had referred to him as a modern sovereign. Grand Duke Henri (1955–) is the eldest son of Jean.

The Environment for Entrepreneurship[3]

Luxembourg makes possible the creation of several types of business entities: (i) *société anonyme* (SA): an anonymous, incorporated company, common across Europe; (ii) *société à responsabilité limitée* (SARL): a firm with limited liability; (iii) 1929-Style Holding Company: a Luxembourg-based SA or SARL, which is largely tax-exempt, according to fiscal legislation passed in July 1929; (iv) *société de participation financière* (SOPARFI): a holding company, the dividend and capital gains of which can be tax-exempt, according to laws of 1990; and a (v) Luxembourg Trading & Commercial Company: a firm which is not a holding company but which nevertheless has SOPARFI tax-exemptions.

Several factors contribute to an environment supportive of entrepreneurship in Luxembourg. Geographically and politically, the location of Luxembourg within the European Union makes it an ideal hub for distribution as well as for investment.

By motorway, Belgium, France, and Germany are never more than 26 kilometres from the capital, namely Luxembourg City — situated along the Alzette River (see Exhibit 14.2). The transportation infrastructure is well developed, with efficient rail links and an international airport six kilometres from Luxembourg City. Luxair is the national flag-carrier.

The financial infrastructure is also very developed. Entrepreneurs in Luxembourg have a wide selection of banks with which to deal. All of the financial institutions are regulated by the Monetary Institute of Luxembourg, locally known by the acronym IML (*Institut Monétaire Luxembourgeois*).

Politically, the stability of the duchy is attractive, and the small size of the country helps make public administration easily accessible. A particular advantage to entrepreneurs based outside Luxembourg is that accounting records need not be kept in the duchy.

Luxembourg is also attractive from a taxation perspective. When compared to other countries in Europe, the social security contributions

[3] This section draws on Dana and Dana (2003).

Exhibit 14.2 The Alzette at Luxembourg City; photo © 2017 Léo-Paul Dana.

are relatively low here. Corporate taxes have a 40% ceiling. In addition to adopting fiscal incentives suggested by the European Union, Luxembourg retained its own. The duchy has over 20 treaties to prevent double taxation.

Finally, the existence of the 1929-style holding company and of SOPARFI benefits add to the attractiveness of Luxembourg as a centre for entrepreneurship. These firms are allowed a wide range of activities, including access to the *Bourse*. Listing on the exchange can take as little as 90 days.

Directors may be of any nationality, and easily-transferred, anonymous, shares may be denominated in any currency, in the absence of any exchange control regulations. A 1929-style holding company can be easily converted into a SOPARFI firm, exempted from taxation or capital gains, dividends and liquidation gains.

It is relatively easy to launch a new enterprise in Luxembourg. Shareholders and directors need not be locals. Shares — issued with or without par value — may be either in bearer-form or registered. The presence of over 100 banks makes credit relatively easy to obtain.

According to Luxembourg's 2014 National Experts Survey (NES), the three biggest enablers of entrepreneurship in Luxembourg were identified as being: (i) physical infrastructure and access to services; (ii) commercial infrastructure; and (iii) government programmes. The most significant constraint was the low level of entrepreneurial education, followed by unfavourable cultural and social norms with regards to a career as entrepreneur. Ben Aoun-Peltier *et al.* (2015) identified initiatives supporting entrepreneurship in Luxembourg, including: (i) The Impactory, which was a platform and factory for members to build their business within a community for entrepreneurship where people go to enterprise; (ii) Business Initiative, which was a non-profit entity that aimed to promote innovative entrepreneurship; and (iii) the Technoport incubator that still exists and provides a physical environment for start-up businesses in IT related projects.

Today, Nyuko provides a dynamic training hub in Luxembourg. With the heading "NETWORK IS KING," the Nyuko community is promoted as the insightful, carefully judged and bold matching *interconnection of people and business sectors*. Through its predecessors Business Initiative and The Impactory, Nyuko has long and solid experience in guiding entrepreneurs to achieve success. Nyuko cooperates with Luxinnovation, National Agency for Innovation & Research.

In summary, Luxembourg is an attractive spot from which to launch European operations. Various initiatives encourage and facilitate entrepreneurship. Furthermore, the 1929-style holding company may hold cash, negotiable instruments, patents, precious metals, and trademarks; it may deposit current assets and finance other firms, which are within arms length. As well, it may borrow capital up to thrice its own issued capital, and it may issue bonds valued up to 10 times its equity. It may also buy, hold, and sell bonds and shares of other enterprises. Very conveniently, it may receive income from licensing agreements. By managing a portfolio via such a company, an entrepreneur benefits from legal exemptions; the portfolio incurs neither capital gains tax nor income tax, in Luxembourg. The absence of exchange controls allows the entrepreneur to direct profits to other jurisdictions, as convenient. This has a considerable impact on international networks of entrepreneurs. With regards to internationalisation of firms based in Luxembourg, Kelley, Singer and Herrington (2016) observed that a third of entrepreneurs in Luxembourg have substantial international sales.

Toward the Future

Ben Aoun-Peltier *et al.* observed, "There seems to be some problems with respect to education system and market structure such as barrier to entry" (2015, p. 14). Nevertheless, despite the lack of abundance in natural endowment, Luxembourg has created a competitive advantage for itself, by means of innovative policies that facilitate entrepreneurship. However, people find more safety in employment with financial and governmental sectors than in entrepreneurship.

As noted by Ben Aoun-Peltier *et al.* "Luxembourgish individuals perceive themselves as more risk adverse and less skilled than other neighbouring countries do even if they perceive better opportunities to start a business" (2015, p. 26). A challenge remains to improve the reputation of entrepreneurs and to increase social acceptance of entrepreneurship — including entrepreneurial failure — such as to encourage people to take entrepreneurial risks. As stated by Ben Aoun-Peltier *et al.* (2015), this implies the modification of cultural and social norms, and the enhancement of entrepreneurial spirit and competencies by developing entrepreneurial education.

Policy-changes may also be on the future agenda. Peroni, Riillo, and Sarracino (2016) suggested that policies to attract highly educated immigrants can promote entrepreneurial initiatives in Luxembourg.

Chapter 15

Monaco

Introduction

Bordering France,[1] between the Alps and the Mediterranean Sea, the Principality of Monaco covers an area of two square kilometres, which is smaller than the Central Park in Manhattan. The constitutional monarchy is governed by the longest reigning dynasty in Europe, the House of Grimaldi. With neither arable land nor mineral resources, Monaco's precious assets include the lack of personal income tax. A brewery, chocolate factory and flourmill have been replaced by high value-added activities in this tiny country that experiences negative unemployment.

Historical Overview

Monaco has belonged to the House of Grimaldi, of Genoa, since 1297. During the 14th century, the Grimaldis "increased their fortunes by levying a *droit de mer*, or sea tribute, on all goods carried by vessels passing within sight of the Rock" (Grosvenor and Grosvenor, 1963, p. 550).

In 1731, the monarchy passed into the female line, to Louise Hippolyte (1697–1731), heiress of Monaco. Her husband, Jacques de Goÿon Matignon, Count of Thorigny (1689–1751) adopted the family name Grimaldi. France annexed Monaco in 1793. In 1815,

[1] See relevant chapter in this volume.

the Congress of Vienna placed the city-state under the protection of the Kingdom of Sardinia. As the Kingdom of Sardinia became the founding state of the new Kingdom of Italy, Monaco was placed under the protection of France.

Grosvenor and Grosvenor wrote, "In the 1860's when Monaco's treasury ran low, Prince Charles III ... sold the rights to his country's struggling casino" (1963, p. 550). Francois Blanc was the entrepreneur who obtained a 50-year operating concession and he sparked a boom in the principality, with the state getting a share of profits from the casino. "Monegasque fishermen beached their boats, exchanged fish for chips, and became nimble-fingered croupiers" (Grosvenor and Grosvenor, 1963, p. 550). Casino profits were high and in 1869 Charles III (1818–1889) abolished taxes in Monaco. Exhibit 15.1

Exhibit 15.1 The casino of Monte Carlo; photo © 2017 Léo-Paul Dana.

features the casino. In 1885 Monaco issued its first postage stamp. Philately eventually contributed 8% of the national budget of Monaco.

Succeeding his grandfather, in 1949, Rainer Louis Henri Maxence Bertrand de Grimaldi (1923–2005) became Prince Rainier III, and was crowned in 1950. In 1955, the editor of *Paris Match* arranged to do a cover story on a meeting between Prince Rainier and the Hollywood "princess" American-born actress Grace Patricia Kelly (1929–1982), second daughter of Philadelphia-entrepreneur John (Jack) Kelly (1889–1960). After a brief encounter, Rainier confided his interest to his private chaplain Father J. Francis Tucker (1889–1972), also from Philadelphia.

Father Tucker arranged for Rainier to share an evening in Philadelphia in December, and persuaded Jack to give Rainier a dowry estimated at $2 million. As Monaco was experiencing a short-term cash flow shortage, the funds were timely.

After an extravagant engagement party in January 1956, Rainier and Grace were married in April, at the Waldorf-Astoria (Exhibit 15.2). Rainier precipitated the industrialisation of his country and was nicknamed the Builder Prince (Edwards, 1992).

A new constitution for Monaco was announced in 1962, maintaining a hereditary monarchy and giving women the right to vote. Grosvenor and Grosvenor observed, "Prince Rainier himself has gone about his business more like an entrepreneur than a monarch, shrewdly and sometimes ruthlessly reshaping the family business that is Monaco" (1963, p. 85).

A consequence of a crisis with Charles de Gaulle (1897–1970), in 1963, Prince Rainier agreed to a treaty with France, requiring French citizens in Monaco to pay income tax to France. Grosvenor and Grosvenor (1963) noted that industry at the time included the production of beer, ceramics, glass, pharmaceuticals, plastics, precision instruments, and tobacco.

In 1982, Princess Grace died due to a car accident. Monaco joined the United Nations, in May 1993.

Rainier III ruled until 2005 when his son Albert II (1958–) rose to the throne. The ruling prince continues to appoint the government.

Exhibit 15.2 The Waldorf-Astoria, New York; photo © 2017 Léo-Paul Dana.

The Environment for Entrepreneurship

Prince Rainier III used tax incentives to develop the economy of his city-state. Yet, not all business is welcome. Enterprises in this city-state are required to be non-polluting, to preserve the quality of life and environment (Spence, 2008).

Given the small size of the country and the high cost of real estate, the Monegasque government intervenes to assist enterprise. The state rents industrial space to local firms, at subsidised rates.

The government also provides local firms with export development programmes. A risk-sharing scheme is available, subsidising expenses in the event that sales are not substantial enough to cover expenses of internationalisation efforts.

Individual entrepreneurs pay no income tax unless they are French citizens. Corporations face a 33% tax on profits, but this can be avoided if a firm can demonstrate that 75% of turnover is generated within the domestic market.

Toward the Future

Industrial clusters of SMEs in Monaco — mostly located in Fontvielle — include: electrical and electronics; food processing; pharma-chemicals; plastics; printing and packaging; steel; and textiles. However, Monaco has a limited industrial base. The domestic market cannot support large production plants with economies of scale. Future research might study options for diversification.

Chapter 16

The Netherlands

Introduction

The Netherlands is the European part of the Kingdom of the Netherlands, which from 1954 to 2010 included the now defunct Netherlands Antilles. In 1986, the Caribbean island of Aruba separated from the Netherlands Antilles becoming an autonomous part of the kingdom; in 2010, Curaçao and Sint Maarten[1] became autonomous countries within the kingdom. Also formerly islands of the Netherlands Antilles, Bonaire, Saba, and Sint Eustatius are special municipalities of the kingdom.

The Netherlands has a surface area of 41,547 square kilometres, including 33,811 square kilometres of land. Its neighbours are Belgium and Germany.[2] Provinces of the Netherlands include Noord (North) Holland, Zeeland, and Zuid (South) Holland. With the exception of several pockets such as Volendam,[3] which were traditionally Catholic, the northern part of the Netherlands is generally inhabited by Protestants. The south is largely Catholic.

The Dutch have long been known for their Calvinistic trading spirit, and for the "Dutch engineering genius" (Kruisinga, 1933, p. 298),

---

[1] For a discussion of entrepreneurship in Sint Maarten, see Dana (1990).

[2] See relevant chapters in this volume.

[3] Volendam was formerly a fishing port on the salt water Zuiderzee, opening to the North Sea; the Zuiderzee was dammed in 1932, forming an inland, freshwater lake, Ijssel Meer. For contemporary accounts and details of the Zuiderzee project, see Kruisinga (1933) and Mumford (1938).

Exhibit 16.1 Built in 1804; photo © 2017 Léo-Paul Dana.

innovation (Borah, 1938), and technology — including windmills (see Exhibit 16.1) that created polders and expanded available land area (Schot, 1998). McDowell wrote, "people of the Netherlands plug away at problems with characteristic ingenuity" (1986, p. 501).

Ulijn, Nagel, and Tan (2001) found that although Dutch and Germans engineers have a common professional culture, the transition from technological orientation to market orientation occurred earlier among Dutch engineers. In another comparison, Ulijn and Fayolle suggested, "The Dutch government does not mingle too much with the national economy affairs ... whereas the French and the German governments do a lot more and protect their much bigger domestic markets" (2004, p. 211).

Comparing France and the Netherlands, Ulijn and Fayolle wrote, "the Netherlands seems to have a stronger entrepreneurial culture ... The Dutch are more impressed with actions than words" (2004, p. 216).

Dutch enterprises have long been important. As an institution, the stock market in Amsterdam is the oldest in the world; Exhibit 16.2 features the 1903 *Beurs van Berlage*, formerly home to the then-called Amsterdam Stock Exchange. Among Dutch entrepreneur success stories are those of: Albert Plesman (1889–1953), founder of KLM Royal Dutch Airlines; Anton Herman Gerard

Exhibit 16.2 Former stock exchange building; photo © 2017 Léo-Paul Dana.

Exhibit 16.3 Fokker F-50; photo © 2017 Léo-Paul Dana.

"Anthony" Fokker[4] (1890–1939), born in the Dutch East Indies and manufacturer of aeroplanes in the Netherlands (see Exhibit 16.3); and beer leader Alfred H. "Freddy" Heineken (1923–2002). Philips, Shell, and Unilever also began here.

Until the early 21st century, policy was directed at getting people to launch enterprises. More recently, policy has been directed toward better-performing entrepreneurs, rather than simply on more individuals being self-employed. The Start Smart programme links firms to coaches; in contrast to the national survival rate of about 50% after five years, this programme yielded a survival rate of 89% after after five years.

Historical Overview

The Netherlands were once a part of the Roman Empire, and ruled by Charlemagne (circa 742–814). During the 15th century, parts of the Netherlands were ruled by dukes of Burgundy; in 1555, these lands came under the Spanish crown, and Dutch Protestants were poorly treated. When William of Orange, German Count of Nassau (1533–1584), inherited vast possessions in the Netherlands, he pushed for freedom of religion. In 1568, the Low Countries demanded autonomy and religious freedom. Villiers noted, "As early

[4] See also Ulijn and Heerkens (1999).

as 1579, a treaty that united the seven northern provinces guaranteed freedom of religion" (1968, p. 532).

McDowell wrote, "the Netherlands has always been a haven for refugees: Jews fleeing the Iberian Inquisitions, Huguenots forced out of France, even English Pilgrims ..." (1986, p. 502). As explained by Rath, "In the sixteenth and seventeenth centuries large groups of Protestants from southern Netherlands and France migrated to Amsterdam ... These immigrants possessed plenty of capital, trading contacts and skills" (2002, p. 149).

"From the end of the sixteenth century on, large groups of Portuguese (Sephardic) Jews arrived in Mokum[5] ... also Ashkenazic Jews from Central and East Europe. These immigrants became involved with trade and industry, partly due to the fact that they were excluded from various occupations by the non-Jewish majority" (Rath, 2002, p. 149). Excluded from traditional guilds, during the late 16th century, Jews established a diamond cutting industry in Amsterdam; for a detailed account see Davenport (1974). Amsterdam remains an important diamond centre; diamond merchants — primarily Jewish — have a high level of trust, and this results in competitive advantage arising from reduced transaction costs.

Rath and Kloosterman noted, "The arrival of Jews from the Iberian Peninsula in the sixteenth century and later from Eastern Europe, and of Roman Catholics from Westphalia throughout the nineteenth century, greatly influenced the Dutch economic landscape as their business acumen enhanced the nation's economic and cultural wealth" (2003, pp. 123–124). Speaking of the Dutch, Sombart wrote "they were fully alive to the gain which the Jews brought" (1913, p. 19).

The 17th century became known as the golden age of the Netherlands. Established in 1602, the innovative *Verenigde Oostindische Compagnie* (United East India Company) issued the world's first corporate stock. This firm combined reduced transaction costs with economies of scale, playing an important role in the Indonesian archipelago; Dana (1999b) provided a history of entrepreneurship in

[5] Nickname for Amsterdam.

Exhibit 16.4 Home of Van Loon family; photo © 2017 Léo-Paul Dana.

Indonesia. Known abroad as the Dutch East India Company, the United East India Company had a monopoly trading spices. The Van Loon merchant family was among those with interests in that company; Exhibit 16.4 features their canal house.

In Amsterdam, the Protestant Zuiderkerk (Exhibit 16.5) was completed in 1614. The Mint Tower (Exhibit 16.6) was built in 1620. The Dutch West India Company was created by Dutch entrepreneurs, in 1621, for the purpose of conducting trade with Africa

Exhibit 16.5 Protestant Zuiderkerk; photo © 2017 Léo-Paul Dana.

and the Americas; on the island of Manhattan, this firm built Fort Amsterdam — which later became New York City. In 1637, the crash of world tulip prices marked the first widely recorded speculative bubble. In 1648, the Dutch Republic became a free, sovereign state. The Dutch West India Company continued trading until 1674. By the end of the century, Amsterdam was the world capital of financial innovation — with the world's first central bank.

In 1795, French revolutionary armies overthrew the Dutch republic and the United East India Company was liquidated the following year. The Dutch kept their independence, albeit under French supervision, until 1815 when Napoléon I (1769–1821) united the former republic and the Belgian provinces, forming the Kingdom of the Netherlands — ruled by Louis (1778–1846) — brother of Napoléon I.

In Amsterdam, the Doelen Hotel (Exhibit 16.7) is said to have been renovated in 1815, becoming the first real hotel of that city. In 1830, Belgium seceded from the Netherlands.

Exhibit 16.6 Mint Tower, built in 1620; photo © 2017 Léo-Paul Dana.

In Amsterdam, during the 19th century, Westphalian Catholics and East European Jews gravitated to the *schmata* (textiles and clothing) business (Raes, 2000). "In the second half of the nineteenth century, Roman Catholic immigrants of Westphalian origin settled in the city" (Rath, 2002, p. 149).

In 1885, the Rijksmuseum moved to its current building (Exhibit 16.8) in Amsterdam. Queen Emma (1858–1934) — regent of the Netherlands from 1890 until 1898, when her daughter Queen Wilhelmina (1880–1962) ascended to the throne — contributed to the popularity of the House of Orange-Nassau.

Exhibit 16.7 The Doelen Hotel; photo © 2017 Léo-Paul Dana.

Exhibit 16.8 Rijksmuseum; photo © 2017 Léo-Paul Dana.

Exhibit 16.9 Dutch cheeses; photo © 2017 Léo-Paul Dana.

Modernisation (Grin *et al.*, 2004) and industrialisation (Kooij, 1997) took place during the late 19th century. The early 20th century in the Netherlands is well documented by Rice (1925).

In 1919, Albert Plesman founded *Koninklijke Luchtvaart Maatschappij* (KLM Royal Dutch Airlines). Sanford (1929) observed that Haarlem was already the centre of the tulip bulb industry, and Alkmaar a centre of cheese trade — important to this day (Exhibit 16.9).

Sanford wrote, "we bumped over the imaginary line which separates Belgium from the Netherlands ... The ugly, prosperous smoke of Belgian factory towns gave place to peaceful meadows where black and white Holstein cattle grazed contentedly and where an occasional windmill flirted us a welcome with its whirling arms" (1929, p. 363).

Sandford wrote of Dutch colonies, "The Nation's rich colonial possessions include vast holdings in the East Indies (Java and

Sumatra, Celebes, Bali, and parts of Borneo, New Guinea and Timor), and Dutch Guiana and the Dutch West Indies in the Western Hemisphere" (1929, p. 364). He described Rotterdam of the times as "a big commercial city and not nearly as 'Hollandesque' as the smaller towns and villages, where old customs and costumes survive" (Sanford, 1929, p. 363).

Kerbey (1940) observed that Rotterdam grew to be Europe's largest port, until its invasion by the Nazis in 1940. Henry (1946) documented World War II in Nazi-occupied Netherlands. Jewish entrepreneur Jacques Goudstikker (1897–1940) was among those fatally injured while trying to escape the Nazis. He was the owner of the Nijenrode estate, dominated by the 13th century castle (Exhibit 16.10), which now serves as campus for Nyenrode Business Universiteit.

The Benelux Customs Union became operative in 1948. Also in 1948, Queen Wilhelmina abdicated in favour of her daughter Juliana (1909–2004).

Exhibit 16.10 Castle at Nijenrode; photo © 2017 Léo-Paul Dana.

Exhibit 16.11 Europe's leading port today; photo © 2017 Léo-Paul Dana.

Clark (1950) and Grosvenor and Neave (1954) discussed the post-war years in the Netherlands. Rath and Kloosterman noted changing demographics, "In the wake of the Second World War, and after the decolonization in Indonesia, a group of Moluccans arrived in 1951 as did cohorts of people of Dutch or Dutch-Asian origin" (2003, p. 125). Thanks to laborious efforts during the post-war years, Rotterdam (Exhibit 16.11) soon regained its rank as the world's busiest port; see Miller (1960) and Graves (1967).

During the 1950s, many Dutch people emigrated from the Netherlands and established themselves — often as entrepreneurs — in Canada, New Zealand, and beyond. In February 1958, at The Hague, a treaty was signed by Belgium, Luxembourg and the Netherlands creating the Benelux Economic Union.

When Israel was invaded in October 1973, the Netherlands took a pro-Israel stance (Davenport, 1974). Following the oil embargo, the Dutch government implemented a ban on Sunday driving. In 1975, Suriname gained its independence. During the 1970s, the

Netherlands continued to welcome immigrants, many of whom created new ventures, "to supply the specific needs of newcomers for food, clothing, and entertainment" (Boissevain and Grotenbreg, 1989, p. 223). In general, however, "small firms were believed to be doomed. The prevalent economic theories of left-wing and mainstream economists alike predicted that only large firms would be able to survive in a modern capitalist economy" (Rath and Kloosterman, 2003, p. 125).

In 1980, Queen Juliana abdicated in favour of her daughter Beatrix (1938–). In 1984, the government launched an Innovation Stimulation Scheme to subsidise small and medium-sized information technology firms. In 1986, the World Economic Forum identified the Netherlands as the most internationally-oriented among 21 Western economies.

Boissevain and Grotenbreg explained, "In the Netherlands, enterprises employing up to 99 employees are considered small or medium-sized" (1987, p. 128). By 1987, "more than 7,000 of the 350,000 registered small and medium-sized businesses in the Netherlands" (Boissevain and Grotenbreg, 1987, p. 105) were ethnic enterprises. Yet, Boissevain and Grotenbreg (1987) noted that self-employment was much *less* common among immigrant groups in the Netherlands, than in mainstream Dutch society.

Boissevain and Grotenbreg (1988) focused on the many immigrants from Suriname who became self-employed in Amsterdam. The authors observed that Hindustani immigrants from Suriname were more parsimonious than Creoles from Suriname, and that the Hindustanis were overwhelmingly active as shopkeepers whereas Creoles from Suriname chiefly owned restaurants and cafés.

In 1991, the merger between ABN and AMRO created the largest bank in the Netherlands, ABN AMRO. Exhibit 16.12 shows its location at Dam Square, in Amsterdam. In 1997, "the Dutch government launched an initiative aimed at supporting start-up firms ... " (Nijkamp, Guldemond, and Teelen, 2004, p. 44). In 2004, KLM Royal Dutch Airlines merged with Air France. Amsterdam remains an important transportation hub (Exhibit 16.13).

Exhibit 16.12 Dam Square; photo © 2017 Léo-Paul Dana.

Exhibit 16.13 Amsterdam's Schiphol Airport; photo © 2017 Léo-Paul Dana.

Focusing on small firm transfers, van Teeffelen, Uhlaner, and Driessen, (2011) revealed that familiarity between seller and buyer rather than kinship or family ties was a key predictor for transfer performance indicators. These authors found that succession planning was strongly related to subjective transfer performance indicator satisfaction.

In 2012, the Dutch government announced that it would abandon its model of multiculturalism that encouraged segregation rather than integration. Dutch Interior Minister Piet Hein Donner presented to parliament a bill reading, "The government shares the social dissatisfaction over the multicultural society model and plans to shift priority to the values of the Dutch people." Roggeveen and van Meeteren (2013) scrutinised social capital invested in Brazilian social networks in Amsterdam.

A milestone for the House of Orange-Nassau, rulers of the Netherlands since 1814, in April 2013 Queen Beatrix abdicated in favour of her son Willem-Alexander Claus George Ferdinand (1967–). One of the three palaces he uses is the Royal Palace of Amsterdam (Exhibit 16.14).

Entrepreneurship is doing well in the Netherlands. Span, van Stel, and van den Berg observed, "Early-stage entrepreneurial activity

Exhibit 16.14 Royal Palace, Amsterdam; photo © 2017 Léo-Paul Dana.

among the adult population aged 18–24 has almost doubled to 13.0% ... the share of the necessity motive in TEA is lowest for those aged 18–24." (2015, p. 3).

The Environment for Entrepreneurship

New ventures, in the Netherlands, have been regulated since the Depression. "In 1935, conditions for establishing an enterprise in Amsterdam were formulated for the first time ... In 1937 the Establishment of Small Business Act came into effect at the national level ... The object of this act and the 1954 Business Establishment Act was to promote orderly entrepreneurial activity" (Boissevain and Grotenbreg, 1989, p. 230).

Until the 1980s, "people who wanted to start a business were legally required to have appropriate qualifications and permits to register" (Rath, 2003, p. 277). Then came a period of deregulation, and eventually support for entrepreneurs. Dana, Korot, and Tovstiga argued that, "generous support for small and medium-sized companies through a network of 18 Innovation Centers attest to a deliberate national policy for promoting the growth of new enterprises. Indeed, many people think that recent economic reforms in the Netherlands offer a successful half-way house between Anglo-American free markets and continental European welfare states. It has even been given a name: the *polder-model*" (2000, p. 192). The polder-model involves policymaking by consensus among the state, employers and unions; see d'Iribane (1989) and Peet (2002).

Villiers wrote about the Dutch, "A nation of individualists? Yes, perhaps — but when necessary, surely the most cooperative individualists in the world" (1968, p. 571). Likewise, the *Netherlands Report on Competition Law and Institutions*, OECD Document DAF/COM D, published in 2005, referred to the Netherlands as a country with a tradition of cooperation.

Dutch entrepreneurs can be excellent team players, as evident from their successful clusters. Among these is the flower industry; Dutch flowers represent 65% of the worldwide exports of cut flowers. Dutch flower producers have innovated at all levels of the value chain, increasing productivity, reducing production costs, improving quality and increasing competitiveness (Pereira and Fernandes, 2006).

Boissevain and Grotenbreg (1987) suggested that *access to a network of contacts is an entrepreneurial resource* in the Netherlands. The authors noted that networks can provide introductions to wholesalers and warning of government inspection, among other things.

Thurik (1993) emphasised the importance of exports in the Netherlands — a country with a small domestic market. He discussed measures to stimulate exports and the hidden potential of small firms.

Kloosterman, van der Leun, and Rath (1998), showed that immigrants to the Netherlands are heavily involved in informal methods of production. They argued that on the demand side, "the scope for informal activities has increased because of trends toward disintegration of activities in manufacturing and especially in service industries, the fragmentation of consumer markets, a gradual emergence of a demand for 'ethnic' products, and also owing to the dynamics of so-called 'vacancy chains'" (1998, p. 249). The authors explained that immigrants "usually set up their businesses in those sectors where informal production could give them a competitive edge. Through their networks of relatives, co-nationals or coethnics they have privileged and flexible access to information, capital and — with relatively low monetary costs — labour" (1998, p. 249).

Kloosterman, van der Leun, and Rath (1999) emphasised the embeddedness of immigrants in their social network coupled with embeddedness in the environment of their host society — mixed embeddedness. In their case study of Islamic butchers, these authors found that complex "configurations of mixed embeddedness enable immigrant businesses to survive — partly by facilitating informal economic activities — in segments where indigenous firms, as a rule, cannot" (1999, p. 253).

Rath and Kloosterman (2003) observed that Amsterdam entrepreneurs from China, India, Pakistan, Suriname, and Turkey, created economies of scope, "Immigrants have been especially active in the food sector ... The *raison d'être* of their businesses originates in part from their capacity to create economies of scope. They sometimes specialize in specific ranges of products, including 'ethnic' or religious products such as kosher or halal food"[6] (Rath and Kloosterman, 2003, p. 123).

During the late 20th century, a crisis facing Philips and DAF Trucks resulted in the creation of 300 new technology-based firms in the Eindhoven area (Noord Brabant province), in the southeast of the Netherlands. When the Dutch entrepreneurial climate was discussed in detail in the 2001 Global Entrepreneurship Monitor (GEM) study (Bosma, Stigter, and Wennekers, 2002), it appeared that potential entrepreneurs were discouraged by negative risk attitudes and by employment conditions and social security, resulting in high opportunity costs in the Netherlands.

The 2003 GEM study revealed that entrepreneurship in the Netherlands was — at the time — relatively low when compared to Belgium, Denmark, Finland, Germany, Greece, Ireland Spain, Sweden, the United Kingdom, and others. Ulijn and Fayolle summarised the situation stating, "starting your own business is perceived as rather difficult, but in the Netherlands less so than in the EU in general" (2004, p. 211). They noted that "the Dutch are per capita (77) more productive than the EU average (65) ... but the Dutch managerial culture seems to lead to a lot less willingness to start your own business (41%) than the USA" (2004, pp. 211–214). Miles, Feulner, and O'Grady (2005) showed that there was a very high fiscal burden of government in the Netherlands.

In their GEM study, Hessels, Bosma, and Wennekers (2005) noted an increase in early-stage entrepreneurship in the Netherlands, but nevertheless noted that entrepreneurial activity in the Netherlands was low; they explained that early-stage entrepreneurs in the Netherlands were less active in consumer oriented sectors compared to other high income countries.

[6] For an explanation, see Kloosterman, van der Leun, and Rath (1998).

Baycan-Levent and Nijkamp (2007) examined ethnic minority entrepreneurs in Amsterdam. They concluded, "Ethnic entrepreneurs constitute a special group in urban economic life with their growing numbers ... ethnic entrepreneurs have become service providers, not only for their own ethnic groups" (Baycan-Levent and Nijkamp, 2007, p. 334).

During the financial crisis, there was an increase of entrepreneurship in the Netherlands. This may be explained by the fact that employment was less plentiful than in the past. Yet, entrepreneurial perceptions deteriorated, as found by the GEM study. In the region of Utrecht, from 2009 to 2013, a workplace innovation project — My Enterprise 2.0 — was implemented with successful outcomes (Oeij *et al.*, 2014).

Kourtit and Nijkamp (2011) emphasised the ethnic diversity of Dutch economy. The 2014 GEM showed a strong increase in entrepreneurial activities, above the average for the European Union. With regards to entrepreneurial activity, Span, van Stel and van den Berg noted, "The Total Early-stage Entrepreneurial Activity (TEA) rate, defined as the percentage of adults between 18 and 64 years of age who are actively trying to start a new business (nascent entrepreneurs) or own and manage a business younger than 3.5 years (young business entrepreneurs), has increased slightly from 9.3% in 2013 to 9.5% in 2014. The increase is entirely due to nascent business entrepreneurship" (2015, p. 3).

Bankruptcies decreased by 16% in the first semester of 2015, compared to the same a year earlier. Terjesen and Lloyd (2015) observed that the Netherlands was among the top five countries whose institutions support female high-growth entrepreneurs.

With regard to perceptions about entrepreneurship as a career, Kelley, Singer, and Herrington noted "only 17% of working-age adults in Puerto Rico think entrepreneurship is a good choice of career ... In Europe, 33% of Finns state these perceptions, while it's 79% in the Netherlands" (2016, p. 15). In 2016, the Netherlands had a score of 74.6 in the Index of Economic Freedom, placing it among the top 16 in the world.

Toward the Future

In contrast to the many places where culture does not accept entrepreneurship as socially desirable activity, Dutch culture views entrepreneurship favourably. Many Dutch people say that they are qualified for entrepreneurship, and they see opportunities. Yet, few choose to pursue an entrepreneurship career. The majority appear to be risk averse.

Social norms in the Netherlands are positive with respect to esteem for entrepreneurs. Earlier barriers to entrepreneurship, including regulation, have been reduced. The formal venture capital market is well developed. Access to physical infrastructure is also good. Other factors, however, decrease the attractiveness of the entrepreneurship sector. Although technical skills (see Exhibit 16.15) are emphasised, education contributes little to entrepreneurship. In contrast to firms that focus on short-term interests of shareholders,

Exhibit 16.15 Technical school in Heerlen; photo © 2017 Léo-Paul Dana.

family-owned MKBs (acronym for *Midden en Klein Bedrijf*) — SMEs — focus on continuity and these will probably continue to be catalysts of innovation.

As emphasised by Van Gils and Zwart (2009) in their study of Belgian and Dutch SMEs, "cooperative agreements are important tools to improve the competitive position of small and medium-sized firms." Span, van Stel, and van den Berg (2015) observed that survival rates of Dutch enterprises are relatively high. This is likely to remain the case.

Chapter 17

Norway

Introduction

Oxholm described the Kingdom of Norway as the "Northernmost civilized country" (1939), p. 493. It covers 324,219 square kilometres of mainland, bounded by Finland, Russia and Sweden[1] to the east, with the North Sea to the west, the Arctic Ocean to the north and the Skagerrak Straits to the south. At the head of a fjord, its capital is Oslo (Exhibit 17.1) — known until 1925 by its Danish name, Christiania. After Bergen, other important centres include Stavanger (Exhibit 17.2) and Trondheim (Exhibit 17.3) — formerly Trondhjem. Norway has had one of the largest shipping fleets in the world.

Norwegian industrialist Hans Nielsen Hauge (1771–1824) participated in numerous ventures, including a mill for which he obtained property rights without payment — in exchange for free use of the mill. Also significant was Sam Eyde (1866–1940), founder of Norsk Hydro. Among more recent success stories is that of Olav Thon (1923–), who worked his way from poor farm-boy to wealthiest resident of Norway. He bought his first building in 1951. Now his Olav Thon Group is the largest private real estate company in Norway. In 2013, he announced he was giving away the largest part of his fortune to a foundation. Erlanger wrote, "Mr. Thon, having

[1] See relevant chapters in this volume; for a discussion of entrepreneurship in Russia, see Dana (2010).

Exhibit 17.1 Oslo; photo © 2017 Léo-Paul Dana.

Exhibit 17.2 Stavanger; photo © 2017 Léo-Paul Dana.

worked since the age of 7 as a shepherd ... thinks young Norwegians have gone soft with oil wealth and the welfare system: 'You can't feed a cat with cream and food in the kitchen and expect him to go catch mice'" (2014, p. 3).

Exhibit 17.3 Neo-classic building from 1925; photo © 2017 Léo-Paul Dana.

At the age of 10, Petter Stordalen (1962–) started working in his father's grocery store. Peter was later involved in the founding of Steen & Strom Invest, one of Norway's largest commercial real estate enterprises and he now owns Nordic Choice Hotels, with 170 high-end hotels making this Scandinavia's largest chain of hotels.

At a smaller scale, Jon Østen Ringi (1954–) and his wife Charlotta Kängstrøm Ringi (1960–) are the 10th generation to operate the Ringi farm — in their family since 1661. They have been producing juice since 1995. In 2001, they launched apple juice in wine bottles, as an alternative to alcoholic beverages.

Historical Overview

In 872, Harold Fairhair (circa 844–933), already ruler of eastern Norway, expanded his realm and established the first Norwegian monarchy, but King Olaf II (995–1030) was deposed in 1028, followed by civil war. Meanwhile, in 982, Erik Thorvaldsson (circa

950–1003) — also known as Eric the Red — reached Greenland and within a few years Norse Vikings became the first farmers in Greenland. The Norse Vikings created a parliament for their independent state, but in 1261 submitted to Norwegian rule in exchange for trade routes. In 1262, Greenland and Iceland came under the control of Norway.

In 1319, Norway was united with Sweden. During the mid-14th century, the Hanseatic League eyed Bergen — Norway's largest city at the time — and German merchants set up a trade colony here, monopolising the city's commerce. In 1397, Denmark, and Norway and Sweden were united under Danish rule. Although Sweden broke away in 1523, Norway remained a Danish province.

During the 16th century, European whalers began trading with Greenlanders. In 1721, Hans Egede (1686–1758), a Norwegian missionary travelled to Greenland to spread Lutheranism (Bobé, 1952; Nuttall, 2005). In 1728, he brought 100 people to a new colony that he named Godthåb, literally "good hope," today known as Nuuk — the capital of Greenland. He is considered the founding father of Nuuk. Exhibit 17.4 shows his home that was built in 1728.

After the Napoleonic Wars, the Treaty of January 14, 1814 transferred Norway from the king of Denmark to the king of Sweden. Although the Norwegians declared themselves independent and elected Prince Christian Frederik of Denmark as their king, foreign powers did not recognise this initiative; Norway subsequently agreed to a union with Sweden under the Swedish king.

Carl XIII of Sweden (1748–1818) ruled as King Carl II of the Norwegian–Swedish union until his death; he was then succeeded by King Carl Johan (1763–1844). In 1825, Carl Johan laid the foundation stone of the Royal Palace (Exhibit 17.5) in Oslo.

As noted by Magga, "From the middle of the 19th century, Norway began a systematic war against everything Saami. The use of the Saami language was forbidden" (1985, p. 17). A section below shall focus on these indigenous people of Norway.

At the south-western end of Norway, Stavanger was largely built of wood (see Exhibit 17.6), and its residents were in constant fear of fire. In 1850, work began building a fire watchtower, called

Exhibit 17.4 House of Hans Egede; photo © 2017 Léo-Paul Dana.

Exhibit 17.5 The Royal Palace; photo © 2017 Léo-Paul Dana.

Exhibit 17.6 Traditional construction; photo © 2017 Léo-Paul Dana.

Valbergtaarnet (Exhibit 17.7). When it was completed in 1853, it was the tallest structure in south-western Norway.

In addition to fire, the sea also posed risk. The open coast of Jæren was a threat for sailors, and Norway devised a national plan to have a safer Norwegian coast. Among others, the Obrestad lighthouse (Exhibit 17.8) was first lit in 1873. Once the lighthouse was automated, in 1991, the last keeper moved away.

Oslo experienced a boom during the 1890s. While visiting the 1893 Chicago World's Fair, Norwegian architect Torolf Prytz (1858–1938) was inspired to design the five-storey Tostrupgården commercial building (Exhibit 17.9). When this modern steel-reinforced high-rise was built in 1896, it was among the first in Oslo to have electric lighting and an elevator. Its façade includes marble from Fauske. Today, it is part of the Olav Thon Group (mentioned above).

Exhibit 17.7 Valbergtaarnet fire watchtower; photo © 2017 Léo-Paul Dana.

Exhibit 17.8 Obrestad lighthouse; photo © 2017 Léo-Paul Dana.

Henry Bucher (1864–1944) designed the Victoria Hotel (see Exhibit 17.10) in Stavanger, in neo-renaissance style. It was completed in 1900.

Kristian Birkeland (1867–1917) and Samuel Eyde (1866–1940) devised a way to use electricity, abundant in Norway, to extract nitrogen from the air. The commercialisation of their technique, in 1905, resulted in the establishment of Norsk Hydro, which became Norway's biggest industrial concern.

Exhibit 17.9 The Tostrupgården; photo © 2017 Léo-Paul Dana.

Following a plebiscite in August 1905, the union with Sweden was officially dissolved that year. Charles of Denmark was elected to be King Haakon VII (1872–1957) of Norway.

In 1925, the Treaty of Svalbard gave Norway sovereignty over the Archipelago of Spitsbergen, now known as Svalbard (see Young, 1978). In 1929, the vessel *S/S* Rogaland (see Exhibit 17.11) was constructed for the Bergen-to-Stavanger coastal passenger service.

Between the world wars, Dennis wrote about Norway, "With almost double the area of the New England States, the kingdom has only three acres in every hundred under the plow, for most of the land is either unproductive or covered with rocks, forests, rivers, and lakes" (1930, p. III). He described Norway as a land of stern reality, "The Norwegians, striving to their utmost, cannot eke out a living from their soil. They must import food. Nor can they depend, as does England, upon the exchange of the products of their factories for the products of other people's farms" (1930, p. 1).

Exhibit 17.10 Victoria Hotel; photo © 2017 Léo-Paul Dana.

Exhibit 17.11 The former *S/S* Rogaland; photo © 2017 Léo-Paul Dana.

In 1940, when the Nazis invaded Norway, the Royal Norwegian Government requisitioned the country's 1,000 privately owned merchant ships for war use; each owner had the choice whether to follow this optional directive and every one did (Morgenstierne, 1943). Henry (1945a) provided a detailed account of the war. In May 1945, Nazis in Norway capitulated.

During the post-war period, Clark (1948b) observed that fish made Stavanger prosperous; at the time, Stavanger was an important fish-canning centre and the town was known as the sardine capital of Norway. (Today, it is Norway's oil capital.)

King Haakon VII died in 1957, succeeded by Olav V (1903–1991). Norwegian anthropologist Fredrik Barth (1928–2016) wrote about family life in a central Norwegian mountain community at the time (Barth, 1960).

In 1965, Norway took over unregistered land in Finnmark (Magga, 1985). This would become a problem for Sámi reindeer herders, discussed below.

In 1972, a referendum was held to decide whether Norway would join the European Community. The majority opted not to join.

In 1978, the Norwegian government passed the Reindeer Management Act. The new Norwegian law made it necessary to have a permit in order to own reindeer, and in the 1980s, authorities stopped issuing new permits.

In 1991, Harald V (1937–) ascended to the thrown. In 1994, Norway voted again to not enter the European Union. Van Stel (2005) observed that in Norway, business ownership rates were lower in 2002 than they had been in 30 years. Norway scored 69.4 in the 2010 Index of Economic Freedom, placing it among the least free economies in Western Europe. In 2016, it scored 70.8, just slightly better.

Indigenous Sámi Entrepreneurship in Norway[2]

In Norway, the Sámi people comprise 96% of the population of Guov'dageai'dno/Kautokeino, 94% of Kárášjohka/Karasjok, 75%

[2] For a detailed overview see Dana (2008).

Exhibit 17.12 Spring round up; photo © 2017 Léo-Paul Dana.

of Unjárga/Nesseby, and 53% of Deatnu/Tana. Eythórsson observed "the relatively sudden 'disappearance' of the coastal Sami from the census records ... when people who had classified themselves as Sami in the pre-war census classified themselves as Norwegians in the first post-war census" (2003, p. 151).

Reindeer herding (Exhibit 17.12) is a traditional form of entrepreneurship among the Sámi people. Beach wrote that the reindeer "has been tamed as a decoy animal to lure its wild brethren into the hunter's grasp. It has been used as a pack animal over bare ground and as a sled-pulling draft animal in winter" (1990, p. 255). Olson described reindeer transport, "In descending a very steep grade, the reindeer is hitched behind the sleigh. The animal resents being pulled by the head and digs his forefeet into the snow, thus providing effective breaks" (1938, p. 512). Shor and Shor elaborated, "In winter the splay-footed beasts pull Lapp *polkas* 10 miles an hour on long trips, easily reach twice that speed on shorter stretches" (1954, p. 280). Until the 1960s, draught reindeer were given names; when too old to travel, they were slaughtered and eaten. Skins were used for clothing.

Although the snowmobile replaced the reindeer for transport (Pelto, 1973), reindeer herding remained a culturally important form of entrepreneurship. Riseth explained, "The production system changed from subsistence pastoralism to a motorized and market-oriented industry, moving away from a near-complete dependence on animal and human muscle power to a degree of dependence on motorized vehicles" (2003, p. 231). Indeed, herding became increasingly mechanical as the reindeer economy became a meat-production business.

Anderson summarised changes, "Where the herder's life once revolved entirely around the reindeer, which provided not only meat and milk but also materials for garments and tools, now the animals more and more are handled as a cash crop. Today the reindeer Lapp needs folding money to buy ever more abundant processed foods, ready-made clothing, automobiles, television sets, and radios." (1977, p. 371). Pelto (1978) described such change as the de-localisation of resources.

As was the case with other indigenous people, activities "became dependent on goods produced outside their sphere of influence, and introduced into their area of residence by external forces" (Müller-Wille, 1978, p. 112). Nevertheless, traditional cultural institutions continue to thrive, including the *sii'dâ* — Bjørklund explained the term as referring "to a group of reindeer owners who live and migrate together, and to the herd of reindeer owned and herded by them" (2004, p. 125). He added, "the *siida* represents a flexible cooperative unit between people and animals" (Bjørklund, 2004, p. 126). In the winter, when a pasture might not sustain a specific herd, a Sámi strategy is frequently to divide the herd into smaller ones and to move each to a different area.

"The strategy of the pastoralists is never to be in a position where the size and composition of the herd is not in proportion to the available labour and pasture" (Bjørklund 2004, p. 126). In summary, the *sii'dâ* is an informal institution uniting people for symbiotic interdependence. It does not claim to be democratic; rather, solutions are reached by consensus and for this reason cooperation is essential.

Exhibit 17.13 Youth with her reindeer; photo © 2017 Léo-Paul Dana.

Bjørklund elaborated on Sámi cultural arrangements that traditionally took care of recruitment into pastoral society — and these traditions continue (see Exhibit 17.13):

> Animals were allocated to children during certain ritual occasions … Along with the gift also came the responsibility of being a reindeer owner. Children learned how to take care of their animals and were thus socialised into the world of reindeer pastoralism. When the time came to marry, both spouses were in possession of knowledge and enough animals — together with the animals given to them as wedding gifts — to make it possible to establish themselves as their own husbandry and perhaps herding unit (2004, p. 133).

Although reindeer are individually owned and herding involves a *sii'dâ* that includes more than one family, the family unit — extended as well as nuclear (Exhibit 17.14) — continues to be central in Sámi entrepreneurship. Anderson elaborated, "In Saami society in Norwegian Lapland, women, once hunters, then herders

Exhibit 17.14 Working as a family, in a *sii'dâ*; photo © 2017 Léo-Paul Dana.

of reindeer alongside men, now manage long-distance networks of trade and politics in reindeer-breeding households. Contemporary Saami women in more sedentary subsistence groups, such as farmers and fishers, market their foraging surpluses and their time to busy nomadic women and to non-Saami settlers" (1983, p. 175).

Sámi people perceive the Reindeer Management Act as a hurdle along with the requirement to have a permit to conduct a traditional activity and the ban on new permits. This is a barrier to entry for indigenous Sámi who were not born to reindeer herders. As expressed by Vesilind, "They want to develop, most Saami say, but not as Norwegians ... " (1983, p. 194).

The Environment for Entrepreneurship

Bergen was an important port since the medieval period; German merchants of the Hanseatic League used to come here to exchange grain for fish. During the Napoleonic Wars, Norwegian trade — largely with England — was damaged when Denmark sided with Napoléon I (1769–1821).

Exhibit 17.15 Fishmongers in Stavanger; photo © 2017 Léo-Paul Dana.

Industry gained importance during the later years of the 19th century. The industrial revolution prompted the creation of new ventures. In 1873, the Stavanger Preserving Co., established the first canning factory in Stavanger, pioneering the concept of tinned sardines. Fish is still important in Stavanger — although not to the extent it was in former times (Exhibit 17.15).

In 1878, A P Foss was established. In 1879, the company Viig & Vraalsen was created. The two merged in 1919, creating Viig & Vraalsen & A P Foss A/S, which became an important manufacturer of articles made of steel, including safes and weights for business and industry. The firm produced for banks, libraries, offices, retailers, and warehouses. A scale produced by this company, in Norway, is featured in Exhibit 17.16.

In 1900, Norway had the third largest merchant fleet in the world. More Norwegians worked in fishing and whaling than in any other sector.

In 1960, Norway joined Austria, Denmark, Portugal, Sweden, Switzerland and the United Kingdom to create the European Free Trade Association (EFTA). While most other EFTA members have since joined the European Union, Norway joined the European Economic Area in 1994.

Spilling (1998) observed that since the mid-1970s, Norway experienced a shift toward smaller units in most sectors of manufacturing;

Exhibit 17.16 Made in Norway; photo © 2017 Léo-Paul Dana.

he identified an industrial decline in Norway and concluded, "Rather than being attributed to the strengths of SMEs, the growing share of SMEs may be interpreted as a result of industrial weakness" (1998, p. 401). Another consideration is that during the 1980s Norway began to prosper from North Sea oil and gas fields, and this provided alternatives to self-employment. In 1985, Bodø Graduate School of Business (now Nord University) launched its major in entrepreneurship as part of its Master of Science in Business programme (Kolvereid and Åmo, 2007). However, unprecedented opportunities arose working with large firms in oil and gas and this may have deterred from ambitions in entrepreneurship; simply, opportunity cost may have been perceived as high.

Weaver, Berkowitz, and Davies (1998) used data from 697 Norwegian SMEs to develop a profitability model to assist government agencies in allocating resources for assistance and support to encourage exporting by SMEs. Spilling and Berg (2000) focused on gender and small business in Norway.

Lundström wrote, "Norway has mainly worked in the Skill area by focusing on knowledge transfer and financing, network building and financing co-operation between R&D and society. However, also in the area of Motivation some measures are taken above all in the school system. Some measures are also targeted at increasing the number of women entrepreneurs" (2003, p. 274).

Lundström elaborated on important facilitators of entrepreneurship in Norway at the time: "SND (The Norwegian Industrial and Development Fund), NFR (The Research Council of Norway) and the SIVA network" (2003, p. 278). (Controlled by the Minister of Trade and Industry, and with the objective of developing an encouraging environment that stimulates industry, SIVA is the state-owned Industrial Development Corporation of Norway, with a nation-wide network of over 100 supportive institutions including research parks and incubators.)

In 2004, Norway launched its Strategy for Entrepreneurship in Education, promoting training for entrepreneurship. This was a coordinated effort involving the Ministry of Education and Research, the Ministry of Trade and Industry and the Ministry of Regional Development and Local Government. The strategy was modified in 2006, such as to motivate educational institutions and municipalities to establish relevant training with the cooperation of various stakeholders, including trade and industry. The training of ethnic entrepreneurs was also made a priority.

Andersson, Nyvold, and Rotefoss (2008) identified government ministries that were actively involved in entrepreneurship policy in

Norway: (i) the Ministry of Education and Research; (ii) the Ministry of Local Government and Regional Development; and (iii) the Ministry of Trade and Industry. In 2008, the Ministry of Labour merged with the Ministry of Trade and Industry.

Despite various efforts, Andersson, Nyvold, and Rotefoss concluded, "Norway has no comprehensive policy document dealing with entrepreneurship. Instead several areas of entrepreneurship have been included as sub topics in the papers and strategy plans presented by the three ministries that deal with Entrepreneurship policy (The Ministry for Education and Research, The Ministry of Trade and Industry and the Ministry of Local Government and Regional Development). The most important public agencies and organizations in the area of entrepreneurship are Innovation Norway, the Industrial Development Corporation (SIVA) and Junior Achievement — Young Enterprise" (2008, p. 30). Notwithstanding the above, Andersson, Nyvold, and Rotefoss wrote, "Norway was one of the first countries to develop a national strategy plan for entrepreneurship in the school system" (2008, p. 31).

Bullvåg *et al.* (2010) found that although entrepreneurship due to necessity increased from 2008 to 2009, the nascent rate of entrepreneurship decreased and female involvement in entrepreneurship decreased in Norway. While very positive about physical infrastructure, the expert panel interviewed for that study pointed to the need for further improvements in the environment for entrepreneurship in Norway. This included reduction of bureaucracy and reduction in the cost of establishing a limited liability firm.

Today, Innovation Norway is the main actor when it comes to offering financial support to entrepreneurs. Complementing SIVA, Innovation Norway is currently the state's most important instrument for innovation and development. Also contributing to the environment for entrepreneurship is Young Enterprise. This nationwide organisation plays an important role in creating awareness of entrepreneurship among young people. In addition, Norway has an important tax scheme, Skattefunn. This is a tax credit scheme to stimulate R&D among privately owned firms.

Toward the Future

Norway was traditionally known as an undiversified exporter of dried cod. So much has changed!

Poelzer wrote, "For most of the 20th century, Norway was a relatively poor country, on the periphery of European political and economic affairs and living under the shadow of its much more powerful neighbour, Sweden" (2013, p. 34). He described Norway as "an ocean-oriented culture" (Poelzer, 2013, p. 36). Indeed, the sea brings much to Norway, including food, offshore fuel and trade routes (see Exhibit 17.17). However, Norway has surpassed Sweden with an increasingly diversified economy — although dominated by raw materials including crude petroleum and natural gas. Hansen and Midtgard (2008) discussed emerging petroleum issues. Nevertheless, Norway ranked number one on the 2015 Legatum Prosperity Index.

Exhibit 17.17 Port Authority; photo © 2017 Léo-Paul Dana.

Norway is Europe's largest petroleum producer. The country also has an abundance of hydro-electric power, an important competitive advantage. There is, however, no reason to be complacent. Alsos *et al.* (2014) observed that Norway had less entrepreneurial activity, fewer nascent entrepreneurs and fewer owners of new firms, in 2013 than in previous years. Notwithstanding strong perceptions of opportunities, an important issue was low perceived capabilities. Furthermore, women involvement was low. Waged employment was attractive, resulting in a high opportunity cost for would-be entrepreneurs.

Fitjar and Rodriguez-Pose (2014) focused firm networking among 1,604 enterprises in Norway. Their study revealed that collaboration is affected by manager-level, firm-level and regional-level variables. Among the findings, education encouraged international collaboration at the expense of local links. These authors recommended balancing policies for boosting regional social capital and R&D with investments in education and fostering open-mindedness.

Alsos *et al.* (2015), reported a continued decrease in entrepreneurship, with women still less involved in entrepreneurship than men. These authors found fewer informal investors and fewer established business owners — perhaps explained by a tight labour market that made salaried employment more attractive.

Nevertheless, a well-developed education system and a highly educated population do enable entrepreneurship in Norway. That said, Alsos *et al.* (2015) reported that Norwegians described themselves as lacking the skills and competences relevant for starting a business. In the future, education can address this.

Given that Alsos *et al.* (2015) found the average Norwegian entrepreneur had relatively low ambitions for the growth and was focused mainly on the domestic market — as opposed to internationalisation — future research may investigate why and future policy may address this issue. Kelley, Singer, and Herrington (2016) noted that despite exhibiting high opportunity perceptions, Norway reports the lowest level of intentions. Future research may investigate causal variables.

Norwegian policy-makers have been discussing a possible ban — effective 2025 — on sales of vehicles that run on fossil fuels. This should give rise to new opportunities for entrepreneurship and research.

In general, Norwegian policy is steering in a positive direction. In the words of Poelzer:

> Only four decades ago, Norway was considered a bit of a backwater in Scandinavia. It lagged behind its Scandinavian neighbours in per capita wealth, education attainment and other economic and social indicators. It had a significantly higher rural population and an economy reliant on traditional industries such as fisheries and agriculture ... Today, Norway is viewed as one of the best countries in the world in which to live ... Norwegians have a high life expectancy ... almost no poverty, low levels of unemployment and high levels of education attainment. The country's vibrant economy, mostly known for its petroleum wealth, is more diversified than most realize ... The Norwegian success story is the combination of those fortunate circumstances and sound policy decisions ... policies of innovation, social inclusion and sound public management ... Norway shows what is possible through smart policy decisions and the strategic use and investment of natural resource revenue (2013, p. 34–37).

Chapter 18

Portugal

Introduction

The Portuguese Republic shares the Iberian Peninsula with Spain,[1] and extends to neighbouring islands, covering 91,905 square kilometres. The Azores archipelago (see Exhibit 18.1) lies 1,600 kilometres from mainland Europe. Major cities of Portugal include the capital, Lisbon (Exhibit 18.2) and Oporto (Porto) — the latter famous for its fortified port wine (Exhibit 18.3).

Portugal was the "earliest and once the greatest of Europe's modern imperial powers" (La Fay, 1965, p. 453). Portugal ruled over Angola, Brazil, Cape Verde (locally known as *Cabo Verde*) Goa, Macao, Mozambique, and beyond. After the independence of Portuguese colonies in Africa, which took place following the revolution of April 25, 1974 — also referred to as the Cravos Revolution — the political and social conditions in the former colonies became problematic. This prompted the exodus of Europeans, who lived in the colonies, to move to the Portuguese mainland. This, in turn, resulted in a huge increase in people seeking employment in Portugal, while jobs became relatively scarce. As a result, many of the so-called *retornados* — returnees from the African colonies — became self-employed, thereby creating new dynamics.

Until the global financial crisis of the early 21st century, Portuguese people tended to prefer the security of employment, over

[1] See relevant chapter in this volume.

Exhibit 18.1 Hotel in Azores; photo © 2017 Léo-Paul Dana.

Exhibit 18.2 Lisbon; photo © 2017 Léo-Paul Dana.

Exhibit 18.3 Fortified port wine; photo © 2017 Léo-Paul Dana.

the risks inherent in entrepreneurship. The general mind-set, in Portugal, reflected an attitude of risk aversion, and the dominance of long-established firms (see Exhibit 18.4) contributed to the barriers to entry.

Although entrepreneurship is socially acceptable in Portugal, it has not been an enticing career path for most Portuguese. Silva and Hall noted, "Portugal is a country where inequalities of power and wealth may hinder the scope for opportunity ... it is further characterised by low tolerance of uncertainty and it is, consequently, a rule oriented country where bureaucracy and controls are very much instituted, a situation in clear contrast with the easiness to accept change and the readiness to take risks ... " (2005, pp. 331, 332).

Historical Overview

Except for a brief period of Spanish rule, Portugal has been independent since the 12th century. In 1500, Portugal colonised Brazil and

Exhibit 18.4 Dominant since the 1930s; photo © 2017 Léo-Paul Dana.

during the 16th century, "Portugal changed the map of the world by her epochal achievements in discovery" (Moore, 1938, p. 133). In 1506, Portugal began ruling Mozambique as part of Portuguese India.

In 1553, officials in Guangdong accepted bribes from the Portuguese who wished to conduct trade in Macao (Dana, 2014). The Japanese were willing to buy Chinese silk, but the Celestial Empire prohibited business dealings between Chinese and Japanese merchants; when Portuguese entrepreneurs discovered this, they prospered as middlemen between the two Asian powers. For discussions of entrepreneurship in middleman minorities, see Auster and Aldrich (1984), Bonacich (1973), Cherry (1990), Dana (1997), and Loewen (1971).

In 1557, China allowed Portuguese merchants to establish homes and warehouses in Macao. The Portuguese supplied ivory from Africa and cotton from Goa, as well as cannons, clocks and mirrors from Europe. In exchange, Chinese entrepreneurs brought porcelain, seed pearls, and silk. Exporting silk from Macao to Japan proved to be highly profitable for the Portuguese entrepreneurs who were happy to be paid in silver. They then used the silver to pay for Chinese goods, which they sold in Europe (Dana, 2014).

John V (1689–1750) — *João V* in Portuguese — was king of Portugal from 1706 until his death. During his reign, diamonds and gold from Brazil enriched Portugal. A mercantile class evolved during the reign of his son Joseph I (1714–1777) — *José I* — dedicated himself to pleasures and delegated power. In 1775, an equestrian statue of Joseph I (Exhibit 18.5) was erected.

In 1846, the *Banco de Lisboa* and the *Companhia de Confiança Nacional* merged and a royal charter created the *Banco de Portugal*, to act as the central bank; in 1891, this bank was given the monopoly to issue bank notes for the Azores and Madeira as well as mainland Portugal. Exhibit 18.6 features its building in Porto, opened in 1934. The bank was nationalised in 1974.

In 1867, the *Teatro da Trindade* (Exhibit 18.7) opened in Lisbon. In 1877, the first telephone lines in Portugal connected

Exhibit 18.5 Statue of Joseph I in Lisbon; photo © 2017 Léo-Paul Dana.

Exhibit 18.6 *Banco de Portugal*; photo © 2017 Léo-Paul Dana.

Carcavelos to Lisbon; a decade later, the concession was transferred to the Anglo Portuguese Telephone Company (Exhibit 18.8).

Spanning the Douro River, at Porto, the Dom Luis I Bridge (Exhibit 18.9) was completed in 1886. At the time, it was longer than any other metal bridge in the world.

In Lisbon, streetcars (Exhibit 18.10) were electrified in 1901. Inspired by the architectural style of Gustave Eiffel (see Chapter 7, this volume), the *Elevador de Santa Justa* — also known in English as the Elevator of Carmo — (Exhibit 18.11) was first opened to the public in 1902. It rises 45 metres over Lisbon. In the same city, the Portuguese Automobile Company commissioned the Auto-Palace (Exhibit 18.12), in 1904; its cast-iron structure was designed by Gustave Eiffel incorporating *art nouveau* tile-work on the façade, with 1907 stained glass windows. Situated at *Rua Alexandre Herculano* 66–68, and completed in 1908, it is still a garage, now owned by Auto-Industrial.

Exhibit 18.7 *Teatro da Trindade*; photo © 2017 Léo-Paul Dana.

Meanwhile, in 1906, the *Banco Totta & Açores* opened a new building (Exhibit 18.13), in Lisbon. The bank is now known as *Banco Santander Totta S.A.*

Although some prospered, poverty and social discontentment led to the Portuguese monarch being deposed in 1910. On October 5, of the same year, Portugal was proclaimed the Portuguese Republic. In 1920, a new town hall (Exhibit 18.14), was built in Porto.

Exhibit 18.8 Anglo Portuguese Telephone Co; photo © 2017 Léo-Paul Dana.

Exhibit 18.9 Dom Luis I Bridge; photo © 2017 Léo-Paul Dana.

Exhibit 18.10 Electric street car in Lisbon; photo © 2017 Léo-Paul Dana.

The creation of a republic was symbolic of the hope for progress, freedom, and social justice. A problem arose when the new regime was incapable of changing the fragile economic, social, and political situation with which Portugal was struggling. As a result, instability and population discontentment escalated. Social institutions lost importance. The state faced budgeting crises, as there was a continuous deficit in the commercial balance. The state sold gold, its currency lost its value, and inflation escalated. Public goods were sold at less than market value. All of these were conducive to military action on May 28, 1926, out of which the New State was created.

The first Catholic church built in Lisbon after the proclamation of the republic was *Nossa Senhora de Fátima* (Exhibit 18.15). It was inaugurated in 1938. In 1951, Angola and Mozambique became

Exhibit 18.11 Elevator of Carmo; photo © 2017 Léo-Paul Dana.

overseas provinces of Portugal. In 1953, the Portuguese ordered indigenous Mozambicans to leave their farms and villages to clear more land for forced cotton growing. Under the supervision of ruthless overseers, each family was also obliged to grow cassava and sorghum. Immigrants from Asia, however, were exempt from forced labour, and were allowed to operate their private small businesses.

According to the 1955 census, 65% of the Europeans in Mozambique were still illiterate at the time. Illiteracy among indigenous Africans in

Exhibit 18.12 The Auto-Palace; photo © 2017 Léo-Paul Dana.

Exhibit 18.13 *Banco Santander Totta*; photo © 2017 Léo-Paul Dana.

Exhibit 18.14 Town hall, Porto; photo © 2017 Léo-Paul Dana.

Exhibit 18.15 *Nossa Senhora de Fátima*; photo © 2017 Léo-Paul Dana.

Mozambique was even higher. In Lisbon, the underground metropolitan subway opened in 1959. *Art nouveau* signage at the station featured in Exhibit 18.16 — a replica of a Hector Guimard (1867–1942) design — was a gift from Paris.

Exhibit 18.16 *Art nouveau* replica; photo © 2017 Léo-Paul Dana.

An independence movement was established in 1962. It came to be known as the *Frente de Liberação de Moçambique* (Front for the Liberation of Mozambique), also referred to as Frelimo. It initiated a violent revolution in 1964. The issue of political, economic and social instability extended to all Portuguese provinces, leading to colonial war. As such, the 1960s was an eventful decade for Portugal, experiencing the colonial war, and also the movement toward the European integration, the internationalisation of the economy and emigration. Four decades of conservative dictatorship ended in a *coup d'état*, in April 1974. In June, the republic announced that it was giving independence to Angola and to Mozambique. Repatriation followed with 471,000 returnees moving from Africa to Portugal.

Graves reported, "Today thousands of small businesses and professional jobs are filled by retornados" (1980, p. 815). While the United Kingdom gave Hong Kongers a British National Overseas Passport, with no entitlement to reside in Britain, Portugal gave Portuguese citizenship to the Macanese.

Economic development escalated in 1986, when Portugal joined the European Economic Community. In 1988, reform of the Community Structural Funds largely benefitted Portugal through the deployment of the Support Community Frames. Operational programmes were defined mostly with structural goals. Then came major investments in infrastructure, and also in the education of the Portuguese — including the working population, the students, the long-term unemployed and the handicapped. Simultaneously, programmes emerged aimed at supporting entrepreneurial initiative and with them the creation of supporting institutions to both the incumbents and the new companies. In 1989, Portugal embarked on a large-scale privatisation programme. The Portuguese currency became fully convertible in 1992.

Studying business ownership in Portugal between 1972 and 2002, Baptista and Thurik (2007) noted that Portugal had a high proportion of microbusinesses created for subsistence. The study revealed that adjustment to new technology actually slowed production.

In July 2002, Portugal launched the Programme for Productivity and Economic Growth, with an axis addressed to supporting innovation, research and development. A concern in 2003 was that inflation in Portugal clearly exceeded the European Union average (Simões, 2004). Portugal scored 64.4 in the 2010 Index of Economic Freedom, placing it among the least free economies in Western Europe.

Unemployment doubled from 8.6% in 2006 to 16.5% in 2013. On the brighter side, the Corruption Perception Index of 2014 ranked Portugal as the least corrupt country in its region. However, public debt continued to be a serious problem.

On the positive side, in 2016 Lisbon hosted the Web Summit. The event had formerly been a Dublin-based event.

The Environment for Entrepreneurship

Traditionally, fishing was of great importance to Portugal, particularly along the coast. Yet, until 1945, tight political control measures clearly threatened entrepreneurial initiative. Measures included: (i) the Colonial Act of 1930; (ii) the Wheat Campaign of 1930–1940; (iii) the Law of Industrial Conditioning, in 1931; (iv) the Law of Economic Restructure, in 1935; (v) the Law of Internal Colonisation, in 1937; (vi) the Law of Hydro-agricultural Promotion, and the Law of Forest Populating, in 1938; (vii) the Law of National Electricity, in 1944; and (viii) the Law of the Industrial Promotion and Reorganisation, in 1945.

The above — coupled with the Law of Import Substitution — created significant restrictions, and most trade was conducted with the colonies. Portugal agreed with its colonies that they would supply the raw materials Portugal would need and in exchange they would receive manufactured products from the mainland. As a result, there was an intensification of the production of primary products, such as cotton, in all the colonies.

Conger (1948) wrote about thousands of self-employed fish peddlers, women known as fishwives. A few years later, Villiers reported, "In Portugal, fishermen are formed into 'companies' perhaps 80 men strong, and the 'companions' (as the members of a company are called) have the right by ancient custom to fish enough to keep their families going and get a share of all profits on the catch. If there are no profits, they still eat" (1954, p. 680). Pickerell (1968) wrote about fishing during the 1960s. Many Portuguese relied on the primary sector — agriculture (see Exhibit 18.17) and fishing — for subsistence.

Since the Portuguese economy had hermetically closed itself to the outside, entrepreneurial spirit was obliterated outside subsistence self-employment. While self-employment still thrives (see Exhibit 18.18),

Exhibit 18.17 Agriculture; photo © 2017 Léo-Paul Dana.

Exhibit 18.18 *Mercado das coleccoes,* Lisbon; photo © 2017 Léo-Paul Dana.

Exhibit 18.19 Fishing fleet; photo © 2017 Léo-Paul Dana.

history changed paths in 1976, as Portugal began to prepare itself to join the European Economic Community a decade later. While primary activities — including agriculture and fishing (see Exhibit 18.19) — remained important, the economy was becoming increasingly diversified.

Commemorating the 500th anniversary of the discovery of an oceanic route to India — by Vasco de Gama (circa 1469–1524) — the 1998 Lisbon World Exposition prompted much investment into Portugal's infrastructure, including airport facilities, motorways and telecommunications. The exhibition's theme was Oceans: A Heritage for the Future. Fourteen international organisations participated along with 143 countries. The improved infrastructure continues to benefit entrepreneurs.

The Institute for the Support to Small and Medium-Sized Enterprises and to Investment — *Instituto de Apoio às Pequenas e Médias Empresas e ao Investimento* (*IAPMEI*) conceives policies, and implements initiatives in its attempts to make Portuguese players more competitive. This institute was among sponsors of the 2001

Global Entrepreneurship Monitor (GEM) Portugal Report, one of the first systematic, large-scale studies of entrepreneurship in Portugal. Although Portugal had relatively open markets and a good infrastructure facilitating entrepreneurship, that GEM study revealed a significant lack of entrepreneurial activity in this country.

The same report ranked Portugal better than Belgium or Germany, but worse than France or Ireland, with regards to entrepreneurial activity. It also found that respondents perceived more entrepreneurship opportunities in Portugal than was the case elsewhere, but acted less on these; the report suggested that this could be evidence of barriers to entrepreneurial activity. There appeared to be powerful barriers to entry, including inflexible employment regulations that put undue strain on entrepreneurs. Constraints included imbalance in governmental programme planning; the lack of effective entrepreneurship training; and underdevelopment in support services. It appeared that training programmes did not always correspond to actual needs. A further constraint appeared to be the difficulty in accessing finance, largely due to lack of awareness of existing sources of capital.

Portugal's second GEM participation was for the 2004 report, with a survey of 1,000 adults on the mainland only. This study revealed that the rate of entrepreneurial activity in Portugal fell from seven entrepreneurs for every 100 people aged 18–64, to four entrepreneurs for every 100 people aged 18–64, i.e., 13th place of 16 European Union countries in GEM and one of the lowest rates of entrepreneurial activity among countries studied. Portugal's entrepreneurs were nearly equally distributed with respect to gender. Issues were identified as: the ineffective allocation of financial support by the government; time-consuming bureaucratic procedures; insufficient education; the concentration of science parks and incubators in only two cities, Lisbon and Porto; poor links between R&D and commercial development; the cost of accessing infrastructure; ineffectiveness of antitrust legislation; and cultural issues.

In 2005, the Jesuit Refugee Service of Portugal began promoting microcredit as incentive for immigrants to become self-employed (Figueirinha, 2008). Comparing immigrants of different ethnicities,

Oliveira (2008) emphasised the unlike self-employment rates among groups.

Silva and Leitão (2009) studied cooperation among firms in Portugal. The study concluded that *firms that established relationships were more capable of developing innovative advances than other enterprises*. The authors proposed that future research be developed on the motivation of firms for engaging in cooperative innovation projects.

The 2013 GEM study found considerable change to have taken place. While austerity measures caused an escalation in unemployment rates, entrepreneurship proved to be a viable alternative; however, in contrast to the past, Portugal's entrepreneurs were no longer evenly distributed with respect to gender. Between eight and nine Portuguese adults in every 100 were early-stage entrepreneurs — a dramatic increase from 2004 and 2010 findings. This could be a result of the implementation of an adjustment programme sponsored by the European Central Bank, the European Union, and the International Monetary Fund. Facilitators were identified as including a programme of access to finance, provided by *IAPMEI*. Nevertheless, that GEM report suggested that government policies were viewed as the most detrimental factor to business creation.

Several clusters have developed in Portugal. These include: the ceramic cluster in the Aveiro; the footwear cluster in São João da Madeira; the furniture cluster in Paços de Ferreira; the textile clusters of Braga and Covilhã; the tourism cluster in the Algarve region; and the wine cluster in Douro. In Aveiro, Braga, Coimbra and Lisbon, there are also knowledge clusters, nurtured by incubators, research centres and technology parks. Portuguese innovators have been providing multinationals with engineering services, tools, and technology. One Portuguese company developed a home security system that uses fingerprints for owner identification. Backed by the European Space Agency, a programme to create "intelligent" clothing is being developed by a Portuguese-led consortium involving several Portuguese firms; equipped with sensors and satellite communication interfaces, the purpose of such clothing is to monitor movements and temperatures in fire-fighting situations.

An innovative initiative pioneered by the municipality of São João da Madeira is that of an industrial heritage cluster for tourism. It combines the preservation of history with new demands. The cluster includes a variety of otherwise unrelated factories — including Viarco, a pencil manufacturer established in 1907, shoe factories that remain competitive thanks to innovation, and the Oliva Creative Factory.

Toward the Future

Much effort has been focused on improving entrepreneurship education, innovation and the small business sector in Portugal — and much has been achieved. Yet, there is still more to do. While the 2013 GEM study suggested that improvements in infrastructure facilitated entrepreneurship in Portugal, Kelley, Singer, and Herrington (2016) reported that a problem identified was, insufficient physical infrastructure. Furthermore, Portuguese business culture is risk-averse; explanatory variables include tight political control measures, which stamped out entrepreneurial spirit during the first half of the 20th century.

Several organisms in Portugal, including *IAPMEI,* have made available services to help budding entrepreneurs. However, these tend to be dispersed, and many would-be entrepreneurs who could use help often lack the knowledge of where to find it.

Simões noted, "many observers have pointed out the absence of a truly co-operative culture as one of the main obstacles to the competitiveness of Portuguese companies" (2004, p. 24). Nevertheless, *physical proximity has allowed entrepreneurs in clusters to benefit from one another. Clusters have had noticeable success in Portugal; clusters of peach-growers date back to medieval times.* Although Spanish peaches have penetrated the Portuguese market, clusters — in general — will likely continue to do well in the future. Areas for improvement appear to be in entrepreneurship education, employment regulation, taxation and issues related to internationalisation.

Pereira (2007) discussed the internationalisation of Portuguese SMEs. Pinho and Martins found that non-exporters considered "the lack of knowledge of potential markets, lack of qualified export personnel, lack of technical suitability, degree of competition in the sector, lack of financial assistance ... and the lack of qualified human resources as the main export barriers" (2010, p. 254).

A further area for concern is very low R&D expenditure; the value of business spending in R&D, as a percentage of GDP, is low when compared to other countries. This usually has a negative impact on national competitiveness.

On the positive side, opportunities include: the introduction of new technologies to revitalise traditional sectors; the further development of existing clusters; and internationalisation by means of symbiotic networking.

Chapter 19

Spain

Introduction

The Kingdom of Spain covers 504,782 square kilometres, mostly on the Iberian Peninsula, and spanning the Balearic Islands of the Mediterranean Sea, and the Canary Islands[1] in the Atlantic Ocean. In Europe, Spain's neighbours are Andorra, France, Gibraltar, and Portugal, while autonomous cities in North Africa share boundaries with Morocco.[2]

Politically, Spain is a decentralised country divided into autonomous communities and cities. The principal language spoken in Spain is Castilian. Languages with official regional status include: Catalan in Catalonia and in the Balearic Islands; Galician in Galicia; and Valencian in the Valencian autonomous community, the capital of which is Valencia (Exhibit 19.1) — an important Mediterranean port, and the third largest city in Spain after Madrid — the nation's capital — and Barcelona, capital of Catalonia.

The Basques constitute an important minority (Abercrombie, 1995; Nolan, 1954) among whom self-employment has traditionally been high (Dana, 1995b). Unlike in France where it has no official recognition, the Basque language has co-official status in Spain's Basque community.

---

[1] Shor and Shor (1955) focus on the Canary Islands.

[2] See relevant chapters in this volume; for a discussion of entrepreneurship in Morocco, see Dana and Dana (2008).

Exhibit 19.1 Valencia; photo © 2017 Léo-Paul Dana.

Spain has many regional differences — some quite subtle. An example is the preparation of fish, important in the Spanish diet. Along the Atlantic, sardines are often fried, while grilling is popular along the Mediterranean. Traditionally, sardines (Exhibit 19.2) were salted for inland demand. Another specialty of Spain with regional variations is cured ham (Exhibit 19.3). Coduras *et al.* (2008) showed that international activity varied greatly among regions of Spain, with 16.1% of Catalonian SMEs exporting, compared to 4.3% of SMEs in Extremadura.

Among innovative entrepreneurs in Spain was Isaac Carasso (1874–1939), a pioneer in the commercialisation of yogurt in the West. Sephardic Jews (of Spanish origin) from Thessaloniki — known as Salonica at the time — the Carasso family moved to Barcelona in 1913, where Isaac was concerned about the high incidence of digestive problems, especially among children. Although yogurt was not well known in Western Europe, Isaac was aware of

Exhibit 19.2 Spanish sardines; photo © 2017 Léo-Paul Dana.

Exhibit 19.3 Spanish ham; photo © 2017 Léo-Paul Dana.

its curative qualities and therefore imported cultures from Bulgaria, where Balkan yogurts were already popular. At first, Isaac's product was sold by pharmacies, as a remedy. In 1919, Isaac established the Danone brand, starting out as a small business in Spain. The name Danone was derived from Isaac's son Daniel (1905–2009), whose nickname in Catalan was Danon. Daniel later established Dannon in the United States. At the age of 103, Daniel died in Paris. Today, Barcelona is classified as a "smart" city; it is considered to be a capital of innovation, a centre for prototyping, a mobile capital, and among the most creative cities in Europe.

Among Spain's leading entrepreneurs is fashion-king Amancio Ortega Gaona (1936–). Owner of the Zara chain and Spain's richest man, he is the founder of the Inditex Group, which has more than 14,000 employees.

Spain has experienced much change in recent years. Spain has been a regular participant of the Global Entrepreneurship Monitor (GEM) study since 2000 and GEM has already had a positive impact here, promoting the reduction of administrative burdens, entrepreneurial attitudes in the educational system, a focus on financing, and the fostering of entrepreneurship.

Historical Overview

The land that is Spain today was formerly divided among three Christian kingdoms in the north, while the south had Moorish rulers. Spain was unified through the marriage of Ferdinand II of Aragon (1442–1516) and Isabella of Castile (1451–1504). After the Moors lost Grenada, Spain became the most powerful country of Europe, controlling much of the Americas.

In 1928, a modernist building (Exhibit 19.4) was inaugurated at Valencia's central market (Exhibit 19.5), selling a variety of fresh produce (Exhibit 19.6). In 1929, the Ibero-American Exposition served as a reunion between Spain and her former colonies; a detailed account appears in Ford (1929). When, in 1931, Spain was proclaimed a republic, King Alfonso XIII (1886–1941) and his family were exiled — including his son Juan de Borbón (1913–1993),

Exhibit 19.4 Market inaugurated 1928; photo © 2017 Léo-Paul Dana.

Exhibit 19.5 More than 8,000 square metres; photo © 2017 Léo-Paul Dana.

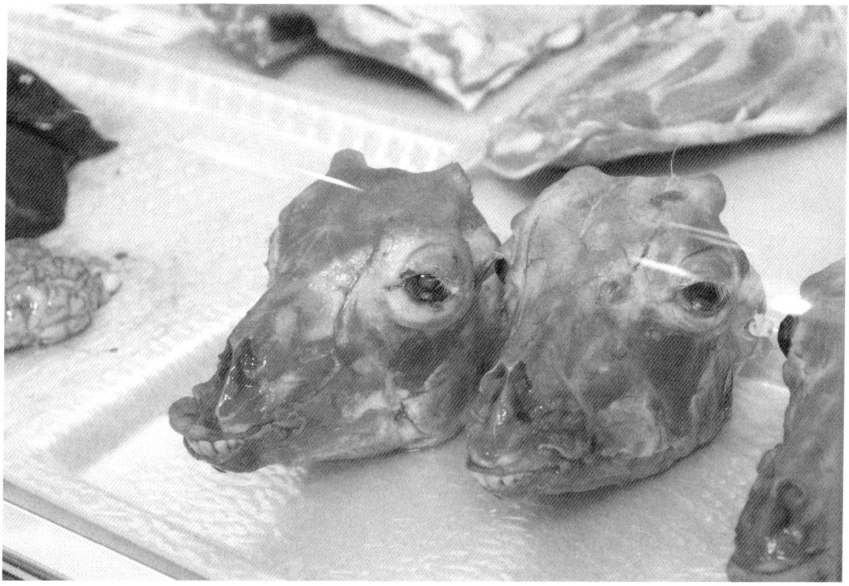

Exhibit 19.6 Fresh produce for sale; photo © 2017 Léo-Paul Dana.

who never became king, but who fathered one. Adams (1929), Kihn (1936), and McBride (1929, 1931) provided accounts of Spain before the Spanish Civil War. Kihn wrote, "Next to agriculture, mining is Spain's most important source of wealth" (1936, p. 410). The war began in July 1936, and in September, General Francisco Franco (1892–1975) was proclaimed chief of state, head of government and generalissimo of the armed forces; for a wartime account of Spain, see McBride (1936). Grandson of Alfonso XIII, Prince Juan Carlos de Bourbon (1938–) was born in Rome, while the monarchy was in exile. The Spanish Civil War ended on April 1, 1939, when Germany and Italy helped Franco crush the republicans.

Although Spain was officially neutral during World War II, Franco supported the Axis. In June 1945, representatives of 50 countries met in San Francisco at the United Nations Conference on International Organisation, and it was unanimously agreed that Spain be excluded from the new United Nations. In August, at the Potsdam conference, the Union of Soviet Socialist Republics, the

United Kingdom and the United States declared Spain to be incompatible with the free world.

On March 1, 1946, France sealed its border with Spain, preventing French and Spanish citizens from passing through. Only nationals of third countries were permitted freedom of movement.

During the 1950s, rural Spain experienced a flight from poverty to Madrid; Putman (1986) provided a discussion of Spain's experience with urbanisation. People also left rural and poor areas such as Andalusia and Extremadura to work in richer and more industrial areas such as the Basque Country and Catalonia (Bover and Velilla, 1999).

Beginning in 1960, excess labour supply in Spain prompted 100,000 workers a year to emigrate to France, Germany, and Switzerland (Bover and Velilla, 1999). In May 1962, Juan Carlos married Princess Sophia of Greece and Denmark (1938–). She then changed her name to Sofía.

In the words of Bryson, "Until well into the 1960s Spain was one of the poorest countries in Western Europe" (1992, p. 8). By the middle of the decade, however, McDowell noted, "Many economists predict that Spain is beginning an economic take-off similar to Italy's after World War II" (1965, p. 297). This had a positive impact on some people, but not on others.

Laxalt reported a Spanish interviewee as saying, "I lost my two sons to progress ... Times are changing ... But I don't know why they should" (1974, p. 796). In 1974, the *Instituto de Estudios Superiores de la Empresa* introduced a course in entrepreneurship (Dana, 1992b).

In 1972, Franco's favourite granddaughter 21-year old Maria del Carmen Martinez-Bordiu (1951–) married 35-year old Prince Alfonso de Bourbon y Dampierre (1936–1989), grandson of King Alfonso XIII. Once Franco died in 1975, and Juan Carlos became king, the Basque, Catalan and Galician languages — that had been officially banned by Franco — reappeared.

In 1978, in response to demands for increased local autonomy, the constitution decentralised power. In 1980, three Spanish provinces, namely Álava, Guipúzcoa, and Vizcaya were united to form the Basque Country Autonomous Community; these were traditionally important areas of industry. Regardless, regional differences remained, and in their study of Galicia, Buechler and Buechler found that, "industrialization in previously rural areas is not an automatic panacea for problems generated by unequal distribution of wealth" (1992, p. 102).

In 1986, Spain joined the European Economic Community, undertook a privatisation programme and began liberalising the economy. Infrastructure (see Exhibit 19.7) was improved. Ports were upgraded (see Exhibit 19.8). Firms became increasingly market-oriented. By the early 1990s, Bryson (1992) noted that the Spanish

Exhibit 19.7 1922 Post & telegraph building; photo © 2017 Léo-Paul Dana.

Exhibit 19.8 Port on the Mediterranean; photo © 2017 Léo-Paul Dana.

society was becoming increasingly secular. Seville — host of the 1929 World's Fair — hosted millions of visitors at Expo '92, which opened in April 1992.

In 1993, the Basque government set to zero, the corporation tax for newly established entrepreneurs. The central government of Spain decided to challenge this move on the premise that it would prejudice neighbouring regions where entrepreneurship is less prevalent and the environment is less conducive to entrepreneurial activity. Red tape was already lean in the Basque Country, while work ethic, entrepreneurial culture and government incentives were keeping Basques at the forefront of economic development. Also in 1993, research found that two-way sub-contracting among Madrid's electronics producers was already substantially higher than among similar firms in Austria and Sweden (Suárez-Villa and Rama, 1996).

In 2008, Spain's long period of economic growth came to an end and the long-lasting property bubble burst. Recession was official (see Exhibit 19.9). In 2009, the Bank of Spain bailed out *Caja Castilla-La Mancha*, an important regional lender.

Exhibit 19.9 Small-scale retailers were hit; photo © 2017 Léo-Paul Dana.

Exhibit 19.10 Bank sold for one euro; photo © 2017 Léo-Paul Dana.

A merger between British Airways and Spain's flag-carrier Iberia was approved in November 2010. In the financial sector, that year, Bankia was created as the merger of several existing regional banks including *Caja Madrid and Castellón y Alicante* (*Bancaja*). In 2011, Sabadell paid one euro to purchase the *Caja de Ahorros del Mediterráneo* (see Exhibit 19.10).

In June 2014, Juan Carlos abdicated in favour of his son, Felipe VI (1968–). In 2015, Spain had an unemployment rate of 22%, among the highest in Europe (Eurostat, 2015). Kelley, Singer, and Herrington noted, "low intentions to start businesses were exhibited in ... Spain ... 5% or less of the population signalled these intentions" (2016, p. 17).

The Environment for Entrepreneurship

Van Auken and de Lema observed, "Economic growth in Spain has primarily been based on the increase of productivity that resulted from intensive capital investment and technical growth ... SMEs have had an important role in Spanish economic growth. During 1996–2000, for example, the number of new firms increased by more than 200,000 firms. The predominance of SMEs in the Spanish economy is evident from the large proportion of the micro-firms relative to other European countries" (2003, p. 19).

SMEs in Spain often work together, and are heavily involved in sub-contracting, sometimes in geographic clusters.[3] Rama, Ferguson, and Melero (2003) noted that over 84% of Spanish electronics production is concentrated in Madrid, Catalonia, and the Basque Country. They elaborated, "while Catalonia specializes in consumer electronics (82% of Spanish production) and the Basque Country in industrial electronics (70%), Madrid is Spain's most important producer of telecommunications equipment (77%) and defence and industrial electronics (59%) ... " (Rama, Ferguson, and Melero 2003, p. 76). As explained by Suárez-Villa and Rama (1996), *Madrid's electronics sector is a complex web of interdependent firms. In contrast, Catalonia has a hub-and-spoke structure, with multinationals ringed by Spanish sub-contractors. The relationship among firms is symbiotic.*

Rama, Ferguson, and Melero noted that, "the small electronics plants located in the Basque Country tend to supply other regional

[3] See also Padmore and Gibson (1997).

industries, such as machine tools, as specialized, or possibly strategic subcontractors ... Linkages between electronics firms are highly concentrated in Madrid and the Basque Country ... In Catalonia, by contrast, the coordination between consumer electronics multinationals and their subcontractors is less intensive" (2003, p. 76). Rama, Ferguson, and Melero added, "while Madrid lacks many of the common socio-cultural values that define classical industrial districts, it is home to a vibrant community of engineering professionals and supporting occupational institutions" (2003, p. 77). Thus, most subcontracting in Madrid's electronics sector can (and does) take place within the Madrid region (Rama and Calatrava, 2002). Rama, Ferguson, and Melero further explained, "Madrid's sampled electronics producers seem to seek complementaries with other companies, not just the flexibility of enlarging their working force during short periods of work overload. This contrasts with the hub-and-spoke district, which relies more on networks of capacity subcontractors. The motivation of externalizing production is not significantly associated with establishment or firm size, suggesting that both small and large producers alike participate in a network characterized by specialized, or collaborative subcontracting" (2003, p. 83).

Suárez-Ortega (2003) studied 286 SMEs in the Spanish wine industry. Their results revealed that perceptions of export barriers decreased as the firm advanced in the export development process.

Coduras *et al.* (2005) revealed that 39% of the Spanish active population perceived the existence of good opportunities in 2004, up from 2003. This indicates an improvement in the climate for the business creation. Yet, the Total Entrepreneurial Activity (TEA) for 2004 was 5.15, down by 23.93% since 2003. This reflected a recession, although not of great magnitude. The recessive economic climate was perhaps partly brought about by the political turmoil that resulted after terrorist attacks in Madrid, in March. Nevertheless, the TEA for 2004 was above average for the European Union member states and very similar to the TEA indexes of Denmark and the Netherlands. The data for 2004 showed that the percentage of businesses that did not have any expectation of expansion fell by 28.2%, suggesting increased hope for growth. In 2004, men were still more

Exhibit 19.11 Women operating newsstand; photo © 2017 Léo-Paul Dana.

than twice as likely to be involved in entrepreneurship as women in Spain and the actual rate of female involvement fell 8.3% with respect to 2003. Nevertheless, women remain involved in microenterprises and are visible in small retail outlets (Exhibit 19.11) Informal investment activity in Spain decreased 24.7% in 2004 with respect to 2003.

Of the eight Spanish regions analysed by the GEM team in 2004 (Andalucía, the Basque Country, Castilla-León, the Canaries, Catalonia, Extremadura, Madrid and Valencia), the least active in terms of entrepreneurship was the region of the Canary Islands. Extremadura — historically the least developed region in Spain — was found to be the most enterprising in 2004. Its TEA index, with 2% above the Spanish average, indicates that the region is gradually catching up with the rest of Spain.

In his comparative study of entrepreneurs in Italy and in Spain, Kantis (2005) found that *networks of Spanish entrepreneurs reflected the greater relative importance of their relatives and friends*, whereas in

Italy, business relations are more common. He found that Spanish business networks are relatively unstable when compared to those in Italy, suggesting that connections are weaker. Among his respondents, those in Spain emphasised to a greater degree than did those in Italy, the influence of the family in shaping attitudes and creating a work ethic.

A long cycle — over a decade — of high growth in Spain, coupled with a building and real estate boom, ended with the global financial crisis. Nevertheless, Defourny and Nyssens (2010) noted that in Spain, "characterized by a strong co-operative tradition" (2010, p. 234), social enterprises were experiencing extra ordinary growth.

Spain scored 69.6 in the 2010 Index of Economic Freedom, placing it among the least free economies in Western Europe. Hadad *et al.* (2012) found Spain's financial sector to be the most efficient of all its sectors. This study also revealed Spain's tourism sector as being more efficient than that of Germany. Tourism is very important for Spain and hotels are prominent (Exhibit 19.12).

Segarra, Papaoikonomou, and Li (2012), listed factors identified as negative, especially in times of crisis: a shortage of skilled employees

Exhibit 19.12 Hotel Londres among others; photo © 2017 Léo-Paul Dana.

and training centres; new and non-traditional competitors; the perceived lack of infrastructures and inefficient use of the existing ones; bureaucratic and regulatory issues; and tax rates.

In 2012, unemployment reached 24%. In June, that year Spain requested loans from the European Union to capitalise Spanish banks. In 2013, more than half of persons aged 15–24 were unemployed. Kelley, Singer, and Herrington (2016) noted that fewer than half the working-age population in Spain saw high status for entrepreneurs.

Toward the Future

De Clercq *et al.* wrote, "Ireland, Spain and Finland score highest for opportunity entrepreneurship" (2004, p. 19). Much has changed since the crisis of 2008 and beyond. Although Spain's openness to the world induced a gradual change in mentality and an increasing social acceptance of entrepreneurs, the economic situation proved challenging.

Cars are Spain's top export; although most Spanish-made cars are exported, Coduras *et al.* found that "the majority of Spanish small and medium exporting companies sell most of their production in the domestic market" (2008, p. 600). Almost a decade later exports by SMEs could still benefit from a boost.

Although Spain has long been an exporter of fish (Exhibit 19.13), fish is a negative net export. Foreign spending on Spanish fish is trailing

Exhibit 19.13 Spanish tuna for sale in Japan; photo © 2017 Léo-Paul Dana.

Exhibit 19.14 Customs; photo © 2017 Léo-Paul Dana.

imports of fish to Spain. Future research may look into this and recommend sustainable policies for the future.

Focusing on socio-cultural factors, Urbano, Toledano, and Ribeiro-Soriano (2011) studied four cases of transnational entrepreneurs in Spain. Given migration trends, it is likely that many opportunities will emerge for future research to focus on transnational entrepreneurs.

In 2014, Spain imported almost $43 billion more than its exports. This may secure jobs at Customs (Exhibit 19.14), but the country needs much more. Future research may investigate how Spain might reduce trade deficits.

Chapter 20

Sweden

Introduction

The Kingdom of Sweden covers 449,964 square kilometres, between Finland and Norway,[1] with shores along the Baltic Sea and also along the Gulf of Bothnia, the Kattegat Sea, the Öresund Strait, and Skagerrak Strait. Sweden's national capital is Stockholm (Exhibit 20.1), a city that spans several islands (Exhibit 20.2). An elaborate ferry service complements the national rail network, which has approximately 11,000 kilometres of electrified rail routes (see Exhibit 20.3). Opened to the public in 2000, the combined railway-and-motorway Öresund Bridge (Exhibit 20.4) — approximately 16 kilometres long — crosses the Öresund Strait, linking Sweden with Denmark.

Famous Swedes include chemist and entrepreneur Alfred Nobel (1833–1896) who patented dynamite in 1867 and established the Nobel Prize. Other prominent Swedish entrepreneurs include: Lars Magnus Ericsson (1846–1926) founder of the telephone manufacturing company bearing his name; Mrs. Wilhelmina Skogh (1849–1926), who pioneered hotels and restaurants for the tourism industry across Sweden; Gustaf Larson (1887–1968) and Assar Gabrielsson (1891–1962) who — in 1927 — cofounded Volvo[2] (see Exhibit 20.5); Mrs. Estrid Ericson (1894–1981) who pioneered

[1] See relevant chapters in this volume.

[2] See Berggren (1993).

Exhibit 20.1 City hall on the far left, Riddarholmskyrkan church to its right, and the German Tyskakyrkan in the middle; photo © 2017 Léo-Paul Dana.

Exhibit 20.2 Aerial view of Stockholm; photo © 2017 Léo-Paul Dana.

design and décor in Sweden, establishing Swedish Tenn in 1924 and operating this firm until 1978; Dr. Ruben Rausing (1895–1983), founder of Tetra Pak — development work for which began in 1943; and Ingvar Kamprad (1926–) who established IKEA in 1943. By the turn of the millennia, Stockholm was acknowledged as the centre of Europe's New Economy (Lynch, 2001).

Exhibit 20.3 Electrified railway; photo © 2017 Léo-Paul Dana.

Tillman and Palander noted, "Together with Switzerland, Sweden tops the global count of multinational companies per capita, a fact which strongly flavours its industrial sector" (2016, p. 230). Long associated as Volvo headquarters, Gothenburg is now also famous for its Lindholmen Science Park for research, innovation and education. (For a study of Swedish science parks, strategy and performance, see Lindelöf and Löften, 2003.)

Sweden has attempted to encourage entrepreneurship; from an institutional-economic perspective, however, important cultural traits and hard institutional factors can be strong inhibitors. Although mind-set may be changing, entrepreneurial behaviour is impeded by stringent employment legislation, coupled with the Swedish tax system (Henrekson, 2005). A large public sector employs more than a third of the workforce, including half the female workforce.

Exhibit 20.4 Öresund Bridge; photo © 2017 Léo-Paul Dana.

Historical Overview

About the people of Gotland — Sweden's largest island in the Baltic — Cerruti wrote, "In the Viking Age (from A. D. 800 to 1050) the Gotlanders were the equals, and the envy, of Swedes, Danes, and Norwegians. By trading, rather than raiding, Gotlanders became the richest Vikings of all" (1973, p. 275).

Exhibit 20.5 Volvo; photo © 2017 Léo-Paul Dana.

At Kalmar Castle, in 1397, Queen Margrethe (1353–1412) of Denmark formed a union with Norway (including the Faroe Islands, Greenland, Iceland, Orkney, and the Shetland Islands) and Sweden (including Finland); later, the medieval castle was modified into a Renaissance palace (Exhibit 20.6). The Kalmar Union lasted until Sweden broke away in 1523.

Clarke noted, "Charles the XIIth, whose policy directed him to preserve the *Laplanders* from mixing with the Swedes, sent engineers, in 1690, to mark, with all possible precision, the southern frontier of *Lapland*" (1824a, p. 328). A forthcoming section shall focus on the Sámi people, the indigenous inhabitants of this area.

In 1773, King Gustav III (1746–1792) founded the Royal Swedish Opera (Exhibit 20.7). The following year, he authorised German-speaking Aron Isak (1730–1817) to establish a Jewish community in Stockholm; see Isak (1897, 1930).

Sweden became a constitutional monarchy in 1809. Clarke wrote his impression of the times, "In their disposition, the *Swedes* are naturally mild and obliging; being rarely provoked to anger, or passionate when disputing with each other" (1824a, p. 238.)

Exhibit 20.6 Kalmar; photo © 2017 Léo-Paul Dana.

Exhibit 20.7 Royal Swedish Opera; photo © 2017 Léo-Paul Dana.

The safety match was invented in Stockholm in 1844. In 1917, entrepreneur Ivar Kreuger (1880–1932) formed Swedish Match, an enterprise that by 1920 controlled 75% of the world's production of matches.

Swedish industry concentrated on heavy, capital-intensive activities, such as heavy engineering, pulp and paper, mines[3] (including iron ore and silver), sawmills, and steel production. The manufacturing of locomotives in Sweden began in 1853.

Poor harvests between 1867 and 1869 caused 80,000 Swedes to leave their country. Brown wrote, "Between 1865 and 1914, a million and a quarter Swedes, unable to make an adequate living at home, emigrated to the United States" (1963, p. 464). Many settled in the American Midwest, especially Minnesota.

During the 1870s, Swedish iron ore and timber contributed to the industrialisation of Europe. Increased demand for such raw materials — abundant in Sweden — brought industrialisation, urbanisation, railway expansion and prosperity to Sweden, which had previously been an agrarian economy.

In 1878, Gustaf de Laval (1845–1913) invented a continuous centrifugal milk and cream separator. In 1883, in partnership with Oscar Lamm (1848–1930), he established the company called AB Separator. In the United States, the De Laval Cream Separator Co., was formed, and this grew into today's Alfa-Laval group.

In 1879, time was standardised across Sweden. This coincided with the expansion of the railroad network. The water tower in Kalmar was completed in 1900. Exhibit 20.8 illustrates the water tower currently used as residential housing.

The peaceful union with Norway was dissolved in 1905. By 1910, 20% of Swedes lived in the United States; in 1910, 8,678 Swedes resided in Seattle. Women in Sweden were granted the right

---

[3] Sweden has a long history of mining and refining metals — as early as the 11th century. During the early 20th century, Sweden had almost 500 mines producing close to 8 million tonnes of ore. By the 1960s these were down to approximately 100 mines producing around 20 million tonnes of ore. In 2013, 16 mines were operating in Sweden and producing about 80 million tonnes of ore. Today, Sweden is the largest producer of iron in the European Union.

Exhibit 20.8 Kalmar water tower; photo © 2017 Léo-Paul Dana.

to vote in 1919, effective 2 years after that. By 1920, the number of Swedes in Seattle had grown to 10,253.

During the 1920s, concern about hard economic times in Sweden spread the fear that immigrants might launch more new ventures in Sweden and thus threaten Swedish firms. Furthermore, high unemployment in Sweden, during the 1920s, propagated the concern that immigrants would compete with Swedes for employment. Consequently, in 1927, legislation restricted immigration into Sweden.

In 1932 the Social Democrats were elected and began building a welfare state with concepts inspired by the "Stockholm School" of Swedish economists. When, during the Depression, farmers were hurt by falling prices, the state agreed to regulate the price of milk; this came to be known as the Cow trade — a term still used to describe political compromises. Nilson (1940) gave an account of rural Sweden during the 1930s.

In 1936, King Gustav V (1858–1950) opened Bromma Airport, less than 8 kilometres from downtown Stockholm. It was the first airport in Europe to have paved runways from the time of its establishment (see Exhibit 20.9). When Scandinavian Airlines Service (SAS) was established in 1946, the new airline's Swedish operations were based here.

Exhibit 20.9 Stockholm Bromma Airport; photo © Saab AB.

With the Saltsjöbaden Accord of 1938, employers and unions established a consensus system of labour relations. This became a pillar of the Swedish economic model.

Sweden's neutrality was respected during World War II and in the autumn of 1943, Swedes and Swedish organisations helped rescue thousands of Danish Jews. Sweden also assisted Norwegian and Hungarian Jews.

During the war, Svenska Aeroplan Aktiebolaget (SAAB) began manufacturing military aircraft, which it did with much success. While the war had a major impact on countries that were forced to focus primarily on the war effort, Sweden's neutrality facilitated the development — in 1944 — of a civilian aeroplane, the Saab 90 Scandia (Exhibit 20.10).

Belt wrote, "In 1945 Sweden had entered the booming world market with the greatest export capacity in Europe. The Continent was war torn and destitute; Swedish factories, untouched by war,

Exhibit 20.10 Saab 90 Scandia; photo © Saab AB.

were already producing a full line of consumer and industrial products ... " (1993, p. 27).

In 1946, Gustav V was king, his son Gustav VI Adolf (1882–1973) was crown prince, and his grandson Gustav Adolf (1906–1947) had four daughters — a concern, because only a male was entitled to be Swedish monarch. Hence the birth of Carl Gustaf (1946–) was welcome as the new-born became third in line to the throne — until 1947, when his father was killed in a plane crash. Gustav V died when Carl Gustaf was four years old and became crown prince.

Meanwhile, in 1948, Sweden proposed the establishment of a Scandinavian defence union, with all members declaring neutrality. At first, Denmark supported the proposal. However, given that the neutrality of Iceland and Norway had been ignored during World War II, these countries felt that a neutral union would not offer them protection.

The post-war years saw great growth in service-sector employment as industrial employment declined. Writing about Sweden during the mid-20th century, Bastide (1954) emphasised the importance for a Swede to have a house that was well built and tasteful (Exhibit 20.11).

During the 1950s and 1960s, the Swedish economy was centralised and highly regulated. Consensus on labour relations and pay contributed to Sweden's prosperity of those decades.

During the 1960s, Sweden experienced considerable immigration from Finland, Greece, Turkey, and Yugoslavia. Until September 3, 1967, drivers in Sweden used the left side of the road. On that day, the switch was made to use the right.

The 1970s brought many changes, including tax reform, infrastructure improvement and rising fuel prices. In 1971, tax reform accelerated the growth in employment among married women in Sweden (Selin, 2009).

Separated from the mainland by Kalmar Strait, Öland — the second largest Swedish island and formerly its own province on the Baltic Sea — relied on ferry services that linked Färjestaden on the island, with Kalmar on the mainland, until 1972. The last ferry was *M/F* Kalmarsund VIII (Exhibit 20.12), made obsolete in

Exhibit 20.11 Traditional houses; photo © 2017 Léo-Paul Dana.

Exhibit 20.12 *M/F* Kalmarsund VIII; photo © 2017 Léo-Paul Dana.

Exhibit 20.13 Öland Bridge; photo © 2017 Léo-Paul Dana.

September 1972, when the Öland Bridge (Exhibit 20.13) — among the longest in Europe — was inaugurated; the following month, this ferry was sold to a firm in Rijeka, Yugoslavia.

The 1970s brought new challenges as the cost of petrol escalated and technology was spreading to countries with low costs of labour. Sweden's industrial competitiveness deteriorated. In 1973, Carl Gustaf ascended to the throne. In 1975, Sweden adopted a new constitution.

Carlsson observed, "Sweden had an outstanding industrial growth record for several decades until the mid-1970s but then suffered economic setbacks ... Industrial output declined for several years, resumed growth in the early 1980s but then stagnated again in the early 1990s" (1996, p. 219). Focusing on industrial dynamics between 1978 and 1994, the same study found, "While manufacturing employment declined by over 20 percent in each country, the number of establishments in manufacturing stayed constant in Sweden and declined by 9% in Ohio while it more than doubled in New Zealand" (Carlsson, 1996, p. 232).

In Sweden, during the early 1980s, the top marginal income tax rate exceeded 80%; coupled with a low differential between wages of skilled and unskilled workers, this undermined the incentive to train. By the end of the decade, the top personal income tax rate in Sweden was reduced to 72%, but this was the highest in the world. A high marginal tax plus a profit tax for companies made it expensive to pay high dividends. Profits were reinvested in companies, resulting in maintaining the existing industrial structure. Little capital was made available for investments in new firms, and this hampered entrepreneurship for many years.

With strict dole entitlement rules, Sweden's carrot and stick policy helped keep both inflation and unemployment low. When, in March 1990, 9% of West European workers were unemployed (no lower than during recession in 1982), the unemployment rate in Sweden was 1.4% — perhaps too low to keep wages and prices stable. A wage explosion was unavoidable. Despite an average pay rise exceeding 10% in 1989 — twice the European average — 1990 started with strikes and demands for a 15% pay hike.

The traditional Swedish model included an unwritten pact between employers and unions to set wages without strikes. All changed when union leaders approached the state for raises, rather than relying on corporate negotiations. In February 1990, the government resigned after its plan for a two-year wage and price freeze was defeated in parliament. Interest rates were already 16% and output stagnating. Swedish productivity fell and in 1991, inflation exceeded 10%. As noted by Bergh (2011), the welfare state was declining. To defend the Swedish crown, in September 1992, the Sveriges Riksbank increased the overnight rate to 500% (Englund, 2015). In 1994, the Swedish Foundation for Small Business Research was founded to initiate and disseminate policy-relevant research, to offer researchers a forum for dialogue, to build relevant networks and to bridge the gap between research and practice. Considerable funding came from the Swedish Ministry of Industry, Employment, and Communications. Sweden became a member of the European Union in 1995.

In 2000, the Global Entrepreneurship Monitor ranked Sweden the 5th least entrepreneurial nation of 21 in its index. Lundström (2003) reported that Sweden had a very large number of solo companies and therefore relatively high values of self-employed and SMEs per 1,000 inhabitants, but low values for SME share of total employment. The same publication explained, "Sweden has for a number of years concentrated much of the resources to the area of Skill. There is a great number of financial programs, counselling services and information systems... not very much is done in the area of Motivation" (Lundström, 2003, p. 27). Noteworthy is that today, as was the case then, Sweden is dominated by few old multinationals.

In 2005, inheritance tax was eliminated in Sweden, and the wealth tax in 2007. A real estate tax reform took place in 2008. To encourage people to work, taxes and hand-outs were reduced. The goal was to raise the employment rate to accelerate growth.

As the post-war baby boomer generation began to approach retirement age, Vikström and Westerberg (2010) suggested that successful succession in small family firms might be a key to sustainability for regional growth, as well as for the firm. The study was based on a survey of 55 small-scale family enterprises in Sweden.

Bergh (2011) studied Sweden's economy since the 19th century, concluding that Sweden grew rich because of well-functioning capitalist institutions. He noted that the decrease in income inequality occurred before the expansion state and was not the result of a welfare state.

Braunerhjelm *et al.* wrote, "In innovation-driven economies, there appears to have been an increase in entrepreneurial intentions between 2002 and 2014 for most countries, Sweden being the exception" (2015, p. 36). They identified a "dramatic and unprecedented fall in Swedish entrepreneurship between 2013 and 2014" (2015, p. 51).

Poelzer observed, "Sweden, the historic economic power of the north, now exports its youth to seek opportunities in Norway" (2013, p. 34). In 2013, public spending as a percentage of GDP was 49%, down from 67% in 1993. When the Norwegian crown fell, so did the attraction to go work in Norway.

Kelley, Singer, and Herrington (2016) noted that, year-by-year from 2013 to 2015, fear of failure decreased in Sweden. They elaborated, however, that despite Exhibiting high opportunity perceptions, Sweden reported a low level of intentions.

In December 2016, the 5th edition of the Global Sustainable Competitiveness Index placed Sweden on the top spot. It was followed by the other Scandinavian nations.

Indigenous Sámi in Sweden

Entrepreneurial intentions are not necessarily equal among different ethnicities in a given country. Furthermore, the perception of opportunity for entrepreneurship is culturally influenced — as illustrated by Dana (1995a). Among the Sámi — indigenous people in Sweden — reindeer herding has long been a cultural symbol as well as a socially desirable form of self-employment.

There has long been interest in the Sámi in Sweden. In the early 19th century, Clarke reported, "The Lapps are said to be more cunning than the Swedes, who consider them as a crafty set of knaves; just as the Gipsies are regarded everywhere. Perhaps their cunning may be principally due to the necessity they are under constantly upon their guard, lest they be maltreated; the people considering them as an inferior order of beings in the creation, and thinking it lawful to make them the objects of contempt and ridicule, using their very name, Lapp, as a term of degradation" (1824b, p. 169).

Brooke (1827) provided an account of a winter in Lapland and Sweden. Von Düben (1873) conducted an ethnographic study of Sámi people in Sweden. In 1919, entrepreneur Torkel Thomasson (1881–1940) launched a newspaper for Sámi people in Sweden.

A significant change occurred, to the advantage of the Sámi, with the Law of July 18, 1928 that made reindeer herding in Sweden an exclusive right of Sámi people. Olson wrote about Sámi people in Sweden making use of the reindeer, "He eats its smoked flesh, drinks its milk, preserves its blood, and sells its meat for a few luxuries, such as salt and snuff, bread, butter, and coffee. He makes tools out of its bones, arm winter boots and clothing from its skin (1928, p. 471)."

An important contribution to the literature about Sámi people in Sweden was Ruong (1937). This study noted that Sámi people were being drawn into the Swedish national economy, and becoming dependent on goods produced outside their sphere of influence, resulting in that which he termed *fjärrkonsumption*, meaning distant consumption.

Manker (1952) provided an account of Swedish contributions to ethnography about Sámi people. Manker (1953) studied the nomadism of Swedish mountain Sámi, a people distinct from forest Sámi.

Hultkrantz (1955) examined Swedish research on the religion and folklore of Sámi people. Whitaker (1955) focused on one Sámi community in Sweden, namely Lainiovuoma. Ruong (1956, 1967) discussed the Sámi community in Sweden, providing a description of the types of husbandry among Sámi in Northern Sweden.

The Reindeer Herding Act of 1971 introduced further changes. Siuruainen and Aikio stated, "the definition of a Lapp in Sweden, for example, presupposes residence in a Lapp village and possession of the accompanying right to herd reindeer" (1977, p. 11). Beach (1980) focused on reindeer management in transition in Northern Sweden. Jahreskog (1982) also focused on the Sámi in Sweden.

Beach (1990) reported Sweden as having more tame reindeer than Finland or Norway, and noted "about 900 active breeders, with family members bringing the total of those directly dependent on herding to approximately 2,700 people" (p. 275). Beach explained, "Unless a non-Saami marries into the herding group, only someone of Saami ancestry has the right to herd reindeer (if his or her parent or grandparent has had herding as a steady livelihood). Possession of the herding right, however, does not mean that one is automatically able to begin herding. According to the Reindeer Herding Act of 1971, anyone eligible to herd must also belong to one of 51 territorial herding collectives called *Samebys* before he or she is permitted to exercise this herding right" (Beach, 1990, p. 275).

Although Finland and Norway granted official status to Sámi language in 1992, the Swedish parliament did the same only seven years later. Beach (1997) revisited the economics of Sámi reindeer management in Sweden, showing that Swedish legislation was applying pressure on Sámi herders to conform to the state's understanding of profitable business, ignoring the cultural value of herding.

Danell (2000) considered directions and priorities of reindeer husbandry research in Sweden. Jernsletten and Klokov (2002) provided a summary of reindeer husbandry in Sweden.

For self-employed herders, access to pasture has long been an issue. A 2011 Supreme Court ruling gave the Sámi in Sweden common law rights to a specific area of land.

The Swedish Reindeer Herding Act regulates the sector, and reindeer husbandry comes under the Swedish Board of Agriculture. Outside Concession Areas where non-Sámi people are allowed to raise reindeer, herding is connected to membership in a Sámi sameby.

The Environment for Entrepreneurship

Merchants who formed a trading alliance with the Hanseatic League weakened early Swedish rulers. In 1397, Sweden came under the Danish crown. Danish rule lasted until an uprising in 1523. Gustavus Vasa (1496–1560) was subsequently elected king of Sweden. He made Sweden Lutheran, he curbed nobility, and ended the nation's economic dependence on the Hanseatic League.

The first savings bank, in Sweden, was opened in Gothenburg in 1820. During the following decades, attempts were made to establish merchant banks; in 1856, the Stockholms Enskilda Bank was founded and this form of banking became successful in Sweden (Elgán and Scobbie, 2015). Working with banks, Swedish entrepreneurs helped shape the environment for entrepreneurship — by bringing to market products that would change the way business was conducted. In 1874, Willgodt Theophil Odhner (1845–1905) invented the world's first practical calculating machine; out of this came the Facit Group, a major manufacturer of computers and office equipment. In 1876, Lars Magnus Ericsson opened a repair shop for telegraph equipment. In 1894, his firm L M Ericsson & Co began manufacturing the wall phone shown in Exhibit 20.14. He also patented the desk phone, the first to combine receiver and mouthpiece in one unit. In 1896, L M Ericsson & Co was transformed into a limited liability company. The enterprise expanded and internationalised. A merger took place in 1918 and the Swedish word for general being *allmänna*, the name "Allmänna Telefon AB L M Ericsson" was adopted for the enlarged firm. However, confusion arose given that *allmänna* sounds like Alemania — meaning Germany in Spanish. For this reason, in 1926, the name was changed to Telefon AB L M Ericsson. Olson wrote, "Sweden has one of the most highly developed telephone systems in the world" (1928, p. 446). She elaborated, "With a highly developed telephone system, business and social matters are handled largely over the wire" (1928, p. 469). The Ericsson group is now a communications giant.

In his study of entrepreneurial activity in Swedish industry between 1919 and 1939, Dahmen (1970) found that two thirds of

Exhibit 20.14 Made in Sweden 1894 to 1917; photo © 2017 Léo-Paul Dana.

the known founders of new firms in the engineering sector were of blue-collar background. He also revealed that the number of firms increased between 1922 and 1932 — suggesting that the increase was due to newly unemployed people creating jobs and improving the image of entrepreneurship, previously shunned in Sweden.

Technological advances continued to shaped environment. The introduction of the forklift and the pallet in 1947 spurred revolutionary change and growth (Hamark, 2014).

To promote closer economic cooperation and free trade, in 1960, Sweden was among the founders of the European Free Trade Association (EFTA). The other founding members were Austria, Denmark, Norway, Portugal, Switzerland, and the United Kingdom.

The following decade brought more change. Lundström noted, "Sweden started the development of a SME policy already in the early 1970s. During this decade many of the main actors still active today (even if under other formal names) were created" (2003, p. 278).

Cerrutti described the changing environment for small-scale farmers in Sweden, "Like the small fisherman, Gotland's small farmer is under pressure. Though Gotland is one of Sweden's most agricultural counties, with 20 percent of the population in farming, its 2,400 farms are dwindling. With too little money and too little land to mechanise, they have been leaving the soil at the rate of 100 a year ... To survive, a small farmer must be something of a superman" (1973, p. 278).

Carlsson noted, "in the late 1970s Sweden instituted a program of industrial subsidies to prevent unemployment in the industries most severely hurt in the aftermath of the 1973–4 oil crisis" (1996, p. 222). In Svappavara — Norrbotten county — all payroll taxes and social insurance contributions were eliminated for the period 1984–1993. Elsewhere in the county, payroll taxes and social insurance contributions payable by employers in selected sectors were reduced.

Gnosjö was Sweden's first fully-fledged industrial district with inter-firm cooperation. Johannisson (1989) observed Swedish enterprises cooperating in sophisticated, local information and production networks; proprietors were developing strong interfirm relations and joint educational programmes. Birley, Cromie and Myers added, "Because the Swedes actively encourage community networking and, because Swedish business founders have a propensity to network, it seems likely that autonomous entrepreneurs in Sweden might be predisposed to networking principles" (1991, p. 60).

The entrepreneurial spirit of Gnosjö became well known. Karlsson and Larsson (1993) investigated the long-run sustainability of the Gnosjö spirit, demonstrating that the manufacturing industry in the region was dominated by successful labour-intensive industries but that employment growth in knowledge-intensive industries was limited. The authors suggested that a causal variable was the lower knowledge-intensity of the labour force in the region, and they predicted that foreign competition would force industries to restructure; they recommended a massive educational campaign to create an arena for entrepreneurs.

Recession, in 1993, hiked unemployment to 8.2%, leading Sweden to reduce its 55% corporate tax rate to a flat 28%. As explained by Lundström, "The SME policy was built upon regional and labor issues from the start. There was not a real interest in the area of SMEs until the structural crises in big firms created great regional and local problems in the early 1990s" (2003, p. 278). In former times, cultural values promoted the thought that being average was good, and the educational network stressed uniformity and discouraged risk-taking and innovation — but time was ripe for change. Lynch (2001) observed that the conformist Swedish tradition of *jantelagen* (not sticking out) was giving way to entrepreneurship becoming socially desirable.

Lundström wrote, "Politicians are to a certain extent questioning the effectiveness of the existing policy measures mainly oriented towards SMEs ... Sweden has rather few financial instruments with grants. Most of them are types of loans with a higher risk than the ordinary financial market is prepared to accept. Another area of great interest during many years has been R&D and different innovation systems" (2003, pp. 265–278).

Jacob, Lundqvist and Hellsmark (2003) noted that some Swedish universities tried to transform themselves into entrepreneurial institutions. These authors focused on the case of Chalmers University of Technology, whose alumni count many successful entrepreneurs. Others should be mentioned too. Entrepreneurial spirit characterises Jönköping International Business School, with considerable entrepreneurship among students, as well as significant publications by scholars. Jönköping University and Lund University — the latter being the top-ranked in Sweden — also have entrepreneurship research traditions that positively impact their pedagogy. While

Linköping University is recognised for its comprehensive entrepreneurial education across disciplines, Luleå University of Technology is increasing its entrepreneurial profile. Successful entrepreneurs also come from KTH Royal Institute of Technology and the Stockholm School of Economics.

Globalisation contributed to shaping the changing environment for entrepreneurship. Blomstermo, Eriksson, and Sharma (2004) provided Swedish perspectives of international entrepreneurship. This country is highly dependent on exports, accounting for approximately half the nation's GDP (Tillman and Palander, 2016).

Johannisson and Wigren (2006) focused on Gnosjö, dominated by multigenerational family businesses — still the only fully-fledged industrial district in Sweden. In this ethnographic study, the authors observed, "norms and values that once guided work-related practices in the Gnosjö region have radically changed. The entry of China as a key player on the global market has amplified the already fierce competition and unemployment has increased to the average Swedish level. The dominant manufacturing industry, forced to invest in more efficient production equipment, offers fewer jobs than before. Gnosjö thus seems to have lost its lead in economic achievement" (Johannisson and Wigren, 2006, p. 189).

In 2006, a new conservative government took office and this would modify the environment for entrepreneurship. Hjalmarsson predicted, "Lower unemployment benefits and social allowance will make it more rewarding to work or to be self-employed in comparison to be unemployed" (2008, p. 36). Although Lundström (2008) observed a shift was taking place from traditional SME policy focus to providing entrepreneurs with skills and production factors, including risk capital and expertise towards focusing more on motivation and opportunity oriented measures, he suggested that this would be a time-consuming process that would continue for several decades.

The merger of Kalmar University with Växjö University, in January 2010, created Linnaeus University in a region dominated by low value-added manufacturing SMEs. Here, entrepreneurship is defined as a dynamic and social process, in which people identify opportunities and act upon them in order to transform ideas into practical and goal-oriented activities in social, cultural, or economic contexts. Influenced by Dyer, Gregersen, and Christensen (2011) who focused on associating, questioning, observing, experimenting and networking, Linnaeus University is attempting to encourage students: to be creative, active, motivated, and environmentally oriented; to challenge habits and identify opportunities; and to increase their belief in their own ability to make a difference.

Berggren and Silver (2010) analysed financial behaviour of SMEs in Sweden. Their findings revealed that SMEs in metropolitan area of Sweden searched for professional investors — although these are not many — while those in smaller municipalities relied on banks as the dominant source of funds. They concluded that policies needed to be tailor-made for unlike regions.

Discussing informal investors, Braunerhjelm *et al.* (2015, 2016) suggested that Sweden was among nations with the largest share of informal investors — a higher share than any of the other innovation-driven countries including the United States. This is debatable, but if it is correct then this implies a somewhat unique environment for entrepreneurship.

Larsson, Thulin, and Skoogberg noted that Sweden had "a relatively large share of entrepreneurship in the extractive sectors compared to the other countries, whereas entrepreneurial activities are more concentrated in the business service sector in the UK and the US" (2016, p. 24). They added, "In innovation-driven economies, there seems to be an increase in entrepreneurial intentions between 2004 and 2015 for most countries, with Sweden being the exception" (2016, p. 32).

Reporting on entrepreneurial intentions of students in Sweden, Durst and Sedenka wrote, "Self-realization and showing off one's own capabilities are the main drivers behind entrepreneurial career intentions. For Swedish students in general to be one's own boss is not important. This may be explained by the more egalitarian and low hierarchy cultural context in Sweden ... Based on these findings one can conclude that start-up and succession intention in Sweden can be improved. Entrepreneurship education at university level should be further stimulated considering specific offers and activities for the different groups of entrepreneurial students" (2016, p. 52–53).

Studying the internationalisation of Swedish SMEs, Naldi and Kuiken (2016) showed that their sample did not exhibit steady export behaviour during the 10-year longitudinal study. Half the SMEs studied stopped exporting, and began again later; based on this, the authors argued that unlike existing models, Swedish SMEs exhibit a non-linear pattern of exporting. In contrast to literature that suggests that family business is risk averse and less prone to internationalise, this study revealed that the most firms that continued to export over time were family-owned, and that family ownership was less common among enterprises that exited permanently.

Toward the Future

Sweden was the first country in Europe to establish a welfare state. Modern-day Swedish governments focused on promoting economic growth while sustaining the very well established system of social welfare. While large firms continue to be dominant (see Exhibit 20.15), small-scale industry (see Exhibit 20.16) and small service providers (see Exhibit 20.17) are also thriving.

Exhibit 20.15 Scania fleet for de-icing; photo © 2017 Léo-Paul Dana.

Exhibit 20.16 Artisanal chocolate production; photo © 2017 Léo-Paul Dana.

Creativity is well-entrenched and here to stay, providing innovative options. Entrepreneurial ideas include finding a new use for old technology; unlike the *M/F* Ursula (Exhibit 20.18) which — after serving as a ferry linking Sweden with Denmark between 1973 to 1997 — went to Mexico, becoming *M/F* Cozumel II, and has since been retired, dismantled and recycled as scrap metal, in contrast, *S/S* Gustaf af Klint (Exhibit 20.19) — a decommissioned survey ship (see Fagerholm, 1964) — now provides ship-board accommodation, in Stockholm.

Lundqvist and Middleton wrote, "in the limited Swedish setting, collective dimensions of entrepreneurship stand out. This nevertheless implies that collective engagements into entrepreneurship of any kind are worthy of more research and recognition" (2010, p. 24). Future research may investigate this further.

Exhibit 20.17 Italian café in Hovmantorp; photo © 2017 Léo-Paul Dana.

Exhibit 20.18 *M/F* Ursula in Helsingborg; photo © 1988 Léo-Paul Dana.

Exhibit 20.19 *S/S* Gustaf af Klint, Stockholm; photo © 2017 Léo-Paul Dana.

Braunerhjelm *et al.* wrote, "Among the innovation-driven countries, Sweden has the highest proportion of the population that considers itself able to identify good business opportunities (70 percent). However, only 37 percent view themselves as having sufficient capabilities to start a business" (2015, p. 11). Even fewer have both the self-confidence and the capital required as well as the capabilities. Future research may investigate *why* this is so, and *how* this problem can be solved.

Although Lundström noted, "Sweden has a number of policy measures directed towards different target groups, mainly women ..." (2003, p. 279), Braunerhjelm *et al.* observed, "Female entrepreneurship declined with more than two percentage points" (2015, p. 22). Future research may focus on issues of female entrepreneurship in Sweden.

Larsson, Thulin, and Skoogberg wrote that, in Sweden, "a relatively low share say that entrepreneurship is a desirable career" (2016, p. 49).

A challenge for the future will be to increase the social desirability of entrepreneurship.

Among the poorest nations of Europe a century ago, Sweden has become a prosperous country and a world leader in innovation, with Stockholm recognised as a hotbed for IT-based entrepreneurship. This success, however, is not a reason to be complacent. Sweden still has a culture of risk aversion and the nation has a limited, although growing, network of angel capital.

Chapter 21

Switzerland

Introduction

Covering 41,285 square kilometres, the Swiss Confederation is landlocked between Austria, France, Germany, Italy, and Liechtenstein.[1] Four languages have equal status here: French, German, Italian, and Romansh. Bergmann noted substantial entrepreneurship disparities among the three largest language areas and wrote, "The different start-up propensities in the three language areas can be explained by structural characteristics of the regional economy" (2011, p. 543).

The 1848 constitution made Bern (Exhibit 21.1) the federal capital; this city is home to the Federal Palace (Exhibit 21.2) and to the central bank (Exhibit 21.3) that decides the republic's monetary policy. The largest city in the country is Zurich (Exhibit 21.4). The largest French-speaking city in Switzerland is Geneva (Exhibit 21.5); this is where Lake Geneva — the country's largest — also known as Lac Léman (Exhibit 21.6) flows into the Rhône River, one of few to drain into the Mediterranean Sea.

Among prominent Swiss entrepreneurs was the Swiss chocolatier and industrialist Philippe Suchard (1797–1884), who opened a chocolate factory in 1826. In 1901, his firm introduced the Milka brand (Exhibit 21.7), acquired in 1990 by Kraft Foods — now Mondelēz International.

[1] See relevant chapters in this volume.

Exhibit 21.1 Bern; photo © 2017 Léo-Paul Dana.

Exhibit 21.2 The Federal Palace; photo © 2017 Léo-Paul Dana.

Exhibit 21.3 The Swiss national bank; photo © 2017 Léo Paul Dana.

Exhibit 21.4 Zurich; photo © 2017 Léo-Paul Dana.

Exhibit 21.5 Geneva; photo © 2017 Léo-Paul Dana.

Exhibit 21.6 Lake Geneva; photo © 2017 Léo-Paul Dana.

In Vevey, Switzerland, Frankfurt-born Henri Nestlé (1814–1890) launched his *farine lactée/Kindermehl* (flour with milk formula) in 1867 (Pfiffner, 1993). Merging with the Anglo-Swiss Condensed Milk Co., in 1905, this enterprise became the Nestlé and Anglo-Swiss Condensed Milk Company, a name it kept until 1947 when

Exhibit 21.7 Milka; photo © 2017 Léo-Paul Dana.

the firm changed its name to Nestlé Alimentana SA. Headquartered in Vevey, Nestlé has 456 factories and over 330,000 employees in 86 countries.

Fritz Hoffman-La Roche (1868–1920) established the Hoffman-La Roche firm in Basel and began producing "cough syrup and a powder for wound treatment in an abandoned ink factory in 1896 ... During the 1930's, it pioneered development of synthetic vitamins" (Abercrombie, 1969, p. 103).

Jean Bindella (1878–1918) began importing Chianti wines to Switzerland in 1909. Today, the Zurich-based family business owns land in Tuscany, where it produces olive oil as well as grappa and wine. This Swiss family owns 40 restaurants and a nightclub in Switzerland. The youngest in the family, Jean Bindella's great-grandson is Christian Bindella (1985–), who originally went to Israel to study, after which he was granted a visa to stay. With Tel Aviv chef Roy Soffer, in 2014 he opened the first Bindella restaurant outside Switzerland — the Bindella Osteria & Bar, in Tel Aviv.

Transnational entrepreneurs have also been significant. Born in Beirut to a banking family established since the time of the Ottoman Empire, Edmond J. Safra (1932–1999) established the Republic National Bank of New York and operated his banking empire from Switzerland. Also foreign-born is Dr. Atilay Ileri (1942–) a Zurich-based attorney-at-law who is a very successful producer of olive oil at the Ab-u Hayat estate of which he is proprietor, in Turkey — the land of his birth.

Multinationals based in Switzerland include ABB, Credit Suisse, Novartis, Swiss Life (Exhibit 21.8), and the largest bank in Switzerland, UBS (see Exhibit 21.9). In New York, Credit Suisse is the primary tenant of the former Metropolitan Life North Building, adjacent to the Met Life Tower (Exhibit 21.10). While Swiss companies have spanned the globe, Switzerland's low corporate taxes have also attracted regional headquarters of foreign firms.

Exhibit 21.8 Swiss Life; photo © 2017 Léo-Paul Dana.

Exhibit 21.9 UBS; photo © 2017 Léo-Paul Dana.

Historical Overview

In ancient times, the Helvetii — a Gallic tribe — lived here. When the Romans, led by Julius Caesar (100BC–44BC), conquered the Helvetti, most of the territory became a province of the Holy Roman Empire — which gave local communities, known as cantons, considerable autonomy. During the 12th century, the Habsburgs (sometimes anglicised to Hapsburgs) came to control the empire with harsher rule.

The Swiss Confederation originated in 1291, the year three cantons formed a union. By 1388, other cantons joined in and helped defeat the Austrians. The 1499 Treaty of Basel led to independence for the Swiss. A loose confederation tied the cantons together, with no central government. By 1513, this included 13 cantons.

Abercrombie wrote, "Craftsmen began building clocks and watches in Geneva more than 400 years ago, and by the early 1700's the industry had spread throughout the Jura Mountains" (1969, p. 98). In 1798

Exhibit 21.10 Credit Suisse in New York; photo © 2017 Léo-Paul Dana.

Napoléon I (1769–1821) invaded and created the centralised Helvetic Republic; the Swiss were forced to abandon their neutrality and to provide troops for Napoléon I. This republic only lasted to 1814. The perpetual neutrality of Switzerland was guaranteed at the Congress of Vienna, in 1815. Inspired by the *Chateau de Chillon* — Chillon Castle (Exhibit 21.11) — in 1816, Lord George Gordon Byron (1788–1824) wrote the poem "The Prisoner of Chillon."

Exhibit 21.11 *Chateau de Chillon*; photo © 2017 Léo-Paul Dana.

In 1839, the watch manufacturer Patek, Czapek & Cie was established. This was a predecessor to Patek, Philippe & Cie and later Patek Philippe SA, founded by Antoine Norbert e Patek (1812–1877) and inventor Adrien Philippe (1815–1894). The firm has been in the hands of the Stern family since 1932 (Foulkes, 2017) with headquarters in Geneva (Exhibit 21.12).

In 1847, civil war raged between Catholic and Protestant cantons. In 1848, the constitution established a federal government. When this was revised in 1874, Article 49 gave religious freedom to all.

In 1863, Swiss businessman Henri Dunant (1828–1910) of Geneva organised the International Cross, which adopted the Swiss flag with colours reversed. The Red Cross has since been very helpful during peace as well as during war (Exhibit 21.13).

Charles d'Este Guelph, also known as Charles II, Duke of Brunswick (1804–1873), was a horseman, linguist and musician. He left his enormous fortune to Geneva, where the Brunswick Monument features a bronze statue of him (Exhibit 21.14).

Industrialisation during the late 19th century prompted development of urban centres. In Zurich, the Hotel National was completed

Exhibit 21.12 Patek Philippe; photo © 2017 Léo-Paul Dana.

and opened in 1877 — at a location that was formerly a sheep pasture. It was enlarged in 1878, and renamed the Grand Hotel National in 1883. It is now the Hotel Schweizerhof (Exhibit 21.15).

During the 19th century, silk weaving was associated with Basel and Zurich, while St. Gallen was a leading centre for embroidery.

Exhibit 21.13 Prisoner of war mail; photo © 2017 Léo-Paul Dana.

Exhibit 21.14 The Duke of Brunswick; photo © 2017 Léo-Paul Dana.

Exhibit 21.15 Hotel Schweizerhof, Zurich; photo © 2017 Léo-Paul Dana.

While machinery manufacturers did well given the demand for relevant machines, the chemical industry developed largely as a result of demand for dyes for textiles (Holmes, 1988). The early 20th century was marked by rapid growth led by the textile industry in Switzerland. The St. Gallen railway station — dating from 1856 — was no longer satisfactory for demand and a new one was built (see Exhibit 21.16).

The 1907 Hague Convention permitted neutral nations to trade with all belligerents. Being industrialised but resource-poor, Switzerland obtained raw materials from various neighbours — throughout the Great War (World War I). Although the Swiss did not fight in that war, in 1918 a sixth of the Swiss population lived below the poverty line. There was a large gap between the working class and those who had valuable assets (see Exhibit 21.17).

During the interwar years, Germany was among Switzerland's most important trading partners and during World War II, export figures to Germany rose sharply. Switzerland conducted relatively little trade with the Allies. When Germany started deporting the Jewish community of France, in August 1942, Switzerland announced the closure of its borders.

During the post-war period, Switzerland experienced an unprecedented economic boom. Many foreign workers, especially Italians, came to Switzerland. In 1971, Swiss women got the right to vote at the national level. The economic boom lasted until the 1970s, when recession caused the influx to dip temporarily.

Exhibit 21.16 Station at St. Gallen; photo © 2017 Léo-Paul Dana.

Exhibit 21.17 Mansion at Creux de Genthod; photo © 2017 Léo-Paul Dana.

In 1999, Switzerland was among the first countries to have a Jewish president — Ruth Dreifuss (1940–). Since then, according to Testarmata and Montecchia, "the Swiss government has expressed its commitment to sustainable development through the introduction of three articles in the Federal Constitution (2, 54, and 73) which seek 'a balanced relationship over time between nature and its ability to renew itself, on the one hand, and the demands placed on it by the human race, on the other'" (2016, p. 239).

In March 2002, the Swiss people voted to join the United Nations — abandoning centuries of political isolationism. Later that month, the nation's flag-carrier, Swissair ceased operations. A new national airline was launched — Swiss International Air Lines.

At the 2009 presidential inauguration of Barack Obama (1961–), First Lady Michelle (1964–) wore linen made in St. Gallen — still an important centre for high-end textiles. Family-owned Filtex AG (Exhibit 21.18) has been manufacturing here for 80 years, and exporting. In 2011, Switzerland launched trade negotiations with China, leading to an agreement in 2013.

Between January 2010 and mid-August 2011, the Swiss currency appreciated 43% against the euro. In response to an escalating,

Exhibit 21.18 Family-owned Filtex; photo © 2017 Léo-Paul Dana.

overvalued currency caused by investors buying Swiss francs to escape the euro-zone's debt crisis, in Sept 2011 the central bank announced it would buy unlimited quantities of foreign currency to secure a minimum exchange rate of SFr 1.20 per euro. The franc then fell from SFr 1.11 to SFr 1.20 per euro. In February 2014, Swiss voters approved new limits on immigration (Eddy, 2014). This reflected concerns about the costs of increasingly open borders.

Baldegger *et al.* wrote, "What is particularly notable is that fear of failure has clearly lessened in the past few years, and in 2014 was even lower than the USA ... Fear of failing is very low in the German-speaking regions (D-CH), yet intentions to found a company are much lower than other language regions. In French-speaking Switzerland (F-CH), there are significantly more people with entrepreneurial intentions, although they are more afraid of failing. In contrast, the successful entrepreneur enjoys an extremely positive status there, and an entrepreneurial career is described as attractive. In the Italian-speaking part of Switzerland (I-CH), the high social status of entrepreneurial activity cannot be transferred to intentions to found a business" (2014, p. iii–iv).

In 2015, the Swiss central bank announced it would let the Swiss franc float freely. That year, 2015 Switzerland's GDP was $685 billion, up from $272 billion in 2000 (World Bank, 2015). The *World Happiness Report* ranked Switzerland the "happiest country, followed by Iceland, Denmark, Norway and Canada" (McGinty, 2015, p. A2).

Baldegger, Wild, and Morel (2016) observed that 79% of internationalising SMEs were doing so incrementally, rather than using a born global strategy; they observed, "the value of goods exported in the first quarter of 2016 grew in most sectors, with companies producing precision instruments, watches and jewellery making a positive mark, along with the machinery, equipment and electronics industries which are heavily dependent on the exchange rate. Together with the increase in new orders received in the first quarter of 2016 in the Swiss machinery, electronics and metal industries, these are signs that the Swiss economy has overcome the test of a strong franc relatively well" (2016, p. 8). In July 2016, Swiss Global

Air Lines — a subsidiary of Swiss International Air Lines — became the first airline to operate the Canadian-built Bombardier CS100 twinjet.

The Environment for Entrepreneurship

The high ratio of multinational companies per capita strongly flavours the environment. Switzerland's stable economy relies heavily on technology-intensive big industry and on numerous large financial institutions; Exhibit 21.19 shows a Graubündner Kantonalbank/ Banca Chantunala Grischuna just across the street from a UBS bank. The abundance of options here creates an opportunity cost for those opting to be entrepreneurs. As noted by Baldegger, Wild, Alberton and Hacklin (2016), only 40% of the Swiss see entrepreneurship as a good career choice, compared to 79.2% of the Dutch.

Entrepreneurs and SMEs are nevertheless important. There are numerous small wineries; Exhibit 21.20 features the Château d'Aigle castle that houses a vine and wine museum. The agricultural sector includes about 600 small-scale cheese-making dairies that contribute toward Switzerland's output of approximately 185,000 tonnes of cheese annually. There are also numerous family farms (Exhibit 21.21).

Exhibit 21.19 Chur; photo © 2017 Léo-Paul Dana.

Exhibit 21.20 Château d'Aigle; photo © 2017 Léo-Paul Dana.

Exhibit 21.21 Swiss farms; photo © 2017 Léo-Paul Dana.

Exhibit 21.22 Self-employed; photo © 2017 Léo-Paul Dana.

Several facilities help individuals to acquire relevant skills, e.g., in Sion, the Ecole Cantonale d'Agriculture teaches agricultural management to self-employed farmers (Dana, 1992b).

Urban self-employment is seldom a necessity here. Although Swiss street performers exist (Exhibit 21.22), many are migrants (see Grill, 2011).

As observed by Thierstein and Wilhem, "Only since the early 1990s, when unemployment rates in Switzerland soared to unprecedented levels, has federal technology and innovation policy begun to design their activities with regards to employment and the establishment of new firms. Now, all across the country, private as well as public incubators facilities, technology and innovation centres have begun to spring up" (2001, p. 315).

The Commission for Technology and Innovation (CTI) is the state's innovation promotion agency. It supports R&D, entrepreneurship, and the development of start-up companies. Among its activities, this agency helps optimise knowledge and technology transfer by means of networks. In 1996, the agency initiated CTI Start-up, helping entrepreneurs with a tailored, hands-on coaching and training process.

Supporting the creation of knowledge-based start-ups in Switzerland, CTI Entrepreneurship is the national training programme. The CTI entrepreneurship programme, Venturelab was launched in 2004; it serves as a training programme for innovative high-tech new ventures.

Becker, Kronthaler, and Wagner (2011), found regions in Switzerland to be unique and distinct with regard to their potential for venture creation, with some having an existing small-firm base and a relatively high number of entrepreneurs. This suggested the possibility of industry concentration consisting of small firms, for example in the agricultural sector, the craft sector and in tourism, together with many entrepreneurial role models. In fact, tourism is not insignificant in Switzerland (see Exhibit 21.23).

Exhibit 21.23 Aarburg Castle, in Aargau; photo © 2017 Léo-Paul Dana.

Wolf, Kaudela-Baum, and Meissner (2012) presented a longitudinal study of innovating cultures among SMEs in central Switzerland. They identified four innovative cultures.

The World Competitiveness Scoreboard 2012 ranked Switzerland the third most competitive after Hong Kong and the United States. Switzerland scored 80.5 in the 2015 Index of Economic Freedom, placing it as the most free in Europe and among the world's five most free countries for which a score was available. Its score moved up to 81, in 2016 — placing it 4th in the world, after Hong Kong, Singapore and New Zealand.

Baldegger *et al.* observed that the overall entrepreneurial framework conditions were generally better in Switzerland than in most other innovation-based economies. They wrote, "Switzerland achieves outstanding results in finance, commercial infrastructure, tertiary education, and knowledge and technology transfer, as well as stable internal market dynamics" (2014, p. ii).

Baldegger *et al.* (2016) assessed the environment for entrepreneurship in Switzerland. They noted that Switzerland had excellent framework conditions for entrepreneurship and that it was rated the most competitive country in the world, according to the Global Competitiveness Report. The same study reported that the National Expert Survey indicated increasing satisfaction with Swiss regulation.

Baldegger *et al.* (2016) summarised enablers of entrepreneurship in Switzerland: (i) the strong R&D sector leading to many new commercial opportunities; (ii) post-secondary education providing adequate preparation for starting-up and growing new firms; and (iii) the presence of and access to physical resources at a price that not discriminating against new, small or growing firms. They noted that Swiss culture did not encourage entrepreneurial risk-taking and discussed constraints including the lack of venture capital, debt finance and funding through Initial Public Offerings and the fact that primary and secondary education did not give enough attention to self-sufficiency, personal initiative and creativity.

Yet, it could be argued that there is much creativity in Switzerland. In addition to technological innovation there is also creative managerial innovation with existing technology. An example is Sharely,

Exhibit 21.24 Liquor with gold flakes; photo © 2017 Léo-Paul Dana.

which allows people to advertise personal goods and earn revenue letting these, to renters with whom they agree on-line. Another example of creativity is that of an SME bottling a liquor containing flakes of gold (Exhibit 21.24).

Examining international activity, Kelley, Singer, and Herrington (2016) indicated that over one-third of entrepreneurs in Switzerland had substantial international sales. Baldegger, Wild, and Morel explained possible causal variables, "The small volume of the Swiss domestic market, the distinctive international orientation of Swiss SMEs, and last but not least, free access to the European market all combine to improve performance. Small and medium-sized enterprises can increase their performance considerably by concentrating on a limited number of market-entry strategies" (2016, p. 47). These authors noted that medium-sized firms were represented more strongly in the East Asian countries and much more frequently in Japan than smaller ones; the same study found that micro and small businesses were more active in the Near and Middle East and in Australia and New Zealand. They also mentioned that the majority of entrepreneurs considered informal networks in international business to be more important than formal ones.

Toward the Future

In a study of human capital among owner–managers of Swiss SMEs, Volery (2008) found different dimensions of personal factors to be significant. That study suggested that public policy directives and educational programmes should recognise significant differences in SME internationalisation. Future policy might also encourage corporate social responsibility. Séraphin observed, "In countries such as Switzerland, where the banking sector relies on its neutrality policy and strong secrecy laws, the promotion of CSR is typically weaker" (2016, p. 14). It may hence be an opportunity for future research to seek viable options.

Baldegger *et al.* (2016) reported that although the Swiss indicate a high perception of opportunities and a positive attitude toward entrepreneurship, they struggled to act accordingly; the authors showed that the entrepreneurial intentions of Swiss inhabitants (7.0%) were under the average (11.4%) for innovation-driven countries including Israel, Norway and the United States. Future research might investigate why this is so and what could/should be done about this. The same study also noted that the typical Swiss entrepreneur was likely to be a man between 35 and 44 years of age. They recommended that significant efforts be made to stimulate entrepreneurship and youth and women to launch their business.

A related opportunity for future research is to investigate why women are under-represented. If it is not by choice, then a suitable alternative could be proposed.

Baldegger *et al.* (2016) also found that, despite excellent framework conditions for entrepreneurship, the potential for young companies to create new jobs in the short term was rather limited. Although unemployment is not a major problem in Switzerland, future research could investigate this issue. The same authors concluded that despite its privileged situation, Switzerland was facing major challenges for the future, as the number of high growth start-ups with the potential to create many jobs remained very small. The authors called for fast growing, specialised firms, creating many new jobs to keep the economy competitive.

Chapter 22

The United Kingdom of Great Britain and Northern Ireland

Introduction

England annexed Wales in 1536. In 1707, the Kingdom of Scotland was united with the Kingdom of England creating the Kingdom of Great Britain. In 1801, the latter formed a legislative union with the Kingdom of Ireland, the result of which was the United Kingdom of Great Britain and Ireland. When the Irish Free State seceded, in 1922, the name was modified to the United Kingdom of Great Britain and Northern Ireland (UK), and the United Kingdom has since shared a border with Ireland.[1]

This kingdom — with a land area of 241,930 square kilometres — consists of England, the capital of which is London (see Worrall, 2000); Northern Ireland — the devolved administration of which is in Belfast; Scotland, with its devolved administration in Edinburgh — which Cerruti (1976) referred to as a capital in search of a country; and Wales — with its devolved administration in Cardiff (Exhibit 22.1).

The Palace of Westminster — with the House of Commons and the House of Lords — is in London. At its north end is the Elizabeth Tower — the tallest four-faced chiming clock in the world (Exhibit 22.2); the clock's bell — known as Big Ben — has a crack that results in a unique chime.

[1] See relevant chapter in this volume.

Exhibit 22.1 Cardiff Castle; photo © 2017 Léo-Paul Dana.

Exhibit 22.2 Elizabeth Tower; photo © 2017 Léo-Paul Dana.

Several British entrepreneurs were key to facilitating future entrepreneurship, by igniting the Industrial Revolution and the Railway Revolution — with neither encouragement nor funding from the state. Josiah Wedgwood (1730–1795), potter and entrepreneur, established the Josiah Wedgwood & Sons Ltd, in 1759 and has since been credited with industrialising the process of pottery manufacturing.

Other prominent British entrepreneurs include John Baring (1730–1816) and Francis Baring (1740–1810) who in 1762 founded the John and Francis Baring Company, forerunner of the Barings Bank, important in Britain's efforts during the American Revolution and later against Napoléon I (1769–1821). This bank financed the Louisiana Purchase — the deal by which the United States bought $15 million of land from France. Also notable is William Blake (1757–1827), a self-employed engraver and acclaimed poet.

Entrepreneurs who were immigrants to the British Isles include Frankfurt-born Nathan Mayer Rothschild (1777–1836) who established a banking dynasty that helped industrialise Europe. Another was Sir Moses Haim Montefiore (1784–1885), a financier originally from Leghorn. Both were Jewish.

In 1823, Englishman George Stephenson (1781–1848) launched a new venture with his son Robert Stephenson (1803–1859); this was the beginning of the Robert Stephenson & Company, the world's first builder of steam locomotives (Smiles, 1860). With these engines, in 1825 the Stockton & Darlington Railway launched the world's first steam-powered public train service. In 1830, Liverpool and Manchester Railway introduced the first high-speed interurban railway with timetabled expresses. For a detailed discussion of the world's first railway system, see Casson (2009b).

Also in 1830, engineer and merchant Charles Tayleur (1785–1854) established the Vulcan Foundry — builders of locomotives — in Lancashire. By the 1930s, the century-old Vulcan Foundry had progressed beyond steam engines and was manufacturing a self-propelled railcar (Exhibit 22.3).

James Kitson (1807–1885) established Kitson & Company in Leeds, in 1837. This firm manufactured steam tram motors

Exhibit 22.3 1939 Vulcan railcar; photo © 2017 Léo-Paul Dana.

Exhibit 22.4 Kitson steam tram motor; photo © 2017 Léo-Paul Dana.

(Exhibit 22.4) to haul streetcars within urban areas. Rather than burn coal, these were designed to be powered by a smokeless fuel — coke. In Glasgow, Walter Neilson (1810–1882) founded Neilson and Company in 1847. This firm's steam engine N°2,306 (Exhibit 22.5) was built in 1878.

Exhibit 22.5 Made in Scotland; photo © 2017 Léo-Paul Dana.

Andrew Carnegie (1835–1919) was born in Dunfermline, the medieval capital of Scotland. His family moved to the United States when he was a child and after several jobs he launched Carnegie Steel Corporation (see Carnegie, 1920).

An observant Jew, Marcus Samuel (1853–1927) created The Shell Transport and Trading Co. In 1907, this firm merged with Royal Dutch — operated by Henri Wilhelm August Deterding (1866–1839) — to form the Royal Dutch Shell Group.

In 1908, Horace Short (1872–1917) joined his brothers Albert Eustace Short (1875–1932) and Hugh Oswald Short (1883–1970) in

Exhibit 22.6 Flying boat cabin; photo © 2017 Léo-Paul Dana.

their family business, adopting the firm name Short Brothers. On the Isle of Sheppey, the newly formed company began aircraft production. In 1948, the enterprise shifted to Northern Ireland. Among the aeroplanes manufactured in Belfast was the Short Bros Solent flying boat, used for intercontinental flights. A replica of the aircraft's cabin is shown in Exhibit 22.6.

William Richard Morris (1877–1963) established Morris Motors Limited. The firm's Morris 8 (Exhibit 22.7) was produced from 1935 to 1948. More recently, Richard Branson (1950–) created the Virgin brand (Exhibit 22.8).

This chapter is about the first nation to experience the industrial revolution. Yet, this was not prompted by state intervention. Nowadays, in the United Kingdom, government is more involved in promoting and facilitating entrepreneurship than was the case in the past. Today, local enterprise partnerships between local authorities

Exhibit 22.7 Morris 8; photo © 2017 Léo-Paul Dana.

Exhibit 22.8 Virgin Atlantic Airbus 340; photo © 2017 Léo-Paul Dana.

and businesses decide on priorities, including investment in infrastructure, office space and facilities. Modern day public policies encourage entrepreneurship, as do business schools.

As will be discussed below, among the earliest powerful forces to shape the environment for entrepreneurship were guilds; these protected existing entrepreneurs but inhibited new ventures. Entrepreneurship was facilitated largely by the development of banks and by early industrialisation — the latter made possible by ample and accessible coal and iron. That said, although this country pioneered the Industrial Revolution and the Railway Revolution, it lagged behind with the Chemical Revolution, the Electricity Revolution, and the Managerial Revolution of the late 19th and early 20th century. The next section shall highlight some historical moments.

Historical Overview

Innes wrote, "Two thousand years ago, what we now call England and Wales was occupied by the Celtic people known as Britons. In the first century after Christ it was conquered by the Romans ... " (1922, p. 2001).

The Romans crossed the English Channel in 43 AD, named their new province Britannia and controlled it until the 5th century. Fyfe wrote about the 5th century, "there was a landing at Ebbsfleet, in the Isle of Thanet, by pirates from Jutland. These pirates were called Angles or English, and with their landing the history of the English people in England began ... they rested their institutions upon the basis of what we should now call peasant proprietorship" (1922, p. 1758).

The Anglo-Saxon era ended in 1066 with the start of Norman rule in England; this was a year during which England had three kings. Edward the Confessor (circa 1003–1066) was succeeded by Harold (circa 1022–1066), who was defeated at the Battle of Hastings by William the Conqueror (1028–1087), a Norman invader.

The *Magna Carta* of 1215 was forced on unpopular King John (1167–1216) by his barons. This guaranteed rights and served as the basis for English institutions (see Thompson, 1948). Feudalism in England declined during the 13th and 14th centuries. Morton wrote, "Economically the decline took the form of an increase in commodity production in agriculture, leading to the break-up of the manor ... The large-scale production of wool for the Flemish market led to the development of trade on an international scale and of merchant capital" (1938 p. 86). As towns grew, craft guilds complemented and also opposed merchant guilds (see Flinn, 1961, Ch 2).

Conflict between England and France from 1337 to 1453 came to be known as the Hundred Years' War. It was extremely costly to the Crown, which became dependent on Jewish moneylenders and later Italian bankers (Terry, 1914). During the 15th century, England shifted from being a wool producer to becoming a cloth manufacturer. After Edward IV (1442–1483) died, his son briefly reigned as Edward V (1470–1483), but the boy's uncle took the throne from him and made himself Richard III (1452–1485).

Henry Tudor (1457–1509) won the throne at the Battle of Bosworth in 1485, ending the Wars of the Roses between his Lancastrian dynasty and their rivals, the House of York. He thus became Henry VII. When he married Elizabeth of York (1466–1503), daughter of Edward IV, he united the two sides of what had been a bloody civil war. Henry VII opened up trade with France and secured England's textile exports to the Netherlands.

The eldest daughter of Henry VII, Margaret Tudor of England (1489–1541) married James IV of Scotland (1473–1513) in 1503. She was the elder sister of the boy who would become Henry VIII (1491–1547). Several Stuart kings later descended from this couple.

Henry VII (1457–1509) outlived his eldest son Arthur Tudor, Prince of Wales (1486–1502). Hence it was Arthur's younger brother, 17-year-old Henry VIII who succeeded his father in April 1509. A few weeks later, Henry VIII married his first of six wives, Catherine of Aragon (1485–1536), the widow of his brother Arthur, and eventually the mother of the girl who — after the death of Henry VIII's successor Edward VI (1537–1553) — would become Queen Mary I (1516–1558).

In 1525, Cardinal Thomas Wolsey (circa 1475–1530) gave his palatial home, Hampton Court (Exhibit 22.9), to Henry VIII. With the support of Wolsey, in 1527, the king asked the pope for an annulment of his marriage. Refusal by the pope, however, led to Henry's breaking with Rome in order to divorce Catherine of Aragon. The dissolution of the monasteries, the creation of the Church of England and centuries of anti-Catholicism were the result (for a detailed account, see Hope, 1894).

Exhibit 22.9 Hampton Court; photo © 2017 Léo-Paul Dana.

In 1533, Henry VIII married his second wife, Anne Boleyn (1501–1536), but had her executed in 1536 — on a pretext of infidelity after she failed to produce a male heir. His third wife was Jane Seymour (circa 1509–1537), the mother of the king's only legitimate son — the future Edward VI, who was born at Hampton Court. When Queen Mary I died in 1558, Anne's daughter became Queen Elizabeth I (1533–1603), who carried out several programmes initiated by her father. Under the protection of the Royal Navy established by Henry VIII, Sir Francis Drake (circa 1540–1596) was among those making profitable voyages, literally travelling around the world. In 1585, Drake set off to plunder Spanish colonies in the New World that his contemporary, Sir Walter Raleigh (circa 1552–1618), proceeded to develop as well as in the American colonies (Tytler, 1853).

With the death of Queen Elizabeth I, the Tudor period came to an end. The queen was succeeded by her first cousin-twice-removed, the Scottish king, James VI (1566–1625), who became known in England as James I of the House of Stuart. The second Stuart king was the second son of James I and Anne of Denmark (1574–1619), Charles I (1600–1649). Following the English Civil War, in 1649, Charles I was beheaded, the monarchy was abolished, and Oliver Cromwell (1599–1658) assumed control of the country. In 1656, Cromwell approved the re-establishment of a Jewish community in England after several centuries (see Vignali, Robinson and Vignali, 2010); the first to come were from the Netherlands and, in 1701, these established the Bevis Marks Synagogue in London.

In Ireland, Cromwell focused on the production of inexpensive food and raw materials for England. By 1660, annual exports of cattle from Ireland to England reached 500,000. When this was seen a competing with English producers, legislation in 1666 banned Irish cattle, dairy products and meat in England. Meanwhile, in 1660, the monarchy was restored with Charles II (1630–1685), a somewhat extravagant king who was succeeded by his Catholic brother James II (1633–1701). The fortunes of England revived considerably following the rejection of James II in favour of the Glorious Revolution; in 1689, James II was replaced by his Protestant daughter Queen Mary II (1662–1694) and her Dutch husband, William III (1650–1702). The Glorious Revolution and its aftermath had a lasting impact on the nation.

With the growth of trade, during the 17th century, insurance gained importance. In London, Edward Lloyd (circa 1648–1713) operated a coffee house where marine insurance could be purchased. Not related to Lloyds Bank (Exhibit 22.10), this was the start of Lloyd's insurance market in 1688. The period from 1688 to 1914 was known as one of innovation, industrialisation and British expansionism (Cain and Hopkins, 1993).

A niece of Charles II, Queen Anne (1665–1714) was the last Stuart monarch. When she died childless, the Georgian era was heralded as she was succeeded by George I (1660–1727) — the first Hanoverian monarch of the Kingdom of Great Britain. "He spoke very little English, preferring to converse in German and French" (Furness, 2013, p. 4). His son George II (1683–1760) was the last British sovereign to fight alongside his soldiers.

Exhibit 22.10 Lloyds, founded in 1765; photo © 2017 Léo-Paul Dana.

The eldest son of George II — Frederick Louis (1707–1751) — died before he did. It was therefore George III (1738–1820) — first Hanoverian monarch to have English as first language — who succeeded his grandfather. In 1768 a vine was planted at Hampton Court Palace, to supply grapes for George III; it is now the largest vine in the world.

Parliament introduced a Stamp Act in 1765, soon replaced by the 1766 Declaratory Act asserting absolute control over colonial government in North America. Beginning in 1767, the Townshend Acts taxed products that could only be imported to the American colonies from England (Thomas, 1987). Blanchard (1992) listed products that were taxed effective 1767: glass, lead, oil, paint, paper, tea, and wines.

In 1773, Parliament authorised the British East India Company to export a quantity exceeding 200 metric tonnes of surplus tea to the American colonies without the usual tariffs. The company could sell its surplus at a price that would undersell American merchants and dominate the colonial trade. Rebellious colonists boarded British ships at Boston harbour and threw 342 chests of tea into the sea at what would become known as the Boston Tea Party; the American Revolution was around the corner. In 1776, Americans declared their independence.

In 1802, Parliament passed an act, forbidding employers to keep apprentices at work beyond 12 hours a day. In 1819, this limit was applied for all labourers younger than 17. Meanwhile, in 1815, the British were jubilant about their victory over Napoléon I at the Battle of Waterloo.

George III was still king when his granddaughter Alexandrina (1819–1901) was born to Prince Edward, Duke of Kent (1767–1820). When the Duke of Kent died, it was her mother's brother Leopold who supported his sister and young Alexandrina — the future Queen Victoria, who was to become the longest-serving British monarch until the 21st century.

In 1820 George IV (1762–1830) succeeded his father, George III. In 1821 the Bank of England adopted the gold standard. When George IV died in 1830, he was succeeded by his brother William IV (1765–1837).

Being a niece of George IV and of William IV, Alexandrina became Queen Victoria (Exhibit 22.11), in 1837, when her father's elder brothers had died leaving no legitimate children. In 1840, she married her cousin Albert of Saxe-Coburg and Gotha (1819–1861). In 1843, the Church of Scotland experienced a division, described in detail by Brown (1884). In 1846, Prime Minister Robert Peel (1788–1850) scrapped the Corn Laws — unpopular since 1815.

In 1851, the Great Exhibition of the Works of Industry of all Nations — brainchild of Prince Albert — was held at the cast iron and glass Crystal Palace at Hyde Park. The emphasis was on the nation's industrial leadership. As discussed in Chapter 7 of this volume, this prompted Napoléon III to issue an imperial decree in 1853 for a similar fair in Paris.

In 1858, Victoria, Princess Royal (1840–1901) — the first child of Queen Victoria and Prince Albert — married Frederick, Crown Prince of Germany and Prussia (1831–1888), later Frederick III,

Exhibit 22.11 Queen Victoria; photo © 2017 Léo-Paul Dana.

German Emperor and King of Prussia (see Chapter 8 in this volume). The second child of Queen Victoria and Prince Albert, namely Albert Edward, Prince of Wales (1841–1910) was married in 1863 to Alexandra of Denmark (1844–1925), and later became Edward VII. It was ironic, if not tragic, that these children of Queen Victoria and Prince Albert found themselves on opposite sides during the Great War (World War I).

In London, in 1863, the world's first underground railway was built, eventually expanding into an elaborate "tube" network. Among the first stops was South Kensington Station (Exhibit 22.12).

Modernisation also affected the countryside. Youatt wrote, "agriculture has improved, the milk of the sheep has ceased to be an article of human sustenance, and has been appropriated to its natural

Exhibit 22.12 South Kensington Station; photo © 2017 Léo-Paul Dana.

purpose, the food of the lamb" (1866, p. 43). Spooner added, "The management and selection of any breed of sheep must after all become a matter of pounds, shillings, and pence" (1874, p. 137).

In 1867, a confederation of British colonies in North America created Canada, with four provinces: New Brunswick, Nova Scotia, Ontario, and Quebec. This was the first country given dominion status. Also in 1867, the Italian bell-tower or campanile-style chimney of India Mill (Exhibit 22.13) was completed in Darwen, Lancashire. It was the tallest and most expensive in the country. The mill became home to thousands of spinning mules — an invention of Samuel Crompton as mentioned above — revolutionising the spinning industry worldwide. This mill kept working until 1991.

Between 1868 and 1880, Benjamin Disraeli (1804–1881) served twice as prime minister for Queen Victoria. As were numerous entrepreneurs of the day, Benjamin Disraeli was of Jewish background (Macknight, 1854) and a member of the above-mentioned Bevis Marks Synagogue in London (Blake, 1966); Britain's Jewish community, the

Exhibit 22.13 Chimney of India Mill; photo © 2017 Léo-Paul Dana.

oldest non-Christian faith group in the kingdom, was very active in trade. In 1868, Queen Victoria gave Benjamin's wife — Mary Anne Disraeli (1792–1872) — the title of Viscountess Beaconsfield. On the suggestion of the prime minister, Queen Victoria adopted the title Empress of India, in 1876.

Located at 122 Cheetham Hill Road, in Manchester, the purpose-built Manchester New Synagogue was completed in 1889 with turrets. The building has been converted for business use and its turrets have been removed (Exhibit 22.14).

Queen Victoria's grandson Albert Victor, Duke of Clarence and Avondale (1864–1892) — son of Albert Edward, Prince of Wales, and Alexandra of Denmark — died engaged to Mary of Teck (1867–1953). The following year, his younger brother George Frederick Ernest Albert (1865–1936) — later George V — married Mary of Teck.

Tower Bridge (Exhibit 22.15) was opened in 1894. It is a symbol of Victorian engineering ingenuity.

Exhibit 22.14 Former synagogue; photo © 2017 Léo-Paul Dana.

Exhibit 22.15 Tower Bridge; photo © 2017 Léo-Paul Dana.

Despite industrialisation and urbanisation, agriculture remained important for the economy. Malden wrote about the sheep business in late 19th century England, "The time to buy is when there is a fair chance of profit, and not when there is little likelihood of gain. The skill of the farmer comes in buying at the right time; he must watch the markets closely, and buy in accordance with the trade … " (1899, p. 3). While some things stayed constant, others changed. Comparing sheep herding in England with the same occupation in Scotland, Malden elaborated, "the terms used to distinguish older sheep are becoming more or less obsolete; but in Scotland and in hill districts generally, where the feeding is not so much forced, the distinguishing terms are still required as much as ever" (1899, p. 28).

In the cities, entrepreneurial activity among Jewish immigrants was accelerated at the turn of the 20th century. Godley (2001) suggested that this was a result of social capital coupled with the Jews' emphasis on righteous behaviour, trust, relationship, and reputation.

When Queen Victoria died, in 1901, her son Albert Edward (1841–1910) became Edward VII, king and emperor (Exhibit 22.16). As his first son Albert Victor (1864–1892) had died, the second son, George Frederick Ernest Albert, became heir apparent who would become George V.

Wrightson observed change in rural England at the beginning of the 20th century, "There is genuine poetry in pastoral life which it would be sad to lose. Nevertheless, agricultural science and literature are between them rapidly taking the romance out of it … It is a pity … only to think of the price of mutton and of wool, or of lambs as fore and hind quarters … The sweetness of pastoral life is going. It is disappearing under the influence of commercial enterprise, the spread of science, and the difficulties of competition" (1905, p. 1).

Along the Leeds to Liverpool Canal, the Trencherfield Mill (Exhibit 22.17) was built in 1907, for the cotton spinning enterprise William Woods & Son Ltd. In 1941, the facility was used to make munitions for the war effort.

Change was also taking place overseas. In 1901, Australia became a dominion when its states united as the Commonwealth of Australia. In 1907, the colonies of New Zealand (facing the

Exhibit 22.16 Edward VII; photo © 2017 Léo-Paul Dana.

Pacific Ocean) and of Newfoundland (with shores on the Atlantic Ocean) and were granted dominion status. At the junction of the Atlantic and the Indian Ocean, the Union of South Africa became a dominion in 1910.

When, in 1910 Edward VII died, his son George became George V, King of the United Kingdom of Great Britain and Ireland and the British Dominions and Emperor of India. Mary of Teck thus became Queen Mary, and their son David (1894–1972) the heir apparent — later Edward VIII.

Exhibit 22.17 Trencherfield Mill; photo © 2017 Léo-Paul Dana.

Exhibit 22.18 Windsor Castle; photo © 2017 Léo-Paul Dana.

In August 1914, the British found themselves at war with Germany, and declared war on the Ottoman Empire in November that year. By 1917, anti-German sentiment led George V to replace his family name — Saxe-Coburg-Gotha — by the name Windsor, after the castle of the same name. With the River Thames in the background, Exhibit 22.18 shows Windsor Castle; from left to right: the Lower Ward; the Middle Ward and Round Tower; and the Upper Ward with the Long Walk.

In 1917, Tsar Nicholas II (1868–1918) lost the Russian Empire; the German Empire of his first cousin Kaiser Wilhelm II (1859–1941) collapsed with World War I. In contrast, their first cousin George V fared well, gaining mandates over protectorates such as Palestine, as a result of the war (see Dana, 2000a). Jan Christiaan Smuts (1870–1950), who obtained dominion status for the new Union of South Africa (later the Republic of South Africa), suggested that the British Empire be known as the British Commonwealth of Nations (Underwood, 1943).

Meanwhile, in 1918, British women aged over 30 were admitted to the franchise — provided they met a property qualification. In 1921, following the Anglo-Irish Treaty that ended the Anglo-Irish war and concluded the partition of Ireland, Londonderry (Exhibit 22.19) became a border city.

Elizabeth Bowes-Lyon (1900–2002) — a daughter of Claude George Bowes-Lyon (1855–1944), 14th Earl of Strathmore and Kinghorne — spent much of her childhood at Glamis Castle (Exhibit 22.20), the earl's ancestral home in Scotland. In 1923, she was engaged to Albert Frederick Arthur George Windsor, Duke of York, (1895–1952) — later George VI. She thus became Duchess of York — later known as Queen Elizabeth and finally as the Queen Mother. The couple had two daughters: (i) Elizabeth Alexandra Mary Windsor (1926–) who would become Queen Elizabeth II; and (ii) Margaret (1930–2002) who was born at Glamis Castle. Fergus Michael Claude Bowes-Lyon (1928–1987) — 17th Earl of Strathmore

Exhibit 22.19 Londonderry, Northern Ireland; photo © 2017 Léo-Paul Dana.

Exhibit 22.20 Glamis Castle, Scotland; photo © 2017 Léo-Paul Dana.

and Kinghorne (Exhibit 22.21) — was a nephew of Elizabeth Bowes-Lyon and cousin of Queen Elizabeth II.

Fyfe wrote, "If anyone who had known England ... in 1885, had chanced to return in 1920, he would have ... found an entirely new class of rich people setting the standards of extravagant living. He would have sought in vain for the owners of many of the historic houses which had been the centres of aristocratic influence ... he would have seen installed ... families ... who had made fortunes in industry or business" (1922, p. 1994).

Exhibit 22.21 Fergus Michael Claude Bowes-Lyon.

Exhibit 22.22 1951 Bedford; photo © 2017 Léo-Paul Dana.

Innes (1922) reported that England produced a fifth of the world's coal. Scotland and Wales also produced considerable coal. In 1925, General Motors took over Vauxhall. This allowed great expansion in production of Vauxhall vehicles, including Bedford trucks (Exhibit 22.22).

Prior to the Statute of Westminster, the British parliament could legislate for the dominions — Australia, Canada, the Irish Free State, New Zealand, Newfoundland, and South Africa. As of 1931, the statue prevented laws from being passed in the United Kingdom for any dominion, without the request of that dominion.

The United Kingdom had three kings in 1936. When George V died in January 1936, David, Prince of Wales, became Edward VIII — but he abdicated, in December of that same year (Gibbs, 1937), to marry Mrs Wallis Warfield Simpson (1896–1986). After this abdication, Edward VIII was given the title Duke of Windsor. His brother Albert, the Duke of York, was proclaimed George VI and his Duchess became Queen Elizabeth while their elder daughter became heir presumptive to become Queen Elizabeth II — presumptive

Exhibit 22.23 Made in Scotland; photo © 2017 Léo-Paul Dana.

because "she could only succeed presuming that no heir apparent, a brother, were born" (Lacey, 1977, p. 89).

Between the world wars, the North British Locomotive Company of Glasgow thrived as the largest locomotive builder in Europe. This firm had been created in 1903 by the merger of three enterprises: (i) Dubs and Company at the Queen's Park Works in Polmadie; (ii) Neilson, Reid and Company at the Hyde Park Works; and (iii) Sharp, Stewart and Company Limited at the Atlas Works in Springburn. North British Locomotive N°24,559 (Exhibit 22.23) was built in 1939 and given Road N°1,236.

When the Nazis invaded Poland in 1939, the United Kingdom declared war on Germany. In 1940, the Nazis bombed Buckingham Palace. Thomas (1991) focused on the eight months early during World War II when the Nazis bombed London. This city was also attacked in 1944 and 1945 by V1 flying bombs and V2 rockets.

Hutchison (1943) reported on Scotland during the war. Hutchison (1944) reported on Wales during war.

During the war years, Manchester's Lower Campfield Market (Exhibit 22.24), — originally opened in 1882 — was used for making blimps for defence. The United Kingdom joined the United

Exhibit 22.24 Former market; photo © 2017 Léo-Paul Dana.

Nations in October 1945. Hutchison (1946) provided an account of post-war Scotland.

In 1947, India and Pakistan obtained their independence from the United Kingdom. Also that year, a nephew of Louis Mountbatten, 1st Earl of Burma (1900–1979), namely Corfu-born Philip of Greece (1921–) — born Philippos Andreou of Schleswig-Holstein-Sonderberg-Glücksburg, son of Prince Andrew of Greece (1882–1944) and Princess Alice of Battenberg (1885–1969) — was naturalised British, with the name Philip Mountbatten. In November 1947, Philip married his third cousin Princess Elizabeth, the elder daughter of George VI.

Princess Elizabeth was in Kenya when her father died. Hemsing wrote, "The most famous visitor of all was a young English girl who arrived on an evening in February 1952 to spend the night at Treetops with her husband. She climbed into the tree one day a Princess, and climbed down the next morning Queen Elizabeth II — her father, George VI had died during the night" (1974, p. 10). Morton (1953) provided coverage of her coronation that took place in 1953.

Also in 1953, Queen Elizabeth II knighted Prime Minister Winston Churchill (1874–1965) who had led the British to victory during World War II. His leadership did not long outlast the war, however, for the next election brought in a Labour government, architects of a welfare state — but in 1951, Churchill was re-elected. Rationing continued until 1954. Churchill was 81 when he retired, in 1955 (McAllister, 2002).

Replacing the name Windsor, in February 1960, Mountbatten-Windsor was proclaimed the surname for male descendants of Queen Elizabeth II who did not have a royal title. The official name of the royal family remained Windsor.

During the 1960s, Leyland was the oldest British manufacturer that was focusing on commercial vehicles. In 1961, it acquired Triumph and diversified into automobiles, while continuing to produce successfully-exported electric-powered trolley-buses (Exhibit 22.25). In 1966, Leyland merged with another automobile manufacturer, Rover. The belief was that bigger was better, but within a few years the firm was seeking a government bailout.

In July 1969, a few days after Georges Pompidou (1911–1974) became president of France, and a couple of weeks before Apollo 11 departed for the moon, Queen Elizabeth II crowned her eldest son Charles Philip Arthur George (1948–), Prince of Wales at a ceremony at Caernarfon Castle.

The Bolton Committee commissioned 18 research reports covering a variety of topics related to small firms in the United Kingdom. Released in late 1971, the seminal Bolton Report influenced small enterprise research in the United Kingdom.

In 1973, Queen Elizabeth's daughter Princess Anne (1950–) married Mark Phillips (1948–). When the couple wanted to purchase an estate in Gloucestershire, Mark's annual salary of approximately £4,000 was insufficient. Although the monarch provided help, Mark was left with a mortgage. Becoming a self-employed farmer, he told the press, "I promised the Queen I would make a profit."

Prime Minister Edward Heath (1916–2005) was able to persuade the public that membership in the European Economic Community was in their interest, and a majority voted for it in the referendum of 1975. During the late 1970s, economic growth came to a standstill and entrepreneurship was the viewed as a way out of

Exhibit 22.25 1962 Leyland; photo © 2017 Léo-Paul Dana.

economic malaise. The New Enterprise Programme was a series of courses and seminars aimed at the potential entrepreneur. The first was held at Manchester Business School in 1977.

In May 1979, Margaret Thatcher (1925–2013) became prime minister. It was the first time a British woman obtained that position. Her government introduced tax advantages with the expectation that the self-employed would work harder; however, actual hours worked dropped as people worked less once their monetary goals were attained. As of 1980, economic policies gave importance to small firms (Storey, 1994), and a programme of privatisation of state assets ensued.

In 1981, the Prince of Wales married Lady Diana Spencer (1961–1997). Dempster and Evans wrote about Prince Charles, "Like his late great-uncle David, the Duke of Windsor, he had a weakness for other men's wives" (1993, p. 41). After the prince and princess were divorced, she died in a car crash in Paris. In 2005, Prince Charles married Camilla Parker Bowles (1947–) — née Camilla Rosemary Shand — great-granddaughter of Alice Keppel (1868–1947), a mistress of Edward VII.

Although later noted as being mainly pro-European, during the 1983 election campaign Tony Blair (1953–) announced that when the Labour Party would come to power it would negotiate withdrawal of the United Kingdom from the European Community. Much later, Sir Norman Fowler stated at the House of Commons: "the present Leader of the Opposition made a specific comment in his election manifesto in 1983, and I do not think the Labour party will be able to challenge this quotation: 'We'll negotiate withdrawal from the EEC which has drained our natural resources and destroyed jobs.'" (House of Commons Debate 9, March 1, 1995, Column 1094). Years after that, *The Telegraph*[2] reminded readers of Blair's election promise: "We will negotiate withdrawal from the EEC which has drained our natural resources and destroyed our jobs."

Vogel explained the desire for protectionism, "In countries where individualistic ideology is strongest, leaders believe that the open market will permit the most rapid adaptation by eliminating companies and sectors that are unable to compete ... However, in societies adhering to the strongest individualistic ideology and with democratic governments, the changes in international competition are now so great that there is a popular clamor for protectionism in declining sectors" (Vogel, 1987, p. 309).

Curran and Burrows (1988) presented a profile of small business owners and the self-employed, the majority of whom worked in con-

[2] *The Telegraph*, "Populist opportunism dressed as patriotism," May, 26, 2001.

struction and services. Also writing at that time, Khan (1988) emphasised that unlike the American environment in which the Minority Business Development Agency helped foster entrepreneurship, the United Kingdom had no similar government agency.

The self-employment rate in the United Kingdom peaked[3] during the early 1990s with approximately 14% of working people being self-employed (Carter and Jones-Evans, 2006). Although the state provided financial, managerial and technical assistance, Westhead and Birley observed skewness in job creation by owner-managed firms and remarked, "only a few provide significant employment" (1995, p. 26). The Scotland Act of 1998 reinstated the Scottish Parliament, allowing the Scots some self-governance within the United Kingdom.

Due to the global financial crisis, a long period of economic growth came to a halt in 2008. The United Kingdom economy was particularly affected by the crisis. Years later, the United Kingdom was still recovering from the deepest recession it had experienced since the 1930s, along with a significant budget deficit.

Binder, Martin, and Coad (2013) found that individuals who moved from regular employment into self-employment experienced an increase in life satisfaction. In a 2014 referendum, Scotland rejected independence from the United Kingdom.

Kelley, Singer, and Herrington (2016) noted that the United Kingdom reported among the highest entrepreneurial employee activity rates. They also observed that although few people were starting businesses, those who were doing so were more likely to state their products or services were innovative.

In June 2016, England and Wales voted for the United Kingdom to leave the European Union (Brexit). In contrast, Scotland voted to remain by 62% and Northern Ireland voted to remain by 56%. As a whole, 52% of voters in the United Kingdom opted for Brexit. In October, Prime Minister Theresa May (1956–) declared she would invoke Article 50 of the Lisbon Treaty by the end of March, 2017,

---

[3] In 2015, the rate reached 15.0% before dropping slightly in early 2016.

for the United Kingdom to leave the union — a move referred to as the world's most complex divorce.

The Environment for Entrepreneurship

Research about entrepreneurship and small business in the United Kingdom is relatively mature, given that this topic has been extensively researched as early as Marshall (1919). This section shall therefore be limited, and far from exhaustive, its primary objective being to provide the reader with a few leads into the very rich literature.

Casson and Godley (2010a) provided an overview of entrepreneurship in Britain from 1830 to 1900. Godley (2001) suggested that Victorian culture contained anti-entrepreneurial values that stifled economic growth. Casson and Godley (2010b) elaborated on entrepreneurship in Victorian Britain. Godley and Casson (2010) provided a history of entrepreneurship during the 20th century in Britain.

Curran and Stanworth (1982) provided a statistical map of the small enterprise sector and Curran and Burrows (1988) presented a national profile of small business owners and the self-employed. A seminal study, Blackburn and Smallbone (2008) charted the development of the field in the United Kingdom, observing its policy orientation. Among many, Curran (2000), and Curran and Storey (2002) examined small business policy in the United Kingdom.

Over the years, numerous aspects of entrepreneurship and its environment were empirically investigated across the United Kingdom, with great variety as to focus. Birley (1985) discussed training introduced to potential entrepreneurs in Manchester. Birley, Cromie, and Myers (1991) studied entrepreneurial networks in Northern Ireland. Burrows 1991 analysed the British petty bourgeoisie, a term used to include the self-employed, whether with or without employees. Mason, Pinch, and Storey (1991) focused on self-employment in Southampton. Hitchens and O'Farrell (1991) compared small manufacturers, 44 in England with 46 in Wales. Marlow (1992) looked at the take-up of business growth training schemes. Rosa, Carter, and Hamilton (1996) examined gender as a determinant of small business performance. Carter and Rosa (1998) focused on farms. Westhead, Wright, and Ucbasaran (2001) examined the internationalisation of new small firms across the United Kingdom. Drakopoulou Dodd, Jack, and Anderson (2002) looked at Scottish entrepreneurial networks. Blackburn (2003) considered innovation in small firms. Williams (2006) investigated the underground economy. Deakins *et al.* (2007), explored the complex and diverse role of social capital in Scotland. Palmer (2007) revisited Britalian entrepreneurs — the subject of his 1972 dissertation. Hamilton, Dana, and Benfell (2008) examined cultural change within families of immigrant entrepreneurs in Manchester. Honig and Dana (2008) looked at entrepreneurial demise in Scotland. Wheeler, Ibeh, and Dimitratos (2008) focused on exports from the United Kingdom. McEvoy and Hafeez (2009) described the regional distribution of five entrepreneurial minorities in England and Wales. Gurău, Lasch, and Dana (2010), focused on human capital in the United Kingdom. Vignali, Robinson, and Vignali (2010) compared Catholics of Lancashire with Jews of Yorkshire. Smallbone, Kitching and Athayde (2010) studied aspects related to competitiveness in London. Jack *et al.* (2010) revisited networking in Scotland. Williams (2011) focused on entrepreneurship and the informal economy in England. Gurău, Dana, and Lasch (2012) studied academic entrepreneurship in the United Kingdom. Smith and McElwee (2013) focused on criminal activity in Scotland. Mason *et al.* (2015) examined high growth firms in Scotland.

Among the earliest powerful forces to shape the environment for entrepreneurship were guilds. Flinn described the Medieval English town, "its occupants were all free men not subject to any lord ... inhabitants were engaged directly or indirectly, principally in industry and trade ... " (1961, p. 24). He elaborated, "one group, the merchants, have invariably become the most powerful by virtue of their grater wealth. Nor have they hesitated to use this power to protect and further their own interests, an action which took the form from the early Middle Ages of an association of traders in each town ... the *Gild Merchant.* Loose forms of gilds of this type appeared in England shortly after the Norman Conquest ... the primary aim of the Gold

Merchant was to restrict competition. This took the form of restricting the right to buy or sell within the town. Membership of a Gild Merchant was not easily obtained" (Flynn, 1961, pp. 26–27). Mumford (1938) explained that from the 16th century on, new monopolies issued in England were not town monopolies but trade monopolies.

Unlike traders on the continent, those in the British Isles often depended on the sea. Harbour boards enhanced the environment for entrepreneurship, by formalising the maintenance and administration of ports. Since its establishment in 1606, the Dover Harbour Board has been developing resources ahead of demand. Dover — 35 kilometres from Calais, France — remains a vital international gateway for passengers and trade. Dover and its chalk cliffs are visible in Exhibit 22.26.

Banks were also important players shaping the environment. In 1694, the establishment of the Bank of England made credit generally easier to obtain than was the case in continental Europe. Whereas the continent was highly regulated, the relative lack of trade barriers between England, Scotland and Wales facilitated trade within Great Britain.

Around the world, governments issue currency. In Scotland, banknotes are issued by the Bank of Scotland, the Clydesdale Bank,

Exhibit 22.26 Dover and its white cliffs; photo © 2017 Léo-Paul Dana.

Exhibit 22.27 Issued by the Clydesdale Bank; photo © 2017 Léo-Paul Dana.

and the Royal Bank of Scotland. Reid (1938) provided a rich history of the Clydesdale Bank; see Exhibit 22.27 for a sample banknote.

With the Industrial Revolution, inventors further shaped the environment. In 1763, Scotsman James Watt (1736–1819) invented the steam engine. Three inventors were responsible for the mechanisation of spinning. James Hargreaves (circa 1720–1778) invented the spinning jenny in 1764. Richard Arkwright (1732–1792) patented the water frame in 1769, and Samuel Crompton (1753–1827) combined the two, creating the spinning mule.

The Industrial Revolution and the factory system changed the environment for the textile industry — initially powered by water, and by steam from the 1820s. Supple wrote, "the British economy ... initiated the Industrial Revolution, without direct intervention of the state ... on the basis of market forces" (1983, p. 173).

Technological advances were shaping the environment for entrepreneurship more so than was the government. In 1771, Richard Arkwright (1732–1792) built the first modern factory producing yarn in England. The steam engine was brought into successful use in 1776 (Innes, 1922).

During the 18th century, landlords "enclosed scattered holdings into compact farms, had introduced new rotational systems based on the use of root-crops, and had greatly increased the size and weight of animals by selective breeding. Such practices became more widespread during the Napoleonic Wars, and enabled England not only to survive the French blockade but to feed a population that grew threefold, from 6,000,000 to 18,000,000 during the century 1750–1850" (Burnett, 1969, p. 10).

Burnett wrote, "By the 1840s, steam-ploughs and steam-threshers were coming to replace the labour of man, manure and artificial fertilisers ... were enriching the soil and increasing yields, while the drainage of heavy clay lands, made possible by the mass-production of non-porous pipes, was bringing ever more land under the plough. Altogether these changes meant a fundamental break with the past and a new concept of landownership for profit rather than pleasure" (1969, p. 10).

Burnett elaborated about the 19th century environment: "Britain ... had certain natural elements which favoured her early industrialisation — coal and iron in great quantity and easily accessible, an old-established cloth industry which supplied a basis of organisational knowledge and experience, a vast colonial market for her goods, a developed banking system and a political structure that encouraged freedom and individual initiative" (1969, pp. 11–12). Industrialisation came at a price, however, as mining for coal scarred the countryside.

On a positive note, coal enabled the development of an unprecedented transportation infrastructure, and this facilitated enterprise. In 1830, Liverpool Road Station in Manchester was opened for train travellers. In London, London Bridge station was opened in 1836 and Euston in 1837. In Manchester, Victoria Station, at Long Millgate, was built in 1844. In 1847, several important lines, including the Manchester and Leeds Railway, merged to create the Lancashire and Yorkshire Railway. In London, Liverpool Street Station (Exhibit 22.28) was built in 1874. Manchester's Victoria Station was enlarged in 1909 (Exhibit 22.29). Casson (2009a) analysed the efficiency of the Victorian British railway network.

In 1873, Butler's Wharf warehouse complex (Exhibit 22.30) was completed, on the River Thames. It included the largest tea warehouse in the world. Cinnamon, grain, rubber, sugar tapioca and tea were traded here. In Manchester, the wholesale fish market (Exhibit 22.31) opened that year.

Exhibit 22.28 Liverpool Street Station; photo © 2017 Léo-Paul Dana.

Infrastructure for international trade was further enhanced in 1875 when — with money borrowed from Lionel Nathan de Rothschild (1808–1879) — Prime Minister Benjamin Disraeli was instrumental in the purchase from Egypt of £4 million worth of shares in the Suez Canal (Dempster and Evans, 1993). This gave the British control of the canal, thereby safeguarding the water route to India. The United Kingdom was to enjoy this freedom until 1956.

Changes in the banking industry also affected the environment for entrepreneurship. In 1878, the collapse of the City of Glasgow Bank ruined local entrepreneurs. This collapse sent shock waves as far as Latin America and the South Pacific (Hunter, 2007). In 1890, the Liverpool Union Bank — established in 1835 to serve the needs of local merchants and brokers associated with the Port of Liverpool — opened a branch at 92 London Road, in Liverpool (Exhibit 22.32). This bank merged into Lloyds in 1900. Barclay and Company Limited was the result of 20 small private family banks joining together in 1896; their Newtown branch, in Wales, dates back to 1899 (Exhibit 22.33).

Exhibit 22.29 Victoria Station, Manchester; photo © 2017 Léo-Paul Dana.

Communications technology also shaped the environment for entrepreneurship. In 1898, Queen Victoria invited Guglielmo Marconi (1874–1937) the Italian entrepreneur who invented the wireless telegraph (see Chapter 12 in this volume) to set up his system in London. With this, he communicated that year from England to France. In 1901, he received the first telegraphic message across the Atlantic. Telegrams would soon become instrumental in international business transactions.

Exhibit 22.30 Butler's Wharf; photo © 2017 Léo-Paul Dana.

Exhibit 22.31 Opened 1873; photo © 2017 Léo-Paul Dana.

Exhibit 22.32 London Road, Liverpool; photo © 2017 Léo-Paul Dana.

As more merchandise was traded, facilities were built for storing goods. In Manchester, the Great Northern Railway Company Goods Station was completed in 1899 — later known as Deansgate Goods Station. Its warehouse (Exhibit 22.34) was redeveloped into a leisure complex starting in 1999.

World War II also affected enterprise. Klemmer wrote about England during the war noting, "Women also are being drawn rapidly into the industrial system" (1941, p. 534). The post-war years saw increased government involvement in the economy. Vogel wrote, "In the 1950s there was a very broad consensus between the Conservatives and mainstream Labour parties supporting a Keynesian stimulus to the economy ... and an extensive role for government planning so that inflation and recession could be avoided" (1987, p. 308). Yet, inflation and recession were not avoided.

Krieger provided an update, "By the 1970s, however, international pressures and growing divisions within domestic political alliances (notably between the Labour Party and the trade union movement) reduced cohesion and heightened ideological ambivalence ... In the 1970s economic growth slowed, and a welfare state consensus that had spanned party identities came undone" (1987, pp. 29–38).

Exhibit 22.33 Barclays in Newtown, Wales; photo © 2017 Léo-Paul Dana.

Migration also prompted change — welcome by some but not by others; for instance, Fisher wrote, "Foreign invasions are changing the face of London, where Middle Eastern garb is a common sight and American fast-food restaurants proliferate" (1979, p. 447).

Ethnic minorities have been important in the United Kingdom's small business sector. Among a multitude of studies are: Barrett and McEvoy (2007); Jones, Ram, and Edwards (2007); Smallbone,

Exhibit 22.34 Completed in 1899; photo © 2017 Léo-Paul Dana.

Ram, and Deakins (2007), Ward and Jenkins (1984), and (Werbner, 2007).

Zwingle wrote about the docks, east of the Tower of London (Exhibit 22.35), at the Isle of Dogs (Exhibit 22.36), "Between 1967 and 1981 commercial pressures forced the docks to close, and shipping moved downstream to Tilbury, where it could be more competitive" (1991, p. 36). This area has been redeveloped as the Docklands.

Whereas in the past, the United Kingdom focused on trade with its colonies and former colonies, in 1973, the United Kingdom joined the European Economic Community (EEC), henceforth engaging in free trade with countries of Europe. For members of the British Commonwealth — a voluntary association of independent sovereign states, each responsible for its own policies, consulting and cooperating in the common interest — entry by the United Kingdom into the EEC was seen as a problem.

SMEs gained importance during the 1980s. Curran described the United Kingdom's "headlong plunge" (1986, p. 54) into a policy of discrimination, in favour of SMEs. Regardless, the growth of imports threatened domestic firms, large and small. Chell and Haworth

Exhibit 22.35 Tower of London; photo © 2017 Léo-Paul Dana.

Exhibit 22.36 The Isle of Dogs; photo © 2017 Léo-Paul Dana.

(1992) noted growing imports and expressed concern about the impact on the clothing manufacturing industry in the United Kingdom.

A rich body of literature developed on inward and outward internationalisation. Crick (2004) and Hall and Tu (2004) provided overviews of internationalisation in the United Kingdom. Sear and Hamilton (2004) focused on internationalisation of English firms.

Danson *et al.* (2008) examined the case of Scotand. Pickernell *et al.* (2008) studied the internationalisation of Welsh SMEs.

Vogel explained the impact of labour disputes. He wrote, "In the United Kingdom, where individualism ... dominates, cleavages between management and labor, and between different social classes, have led to serious strikes that have hindered prompt response to economic adversity. These difficulties have been greatly exacerbated by England's loss of its colonies, and the decline of its geopolitical influence and its economic competitiveness" (1987, p. 308). This is technically incorrect as it was not England that lost colonies, but rather the United Kingdom.

Clark and Drinkwater (2010) observed falling rates of self-employment among Chinese and Indians in the United Kingdom. Although those authors suggested that this was due to increased opportunities in paid employment, it can be argued that this was only a partial explanation and that the crucial point is generational transition. British-raised and educated members of the Chinese and Indian communities understand the way United Kingdom society and its economy and job-market function — better than did their overseas-born parents. Furthermore, educational qualifications help the new generation exploit this knowledge.

The oil boom contributed to Aberdeen (Exhibit 22.37) — also known as Granite City, because of its many granite buildings — being ranked the British city best placed in 2011 to grow out of the downturn. It was ranked second of 63 cities for employment and identified as having a good private business base. The city has since dropped to 10th in the 2016 Good Growth for Cities index, which measures the performance of 42 United Kingdom cities.

Young (2013) made policy recommendations for enterprises employing fewer than 25 people. This suggested the establishment of a Supporting Small Business Charter with an award scheme to incentivise business schools to work with small firms, in an advisory capacity and through helping place students with small businesses. The same report also proposed a growth vouchers programme and growth loans, as well as start-up loans.

Exhibit 22.37 Aberdeen, Scotland; photo © 2017 Léo-Paul Dana.

In December 2013, "the United Kingdom Government launched the scheme Small Business: GREAT Ambition in December 2013 — a series of measures designed to make it easier for small businesses to expand which dovetail into the national initiative" (Herrington, 2016, p. 41). In 2014, Small Business Charter (SBC) brought together business schools and SMEs across the United Kingdom to create sustainable growth. In 2017 Leeds was the fastest growing city in the United Kingdom. The city's Kirkgate Market (Exhibit 22.38) is the largest indoor market in Europe — a base for several hundred entrepreneurs.

Toward the Future

Beresford wrote, "The UK economy today is largely driven by the service industry, though manufacturing still accounts for around 10% of GDP, which totalled $2.5 trillion in 2013. Agriculture is highly mechanized and intensive, growing around 60% of the UK's food" (2016, p. 246).

With reference to the earliest stage of entrepreneurship, nascent entrepreneurship, Braunerhjelm *et al.* (2015) observed that while the

Exhibit 22.38 Kirkgate Market, Leeds; photo © 2017 Léo-Paul Dana.

United States dominated with almost 10% of the adult population involved in setting up a business, the United Kingdom ranked second. This may seem rosy, but is no reason to be complacent. The same study observed entrepreneurship becoming increasingly prevalent among the elderly. It also reported that relatively more men in the United Kingdom were starting their businesses out of necessity. Future research might investigate the causal variables. Are senior men being pushed to self-employment to cope with rising prices?

Hart, Bonner, and Levie (2016) also discussed positive observations, e.g., that 9.6% of working age adults expected to start a business within the following three years — similar to that observed in Germany (9.2%). They nevertheless identified deficiencies too. For instance, 4.0% of the adult population in the United Kingdom were nascent entrepreneurs actively trying to start a business in 2015, but this was significantly less than the rate in 2014 and less than half the 8.3% in the United States. The same study observed that the opportunity Total Early-stage Entrepreneurial Activity (TEA) was down significantly from 7.0% in 2014 to 5.3% in 2015. It also revealed that the start-up skills perception rate in the United Kingdom was down from 38.4% in 2014 to 37.5% in 2015, while the rate in Germany remained stable and that in the United States increased by 3%. The gap in skills perception between the United Kingdom and the United States thus widened to 10% points. Future research might investigate this further — identifying what might be learned from the American experience.

With Brexit events evolving, timing is ideal for future research focusing on the impact of Brexit on new venture creation, failure rates of SMEs and related issues. New opportunities for research are likely to arise as events unfold.

Chapter 23

Entrepreneurship in Western Europe

Toward an Understanding of Overlapping Layers

Entrepreneurship is a vast field — with bankers, developers, engineers, industrialists and inventors — as discussed in the preceding chapters. The organ grinder illustrated in Chapter 1, Alexandre-Gustave Eiffel (1832–1923) whose tower is shown in Chapter 7, Lars Magnus Ericsson (1846–1926) mentioned in Chapter 20, Frankfurt-born Nathan Mayer Rothschild (1777–1836) discussed in Chapter 22, and the musician in Exhibit 23.1 all share in common, the fact that each of them created his own job. Yet, there is significant variation with regards to the scope of their respective enterprises.

Some individuals seek to make their firms grow. Others supplement their salary or pension with part-time self-employment. Among the Sámi people, reindeer herding is a culturally attractive occupation that pulls many to self-employment, but some are pushed — out of economic need — to also seek employment for the purpose of supplementing meagre revenue from herding.

In addition to the above differences at the micro-level, the preceding chapters have shown that entrepreneurship varies greatly at the macro level. The phenomenon is greatly influenced by context — including historically rooted values, as well as a variety of regulatory conditions. Chan and Justis (1992) correctly predicted the importance

Exhibit 23.1 Self-employed; photo © 2017 Léo-Paul Dana.

of cultural differences in Europe, with local preferences over a "pan-European" (1992, p. 85) ideal. As suggested by Braunerhjelm *et al.* "there is no one-size-fits-all avenue for making individuals aware of entrepreneurial opportunities" (2015, p. 36).

At the macro-economic level, Europe is rich with contrasts. Tiny Monaco concentrates on high value-added activities. Large countries such as Finland and Sweden prosper from their natural resources. Norway and the United Kingdom dominate the oil and gas sector. Denmark focuses on sustainability.

On the European mainland, the Rhineland model has a strong focus on long-term relationships, employees are empowered, and firms are less steered by headquarters than is the case in the United Kingdom. Under the Nordic model, taxes are high in order to pay for social protection and universal welfare provision. Yet, distinctions are not water-tight.

Horizontal networking is widespread in Western Europe. In contrast, vertical networking is less visible in the north than it is in the south of Europe.

In former colonial powers, demographics reflect colonial history. Several countries have notable internal differences among their constituent regions. Iceland is relatively homogeneous.

As observed by Kaynak and Jallat, "Throughout history, Europe has been able to retain its multitude of cultures, varied social organizations, distinct forms of expression, and disparate modes of thought" (2004, p. 4). Yet, these do not necessarily follow national boundaries. Madrid's electronics sector is a complex web of interdependent firms; also in Spain, Catalonia has a hub-and-spoke structure, with sub-contractors ringed around larger firms.

History reveals that Europe is not simply the sum of discrete entities. Rather, Europe has been shaped by migrations, wars and changing borders, with fuzzy integration over time.

Different linguistic groups are artificially compressed within or split by modern state borders. Belgium's Wallonia is linguistically closer to France than to Belgium's Flanders.

Likewise cultural similarities cross borders. The Meuse-Rhine is a cross-border region of cooperation.

Furthermore, economic development is also affected by geography. The airport serving Basel, Switzerland, is physically in France.

Indeed, present-day geo-political divisions such as nation-states do not necessarily coincide with specific cultures or economic realities. Unlike the United States that can be described as a melting pot, or Canada that is a mosaic, Europe might best be described in terms of overlapping layers.

Observing the Trends

We know, from history, that Europe has always been in the process of changing. Immigration continues to change demographics. Occupational clustering evolves as members of minorities become self-employed (Ward and Jenkins, 1984). We continue to see coethnic solidarity, as did Boissevain and Grotenbreg (1987). Many entrepreneurs choose to operate in the large sector of grey market activity — the focus of Williams (2006) among others. Chains have accelerated the desertification of villages and the need for transport — causing a growing carbon footprint.

Simultaneously, younger overarching trends are evident. Although Charles de Gaulle (1890–1970) spoke of *L'Europe des Nations*, today it seems to make increasing sense to think of *l'Europe des Régions,* with regions gaining importance over nation-states. Findings confirm, "The New Europe is characterised by two overarching trends: (1) the reduced importance of the nation-state as the relevant unit around which international business activity is organized and collected; and (2) the diminishing importance of the stand-alone firm as the principal unit of business competition" (Dana, Bajramovic, and Wright, 2005, p. 102).

Inter-firm cooperation can overcome resource constraints faced by stand-alone firms; entrepreneurs have long cooperated to various degrees, depending on the context (Dana, 2000a). In the Occident, the shift from independence to interdependence and coopetition began accelerating in the late 20th century (Acs and Yeung, 1999; Lado, Boyd, and Hanlon, 1997; Lodge and Vogel, 1987). Today, Europe's emerging, highly specialised and competitive SMEs are qualitatively different from those of the 20th century.

Entrepreneurs often choose to operate in a cluster. As stated by Rocha and Sternberg, "Clusters are a richer industrial dimension than industrial agglomerations, including not only spatial proximity but also inter-organisational relations. Interaction is driven ... by interpersonal and associational relations among people and firms within the cluster. This interaction provides established relationships and complementary linkages, two differential mechanisms to start businesses that are not present in industrial agglomerations" (2005, p. 288).

Clustering facilitates access to role models, information, tacit knowledge, assistance, and skills. By providing a critical mass, clusters allow strong joint initiatives; by means of clustering and networking with other firms — that could otherwise be competitors — competitiveness is increased. As noted by Porter (1998a), clusters increase productivity in a geographic area; they drive innovation, and stimulate new venture creation. As discussed by Rocha (2004), clusters provide the synergy of geographic proximity, an inter-firm network, and an organisational or institutional network.

It is important to note, however, that clusters are not a new phenomenon; endowed with high quality clay, Saint Jean de Fos (near Montpellier) is known to have had a pottery cluster in the Middle Ages. What is new is their evolved sophistication. Clustered entrepreneurs are able to draw upon the pooled capabilities and knowledge stock of their entire cluster, instead of developing the required knowledge themselves. Many have documented the positive impact of clusters on entrepreneurship, including: Maskell and Malmberg (1999); Piore and Sable (1984); and Pyke, Becattini, and Sengenberger (1992).

Newer than clusters are the concepts of symbiotic marketing and coopetition. Subcontractors in Austria — united in the form of an association — have symbiotic relationships with other firms. Likewise, Finland's network of technology and science parks promotes symbiotic entrepreneurship, as do formal networks in Ireland and elsewhere. What we see is that the classic, independent entrepreneur of former times is yielding to increased cooperation and networking. This is important to recognise because entrepreneurs will require new strategies to help develop and maintain *network* capabilities, in addition to their own internal competencies. Whereas it used to be advantageous to compete for market share, at the expense of other firms, symbiotic entrepreneurship allows cooperating firms to enlarge the market size — with multiple firms benefitting. Such symbiotic entrepreneurship is especially useful in R&D management.

Also important is that the lack of cooperation has become an obstacle. Simões noted, "Many observers have pointed out the absence of a truly co-operative culture as one of the main obstacles to the competitiveness of Portuguese companies" (2004, p. 24).

Implications for Public Policy

Peterson (1988) described entrepreneurship policies as fitting into categories: (i) laissez-faire; (ii) a limited environmental approach; and (iii) strategic interventionism. During the late 1980s, scholars debated with regards to which of these was "better." It is clear now that policy should be context-specific in order to be effective. Unequal constraints in different regions of Europe make it impossible for a uniform policy to be applicable across the many cultures residing here. To be effective, policy will need to reflect local needs — often a function of cultural and historical context. As written by Smallbone, "Of course, there are good reasons why one would expect some variation between countries and regions in the types and strengths of policy intervention used, on the basis that the level of entrepreneurship itself can vary considerably between regions and between countries ... just as context is important for the study of entrepreneurship, it is also important for a study of entrepreneurship policy" (2016, pp. 3–8).

As argued by Ring *et al.* (2005), governments have a considerable impact on entrepreneurship. Smallbone concurred, "Whilst entrepreneurship results from the creativity, drive and skills of individuals, rather than from the actions of government, government policies and actions are a key influence on the external environment in which entrepreneurship takes place; in some cases constraining it, in others facilitating it" (2016, p. 2).

While many agree that a conducive environment fosters entrepreneurship, there is no consensus as to the optimal degree of regulation to enact and to enforce, such that the benefits to society exceed the costs of compliance. Mill (1869) argued that the only purpose for which power can be rightfully exercised over a member of society, against his will, is to prevent harm onto others. While some regulation is required to ensure order, excessive intervention is counter-productive; to benefit an economy, tax systems should reward success. McMillan explained, "decentralized — that is, market-based — decision-making is essential for economic success" (2002, p. 149). As stated by Blond and Pabst, "Only a radical decentralization of power and money can tie the universal hopes of the European project to each particular citizen. The EU should abandon centrally imposed determinations in favour of local discernment" (2005, p. 6). Indeed, to be effective, policies must be culturally sensitive.

Relevance is also importance. Rath and Swagerman observed, "At the moment, ethnic entrepreneurship is not an important part of the European integration policy for migrants" (2011, p. 96). Given recent immigration waves, ethnic entrepreneurship should be on the agenda. Governments should also include visible one-stop agencies for potential entrepreneurs, and the availability of microfinancing.

Toward Future Research

Chapter 1 mentioned that the making of wine varies from one country to another. In addition to relevant public policy that is not uniform, culture-induced regulation or tradition also come into play. Ribéreau-Gayon *et al.* explained, "Adjusting SO2 concentrations in wine raises many concerns. .... Today, French wines are under EC legislation ... 160 mg/l for most red wines and 210 mg/l for the majority of white wines ... In practice, the concentration used is even lower. For French white wines ... the average concentration is 105 mg/l; for red wines it is 75 mg/l ... In certain countries the regulation of sulphur dioxide dictates a common limit for all wines. For example, this value is 350 mg/l in the USA, in Canada, in Japan and in Australia" (Ribéreau-Gayon *et al.*, 2000, p. 180). Likewise, motivations for entrepreneurship vary, as do objectives. In terms of future research, there is no limit.

We see some convergence in Europe, largely on macro level issues. Technology is becoming increasingly similar. Yet, Europeans are maintaining cultural uniqueness, and entrepreneurship depends on cultural context. Different countries have differing levels of start-ups. Can this be partly explained by differences in perception of opportunities for entrepreneurship, and by motivation, both culturally influenced? Emirbayer and Goodwin observed that researchers have "inadequately theorized the causal role of ideals, beliefs, and values of the actors that strive to realize them, as a result it has neglected the cultural and symbolic moment in the very determination of social action" (1994, p. 1446). Likewise, Jagd noted, "most of network research has, in the tradition of social network theory, focused on structural aspects of networks leaving the cultural aspects of networks inadequately analysed" (2005, p. 47.) Future research might investigate the cultural causal variables behind networks.

Opportunities for future research were also identified in individual chapters. The impact of dissimilar entrepreneurship policy models can be compared. Research could focus on cultural variables, social capital and cultural capital, among contextual causal variables. Research could also compare different ethnic groups, including Swedes in Finland and the indigenous Sámi.

Another exciting topic for future research is the study of collective entrepreneurship, which has become important in France, among other places; as discussed in Chapter 7, this involves entrepreneurial individuals who enterprise together, with common resources. Regional differences are also fascinating, for example, contrasting areas of former East Germany with those of former West Germany. Also interesting is to understand the impact of religion on entrepreneurship, and to understand the impact of entrepreneurship on the environment.

Other relevant topics include the relationships between entrepreneurship and cooperation, corruption, outsourcing, sustainability, the undeclared economy, and interfirm relationships. As noted by Miles, Miles, and Snow, "because cooperative behaviour ultimately involves the pursuit of self-interest, it requires periodic or even continual assessment by each participant of the amount of trust and commitment of the other party" (1995, p. 40). Often, Western management puts much effort in monitoring a transaction. In contrast, where a strong relationship exists, problems can always be solved; in cooperative circles, it is more crucial to monitor a relationship than a transaction (Dana, 2000b).

References

Abercrombie, Thomas J. (1969), "Switzerland, Europe's High-rise Republic," *National Geographic 136* (1), pp. 68–113.

Abercrombie, Thomas J. (1995), "The Basques: Europe's First Family," *National Geographic 188* (5), November, pp. 74–97.

Abetti, Pier A., Joyce O'Connor, Lisa M. Ehid, Joseph L. Rocco, and Barry J. Sanders (1987), "A Tale of Two Parks: Key Factors Influencing the Location Decision Process of New Entrepreneurial Companies at Rensselaer (New York State) and Plassey (Ireland) Technology Parks," in Neil C. Churchill, John A, Hornaday, Bruce A. Kirchhoff, O. Jay Krasner, and Karl H. Vesper, Eds., *Frontiers of Entrepreneurship Research*, Wellesley, Massachusetts: Babson College, pp. 26–43.

Acs, Zoltan J., and Bernard Yeung (1999), "Entrepreneurial Discovery and the Global Economy," *Global Focus 11* (3), pp. 63–71.

Acs, Zoltan J., László Szerb, and Erkko Autio (2016), *Global Entrepreneurship and Development Index 2015*, London: Springer.

Adams, Harriet Chalmers (1929), "Barcelona, Pride of the Catalans," *National Geographic 55* (3), March, pp. 373–402.

Adler, Marcus Nathan (1907), *The Itinerary of Benjamin of Tudela: Critical Text, Translation and Commentary*, London: Oxford University Press.

Aðalsteinsson, Gylfi Dalmann, and Runólfur Amári Steinþórsson (2015), "LYSI in Iceland: Purifying the Gold of the Sea," in Godfrey Baldacchino, Ed., *Entrepreneurship in Small Island States and Territories*, New York and London: Routledge, pp. 154–163.

Alberoni, Francesco (2013), *Pietro Barilla: "Tutto è fatto per il futuro, andate avanti con coraggio," Biografia di un grande imprenditore*, Milan: Rizzoli.

Alderman, Liz (2013), "Italy's Travails Are Hitting Small Firms the Hardest," *International Herald Tribune*, 12 March, p. 1.

Aldrich, Howard E. (1999), *Organizations Evolving*, London: Sage.

Alsos, Gry Agnete, Tommy Høyvarde Clausen, Espen John Isaksen, Bjørn Willy Åmo, and Erlend Bullvåg (2014), *Entreprenørskap i Norge 2013*, Bodø: Handelshøgskolen i Bodø.

Alsos, Gry Agnete, Tommy Høyvarde Clausen, Espen John Isaksen, and Bjørn Willy Åmo (2015), *Entreprenørskap i Norge 2014*, Bodø: Handelshøgskolen i Bodø.

Amatori, Franco, and Andrea Colli (2004), "Entrepreneurship: The Italian Story," in Guido Corbetta, Morton Huse, and Davide Ravasi, Eds., *Crossroads of Entrepreneurship*, Boston: Kluwer Academic, pp. 243–261.

Anderson, Myrdene (1983), "Woman as Generalist, as Specialist, and as Diversifier in Saami Subsistence Activities," *Humboldt Journal of Social Relations 10* (2), Spring/Summer, pp. 175–197.

Anderson, Sally (1977), "Norway's Reindeer Lapps," *National Geographic 152* (3), September, pp. 364–379.

Andersson, Marlén, Carl Erik Nyvold, and Beate Rotefoss (2008), "Entrepreneurship Policy in Norway: Recent Developments," Anders Lundström, Ed., *Entrepreneurship Policy in the Nordic Countries: Perspectives of the Development Since 2003*, Oslo: Norden Nordic Innovation Centre, pp. 30–35.

Antonelli, Marta, and Chiara Corbo (2016), "Italy," in Wayne Visser, Ed., *The World Guide to Sustainable Enterprise, Volume 3 Europe*, Sheffield, United Kingdom: Greenleaf, pp. 139–145.

Apfelthaler, Gerhard, Thomas Schmalzer, Ursula Schneider, and Rene Wenzel (2008), *Global Entrepreneurship Monitor: Bericht 2007 zur Lage des Unternehmertums in Österreich*, Graz: FH Joanneum.

Arenius, Pia, Erkko Autio, and Anne Kovalainen (2004), *Global Entrepreneurship Monitor*, Espoo: Helsinki University of Technology.

Arenius, Pia, Erkko Autio, Anne Kovalainen, and Paul Davidson Reynolds (2001), *Global Entrepreneurship Monitor: 2001 Finnish Executive Report*, Espoo: Helsinki University of Technology.

Audretsch, David B., and Michael Fritsch (1994), "The Geography of Firms Births in Germany," *Regional Studies 28* (4), pp. 359–365.

Auster, Ellen, and Howard E. Aldrich (1984), "Small Business Vulnerability, Ethnic Enclaves and Ethnic Enterprise," in Robin Ward and Richard Jenkins, Eds., *Ethnic Communities in Business: Strategies for Economic Survival*, Cambridge: Cambridge University Press, pp. 39–54.

Austrian Institute for SME Research (1996), *Barrieren für potentielle Unternehmensgründer*, Vienna: Austrian Institute for SME Research.

Bachinger, Karl (1987), "Österreich 1918–1945," in Karl Bachinger, Hildegard Hemetsberger-Koller, and Herbert Mathis, Eds., *Grundriß der österreichischen Sozial- und Wirtschaftsgeschichte von 1848 bis zur Gegenwart*, Vienna: ÖBV.

Bagnasco, Arnaldo, and Marcello Messori (1975), *Tendenze dell'economia Periferica*, Turin: Editoriale Valentino.

Baldacchino, Godfrey (2005), "Successful Small-scale Manufacturing: A Comparative Assessment across Five European Island Regions," *Bank of Valletta Review 31*, pp. 17–31.

Baldegger, Rico J., Pascal Wild, Siegfried Alberton, and Fredrik Hacklin (2014), *Global Entrepreneurship Monitor 2014: Report on Switzerland*, Fribourg: Institute for Entrepreneurship and SMEs at the School of Management.

Baldegger, Rico J., Pascal Wild, Siegfried Alberton, and Fredrik Hacklin (2016), *Global Entrepreneurship Monitor 2015/2016: Report on Switzerland*, Fribourg: Institute for Entrepreneurship and SMEs at the School of Management.

Baldegger, Rico J., Pascal Wild, and Benoît Morel (2016), *Swiss International Entrepreneurship Survey 2016: Results of the Study on the Internationalization of Swiss SMEs*, Bern and Zurich: PostFinance Ltd and Bisnode D&B Switzerland.

Bamford, Julia (1987), "The Development of Small Firms, the Traditional Family and Agrarian Patterns in Italy," in Robert Goffee and Richard Scase, Eds., *Entrepreneurship in Europe: The Social Processes*, London: Croom Helm, pp. 12–25.

Baptista, Rui, and Peter Swann (1998), "Do Firms in Clusters Innovate More?" *Research Policy 27*, pp. 525–540.

Baptista, Rui, and A. Roy Thurik (2007), "The Relationship between Entrepreneurship and Unemployment: Is Portugal an Outlier?" *Technological Forecasting and Social Change 74*, pp. 75–89.

Barrett, Giles A., and David McEvoy (2007), "Temporal and Geographical Variations in Ethnic Minority Business: Thirty Years of Research in the United Kingdom," in Léo-Paul Dana, Ed., *Handbook of Research on Ethnic Minority Entrepreneurship: A Co-evolutionary View on Resource Management*, Cheltenham, United Kingdom: Edward Elgar, pp. 337–359.

Barth, Fredrik (1960), "Family Life in a Central Norwegian Mountain Community," in Thomas D. Eliot and Arthur Hillman, Eds., *Norway Families*, Philadelphia: University of Pennsylvania Press, pp. 81–107.

Barth, Fredrik, Ed., (1963), *The Role of the Entrepreneur in Social Change in Northern Norway*, Bergen: Årbok for Universitetet i Bergen.

Barth, Fredrik (1967), "On the Study of Social Change," *American Anthropologist 69* (6), December, pp. 661–669.

Barzini, Luigi (1987), *The Italians*, London: Hamish Hamilton.

Bastide, François-Régis (1954), *Suède*, Paris, France: Editions du Seuil.

Baycan-Levent, Tüzin, and Peter Nijkamp (2007), "Ethnic Minority Entrepreneurs in European Cities: A Comparative Study of Amsterdam," in Léo-Paul Dana, Ed., *Handbook of Research on Ethnic Minority Entrepreneurship: A Co-evolutionary View on Resource Management*, Cheltenham, United Kingdom: Edward Elgar, pp. 323–336.

Beach, Hugh (1990), "Comparative Systems of Reindeer Herding," in John G. Galaty and Douglas L. Johnson, Eds., *The World of Pastoralism: Herding Systems in Comparative Perspective*, New York: Guildford Press, pp. 253–298.

Beach, Hugh (1997), "Negotiating Nature in Swedish Lapland: Ecology and Economics of Saami Reindeer Management," in Eric Alden Smith and Joan McCarter, Eds., *Contested Arctic: Indigenous Peoples, Industrial States, and the Circumpolar Environment*, Seattle: University of Washington Press, pp. 122–149.

Becattini, Giacomo (2004), *Industrial Districts: A New Approach to Industrial Change*, Cheltenham, United Kingdom: Edward Elgar.

Becattini, Giacomo, Marco Bellandi, Babi Ottati, and Fabio Sforzi (2003), *From Industrial Districts to Local Development: An Itinerary of Research*, Cheltenham, United Kingdom: Edward Elgar.

Becker, Katharina, Franz Kronthaler, and Kerstin Wagner (2011), "The Entrepreneurship Potential within Swiss Regions: A Comparison Based on Cluster Analysis," in Mario Raposo, David Smallbone, Karoly Balaton and Lilla Hortovanyi, Eds., *Entrepreneurship, Growth and Economic Development: Frontiers in European Entrepreneurship Research*, Cheltenham, United Kingdom: Edward Elgar, pp. 180–204.

Bell, Jim, David Demick, Ian Callaghan, and Aidan O'Reilly (2004), "Irish Perspectives on Developing International Entrepreneurs," in Léo-Paul Dana, Ed., *Handbook of Research on International Entrepreneurship*, Cheltenham, United Kingdom: Edward Elgar, pp. 499–511.

Belletante, Bernard, Nadine Levratto, and Bernard Paranque (2001), *Diversité Economique et Modes de Financement des PMEs*, Paris: L'Harmattan.

Belshaw, Cyril S. (1955), "The Cultural Milieu of the Entrepreneur: A Critical Essay," *Explorations of Entrepreneurial History* 7 (3), February, pp. 146–163.

Belt, Don (1993), "Sweden: In Search of a New Model," *National Geographic* 184 (2), August, pp. 2–35.

Ben Aoun-Peltier, Leïla, Peter R. Höck, Chiara Peroni, and Cesare A. F. Riillo (2015), *Global Entrepreneurship Monitor: Luxembourg 2014*, Luxembourg: Institut National de la Statistique et des Etudes Economiques.

Benoit, Bertrand (2004), "Growing Apart: 15 Years After the Wall's Fall, Germany's Two Halves Diverge," *Financial Times*, Thursday, September 23, p. 11.

Beresford, James (2016), "United Kingdom," in Wayne Visser, Ed., *The World Guide to Sustainable Enterprise, Volume 3 Europe*, Sheffield, United Kingdom: Greenleaf, pp. 246–253.

Berggren, Björn, and Lars Silver (2010), "Financing Entrepreneurship in Different Regions: The Failure to Decentralise Financing to Regional Centres in Sweden," *Journal of Small Business and Enterprise Development* 17 (2), pp. 230–246.

Berggren, Christian (1993), *The Volvo Experience: Alternatives to Lean Production in the Swedish Auto Industry*, London: Palgrave Macmillan.

Bergh, Andreas (2011), "The Rise, Fall and Revival of the Swedish Welfare State: What are the Policy Lessons from Sweden?" IFN Working Paper No. 873, Stockholm: Research Institute of Industrial Economics.

Bergmann, Heiko (2011), "Entrepreneurship Disparities within Switzerland: Do Tax and Language Differences Play a Role?" *Entrepreneurship & Regional Development 23* (7–8), pp. 523–548.

Bergmann, Heiko, and Rolf Sternberg (2005), "The Changing Face of Entrepreneurship in Germany — Recent Policy Changes and their Regional Implications," Paper presented at the 2nd GEM Research Conference in Hungary, May.

Berlinski, Claire (2005), "To Hell with Europe!" *The Gazette* (Montreal), Sunday, June 12, p. A-17.

Bertaud, Jean-Paul, Jean Leflon, Georges Lefranc, Alain Melchior-Bonnet, and Pierre Mermet (1976), *La Revolution Française,* Paris: Larousse.

Beyer, Norbert, Walter Hämmerle, and Stefan Garbislander (2005), *Ein-Personen-Unternehmen in Tirol. Situation und Zukunftsperspektiven.* Tiroler regionalpolitische Studien Nr. 27; Innsbruck: Wirtschaftskammer Tirol.

Bianchi, Carmine, and Graham Winch (2006), "Unleashing Growth Potential in 'Stunted' SMEs: Insights from Simulator Experiments," *International Journal of Entrepreneurship and Small Business 3* (1), pp. 92–105.

Bianchi, Giuliano (1990), "Innovating in the Local Systems of Small Medium Sized Enterprises: The Experience of Tuscany," *Entrepreneurship & Regional Development* 2, pp. 57–69.

Bianchi, Giuliano (1998), "Requiem for the Third Italy? Rise and Fall of a Successful Concept," *Entrepreneurship & Regional Development 10*, pp. 93–116.

Binder, Martin, and Alex Coad (2013), "Life Satisfaction and Self-employment: A Matching Approach," *Small Business Economics 40* (4), pp. 1009–1033.

Birley, Sue (1985), "Encouraging Entrepreneurship: Britain's New Enterprise Program," *Journal of Small Business Management 23* (4), pp. 6–12.

Birley, Sue, Stan Cromie, and Andrew Myers (1991), "Entrepreneurial Networks: Their Emergence in Ireland and Overseas," *International Small Business Journal 9* (4), pp. 56–74.

Bjørklund, Ivar (2004), "Saami Pastoral Society in Northern Norway: The National Integration of an Indigenous Management System," in David G. Anderson and Mark Nuttall, Eds., *Cultivating Arctic Landscapes: Knowing and Managing Animals in the Circumpolar North,* New York & Oxford: Berghahn, pp. 124–135.

Blackburn, Robert A., Ed., (2003), *Intellectual Property and Innovation Management in Small Firms,* London and New York: Routledge.

Blackburn, Robert A., and David Smallbone (2008), "Researching Small Firms and Entrepreneurship in the UK: Developments and Distinctiveness," *Entrepreneurship: Theory & Practice 32* (2), pp. 267–288.

Blake, Robert (1966), *Disraeli.* London: Eyre and Spottiswoode.

Blanchard, Margaret A. (1992), "Free Expression and Wartime: Lessons from the Past, Hopes for the Future," *Journalism & Mass Communication Quarterly 69* (1), pp. 5–17.

Blim, Michael L. (1992), "Small-Scale Industrialization in a Rapidly Changing World Market," in Frances Abrahamer Rothstein and Michael L. Blim, Eds., *Anthropology and the Global Factory: Studies of the New Industrialization in the Late Twentieth Century,* New York: Bergin & Garvey, pp. 85–101.

Blomstermo, Anders, Kent Eriksson, and D. Deo Sharma (2004), "Swedish Perspectives of International Entrepreneurship," in Léo-Paul Dana, Ed., *The Handbook of Research on International Entrepreneurship,* Cheltenham, United Kingdom: Edward Elgar, pp. 564–579.

Blond, Phillip, and Adrian Pabst (2005), "A Fresh Vision: Europe Needs to Think Locally," *International Herald Tribune,* Saturday, June 25, p. 6.

Bobé, Louis (1952), *Hans Egede: Colonizer and Missionary of Greenland,* Copenhagen: Rosenkilde and Bagger.

Boesso, Giacomo, Francesco Favotto, Andrea Menini, and Kamalesh Kumar (2009), "Strategic Innovativeness of SMEs vs. Large MNEs: Functional Yogurts in Italy," *Rivista Piccola Impresa 2,* pp. 29–49.

Böhmer, Gérard (1979), "Portrait du Mois: Jean, Grand-Duc de Luxembourg," *Historama* 336, pp. 58–59.

Boissevain, Jeremy, and Hanneke Grotenbreg (1987), "Ethnic Enterprise in the Netherlands: The Surinamese of Amsterdam," in Robert Goffee and Richard Scase, Eds., *Entrepreneurship in Europe: The Social Processes*, London: Croom Helm, pp. 105–130.

Boissevain, Jeremy, and Hanneke Grotenbreg (1988), "Culture, Structure, and Ethnic Enterprise: The Surinamese of Amsterdam," in Malcolm Cross and Han Entzinger, Eds., *Lost Illusions: Caribbean Minorities in Britain and the Netherlands,* London: Routledge, pp. 221–249.

Boissevain, Jeremy, and Hanneke Grotenbreg (1989), "Entrepreneurs and the Law: Self-employed Surinamese in Amsterdam," in June Starr and Jane F. Collier, Eds., *History and Power in the Study of Law: New Directions in Legal Anthropology,* Ithaca: Cornell University Press, pp. 223–251.

Bolton, Bill K., and John L. Thompson (2004), *Entrepreneurs: Talent, Temperament, Technique,* 2nd edition, Oxford: Elsevier Butterworth-Heinemann.

Bonacich, Edna (1973), "A Theory of Middleman Minorities," *American Sociological Review 38* (5), October, pp. 583–594.

Booth, Robert (1981), "Liechtenstein: A Modern Fairy Tale," *National Geographic 159* (2), February, pp. 273–284.

Borah, Leo A. (1938), "Some Odd Pages from the Annals of the Tulip: A 'Made' Flower of Unknown Origin Took Medieval Europe by Storm and Caused a Financial Panic in the Netherlands," *National Geographic 64* (3), September, pp. 321–344.

Bosma, Niels S., Tine Holvoet, and Hans Crijns (2014), *Global Entrepreneurship Monitor 2013 Report for Belgium & Flanders*, Leuven: Steunpunt Ondernemen en Regionale Economie.

Bosma, Niels S., Heleen W. Stigter, and A. R. M. Wennekers (2002), *The Long Road to the Entrepreneurial Society: Global Entrepreneurship Monitor in the Netherlands*, Zoetermeer: EIM.

Bover, Olympia, and Pilar Velilla (1999), *Migrations in Spain: Historical Background and Current Trends*, Madrid: Banco de Espana.

Bowie, Beverley M. (1959), "Building a New Austria: Looted, Pillaged, and Occupied. Eastern Austria remains the gay land of Mozart and Strauss while striding toward recovery," *National Geographic 115* (2), February, pp. 172–213.

Bradford, Ernle (1970), "Denmark's Faeroes, Isles of Maybe," *National Geographic 138* (3), September, pp. 410–442.

Bradley, La Verne (1947), "Scenes of Postwar Finland," *National Geographic 92* (2), August, pp. 233–264.

Braunerhjelm, Pontus, Carin Holmquist, Johan P. Larsson, Lisa Silver, and Per Thulin (2015), *The Entrepreneurial Code: A Comparative Study of Entrepreneurial Dynamics in China, Europe and the US*, Stockholm: Swedish Entrepreneurship Forum.

Braunerhjelm, Pontus, Johan P. Larsson, Per Thulin, and Ylva Skoogberg (2016), *The Entrepreneurial Challenge: A Comparative Study of Entrepreneurial Dynamics in China, Europe and the US*, Stockholm: Swedish Entrepreneurship Forum.

Britton, Wright (1969), "Sailing Iceland's Rugged Coasts," *National Geographic 136* (2), August, pp. 228–265.

Brixy, Udo, and Susanne Kohaut (1999), "Employment Growth Determinants in New Firms in Eastern Germany," *Small Business Economics 13*, pp. 155–170.

Brooke, Sir Arthur de Capell (1827), *A Winter in Lapland and Sweden*, London: J. Bodwell.

Brown, Andrew H. (1963), "Sweden, Quiet Workshop for the World," *National Geographic 123* (4), April, pp. 451–491.

Brown, Thomas (1884), *Annals of the Disruption*, Edinburgh: Macniven & Wallace.

Brüderl, Josef, and Peter Preisendörfer (1998), "Network Support and the Success of Newly Founded Businesses," *Small Business Economics 10*, pp. 213–225.

Brüderl, Josef, Peter Preisendörfer, and Rolf Ziegler (1992), "Survival Chances of Newly Founded Business Organizations," *American Sociological Review 57* (2), pp. 227–242.

Brüderl, Josef, Peter Preisendörfer, and Rolf Ziegler (2007), *Erfolgschancen neugegründeter Betriebe*, 3rd edition, Berlin: Duncker and Humblot.

Brusco, Sebastiano (1986), "Small Firms and Industrial Districts: The Experience of Italy," in David Keeble and Egbert Wever, Eds., *New Firms and Regional Development in Europe*, London: Croom Helm, pp. 184–202.

Bryson, Bill (1992), "The New World of Spain," *National Geographic 181* (4), April, pp. 3–33.

Bryson, Bill (1995), "Essence of Provence," *National Geographic 188* (3), September, pp. 52–77.

Bryson, Bill (1996), "Gibraltar," *National Geographic 190* (5), November, pp. 54–71.

Buckley, Peter J. (1997), "International Technology Transfer by Small and Medium-Sized Enterprises," *Small Business Economics 9*, pp. 67–78.

Buechler, Hans C., and Judith-Maria Buechler (1992), "Spanish Galician Industrialization and the Europe of 1992: A Contextual Analysis," in Frances Abrahamer Rothstein and Michael L. Blim, Eds., *Anthropology and the Global Factory: Studies of the New Industrialization in the Late Twentieth Century*, New York: Bergin & Garvey, pp. 102–118.

Bullvåg, Erlend, Lars Kolvereid, Terje Mathisen, and Bjørn Willy Åmo (2010), *Entreprenørskap i Norge 2009*, Bodø: Handelshøgskolen i Bodø.

Bundesministerium für Wirtschaft und Arbeit (2005), *Mittelstandsbericht 2002/03. Bericht über die Situation der kleinen und mittleren Unternehmungen der gewerblichen Wirtschaft* (Medium-sized businesses report 2002/03: Report about the situation of the small and medium-sized businesses of the industrial economy), Vienna: Federal Ministry of Economy and Labour.

Burgess, Philip (1999), *Human Environmental Interactions in Upper Lapland, Finland*, Rovaniemi, Finland: Arctic Centre, University of Lapland.

Burke, Andrew E., Ed., (1995), *Enterprise and the Irish Economy*, Dublin: Oak Tree Press.

Burnett, John (1969), *The Challenge of the Nineteenth Century*, New York: Paul Hamlyn.

Burrows, Roger (1991), "Who Are the Contemporary British Petty Bourgeoisie?," *International Small Business Journal* 9 (2), pp. 12–25.

Cain, Peter J., and Antony Gerald Hopkins (1993), *British Imperialism: Innovation and Expansion 1688–1914*, London: Longman.

Cantillon, Richard (1755), *Essai sur la nature du commerce en général*, London and Paris: R. Gyles; translated (1931), by Henry Higgs, London: MacMillan and Co.

Capaldo, Guido (1997), "Entrepreneurship in Southern Italy: Empirical Evidence of Business Creation by Young Founders," *Journal of Small Business Management* 35 (3), pp. 86–92.

Carlsson, Bo (1996), "Differing Patterns of Industrial Dynamics: New Zealand, Ohio, and Sweden, 1978–1994," *Small Business Economics 8*, pp. 219–234.

Carnegie, Andrew (1920), *Autobiography of Andrew Carnegie*, Boston: Houghton Mifflin.

Carter, Sara, and Dylan Jones-Evans (2006), *Enterprise and Small Business: Principles, Practice and Policy*, Harlow, UK: FT Prentice Hall.

Carter, Sara, and Peter Rosa (1998), "Indigenous Rural Firms: Farms in the UK," *International Small Business Journal 16* (4), pp. 15–27.

Casson, Marc C. (1982), *The Entrepreneur: An Economic Theory,* New York: Barnes & Noble.

Casson, Mark C. (2009a), "The Efficiency of the Victorian British Railway Network: A Counterfactual Analysis," *Networks and Spatial Economics 9* (3), pp. 339–378.

Casson, Mark C. (2009b), *The World's First Railway System: Enterprise, Competition and Regulation on the Railway Network in Victorian Britain,* Oxford: Oxford University Press.

Casson, Mark C., and Andrew C. Godley (2010a), "Entrepreneurship in Britain 1830–1900," in David S. Landes, Joel Mokyr, and William J. Baumol, Eds., *The Invention of Enterprise: Entrepreneurship from Ancient Mesopotamia to Modern Times*, Princeton: New Jersey: Princeton University Press, pp. 211–242.

Casson, Mark C., and Andrew C. Godley (2010b), "Entrepreneurship in Victorian Britain," in Mark C. Casson, Ed., *Entrepreneurship: Theory, Networks and History,*" Cheltenham, United Kingdom: Edward Elgar, pp. 288–325.

Castelot, André (1971), *L'Histoire de Napoléon Bonaparte: Le Grand Empire,* Paris: Presses Pocket.

Cerruti, James (1973), "Gotland: Sweden's Treasure Island," *National Geographic 144* (2), pp. 268–288.

Cerruti, James (1976), "Edinburgh: Capital in Search of a Country," *National Geographic 150* (2), pp. 274–296.

Cerruti, James (1979), "Belgium: One Nation Divisible," *National Geographic 155* (3), March, pp. 314–341.

Chan, Peng S., and Robert T. Justis (1992), "Franchising in the EC: 1992 and Beyond," *Journal of Small Business Management 30* (1), January, pp. 83–88.

Chandler, Douglas (1938), "Belgium — Europe in Miniature," *National Geographic 73* (4), April, pp. 398–450.

Chanut-Guieu, Cécile, and Gilles Guieu (2014), "High Growth Trajectories in Small and Medium Sized Enterprises: A Comparative Study," *Journal of Small Business and Entreprise Development 21* (4), pp. 623–637.

Chater, Melville (1925), "Through the Back Doors of Belgium," *National Geographic 47* (5), May, pp. 499–540.

Chater, Melville (1929), "The Danube, Highway of Races: From the Black Forest to the Black Sea, Europe's Most Important River Has Borne the Traffic of Centuries," *National Geographic 56* (6), December, pp. 643–698.

Chell, Elizabeth, and Jean M. Haworth (1992), "The Competitive Performance of SMEs in the UK Clothing Industry," *International Small Business Journal 10* (3), pp. 11–24.

Cherry, Robert (1990), "Middleman Minority Theories: Their Implications for Black-Jewish Relations," *The Journal of Ethnic Studies 17* (4), Winter, pp. 117–138.

Christiansen, Fredrik, and David Lusseau (2015), "Linking Behavior to Vital Rates to Measure the Effects of Non-Lethal Disturbance on Wildlife," *Conservation Letters 8* (6), pp. 424–431.

Cienski, Jan, and Ralph Atkins (2010), "Germany Spreads Benefits of Revival to Neighbours in East," *Financial Times,* November 12, p. 3.

Clark, Deena (1951), "Iceland Tapestry," *National Geographic 100* (5), November, pp. 599–630.

Clark, Ken, and Stephen Drinkwater (2010), "Recent Trends in Minority Ethnic Entrepreneurship in Britain," *International Small Business Journal 28* (2), pp. 131–146.

Clark, Sydney (1948a), "Luxembourg, Survivor of Invasions," *National Geographic 93* (6), June, pp. 791–810.

Clark, Sydney (1948b), "Norway Cracks Her Mountain Shell," *National Geographic 94* (2), August, pp. 171–211.

Clark, Sydney (1950), "Mid-Century Holland Builds Her Future," *National Geographic 98* (6), December, pp. 747–778.

Clarke, Edward Daniel (1824a), *Travels in Various Countries of Europe Asia and Africa: Scandinavia,* Volume 9, London: T. Cadell.

Clarke, Edward Daniel (1824b), *Travels in Various Countries of Europe Asia and Africa: Scandinavia,* Volume 10, London: T. Cadell.

Clute, Robert Eugene (1962), *The International Legal Status of Austria 1938–1955,* The Hague: M. Nijhoff.

Cockburn, Andrew (2003), "21st Century Slaves," *National Geographic 204* (3), September, pp. 2–25.

Coduras, Alicia, Ignacio de la Vega, Rachida Justo, and Cristina Cruz (2005), *Global Entrepreneurship Monitor Report*, Madrid: Instituto de Empresa.

Coduras, Alicia, Cristina Cruz, Ignacio de la Vega, and Rachida Justo (2008), "The Internationalization of Small and Medium Firms in Spain," in Léo-Paul Dana, Isabell M. Welpe, Mary Han, and Vanessa Ratten, Eds., *Handbook of Research on European Business and Entrepreneurship: Towards a Theory of Internationalization*, Cheltenham, United Kingdom: Edward Elgar, pp. 598–617.

Collinder, Björn (1949), *The Lapps*, Princeton, New Jersey: Princeton University Press, for the American Scandinavian Foundation.

Conger, Clement E. (1948), "Portugal is Different," *National Geographic 94* (5), November, pp. 583–622.

Conly, Robert Leslie (1970), "Luxembourg, the Quiet Fortress," *National Geographic 138* (1), July, pp. 69–126.

Conniff, Richard (1994), "Ireland on Fast Forward," *National Geographic 186* (3), September, pp. 2–36.

Coquery, Natacha (1997), "The Aristocratic *Hôtel* and Its Artisans in Eighteenth-century Paris: The Market Ruled by Court Society, in Geoffrey Crossick," Ed., *The Artisan and the European Town, 1500–1900,* Aldershot and Brookfield, Vermont: Ashgate, pp. 92–115.

Corbetta, Guido, Alexandra Dawson, and Giovanni Valentini (2009), *Global Entrepreneurship Monitor — Italy*, Milan: Bocconi University.

Crick, Dave (2004), "The Internationalization Process of Firms in the United Kingdom," in Léo-Paul Dana, Ed., *The Handbook of Research on International Entrepreneurship,* Cheltenham, United Kingdom: Edward Elgar, pp. 580–595.

Culasso, Francesca, Laura Broccardo, Elisa Giacosa, and Alberto Mazzoleni (2012), "Corporate Governance in Listed Italian Family Firms: Impact on Performance and Comparison with Not Family Firms," *Journal of Management and Change 29* (1), pp. 67–88.

Curran, James (1986), *Bolton, Fifteen Years On: A Review and Analysis of Small Business Research in Britain 1971–1986*, London: Small Business Research Trust.

Curran, James (2000), "What is Small Business Policy in the UK for? Evaluation and Assessing Small Business Policies," *International Small Business Journal 18* (3) pp. 36–50.

Curran, James, and Roger Burrows (1988), *Enterprise in Britain: A National Profile of Small Business Owners and the Self-employed,* London: Small Business Research Trust.

Curran, James, and John Stanworth (1982), "The Small Firm in Britain: Past, Present and Future," *European Small Business Journal 1* (1), pp. 16–25.

Curran, James, and David J. Storey (2002), "Small Business Policy in the United Kingdom: The Inheritance of the New Small Business Service and Implications for its Future Effectiveness," *Environment and Planning C: Government and Policy 20* (2), pp. 163–177.

Daes, Erica-Irene (2003), "Globalization, Intellectual Property and Indigenous Peoples," in Svein Jentoft, Henry Minde, and Ragnar Nilsen, Eds., *Indigenous Peoples: Resource Management and Global Rights,* Delft, The Netherlands: Eburon Academic, pp. 67–73.

Dahmen, Erik (1970), *Entrepreneurial Activity and the Development of Swedish Industry, 1919–1939,* Homewood, Illinois: Richard D. Irwin.

Dana, Léo-Paul (1987), "Entrepreneurship and Venture Creation — An International Comparison of Five Commonwealth Nations," *Frontiers of Entrepreneurship Research*, pp. 573–583.

Dana, Léo-Paul (1990), "Saint Martin/Sint Maarten: A Case Study of the Effects of Politics and Culture on Economic Development," *Journal of Small Business Management 28* (4), October, pp. 91–98.

Dana, Léo-Paul (1992a), "A Look at Small Business in Austria," *Journal of Small Business Management 30* (4), October, pp. 126–130.

Dana, Léo-Paul (1992b), "Entrepreneurial Education in Europe," *Journal of Education for Business 68* (2), November-December, pp. 74–78.

Dana, Léo-Paul (1993a), "An Analysis of Strategic Intervention Policy in Namibia," *Journal of Small Business Management 31* (3), July, pp. 90–95.

Dana, Léo-Paul (1993b), "Mediterranean Warmth and British Discipline," *La Voix Sépharade 23* (2), March-April, p. 48.

Dana, Léo-Paul (1995a), "Entrepreneurship in a Remote Sub-Arctic Community: Nome, Alaska," *Entrepreneurship: Theory & Practice, 20* (1), Fall, pp. 55–72. Reprinted in Norris Krueger, Ed., *Entrepreneurship: Critical Perspectives on Business and Management,* Volume IV, London: Routledge, 2002, pp. 255–275.

Dana, Léo-Paul (1995b), "Entrepreneurship in the Basque Country: An Ethnographic Account," *Entrepreneurship, Innovation, and Change 4* (1), March, pp. 69–76.

Dana, Léo-Paul (1996), "Influence du Facteur Culturel sur la Très Petite Entreprise à Strasbourg," *Journal of Small Business & Entrepreneurship 13* (2), Summer, pp. 81–94.

Dana, Léo-Paul (1997), "The Origins of Self-Employment," *Canadian Journal of Administrative Sciences/Revue Canadienne des Sciences de l'Administration 14* (1), April, pp. 99–104.

Dana, Léo-Paul (1999a), "Business and Entrepreneurship in Bosnia-Herzegovina," *Journal of Business & Entrepreneurship 11* (2), October, pp. 105–118.

Dana, Léo-Paul (1999b), *Entrepreneurship in Pacific Asia,* Singapore, London and Hong Kong: World Scientific.

Dana, Léo-Paul (2000a), *Economies of the Eastern Mediterranean Region: Economic Miracles in the Making*, Singapore, London and Hong Kong: World Scientific.

Dana, Léo-Paul (2000b), "International Management: Culture is of the Essence in Asia," *Financial Times*, Mastering Management Special Section, November 27, pp. 12–13.

Dana, Léo-Paul (2002), "Entrepreneurship & Public Policy in Gibraltar," *International Journal of Entrepreneurship and Innovation Management 2* (1), pp. 38–42.

Dana, Léo-Paul (2005), "Sheep Farm in the Pyrenees," in Timothy S. Hatten, *Small Business Management: Entrepreneurship & Beyond,* 3rd edition, Boston: Houghton Mifflin, pp. 351–352.

Dana, Léo-Paul (2006), "A Historical Study of the Traditional Livestock Merchants of Alsace," *British Food Journal 108* (7), July, pp. 586–598.

Dana, Léo-Paul (2007), "Promoting SMEs in Africa: Some Insights from An Experiment in Ghana and Togo," *Journal of African Business 8* (2), October, pp. 151–174.

Dana, Léo-Paul (2008), "Community-based Entrepreneurship in Norway," *International Journal of Entrepreneurship and Innovation* 9 (2), June, pp. 77–92.

Dana, Léo-Paul (2010), *When Economies Change Hands: A Survey of Entrepreneurship in the Emerging Markets of Europe from the Balkans to the Baltic States*, New York: Routledge.

Dana, Léo-Paul (2014), *Asian Models of Entrepreneurship — From the Indian Union and Nepal to the Japanese Archipelago: Context, Policy and Practice*, 2nd Edition, Singapore & London: World Scientific.

Dana, Léo-Paul, and Robert Brent Anderson, Eds., (2007), *Indigenous Entrepreneurship*, Cheltenham, United Kingdom: Edward Elgar.

Dana, Léo-Paul, Mark B. Bajramovic, and Richard W. Wright (2005), "Chapter 5: A New Paradigm of Multipolar Competition and Its Implications for Entrepreneurship in Europe," in Alain Fayolle, Paula Kyrö, and Jan Ulijn, Eds., *Entrepreneurship Research in Europe: Outcomes and Perspectives,* Cheltenham, United Kingdom: Edward Elgar, pp. 102–117.

Dana, Léo-Paul, and Teresa E. Dana (2003), "Innovative Policies for Entrepreneurship: The Principality of Liechtenstein & the Grand Duchy of Luxembourg," *International Journal of Entrepreneurship and Innovation Management 3* (3), June, pp. 295–302.

Dana, Léo-Paul, and Teresa E. Dana (2007), "How do Self-employed Sámi People Perceive the Impact of the EU & Globalisation?" *International Journal of Business and Globalisation 1* (1), pp. 3–19.

Dana, Léo-Paul, and Teresa E. Dana (2008), "Ethnicity & Entrepreneurship in Morocco: A Photo-ethnographic Study," *International Journal of Business and Globalisation 2* (3), pp. 209–226.

Dana, Léo-Paul, Hamid Etemad, and Richard W. Wright (2008), "Toward a Paradigm of Symbiotic Entrepreneurship," *International Journal of Entrepreneurship and Small Business 5* (2), pp. 109–126.

Dana, Léo-Paul, Len Korot, and George Tovstiga (2000), "Toward a Transnational Techno-culture: An Empirical Investigation of Knowledge Management," in Hamid Etemad and Richard W. Wright, Eds., *Globalization and Entrepreneurship: Policy and Strategy Perspectives,* Cheltenham, United Kingdom: Edward Elgar, pp. 183–204.

Dana, Léo-Paul, and Ivan H. Light (2011), "Two Forms of Community Entrepreneurship among Reindeer Herding Entrepreneurs in Finland," *Entrepreneurship & Regional Development, 23* (5–6), June, pp. 331–352.

Dana, Léo-Paul, and Jan Age Riseth (2011), "Reindeer Herders in Finland: Pulled to Community-based Entrepreneurship and Pushed to Individualistic Firms," *The Polar Journal 1* (1), June, pp. 99–114.

Dana, Teresa E., and Liisa Remes (2005), "Entrepreneurship among the Sámi People of Finland," *Journal of Small Business & Entrepreneurship 18* (2), Spring, pp. 189–200.

Danell, Öje (2000), "Status, Directions and Priorities of Reindeer Husbandry Research in Sweden," *Polar Research 19* (1), pp. 111–115.

Danson, Mike, Ewa Helinska-Hughes, Michael Hughes, and Geoff Whittam (2008), "Supporting SMEs in Scotland: Strategies for Internationalizing," in Léo-Paul Dana, Isabell M. Welpe, Mary Han, and Vanessa Ratten, Eds., *Handbook of Research on European Business and Entrepreneurship: Towards a Theory of Internationalization*, Cheltenham, United Kingdom: Edward Elgar, pp. 700–717.

Davenport, William (1974), "Amiable Amsterdam," *National Geographic 145* (5), May, pp. 682–705.

Davenport, William (1980), "Bordeaux: Fine Wines and Fiery Gascons," *National Geographic 158* (2), August, pp. 233–259.

De Clercq, Dirk, Sophie Manigart, Bart Clarysse, Hans Crijns, Mathieu de Sutter, and Frank Verzele (2002), *The Global Entrepreneurship Monitor Executive Report for Belgium 2003,* Ghent: Ghent University.

De Clercq, Dirk, Sophie Manigart, Hans Crijns, Bart Clarysse, Frank Verzele, and David Zegers (2004), *The Global Entrepreneurship Monitor Executive Report for Belgium & Wallonia 2003,* Ghent: Ghent University.

De Marchi, Valentina, and Roberto Grandinetti (2014), "Industrial Districts and the Collapse of the Marshallian Model: Looking at the Italian Experience," *Competition and Change 18* (1), pp. 70–87.

De Roover, Raymond (1963), *The Rise and Decline of the Medici Bank, 1397–1494,* Cambridge, Massachusetts: Harvard University Press.

Deakins, David, Mohammed Ishaq, David Smallbone, Geoff Whittam, and Janette Wyper (2007), "Ethnic Minority Businesses in Scotland and the Role of Social Capital," *International Small Business Journal 25* (3), pp. 307–326.

Defourny, Jacques, and Marthe Nyssens (2010), "Social Enterprise in Europe: At the Crossroads of Market, Public Policies and Third Sector," *Policy and Society 29* (3), pp. 231–242.

Degadt, Jan (2008), "Internationalization of SMEs in Belgium," in Léo-Paul Dana, Isabell M. Welpe, Mary Han, and Vanessa Ratten, Eds., *Handbook of Research on European Business and Entrepreneurship: Towards a Theory of Internationalization,* Cheltenham, United Kingdom: Edward Elgar, pp. 77–93.

Deimel, Klaus, Sascha Kraus, and Sebastian Reiche (2009), "Strategic Management in the German Strategic Management in the German 'Mittelstand' — An Empirical Investigation," in Sascha Kraus and Matthias Fink, Eds., *The Management of Small and Medium Enterprises,* London: Routledge, pp. 38–55.

Del Monte, Alfredo, and Domenico Scalera (2001), "The Life-duration of Small Firms Born with a Start-up Programme: Evidence from Italy," *Regional Studies 35* (1), pp. 11–21.

Dempster, Nigel, and Peter Evans (1993), *Behind Palace Doors: Marriage and Divorce in the House of Windsor*, New York: G. P. Putnam's Sons.

Denby, Elaine (2002), *Grand Hotels: Reality and Illusion*, London: Reaktion.

Dennis, Alfred Pearce (1930), "Norway, A Land of Stern Reality: Where Descendants of the Sea Kings of Old Triumphed Over Nature and Wrought a Nation of Arts and Crafts," *National Geographic 58* (1), July, pp. 1–36.

Desmond, Shaw (1920), "Denmark: The Democratic Danes and Their Homeland," in John Alexander Hamerton, Ed., *Peoples of All Nations: Their Life Today and the Story of Their Past*, London: Educational Book Co., pp. 1575–1618.

Drakopoulou Dodd, Sarah, Sarah Jack, and Alistair R. Anderson (2002), "Scottish Entrepreneurial Networks in International Context," *International Small Business Journal 20* (2), pp. 213–219.

Ducros, Christine, Jean-Yves Guérin, and Brunot Jacquot (2004), "Tous Entrepreneurs!" *Le Figaro Entreprises*, September 13, pp. 18–23.

Durst, Susanne, and Thomas Henschel (2014), "Governance in Small Firms: A Country Comparison of Current Practices," *International Journal of Entrepreneurship and Small Business 21* (1), pp. 16–32.

Durst, Susanne, and Jan Sedenka (2016), *Entrepreneurial Intentions and Behaviour of Students attending Swedish Universities Global University Entrepreneurial Spirit Students' Survey 2016 — National Report Sweden*, Skövde: University of Skövde.

Dyer, Jeff, Hal B. Gregersen, and Clayton M. Christensen (2011), *The Innovator's DNA: Mastering the Five Skills of Disruptive Innovators*, Cambridge, Massachusetts: Harvard Business Press.

Eddy, Melissa (2014), "Swiss Voters Approve New Limits on Immigration," *International New York Times*, Monday February 10, p. 1–3.

Edvardsson, Ingi Runar (2006), "Knowledge Management and SMEs: The Case of Icelandic Firms," *Knowledge Management Research & Practice 4* (4), pp. 275–282.

Edvardsson, Ingi Runar (2009), "Is Knowledge Management Losing Ground? Developments among Icelandic SMEs," *Knowledge Management Research & Practice 7* (1), pp. 91–99.

Edvardsson, Ingi Runar, Gudmundur Kristjan Oskarsson, and Sigrun Versteinsdottir (2011), "Enhancing Customer Services and Core Competencies: Outsourcing in Icelandic Service SMEs," *International Journal of Entrepreneurship and Small Business 14* (3), pp. 313–333.

Edwards, Anne (1992), *The Grimaldis of Monaco*, New York: William Morrow & Co.

Edwards, Walter Meayers (1951), "France's Past Lives in Languedoc," *National Geographic 100* (1), July, pp. 1–43.

Egan, Maurice Francis (1922), "Denmark and the Danes," *National Geographic 42* (2), August, pp. 115–164.

Ehmer, Josef (1997), "Worlds of Mobility: Migration Patterns of Viennese Artisans in the Eighteenth Century," in Geoffrey Crossick, Ed., *The Artisan and the European Town, 1500–1900*, Aldershot and Brookfield, Vermont: Ashgate, pp. 172–199.

Einarsson, Agust (2004), "The Economic Contribution of the Cultural Sector of a Small Society in a Global Context," *Review of International Comparative Management 5*, pp. 131–143.

El-Namaki, M. S. S. (1992), "Europe After Integration: Existing and Prospective Propensities to Enterprise in Four EC Countries at Different Stages of Economic Growth," *Entrepreneurship, Innovation, and Change 1* (1), March, pp. 87–96.

Elgán, Elisabeth, and Irene Scobbie (2015), *Historical Dictionary of Sweden*, Lanham Maryland: Rowman & Littlefield.

Ellis, Tania, and Annika Rømer (2016), "Denmark," in Wayne Visser, Ed., *The World Guide to Sustainable Enterprise, Volume 3 Europe*, Sheffield, United Kingdom: Greenleaf, pp. 71–77.

Ellis, William S. (1984), "Surviving, Italian Style," *National Geographic 165* (2), February, pp. 185–209.

Elo, Maria (2015), "Diaspora Networks in International Business: A Review on an Emerging Stream of Research," in Jorma Larimo, Niina Nummela, and Tuija Mainela, Eds., *Handbook on International Alliance and Network Research*, Cheltenham, United Kingdom: Edward Elgar, pp. 13–41.

Ely, Richard T., and Ralph H. Hess (1893), *Outline of Economics*, New York: Macmillan.

Emirbayer, Mustafa, and Jeff Goodwin (1994), "Network Analysis, Culture, and the Problem of Agency," *American Journal of Sociology 99* (6), pp. 1411–1454.

Englund, Peter (2015), "The Swedish 1990s Banking Crisis: A Revisit in the Light of Recent Experience," paper prepared for the Riksbank Macroprudential Conference, Stockholm 23–24 June.

Enterprise Strategy Group (2004), *Ahead of the Curve: Ireland's Place in the Global Economy*, Dublin: Forfás.

Erlanger, Steven (2014), "In Left-leaning Norway, Billionaire Goes in Opposite Direction," *International New York Times,* February 10, p. 3.

Esteban, Pere, Philip D. Jones, Javier Martín-Vide, and Montse Mases (2005), "Atmospheric Circulation Patterns Related to Heavy Snowfall Days in Andorra, Pyrenees," *International Journal of Climatology 25*, pp. 319–329.

Eurostat (2015), *Unemployment Statistics 2015*, Luxembourg: Eurostat.

Eythórsson, Einar (2003), "The Coastal Sami: a 'Pariah Caste' of the Norwegian Fisheries? A Reflection on Ethnicity and Power in Norwegian Resource Management," in Svein Jentoft, Henry Minde, and Ragnar Nilsen, Eds., *Indigenous Peoples: Resource Management and Global Rights,* Delft, The Netherlands: Eburon Academic, pp. 149–162.

Fagerholm, P. O. (1964), "'Gustav af Klint', a New Old Swedish Survey Ship with New Survey Boats," *International Hydrographic Review 41* (2), pp. 23–30.

Farmer, Richard N., and Barry M. Richman (1965), *Comparative Management and Economic Progress,* Homewood, Illinois: Richard D. Irwin.

Fayolle, Alain (2000), "L'Enseignement de l'Entrepreneuriat dans le Système Educatif Supérieur Français: Un Regard sur la Situation Actuelle," *Gestion 2000* (3), pp. 77–95.

Fayolle, Alain (2004), "French Perspectives of International Entrepreneurship," in Léo-Paul Dana, Ed., *Handbook of Research on International Entrepreneurship,* Cheltenham, United Kingdom: Edward Elgar, pp. 431–454.

Fayolle, Alain, Paula Kyrö, and Jan Ulijn (2005), "The Entrepreneurship Debate in Europe: A Matter of History and Culture?" in Alain Fayolle, Paula Kyrö, and Jan Ulijn, Eds., *Entrepreneurship Research in Europe: Outcomes and Perspectives,* Cheltenham, United Kingdom: Edward Elgar, pp. 1–31.

Fehrenbach, Silke, and Maria Lauxen-Ulbrich (2006), "A Gender View on Self-Employment in Germany," *International Journal of Entrepreneurship and Small Business 3* (5), pp. 572–593.

Fernsworth, Lawrence A. (1933), "Andorra: Museum of Feudal Europe," *National Geographic 64* (4), October, pp. 493–512.

Fertala, Nikolinka (2003), "Immigrants' Propensity to Self-Employment in Germany," *Journal of Transforming Societies and Economies 4* (38), pp. 30–40.

Fertala, Nikolinka (2007), "Immigrant Entrepreneurs in Hamburg," in Léo-Paul Dana, Ed., *Handbook of Research on Ethnic Minority Entrepreneurship: A Co-evolutionary View on Resource Management,* Cheltenham, United Kingdom: Edward Elgar, pp. 511–433.

Fibonacci, Leonardo (1854), *Tre Scritti Inediti*, Florence: Baldassarre Boncompagni.

Figueirinha, Susana (2008), "JRS and Microcredit," *Migrações 3*, October, pp. 263–267.

Fink, Matthias, Rainer Harms, and Sascha Kraus (2008), "Cooperative Internationalization of SMEs: Self-commitment as a Success Factor for International Entrepreneurship," *European Management Journal 26* (6), pp. 429–440.

Fink, Matthias, and Slawomir Teodorowicz (2008), "Trust-based Cooperation as a Driver for the Internationalization of SMEs: Empirical Evidence from Austria," in Léo-Paul Dana, Isabell M. Welpe, Mary Han, and Vanessa Ratten, Eds., *Handbook of Research on European Business and Entrepreneurship: Towards a Theory of Internationalization,* Cheltenham, United Kingdom: Edward Elgar, pp. 42–56.

Fisher, Allan C. (1979), "Pilgrimage Through Two Englands," *National Geographic 156* (4), pp. 442–482.

Fitjar, Rune Dahl, and Andrés Rodriguez-Pose (2014), "The Geographical Dimension of Innovation Collaboration: Networking and Innovation in Norway," *Urban Studies 51* (12), pp. 2572–2595.

Fitzsimons, Paula, and Colm O'Gorman (2004), *The Irish Report: How Entrepreneurial is Ireland?* Dublin: University College.

Fitzsimons, Paula, and Colm O'Gorman (2009), *Entrepreneurship in Ireland 2008,* Dublin: Dublin City University.

Fitzsimons, Paula, and Colm O'Gorman (2014), *Entrepreneurship in Ireland 2013,* Dublin: Enterprise Ireland.

Fitzsimons, Paula, and Colm O'Gorman (2015), *Entrepreneurship in Ireland 2014,* Dublin: Enterprise Ireland.

Fleischer, Jørgen (2003), *A Short History of Greenland,* Copenhagen: Aschehoug.

Flinn, Michael W. (1961), *An Economic and Social History of Britain 1066–1939,* London: Macmillan & Co.

Fontaine, Pascal (2000), *A New Idea for Europe: The Schuman Declaration 1950–2000,* Luxembourg: Office for Official Publications of the European Communities.

Ford, Richard (1929), "Seville, More Spanish than Spain: The City of the Ibero-American Exposition, Which Opens This Spring, Presents a Tapestry of Many Ages and of Nations Old and New," *National Geographic 55* (3), March, pp. 273–310.

Fotopoulos, Georgios, and Nigel Spence (1998), "Accounting for Net Entry into Greek Manufacturing by Establishments of Varying Size," *Small Business Economics 11*, pp. 125–144.

Foulkes, Nicholas (2017), *Patek Philippe: The Authorized Biography,* New York: Penguin Random House.

Frank, Hermann, Alexander Kessler, Christian Korunka, and Manfred Lueger (2002), *Von der Gründungsidee zum Unternehmenserfolg. Eine empirische Analyse von Entwicklungsverläufen österreichischer Gründungen. Veröffentlichungen zur Mittelstandspolitik* 6; Vienna: Federal Ministry of Economics and Labour of the Republic of Austria.

Fraser, Lindley M. (1937), *Economic Thought and Language,* London: A & C Black.

Friedrichs, Christopher R. (1997), "Artisans and Urban Politics in Seventeenth-century Germany," in Geoffrey Crossick, Ed., *The Artisan and the European Town, 1500–1900,* Aldershot and Brookfield, Vermont: Ashgate, pp. 41–55.

Fritsch, Michael, Alexander Kritikos, and Alina Rusakova (2012), "Who Starts a Business and Who is Self-Employed in Germany?" Discussion Paper 1184, Berlin: German Institute for Economic Research (DIW).

Fritsch, Michael, Alexander Kritikos, and Alina Sorgner (2015), "Why Did Self-employment Increase So Strongly in Germany?" *Entrepreneurship and Regional Development 27*, pp. 307–333.

Fritsch, Michael, and Pamela Müller (2004), "Effects of New Business Formation on Regional Development over Time," *Regional Studies 38* (8), pp. 961–976.

Fritsch, Michael, and Jürgen Schmude (2006), *Entrepreneurship in the Region,* Boston: Springer.

Furness, Hannah (2013), "Colourful Legacy of the Long Line of Royal Georges," *The Daily Telegraph*, Thursday, July 25, p. 4.

Fyfe, Hamilton (1922), "England: Survey of English Life & Character," in John Alexander Hammerton, Ed., *Peoples of All Nations: Their Life Today and the Story of Their Past*, London: Educational, pp. 1757–2000.

Galenson, Walter (1952), *The Danish System of Labor Relations: A Study in Industrial Peace*. Cambridge, Massachusetts: Harvard University Press.

Garofoli, Gioacchino (1994), "New Firm Formation and Regional Development: The Italian Case," *Regional Studies 28* (4), pp. 381–393.

Gartner, William B. (1989), "Some Suggestions for Research on Entrepreneurial Traits and Characteristics," *Entrepreneurship: Theory & Practice 14*, pp. 27–37.

Gartner, William B. (1990), "What Are We Talking about When We Talk about Entrepreneurship?" *Journal of Business Venturing 5* (1), pp. 15–28.

Getzner, Michael, Gottfried Haber, and Erich Schwarz (2004), *Gesamtwirtschaftliche Effekte der Unternehmensgründungen in Österreich 2003. Forschungsbericht. Version 2.13.* (Macroeconomic effects of enterprise foundations in Austria in 2003. Survey-report), Klagenfurt: Institut für Wirtschaftwissenschaften Universität Klagenfurt.

Gibbs, Philip (1937), *Ordeal in England: England Speaks Again*, London: William Heinemann.

Glassey, Frank P. S. (1925), "Helsingfors — A Contrast in Light and Shade," *National Geographic 47* (5), May, pp. 597–612.

Glassman, Ulrich, and Helmut Voelzkow (2001), "The Governance of Local Economies in Germany," in Colin Crouch, Patrick Le Galès, Carlo Trigilia, and Helmut Voelzkow, Eds., *Local Production Systems in Europe, Rise or Demise?* Oxford, United Kingdom: Oxford University Press, pp. 79–116.

Godley, Andrew C. (2001), *Jewish Immigrant Entrepreneurship in New York and London 1880–1914*, New York: Palgrave.

Godley, Andrew C., and Mark C. Casson (2010), "History of Entrepreneurship: Britain 1900–2000," in David S. Landes, Joel Mokyr, and William J. Baumol, Eds., *The Invention of Enterprise: Entrepreneurship from Ancient Mesopotamia to Modern Times*, Princeton: New Jersey: Princeton University Press, pp. 243–272.

Graves, William (1967), "The Rhine," *National Geographic 131* (4), April, pp. 449–499.

Graves, William (1968), "Finland: Plucky Neighbor of Soviet Russia," *National Geographic 133* (5), May, pp. 587–629.

Graves, William (1974), "Denmark: Field of the Danes," *National Geographic 145* (2), February, pp. 245–275.

Graves, William (1980), "After an Empire...Portugal," *National Geographic 158* (6), December, pp. 804–831.

Grichnik, Dietmar, and Robert D. Hisrich (2005), "Entrepreneurship Education needs Arising from Entrepreneurial Profiles in Unified Germany — An International Comparison," *Piccola Impresa/Small Business Management 3*, pp. 101–127.

Grill, Jan (2011), "From Street Busking in Switzerland to Meat Factories in the UK: A Comparative Study of Two Roma Migration Networks from Slovakia," in Deema Kaneff and Frances Pine, Eds., *Global Connections and Emerging Inequalities in Europe*, London: Anthem Press, pp. 79–102.

Grimond, John (1990), "Italy Survey," insert in *The Economist*, May 26.

Grin, John, Francisca Felix, Bram Bos, and Sierk Spoelstra (2004), "Practices for Reflexive Design: Lessons from a Dutch Programme on Sustainable Agriculture," *International Journal of Foresight and Innovation Policy 1* (1/2), pp. 126–149.

Grocott, Chris, and Gareth Stockey (2012), *Gibraltar: A Modern History,* Cardiff: University of Wales Press.

Groen, Aard, Jan Ulijn, and Alain Fayolle (2006), "Educational Diversity in Technology Entrepreneurship: Some Experiences from France and the Netherlands," *International Journal of Entrepreneurship and Small Business 3* (5), pp. 517–537.

Grosvenor, Gilbert M., and Donna Kerkam Grosvenor (1963), "Miniature Monaco," *National Geographic 123* (4), April, pp. 546–573.

Grosvenor, Gilbert M., and Charles Neave (1954), "Helping Holland Rebuild Her Land," *National Geographic 106* (3), September, pp. 365–413.

Guesnier, Bernard (1994), "Regional Variations in New Firm Formation in France," *Regional Studies 28* (4), pp. 347–358.

Gundolf, Katherine, and Annabelle Jaouen (2005), "Patterns and Coordination of Collective Action in Small and Very Small Business: The Case of a Tourist Village in the Pyrenees," *International Journal of Entrepreneurship and Small Business 2* (4), pp. 392–403.

Gurău, Călin, Léo-Paul Dana, and Frank Lasch (2012), "Academic Entrepreneurship in UK Biotechnology Firms," *Journal of Enterprising Communities: People and Places in the Global Economy* 6 (2), pp. 154–168.

Gurău, Călin, Frank Lasch, and Léo-Paul Dana (2010), "Human Capital for Successful Entrepreneurial Ventures: The Profile of the Top Management Team (TMT) in UK Biopharmaceutical SMEs," *International Journal of Entrepreneurship and Small Business 11* (4), December, pp. 436–454.

Haberfellner, Regina (2003), "Austria: Still a Highly Regulated Economy," in Robert Kloosterman and Jan Rath, Eds., *Immigrant Entrepreneurs: Venturing Abroad in the Age of Globalization,* Oxford: Berg, pp. 213–232.

Hadad, Sharon, Yossi Hadad, Miki Malul, and Mosi Rosenboim (2012), "Measuring and Ranking Structural Economic Efficiency: Exploring the Case of Spain Compared to Germany," *World Review of Entrepreneurship, Management and Sustainable Development 8* (1), pp. 13–22.

Haetta, Odd Mathis (1996), *The Sami: An Indigenous People of the Arctic,* translated by Ole Petter Gurholt, Vaasa, Finland: Davvi Girji.

Hall, Graham, and Ciwen Tu (2004), "Internationalization and Size, Age and Profitability in the United Kingdom," in Léo-Paul Dana, Ed., *The Handbook of Research on International Entrepreneurship,* Cheltenham, United Kingdom: Edward Elgar, pp. 596–613.

Haller, Dieter (2003), "Place and Ethnicity in Two Merchant Diasporas: a Comparison of Sindhis and Jews in Gibraltar," *Global Networks 3* (1), pp. 75–96.

Hallgrímsdóttir, Berglind, and Charlotte Sigurdardóttir (2003), "The Case of Iceland," in Anders Lundström, Ed., *Towards an Entrepreneurship Policy: A Nordic Perspective,* Oslo: Nordic Innovation Centre, pp. 145–176.

Hamark, Jesper (2014), "Technology and Productivity in the Port of Gothenburg c 1850–1965," *International Journal of Maritime History 26* (2), pp. 265–287.

Hamilton, Robert T., Léo-Paul Dana, and Camilla Benfell (2008), "Changing Cultures: An International Study of Migrant Entrepreneurs," *Journal of Enterprising Culture 16* (1), March, pp. 89–105.

Hanna, Victoria, and Kathryn Walsh (2008), "Interfirm Cooperation among Small Manufacturing Firms," *International Small Business Journal 26* (3), pp. 299–321.

Hansen, Ove Heitmann, and Mette Ravn Midtgard (2008), "Going North: The New Petroleum Province of Norway," in Aslaug Mikkelsen and Oluf Langhelle, Eds., *Arctic Oil and Gas: Sustainability at Risk? Arctic Oil and Gas: Sustainability at Risk?* London and New York: Routledge, pp. 200–239.

Hanson, Earl (1928), "The Island of the Sagas," *National Geographic 53* (4), pp. 499–511.

Hansson, Agnar, Halla Tómasdóttir, Guðrún Mjöll Sigurðardóttir, Lúðvík Elíasson, and Rögnvaldur J. Sæmundsson (2002), *Global Entrepreneurship Monitor 2002: Ísland,* Reykjavík: Reykjavík University.

Harrison, Bennett (1992), "Industrial Districts: Old Wine in New Bottles?" *Regional Studies 26*, pp. 469–483.

Hart, Mark, Karen Bonner, and Jonathan Levie (2016), *Global Entrepreneurship Monitor United Kingdom 2015 Monitoring Report,* London: Global Entrepreneurship Research Association.

Hart, Mark, and Graham Gudgin (1994), "Spatial Variations in New Firm Formation in the Republic of Ireland, 1980–1990," *Regional Studies 28* (4), pp. 367–380.

Hau, Michel, and Nicolas Stoskopf (2005), *Les Dynasties Alsaciennes: du XVIIe siècle à nos jours,* Paris: Perrin.

Haunschild, Ljuba, Frank Wallau, Hans-Eduard Hauser, and Hans-Jürgen Wolter (2007), *Die volkswirtschaftliche Bedeutung der Familienunternehmen, Gutachten im Auftrag der Stiftung Familienunternehmen, Institut für Mittelstandsforschung Materialien,* Nr. 172, Bonn: Institut für Mittelstandsforschung.

Hemsing, Jan (1974), *Treetops Outspan Paxtu,* Nairobi: Sealpoint.

Henrekson, Magnus (2005), "Entrepreneurship: A Weak Link in the Welfare State?" *Industrial and Corporate Change 14* (3), pp. 437–467.

Henry, Thomas R. (1945a), "The White War in Norway," *National Geographic 88* (5), November, pp. 617–640.

Henry, Thomas R. (1945b), "War's Wake in the Rhineland," *National Geographic 88* (1), July, pp. 1–32.

Henry, Thomas R. (1946), "Holland Rises from War and Water," *National Geographic 89* (2), February, pp. 237–260.

Henschel, Thomas (2006), "Risk Management Practices in German SMEs: An Empirical Investigation," *International Journal of Entrepreneurship and Small Business 3* (5), pp. 554–571.

Henschel, Thomas, and Susanne Durst (2016), "Risk Management in Scottish, Chinese and German Small and Medium-sized Enterprises: A Country Comparison," *International Journal of Entrepreneurship and Small Business 29* (1), pp. 112–132.

Herbert, Ulrich (1990), *A History of Foreign Labor in Germany, 1880–1980: Seasonal Workers, Forced Laborers, Guest Workers*, Ann Arbor: University of Michigan Press.

Herrington, Michael (2016), *Global Entrepreneurship Monitor Policy Briefs*, London: GEM Consortium.

Hessels, Jolanda, Niels Bosma, and Sander Wennekers (2005), *Nieuw Ondernemerschap in Herstel: Global Entrepreneurship Monitor 2004*, Zoetermeer: EIM.

Hildebrand, Jesse Richardson (1932), "Royal Copenhagen, Capital of a Farming Kingdom," *National Geographic 61* (2), pp. 217–250.

Hinz, Thomas (1998), *Betriebsgründungen in Ostdeutschland*, Berlin: Edition Sigma.

Hitchens, David, and Patrick O'Farrell (1991), "Comparative Performance of Small Manufacturing Firms Located in South Wales and Two English Regions," *International Small Business Journal 9* (2), pp. 64–70.

Hjalmarsson, Dan (2008), "Entrepreneurship Policy in Sweden: Recent Development," in Anders Lundström, Ed., *Entrepreneurship Policy in the Nordic Countries: Perspectives of the Development since 2003*, Oslo, Norway: Norden Nordic Innovation Centre, pp. 36–44.

Hofstede, Geert (1980), *Culture's Consequences: International Differences in Work-Related Values*, Beverly Hills, California: Sage.

Hofstede, Geert, Niels G. Noorderhaven, A. Roy Thurik, Lorraine M. Uhlaner, Alexander R. M. Wennekers, and Ralph E. Wildeman (2004), "Culture's Role in Entrepreneurship: Self-employment Out of Dissatisfaction," in Terrence E. Brown and Jan Ulijn, Eds., *Innovation, Entrepreneurship and Culture: The Interaction between Technology, Progress and Economic Growth*, Cheltenham, United Kingdom: Edward Elgar, pp. 162–203.

Holmes, Madelyn (1988), *Forgotten Migrants: Foreign Workers in Switzerland Before World War I*, Cranbury, New Jersey: Associated University Presses.

Honig, Benson, and Léo-Paul Dana (2008), "Communities of Dis-entrepreneurship: A Comparative Cross-national Examination of Two Cases of Entrepreneurial Demise," *Journal of Enterprising Communities: People and Places in the Global Economy* 2 (1), pp. 5–20.

Hope, Anne Fulton (1894), *The First Divorce of Henry VIII as Told in the State Papers*, London: Kegan Paul, Trench, Trübner & Co.

Hosmer, Dorothy (1941), "Rhodes, and Italy's Aegean Islands," *National Geographic 79* (4), April, pp. 449–480.

Hultkrantz, Åke (1955), "Swedish Research on the Religion and Folklore of the Lapps," *The Journal of the Royal Anthropological Institute of Great Britain and Ireland 85* (1/2), pp. 81–99.

Hume, Edgar Erskine (1949), "Italy Smiles Again," *National Geographic 95* (6), June, pp. 693–732.

Hume, Edgar Erskine (1951), "The Palio of Siena," *National Geographic 100* (2), August, pp. 231–244.

Hundt, Christian, and Rolf Sternberg (2014), "How Did the Economic Crisis Influence New Firm Creation? A Multilevel Approach Based Upon Data from German Regions," *Jahrbücher für Nationalökonomie und Statistik/Journal of Economics and Statistics 234* (6), pp. 722–756.

Hunnisett, Stanley F., and Jukka Pennanen (1991), "Saami, Gypsies, Indians, and Immigrants," *Ethnos 1991* (3–4), pp. 210–223.

Hunter, Ian (2007), *Age of Enterprise: Rediscovering the New Zealand Entrepreneur 1880–1910*, Auckland: Auckland University Press.

Huntington, Samuel P. (1993), "The Clash of Civilization," *Foreign Affairs 72* (3), pp. 22–49.

Huntington, Samuel P. (1996), *The Clash of Civilization and the Remaking of World Order*, New York: Simon and Schuster.

Hürlimann, Marcel, Ramon Copons, and Joan Altimir (2006), "Detailed Debris Flow Hazard Assessment in Andorra: A Multidisciplinary Approach," *Geomorphology 78* (3–4), August, pp. 359–372.

Hutchison, Isobel Wylie (1928), "A Walking Tour across Iceland," *National Geographic* 53 (4), pp. 467–497.

Hutchison, Isobel Wylie (1943), "Scotland in Wartime," *National Geographic 83* (6), pp. 723–743.

Hutchison, Isobel Wylie (1944), "Wales in Wartime," *National Geographic 85* (6), pp. 751–768.

Hutchison, Isobel Wylie (1946), "Bonnie Scotland, Postwar Style," *National Geographic 89* (5), pp. 545–601.

Hutchison, Isobel Wylie (1949), "2,000 Miles Through Europe's Oldest Kingdom," *National Geographic 95* (2), February, pp. 141–180.

Hutchison, Isobel Wylie (1951), "A Stroll to Venice," *National Geographic 100* (3), September, pp. 378–410.

Hyland, Andrew, Cheryl Higbee, Louise Hassan, Geoffrey T. Fong, Ron Borland, K. Michael Cummings, and Gerard Hastings (2008), "Does Smoke-free Ireland Have More Smoking Inside the Home and Less in Pubs than the United Kingdom? Findings from the International Tobacco Control Policy Evaluation Project," *The European Journal of Public Health 18* (1), pp. 63–65.

Ingold, Tim (1976), *The Skolt Lapps Today,* Cambridge: Cambridge University Press.

Ingold, Tim (1980), *Hunters, Pastoralists and Ranchers,* Cambridge: Cambridge University Press.

Innes, Arthur D. (1922), "England: The Political History of the English People," in John Alexander Hammerton, Ed., *Peoples of All Nations: Their Life Today and the Story of Their Past*, London: Educational, pp. 2001–2015.

International Labour Organisation (1925), *International Labour Directory 1925,* Geneva: International Labour Organisation.

Isak, Aron (1897), *Aron Isaks sjelfbiografi, efter författares handskrift utg. af Israelitiska litteratur-sällskapet,* Stockholm: Joseph Seligmann.

Isak, Aron (1930), *Denkwürdigkeiten des Aron Isak, 1730–1817,* memoirs edited by Z. Holm and Martin Buber, Berlin: Der Heine-Bund.

Jääskö, Outi (1999), "Women's Position in Reindeer Herding Economy: An Environmental Factor," in Ludger Müller-Wille, Ed., *Human Environmental Interactions: Issues and Concerns in Upper Lapland, Finland,* Rovaniemi: Arctic Centre, University of Lapland, pp. 35–40.

Jack, Sarah, Susan Moult, Alistair R. Anderson, and Sarah Dodd (2010), "An Entrepreneurial Network Evolving: Patterns of Change," *International Small Business Journal 28* (4), pp. 315–337.

Jacob, Merle, Mats Lundqvist, and Hans Hellsmark (2003), "Entrepreneurial Transformations in the Swedish University System: The Case of Chalmers University of Technology," *Research Policy 32*, pp. 1555–1568.

Jafarov, Elkhan (2015), *The Role of Diaspora Networks in Opportunity Exploitation by Ethnic Entrepreneurs in Finland,* Turku: Turku School of Economics.

Jagd, Søren (2005), "The 'Network Ethic' and the New Spirit of Capitalism in French Sociology of Capitalism," in Sokratis M. Koniordos, Ed., *Networks, Trust and Social Capital: Theoretical and Empirical Investigations from Europe,* Aldershot, United Kingdom: Ashgate, pp. 47–69.

Jahreskog, Birgitta, Ed., (1982), *The Sami National Minority in Sweden*, Stockholm: Almqvist and Wiksell International.

Jansen, Dorothea, and Mike Weber (2003), *Zur Organisation des Gründungserfolgs*, Wiesbaden: VS-Verlag.

Jennings, Gary (1974), "Bavaria: Mod, Medieval — and Bewitching," *National Geographic 145* (3), March, pp. 409–431.

Jenniskens, Ineke, Jan Ulijn, and Simon Tywuschik (2011), "Cultural Capital and European Entrepreneurship Research: A Plea for a Paradigm Focusing on National, Corporate and Professional Cultural Capital," *International Journal of Entrepreneurship and Small Business 14* (1), pp. 39–55.

Jernsletten, Johnny-Leo L., and Konstantin Klokov (2002), *Sustainable Reindeer Husbandry*, Tromsø: University of Tromsø Centre for Saami Studies.

Johannisson, Bengt (1989), "Beyond Industrial Policy," presented at 16th conference of the European Council for Small Business, September.

Johannisson, Bengt, and Caroline Wigren (2006), "The Dynamics of Community Identity Making in an Industrial District: The Spirit of Gnosjö Revisited," in Chris Steyaert and Daniel Hjorth, Eds., *Entrepreneurship as Social Change: A Third New Movements in Entrepreneurship*, Cheltenham, United Kingdom: Edward Elgar, pp. 188–209.

Johansson, Edvard (2000), "Self-employment and the Predicted Earning Differential — Evidence from Finland," *Finnish Economic Papers 13* (1), Spring, pp. 45–55.

Jones, Trevor, Monder Ram, and Paul Edwards (2007), "Ethnic Minority Business and the Employment of Illegal Immigrants in Birmingham," in Léo-Paul Dana, Ed., *Handbook of Research on Ethnic Minority Entrepreneurship: A Co-evolutionary View on Resource Management*, Cheltenham, United Kingdom: Edward Elgar, pp. 405–424.

Jónsson, Eyþór Ívar (2008), "Entrepreneurship Policy in Iceland — Recent Developments," in Anders Lundström, Ed., *Entrepreneurship Policy in the Nordic Countries — Perspectives of the Development since 2003*, Oslo: Nordic Innovation Centre, pp. 23–29.

Jónsson, Eyþór Ívar (2010), *The Role of the Board in SMEs: Evidence from Iceland*, Reykjavík: Félagsvísindastofnun Háskóla Íslands.

Jónsson, Örn D., and Rögnvaldur J. Saemundsson (2006), "Isolation as a Source of Entrepreneurial Opportunities: Overcoming the Limitations of Isolated Micro-states," in Craig S. Galbraith and Curt H. Stiles, Eds., *Developmental Entrepreneurship: Adversity, Risk, and Isolation*, Amsterdam: Elsevier, pp. 217–234.

Jordine, Melissa R. (2007), *The Dispute Over Gibraltar*, New York: Chelsea House.

Judge, Joseph (1972), "Venice Fights for Life," *National Geographic 142* (5), November, pp. 591–631.

Juillard, Emile (1947), *Atrocités Allemandes dans les Camps de Concentration*, Lyon: Joannès Desvigne & Cie.

Kammerman, Eugene L. (1956). "The Camargue, Land of Cowboys and Gypsies," *National Geographic 109* (5), pp. 667–699.

Kanein, Werner, and Günter Renner (1988), *Ausländerrecht, Kommentar*, 4th edition, Munich: C. H. Beck.

Kantis, Hugo (2005), "The Emergence of Dynamic Ventures in Latin America, Southern Europe and East Asia: An International Comparison," *International Journal of Entrepreneurship and Small Business* 2 (1), pp. 34–56.

Karlsson, Charlie, and Jan Larsson (1993), "A Macro View of the Gnosjo Entrepreneurial Spirit," *Entrepreneurship & Regional Development* 5 (2), pp. 117–140.

Kaufmann, Hans-Rüdiger (2008), "Internationalization of SMEs in Liechtenstein," in Léo-Paul Dana, Isabell M. Welpe, Mary Han, and Vanessa Ratten, Eds., *Handbook of Research on European Business and Entrepreneurship: Towards a Theory of Internationalization*, Cheltenham, United Kingdom: Edward Elgar, pp. 386–409.

Kaynak, Erdener, and Frédéric Jallat (2004), "Marketing in Western Europe: A Monolith or a Multidimensional Market," *Journal of Euromarketing 14* (1–2), pp. 1–14.

Kelley, Donna J., Slavica Singer, and Mike Harrington (2012), *The Global Entrepreneurship Monitor: 2011 Global Report*, Babson Park, Massachusetts: GEM Consortium.

Kelley, Donna J., Slavica Singer, and Mike Herrington (2016), *2015/16 Global Report*, Babson College: GEM Consortium.

Kemp, Ron, and Clemens Lutz (2006), "Perceived Barriers to Entry: Is There Any Difference between Small, Medium-Sized and Large Companies?" *International Journal of Entrepreneurship and Small Business*, *3* (5), pp. 538–553.

Kenney, Nathaniel T. (1961), "United Italy Marks Its 100th Year," *National Geographic 120* (5), November, pp. 593–649.

Kerbey, McFall (1940), "Behind Netherlands Sea Ramparts," *National Geographic 77* (2), February, pp. 255–290.

Khan, Golam Mostafa (1988), "Size and Growth of Asian-owned Incorporated Companies in Britain," *International Small Business Journal* 7 (1), pp. 10–28.

Kihn, W. Langdon (1936), "A Palette from Spain," *National Geographic* 69 (3), March, pp. 407–440.

Klandt, Heinz (1987), "Trends in Small Business Start-up in West Germany," in Robert Goffee and Richard Scase, Eds., *Entrepreneurship in Europe: The Social Processes*, London: Croom Helm, pp. 26–38.

Klandt, Heinz (1997), "State of the Art of Entrepreneurship and SME Research and Education in Germany," in Hans Landström, Hermann Frank, and Jose M. Veciana, Eds., *Entrepreneurship and Small Business Research in Europe: An ESCB Survey*, Brookfield, Vermont: Avebury, pp. 112–137.

Klandt, Heinz (2004), "Entrepreneurship Education and Research in German-Speaking Europe," *Academy of Management Learning and Education 3* (3), pp. 293–301.

Klemmer, Harvey (1941), "Everyday Life in Wartime England," *National Geographic 79* (4), pp. 497–534.

Klemmer, Harvey (1948), "Belgium Comes Back," *National Geographic 93* (5), May, pp. 575–614.

Kloosterman, Robert, Joanne van der Leun, and Jan Rath (1998), "Across the Border: Immigrants' Economic Opportunities, Social Capital and Informal Business Activities," *Journal of Ethnic and Migration Studies 24* (2), April, pp. 249–268.

Kloosterman, Robert, Joanne van der Leun, and Jan Rath (1999), "Mixed Embeddedness: (In)formal Economic Activities and Immigrant Businesses in the Netherlands," *International Journal of Urban and Regional Research 23* (2), pp. 252–266.

Kolvereid, Lars, and Bjørn Willy Åmo (2007), "Entrepreneurship among Graduates from Business Schools: a Norwegian Case," in Alain Fayolle, Ed., *Handbook of Research in Entrepreneurship Education: Contextual Perspectives,* Cheltenham, United Kingdom: Edward Elgar, Volume 2, pp. 207–220.

Kontos, Maria (2003), "Self-employment Policies and Migrants' Entrepreneurship in Germany," *Entrepreneurship & Regional Development 15* (2), pp. 119–135.

Kontos, Maria (2007), "Immigrant Entrepreneurs in Germany," in Léo-Paul Dana, Ed., *Handbook of Research on Ethnic Minority Entrepreneurship: A Co-evolutionary View on Resource Management,* Cheltenham, United Kingdom: Edward Elgar, pp. 445–463.

Kooij, Pim (1997), "Artisans and the Labour Market in Dutch Provincial Capitals Around 1900," in Geoffrey Crossick, Ed., *The Artisan and the European Town, 1500–1900,* Aldershot and Brookfield, Vermont: Ashgate, pp. 239–256.

Kossman-Putto, Johanna Adriana, and Ernst H. Kossman (1996), *The Low Countries: History of the Northern and Southern Netherlands,* translated by Jane Fenoulhet, Theo Hermans, and Paul Vincent, Rekkem, Belgium: Flemish-Netherlands Foundation.

Kourtit, Karima, and Peter Nijkamp (2011), "The New Dutch Economy: New and Colourful Entrepreneurship," in Marco van Gelderen and Enno Masurel, Eds., *Entrepreneurship in Context,* London: Routledge, pp. 187–201.

Kraus, Sascha, Rainer Harms, and Erich Schwarz, (2008), "Strategic Business Planning and Success in Small Firms," *International Journal of Entrepreneurship and Innovation Management 8* (4), pp. 381–396.

Kraus, Sascha, and Erich Schwarz (2007), "The Role of Pre-Start-Up-Planning in New Small Business," *International Journal of Management and Enterprise Development 4* (1), pp. 1–17.

Kraus, Sascha, and Arndt Werner (2012), "Nascent Migrant Entrepreneurship in Germany: Is There a Culturing effect?" *International Journal of Entrepreneurship and Small Business 15* (3), pp. 320–339.

Krieger, Joel (1987), "The United Kingdom: Symbiosis or Division," in George Lodge and Ezra F. Vogel, Eds., *Ideology and National Competitiveness: An*

Analysis of Nine Countries, Boston, Massachusetts: Harvard Business School Press, pp. 29–53.

Kruisinga, J. C. M. (1933), "A New Country Awaits Discovery: The Draining of the Zuider Zee Makes Room for the Excess Population of the Netherlands," *National Geographic 64* (3), September, pp. 293–320.

Kurtoglu, Filiz (2007), "Immigrant Entrepreneurs in Austria," in Léo-Paul Dana, Ed., *Handbook of Research on Ethnic Minority Entrepreneurship: A Co-evolutionary View on Resource Management*, Cheltenham, United Kingdom: Edward Elgar, pp. 425–432.

La Fay, Howard (1965), "Portugal at the Crossroads," *National Geographic 128* (4), October, pp. 453–501.

La Fay, Howard (1966), "Gibraltar — Rock of Contention," *National Geographic 130* (1), July, pp. 102–121.

Lacey, Robert (1977), *Majesty: Elizabeth II and the House of Windsor*, New York and London: Harcourt Brace Jovanovich.

Lacroix, Thomas, and Antoine Dumont (2015), "Moroccans in France: Their Organizations and Activities Back Home," in Alejandro Portes and Patricia Fernández-Kelly, Eds., *The State and the Grassroots*, New York: Berghahn pp. 212–235.

Lado, Augustine A., Nancy G. Boyd, and Susan C. Hanlon (1997), "Competition, Cooperation, and the Search for Economic Rents: A Syncretic Model," *Academy of Management Review 22* (1), pp. 110–141.

Landler, Mark (2005), "For Europe, the Costs of a Weak Germany: Berlin Can No Longer be EU Sugar Daddy," *International Herald Tribune*, June 25, p. 1.

Landström, Hans (1999), "The Roots of Entrepreneurship Research," *New England Journal of Entrepreneurship 2* (2), Fall, pp. 9–20.

Lasch, Frank, and Said Yami (2008), "The Nature and Focus of Entrepreneurship in France over the Last Decade: A French Touch?" *Entrepreneurship: Theory & Practice 32* (2), pp. 339–360.

Laurent, André (1983), "A Cultural Diversity of Western Conceptions of Management," *International Studies of Management and Organization 13*, Spring/Summer, pp. 75–96.

Laxalt, Robert (1966), "Basque Sheepherders: Lonely Sentinels of the American West," *National Geographic 129* (6) June, pp. 870–888.

Laxalt, Robert (1968), "Land of the Ancient Basques," *National Geographic 134* (2), August, pp. 240–277.

Laxalt, Robert (1974), "The Enduring Pyrenees," *National Geographic 146* (6), December, pp. 794–819.

Le Galès, Yann (2010), "Sarkozy: 'Les PME sont le fer de lance de la croissance," *Le Figaro*, June 10, p. 20.

Lee, Susan E., Malcolm C. Press, John A. Lee, Tim Ingold, and Terhi Kurttila (2000), "Regional Effects of Climate Change on Reindeer: A Case Study of the Muotkatunturi Region in Finnish Lapland," *Polar Research 19* (1), pp. 99–105.

Lefèvre-Utile, Patrick (1995), *L'Art du Biscuit*, Vanves: Fernand Hazan.

Lehnert, Nicole (2003), "Existenzgründungen durch Migranten in Deutschland: Ergebnisse des DtA-Gründungsmonitors 2002," in Deutsche Ausgleichsbank, Ed., *Wirtschaftsdynamik durch Existenzgründungen Migranten*, Bonn: Deutsche Ausgleichsbank, pp. 39–54.

Lehti, Matti, and Kauko Aromaa (2002), *Trafficking in Human Beings, Illegal Immigration and Finland*, Helsinki: Helsinki University Press.

Lehtola, Veli-Pekka (2002), *The Sámi People: Traditions in Transition*, Inari: Kustannus-Puntsi.

Leicht, René, Markus Leiss, and Silke Fehrenbach (2005), "Social and Economic Characteristics of Self-Employed Italians in Germany," *International Journal of Migration Studies 62* (158), pp. 285–307.

Lepoutre, Jan, Olivier Tilleuil, Miguel Meuleman, and Hans Crijns (2009), *Global Entrepreneurship Monitor Rapport voor Vlaanderen & België*, Ghent and Leuven: Autonomous Management School of Ghent University and Katholicke Universiteit Leuven.

Leung, Maggi W. H. (2007), "Migrant Entrepreneurship in Germany," in Léo-Paul Dana, Ed., *Handbook of Research on Ethnic Minority Entrepreneurship: A Co-evolutionary View on Resource Management*, Cheltenham, United Kingdom: Edward Elgar, pp. 464–487.

Levathes, Louise E. (1987), "Iceland: Life Under the Glaciers," *National Geographic 171* (2), February, pp. 184–215.

Light, Ivan H., Shahamak Rezaei, and Léo-Paul Dana (2013), "Ethnic Minority Entrepreneurs in the International Carpet Trade," *International Journal of Entrepreneurship and Small Business 18* (2), pp. 125–153.

Lindelöf, Peter, and Hans Löfsten (2003), "Science Park Location and New Technology-Based Firms in Sweden: Implications for Strategy and Performance," *Small Business Economics 20*, pp. 245–258.

Lindquist, Willis (1940), "On Danish By-lanes," *National Geographic 77* (1), pp. 1–34.

Lodge, George C., and Ezra F. Vogel, Eds., (1987), *Ideology and National Competitiveness: An Analysis of Nine Countries*, Boston, Massachusetts: Harvard Business School Press.

Loewen, James W. (1971), *The Mississippi Chinese: Between Black and White*, Cambridge, Massachusetts: Harvard University Press.

Long, George W. (1951), "Occupied Austria, Outpost of Democracy," *National Geographic 99* (6), June, pp. 749–790.

Luciani, Patrick (1987), "Small Business, Italian-Style: Low-key, but High-tech, Small Companies Lead the Italian Economic Renaissance," *Small Business*, May, pp. 34–43.

Lundqvist, Mats A., and Karen L. Williams Middleton (2010), "Promises of Societal Entrepreneurship: Sweden and Beyond," *Journal of Enterprising Communities: People and Places in the Global Economy 4* (1), pp. 24–36.

Lundström, Anders (2003), "Results and Summary," in Anders Lundström, Ed., *Towards an Entrepreneurship Policy: A Nordic Perspective,* Oslo: Nordic Innovation Centre, pp. 265–289.

Lundström, Anders, Ed., (2008), *Entrepreneurship Policy in the Nordic Countries: Perspectives of the Development since 2003,* Oslo, Norway: Norden Nordic Innovation Centre.

Luostarinen, Reijo, and Mika Gabrielsson (2004), "Finnish Perspectives of International Entrepreneurship," in Léo-Paul Dana, Ed., *The Handbook of Research on International Entrepreneurship,* Cheltenham, United Kingdom: Edward Elgar, pp. 383–403.

Lynch, David J. (2001), "'Entrepreneur' No Longer a Dirty Word in Sweden: Traditions Change, Start-ups Sprout," *USA Today,* Friday 30 March, p. 9A.

Ma Mung, Emmanuel, and Thomas Lacroix (2003), "France: The Narrow Path," in Robert Kloosterman and Jan Rath, Eds., *Immigrant Entrepreneurs: Venturing Abroad in the Age of Globalization,* Oxford: Berg, pp. 173–194.

Macknight, Thomas (1854), *The Right Honourable Benjamin Disraeli: A Literary and Political Biography,* London: Richard Bentley.

MacLeish, Kenneth (1966), "River of Counts and Kings: The Loire," *National Geographic 129* (6), June, pp. 822–869.

Magatti, Mauro (2003), "Italy: Between Legal Barriers and Informal Arrangements," in Robert Kloosterman and Jan Rath, Eds., *Immigrant Entrepreneurs: Venturing Abroad in the Age of Globalization,* Oxford: Berg, pp. 147–172.

Magga, Ole Henrik (1985), "Are We Finally to Get Our Rights? On the Work to Secure the Saami Peoples' Rights," in Jens Brøsted, Jens Dahl, Andrew Gray, Hans Christian Gulløv, Georg Henriksen, Jørgen Brøchner Jørgensen, and Inge Kleivan, Eds., *Native Power: The Quest for Autonomy and Nationhood of Indigenous Peoples,* Bergen, Norway: Universitetsforlaget, pp. 15–22.

Maggioni, Vincenzo, Mario Sorrentino, and Mary Wlliams (1999), "Mixed Consequences of Government Aid for New Venture Creation: Evidence from Italy," *Journal of Management and Governance 3,* pp. 287–305.

Mahlamäki-Kultanen, Seija (2005), "Gender and Sector Effects on Finnish Rural Entrepreneurs' Culture: Some Educational Implications," in Alain Fayolle, Paula Kyrö, and Jan Ulijn, Eds., *Entrepreneurship Research in Europe: Outcomes and Perspectives,* Cheltenham, United Kingdom: Edward Elgar, pp. 292–312.

Majocchi, Antonio, and Antonella Zucchella (2003), "Internationalization and Performance: Findings from a Set of Italian SMEs," *International Small Business Journal 21* (3), pp. 249–268.

Malaise, N. (1988), *Conditions de Travail et Petites et Moyennes Entreprises,* Dublin: Fondation européenne pour l'amélioration des conditions de vie et de travail.

Malden, Walter J. (1899), *Sheep Raising and Shepherding: A Handbook of Sheep Farming,* London: L. Upcott Gill.

Mandl, Irene (2004), *Business Transfers and Successions in Austria*, Vienna: Austrian Institute for SME Research.

Manker, Ernst Mauritz (1952), "Swedish Contributions to Lapp Ethnography," *Royal Anthropological Institute Journal 82*, pp. 39–54.

Manker, Ernst Mauritz (1953), *The Nomadism of the Swedish Mountain Lapps: The Siidas and Their Migratory Routes in 1945*, translated by Robert N. Pehrson, Stockholm: Hugo Gebers Förlag.

Manuel, George, and Michael Posluns (1974), *The 4th World: An Indian Reality*, New York: Free Press.

Marden, Luis (1955), "Bruges, the City the Sea Forgot: Belgium's Chief Port and World-trade Center in Medieval Days Relives Its Past in Brilliant, Reverent Pageantry," *National Geographic 107* (5), May, pp. 631–665.

Marlow, Susan (1992), "The Take-up of Business Growth Training Schemes by Ethnic Minority-owned Small Firms in Britain," *International Small Business Journal 10* (4), pp. 34–46.

Marsh, Peter (2004), "Customisation: Mass-produced for Individual Tastes," *Financial Times,* April 22, p. 8.

Marshall, Alfred (1890), *Principles of Economics: An Introductory Text*, London: Macmillan.

Marshall, Alfred (1919), *Industry and Trade: A Study of Industrial Technique and Business Organization and of Their Influence on the Conditions of Various Classes and Nations,* London: Macmillan.

Maskell Peter, and Anders Malmberg (1999), "Localised Learning and Industrial Competitiveness," *Cambridge Journal of Economics 23*, pp. 167–185.

Mason, Colin, Ross Brown, Mark Hart, and Michael Anyadike-Danes (2015), "High Growth Firms, Jobs and Peripheral Regions: The Case of Scotland," *Cambridge Journal of Regions, Economy and Society 8* (2), pp. 343–358.

Mason, Colin, Steven Pinch, and Angele Storey (1991), "Self-employment in a British City: An Analysis of Household Survey Data," *International Small Business Journal 10* (1), pp. 27–43.

Mattiacci, Alberto, Christian Simoni, and Lorenzo Zanni (2008), "Italian SME International Strategies: State of the Art and Some Empirical Evidences," in Léo-Paul Dana, Isabell M. Welpe, Mary Han, and Vanessa Ratten, Eds., *Handbook of Research on European Business and Entrepreneurship: Towards a Theory of Internationalization,* Cheltenham, United Kingdom: Edward Elgar, pp. 337–365.

Mauco, Georges (1932), *Les Etrangers en France: Etude Géographique sur leur Rôle dans l'activité Economique*, Paris: Armand Collin.

Mayer, Nonna (1987), "Small Business and Social Mobility in France," in Robert Goffee and Richard Scase, Eds., *Entrepreneurship in Europe: The Social Processes*, London: Croom Helm, pp. 39–59.

McAllister, John F. O. (2002), "Golden Jubilee: Elizabeth II," *Time*, Canadian edition, June 23, pp. 40–49.

McBride, Harry A. (1929), "On the Bypaths of Spain," *National Geographic 55* (3), March, pp. 311–372.

McBride, Harry A. (1931), "Pursuing Spanish Bypaths Northwest of Madrid," *National Geographic 59* (1), January, pp. 121–130.

McBride, Ruth Q. (1936), "Turbulent Spain," *National Geographic 70* (4), October, pp. 397–427.

McCall, Grant (1980), "Four Worlds of Experience and Action," *Third World Quarterly 2* (3), pp. 536–545.

McCarry, John (1992), "Milan: Where Italy Gets Down to Business," *National Geographic 182* (6), December, pp. 90–122.

McDonald, Michael Dwyer, and Frank Wendt (1994), "Italy's Black Economy: Corporate Indiscretion," *Management Decision 32* (3), pp. 49–52.

McDowell, Bart (1965), "The Changing Face of Old Spain," *National Geographic 127* (3), March, pp. 291–339.

McDowell, Bart (1986), "The Dutch Treat," *National Geographic 170* (4), October, pp. 501–525.

McEvoy, David, and Khalid Hafeez (2009), "Ethnic Enclaves or Middleman Minority? Regional Patterns of Ethnic Minority Entrepreneurship in Britain," *International Journal of Business and Globalisation 3* (1), pp. 94–110.

McGinty, Jo Craven (2015), "Happiness Gauges Show Money Isn't Everything," *The Wall Street Journal*, August 22–23, p. A2.

McGrath, Rita Gunter, Ian C. MacMillan, and Sari Scheinberg (1992), "Elitists, Risk-Takers, and Rugged Individualists? An Exploratory Analysis of Cultural Differences Between Entrepreneurs and Non-Entrepreneurs," *Journal of Business Venturing* 7, pp. 115–135.

McMillan, John (2002), *Reinventing the Bazaar: The Natural History of Markets,* New York: W. W. Norton & Co.

Meulemans, Dirk (2000), "Developing Startpunt, a Business Incubator for the Social Economy," in Dirk Deschoolmeester, Daniel De Steur, Kathy Gillis, and Tom Schamp, Eds., *Entrepreneurship Under Difficult Circumstances*, Seminar Proceedings of the 30th European Small Business Seminar, Gent, Belgium, September 20–22, pp. 95–105.

Miles, Marc A., Edwin J. Feulner, and Mary Anastasia O'Grady (2005), *2005 Index of Economic Freedom,* Washington, DC: The Heritage Foundation.

Miles, Raymond E., Grant Miles, and Charles C. Snow (2005), *Collaborative Entrepreneurship: How Communities of Networked Firms Innovation to Create Economic Wealth*, Stanford: Stanford University Press.

Mill, John Stuart (1848), *The Principles of Political Economy with Some of Their Applications to Social Philosophy*, London: John W. Parker, Volumes 1 & 2; revised 1886, London: Longmann, Green.

Mill, John Stuart (1869), *On Liberty,* London: Longman, Roberts and Green.

Miller, Helen Hill (1960), "Rotterdam — Reborn From Ruins," *National Geographic 118* (4), October, pp. 526–553.

Mingels, Guido (2014), "Island: Zurück im Glück," *Der Spiegel 2014* (2), January 6, pp. 86–89.

Minniti, Maria (2005), "An Empirical Assessment of Entrepreneurial Behaviour: The Case of Italy," *Global Business and Economics Review 7* (1), pp. 31–46.

Minniti, Maria, and Patrizia Venturelli (2000), *Global Entrepreneurship Monitor National Assessment: Italy 2000 Executive Report*, Wellesley: Babson College.

Mitchell, Carleton (1970), "Capri, Italy's Enchanted Rock," *National Geographic 137* (6), June, pp. 795–809.

Moore, W. Robert (1938), "Castles and Progress in Portugal," *National Geographic 73* (2), February, pp. 133–188.

Moore, W. Robert (1943), "The Coasts of Normandy and Brittany," *National Geographic 84* (2), August, pp. 205–224.

Morgenstierne, Wilhelm (1943), "Norway, an Active Ally," *National Geographic 83* (3), March, pp. 333–357.

Morton, Arthur Leslie (1938), *A People's History of England*, London: Victor Gollancz.

Morton, Henry Vollam (1953), "In the London of the New Queen," *National Geographic 104* (3), pp. 291–342.

Moskowitz, Sanford L. (2008), "Internationalization of Small and Medium-sized Firms (SMEs) in a Western European Service Economy: The Case of Andorra," in Léo-Paul Dana, Isabell M. Welpe, Mary Han, and Vanessa Ratten, Eds., *Handbook of Research on European Business and Entrepreneurship: Towards a Theory of Internationalization*, Cheltenham, United Kingdom: Edward Elgar, pp. 31–41.

Muffatto, Moreno, Patrizia Garengo, Donato Iacobucci, Alessandra Micozzi, Michael Sheriff, and Saadat Saeed (2015), *Global Entrepreneurship Monitor Italia 2014*, Padua: Università degli Studi di Padova.

Mugler, Josef (1998), *Betriebswirtschaftslehre der Klein- und Mittelbetriebe*, Vienna: Springer.

Mulhern, Alan (1995), "The SME Sector in Europe: A Broad Perspective," *Journal of Small Business Management 33* (3), July, pp. 83–87.

Müller-Wille, Ludger (1978), "Cost Analysis of Modern Hunting among the Inuit of the Canadian Central Arctic," *Polar Geography 2* (2), pp. 104–114.

Müller-Wille, Ludger (1987), "Indigenous People, Land-use Conflicts, and Economic Development in Circumpolar Lands," *Arctic and Alpine Research 19* (4), pp. 351–356.

Müller-Wille, Ludger, and Pertti J. Pelto (1971), "Technological Change and Its Impact in Arctic Regions: Lapps Introduce Snowmobiles into Reindeer Herding, *Polarforschung 41*, pp. 142–148.

Mumford, Lewis (1938), *The Culture of Cities,* New York: Harcourt Brace Jovanovich.

Musgrave, Elizabeth (1997), "Women and the Craft Guilds in Eighteenth-century Nantes," in Geoffrey Crossick, Ed., *The Artisan and the European Town, 1500–1900,* Aldershot and Brookfield, Vermont: Ashgate, pp. 151–171.

Naldi, Lucia, and Andrea Kuiken (2016), *International Market Exit and Re-entry: An Empirical Study of Export Patterns of Swedish SMEs*, Örebro, Sweden: Entreprenörskapsforum.

Nasmith, George, G. (1919), *Canada's Sons and Great Britain in the World War,* Toronto: John C. Winston.

Nekka, Hadj, and Alain Fayolle (2010), "Muslim Entrepreneurs in France," in Léo-Paul Dana, Ed., *Entrepreneurship & Religion*, Cheltenham, United Kingdom: Edward Elgar, pp. 296–312.

Ní Bhrádaigh, Emer (2007), "Entrepreneurship in the Gaeltachtaí of Ireland," in Léo-Paul Dana and Robert Brent Anderson, Eds., *Indigenous Entrepreneurship,* Cheltenham, United Kingdom: Edward Elgar, pp. 211–231.

Nijkamp, Peter, Cher Guldemond, and Hugo Teelen (2004), "The Importance of Venture Capital for High-tech Development Experiences from the Netherlands and Israel," *International Journal of Entrepreneurship and Innovation Management 4* (1), pp. 41–49.

Nilson, Elizabeth W. (1940), "Rural Sweden Through American Eyes," *National Geographic 77* (6), June, pp. 795–814.

Niskanen, Kirst (2001), "Theoretical Issues: Gender Economics in Action: Rural Women's Economic Citizenship in Finland during the Twentieth Century," *Journal of Women's History 13* (2), Summer, pp. 132–152.

Nolan, John E. H. (1954), "In the Land of the Basques," *National Geographic 105* (2), February, pp. 147–187.

Nothdurft, William E. (1992), *Going Global: How Europe Helps Small Firms Export,* Washington, DC: Brookings Institution.

Nummela, Niina (2004), "Three Case Studies from Finland," in Léo-Paul Dana, Ed., *The Handbook of Research on International Entrepreneurship,* Cheltenham, United Kingdom: Edward Elgar, pp. 404–430.

Nuttall, Mark (2005), "Greenland," in Mark Nuttall, Ed., *Encyclopedia of the Arctic,* New York, New York: Routledge, pp. 778–785.

Nziali, Emeran, and Alain Fayolle (2013), *L'entrepreneuriat en France: Une Comparaison Internationale,* Lyon: E M Lyon Business School.

Obrecht, Jean-Jacques (2002), "The Public System of Incubators in France," in Peter C. van der Sijde, Birgit Wirsing, Rudi Cluyvers and Annemarie Ridder, Eds., *New Concepts for Academic Entrepreneurship*, Twente: Twente University Press.

Obrecht, Jean-Jacques (2005), "L'Entrepreneuriat International: Un Rhizome Vigoureux dans un Terrain Nouveau," *Les Sciences de Gestion au Cœur du*

Développement, Actes du Colloque International INSCAE, Antananarivo, Madagascar, November 2–4.

Obrecht, Jean-Jacques (2016), "Sustainable Entrepreneurship Education: A New Field for Research in Step with the Effectual Entrepreneur," *International Journal of Entrepreneurship and Small Business 29* (1), pp. 83–102.

Oeij, Peter, Ernest de Vroome, Astrid Bolland, Rob Grundemann, and Lex van Teeffelen (2014), "Investing in Workplace Innovation Pays Off for SMEs: A Regional Innovation Initiative from the Netherlands," *International Journal of Social Quality 4* (2), pp. 86–106.

Ohlson, Birger (1960), "Settlement and Economic Life in Enotekiö — A Parish in the Extreme North of Finland," *Fennia 84*, pp. 21–46.

Oliveira, Cararina Reis (2008), "The Determinants of Immigrant Entrepreneurial Strategies in Portugal," *Migrações 3*, October, pp. 101–128.

Olson, Alma Luise (1928), "Sweden, Land of White Birch and White Coal," *National Geographic 54* (4), October, pp. 441–484.

Olson, Alma Luise (1938), "The Farthest-North Republic: Olympic Games and Arctic Flying Bring Sequestered Finland into New Focus of World Attention," *National Geographic 74* (4), October, pp. 499–534.

Oxholm, Axel H. (1939), "Country Life in Norway: The Beneficent Gulf Stream Enables One-third of the People in a Far-north, Mountainous Land to Prosper on Farms," *National Geographic 75* (4), April, pp. 493–528.

Paché, Gilles (1996), "The Small Producer in the French Food Distribution Channel," *Journal of Small Business Entrepreneurship* (2), April, pp. 84–88.

Padmore, Tim, and Hervey Gibson (1997), "Modelling Systems of Innovation: A Framework for Industrial Cluster Analysis in Regions," *Research Policy 26*, pp. 625–641.

Paine, Robert (1984), "Norwegians and Saami: Nation-State and Fourth World," in Gerald L. Gold, Ed., *Minorities and Mother Country Imagery*, St. John's, Newfoundland, Canada: Memorial University, pp. 211–248.

Paine, Robert (1985), "The Claim of the Fourth World," in Jens Brøsted, Jens Dahl, Andrew Gray, Hans Christian Gulløv, Georg Henriksen, Jørgen Brøchner Jørgensen, and Inge Kleivan, Eds., *Native Power: The Quest for Autonomy and Nationhood of Indigenous Peoples*, Bergen, Norway: Universitetsforlaget, pp. 49–66.

Paine, Robert (1994), *Herds of the Tundra: A Portrait of Saami Reindeer Pastoralism*, Washington, DC, and London: Smithsonian Institution Press.

Palmer, Robin (2007), "Italians in Britain: 'Britalian Culture Entrepreneurs' Revisted," in Léo-Paul, Ed., *Handbook of Research on Ethnic Minority Entrepreneurship: A Co-evolutionary View on Resource Management*, Cheltenham, United Kingdom: Edward Elgar, pp. 360–374.

Pang, Ching Lin (2003), "Belgium: From Proletarians to Proteans," in Robert Kloosterman and Jan Rath, Eds., *Immigrant Entrepreneurs: Venturing Abroad in the Age of Globalization*, Oxford: Berg, pp. 195–212.

Parmentier, Antoine-Augustin (1789), *Traité sur la Culture et les Usages des Pommes de Terre, de la Patate, et du Topinambour,* Paris: Barrois.

Pascal, Blaise (1701), *Pensées sur la Religion, et sur Quelques Autres Sujets. Augmentée de beaucoup de pensées, de la vie de l'auteur, & de quelques dissertations*, Amsterdam: Pierre Mortier.

Patric, John (1940), "Italy, from Roman Ruins to Radio," *National Geographic 77* (3), March, pp. 347–394.

Pattisson, Naomi, and Adam Lindgreen (2004), "Success and Failures in the Dairy Industry: South West England and North West France," *British Food Journal 106* (6), pp. 422–435.

Peet, John (2002), "Model Makers: A Survey of the Netherlands," insert in *The Economist*, May 4.

Peet, John (2005), "Addio, Dolce Vita," insert in *The Economist*, November 26.

Pelto, Pertti Juho (1973), *The Snowmobile Revolution: Technology and Social Change in the Arctic,* Menlo Park, California: Cummings.

Pelto, Pertti Juho (1978), "Ecology, De-localization and Social Change," in Ludger Müller-Wille, Pertti J. Pelto, Linna Müller-Wille, and Regna Darnell, Eds., *Consequences of Economic Change in Circumpolar Regions,* Edmonton, Alberta, Canada: Boreal Institute for Northern Studies, pp. 29–36.

Pelto, Pertti Juho, and Ludger Müller-Wille (1972/1973), "Reindeer Herding and Snowmobiles: Aspects of a Technological Revolution," *Folk 14–15*, pp 119–144.

Peltoniemi, Mirva (2009), "Entrepreneurship and Innovation within Creative Industries: A Case Studies on the Finnish Games Industry," *International Journal of Entrepreneurship and Small Business 7* (4), pp. 420–430.

Pereira, Elisabeth T. (2007), "The Internationalisation of Portuguese SMEs," *International Journal of Business and Globalisation 1* (3), pp. 369–390.

Pereira, Elisabeth T., and António Jorge Fernandes (2006), "Clusters Development as a Factor of Competitive Advantage," *International Journal of Entrepreneurship and Small Business 3* (2), pp. 266–276.

Pereira, Elisabeth T., António Jorge Fernandes, and Henrique Manuel Morais Diz (2004), "Evolutionary Economics: Application to the Case of Ceramics Industry in the Portuguese District of Aveiro," presented at the conference, New Economic Windows 2004: Complexity Hints for Economic Policy, University of Salerno, Salerno, Italy, September.

Perier, Mme (1842), *Pensées de Pascal, Précédées de sa Vie par Mme Perier, sa Soeur, Suivies d'un Choix des Pensées de Nicole, et son Traité de la Paix avec les Hommes*, Paris: Librairie de Firmin Didot Frères, Imprimeur de l'Institut.

Peroni, Chiara, Cesare A. F. Riillo, and Francesco Sarracino (2016), "Entrepreneurship and Immigration: Evidence from GEM Luxembourg," *Small Business Economics 46* (4), pp. 639–656.

Peters, Mike, Stefan Märk, and Sascha Kraus (2011), "The Influences of Family on the Everyday Business of a Family Firm Entrepreneur," *International Journal of Entrepreneurship and Small Business 12* (1), pp. 82–100.

Peterson, Rein (1988), "Understanding and Encouraging Entrepreneurship Internationally," *Journal of Small Business Management 26* (2), pp. 1–7.

Peterson, Rein, and Mari A. Peterson (1981), "The Impact of Economic Regulation and Paperwork," *Regulation Reference Working Paper Series,* Ottawa, Canada: Economic Council of Canada.

Pfiffner, Albert (1993), *Henri Nestlé (1814–1890): Vom Frankfurter Apothekergehilfen zum Schweizer Pionierunternehmer,* Zurich: Chronos-Verlag.

Pichler, J. Hanns, and Walter Bornett (2005), "Wirtschaftliche Bedeutung der kleinen und mittleren Unternehmen (KMU) in Österreich," in Reinbert Schauer, Norbert Kailer, and Birgit Norbert, Eds., *Mittelständische Unternehmen*; Linz, Austria: Trauner.

Pickerell, James H. (1968), "Dory on the Banks: A Day in the Life of a Portuguese Fisherman," *National Geographic 133* (4), April, pp. 573–583.

Pickernell, David, David Brooksbank, Helena Snee, Farid Ullah, and Dylan Jones-Evans (2008), "Internationalization of Welsch SMEs: The Role of Wales Trade International," in Léo-Paul Dana, Isabell M. Welpe, Mary Han, and Vanessa Ratten, Eds., *Handbook of Research on European Business and Entrepreneurship: Towards a Theory of Internationalization*, Cheltenham, United Kingdom: Edward Elgar, pp. 718–739.

Pinho, José Carlos, and Lurdes Martins (2010), "Exporting Barriers: Insights from Portuguese Small- and Medium-sized Exporters and Non-exporters," *Journal of International Entrepreneurship 8*, pp. 254–272.

Piore, Michael J., and Charles F. Sabel (1984), *The Second Industrial Divide,* New York: Basic Books.

Poelzer, Greg (2013), "Saskatchewan Vikings," *Policy Options,* March, pp. 34–37.

Porter, Michael E. (1990), *The Competitive Advantage of Nations,* New York: Free Press.

Porter, Michael E. (1998a), "Clusters and the New Economics of Competition," *Harvard Business Review 76* (6), November-December, pp. 77–90.

Porter, Michael E. (1998b), *On Competition,* Boston, Massachusetts: Harvard Business School Press.

Portes, Alejandro, and William Haller (2005), "The Informal Economy," in Neil J. Smelser and Richard Swedberg, Eds., *The Handbook of Economic Sociology,* Princeton: Princeton University Press, pp. 403–425.

Potts, Neil (2000), "Will the Single European Market Make Us All Richer and Happier?" *European Business Review 12* (6), pp. 332–336.

Putman, John J. (1977), "West Germany: Continuing Miracle," *National Geographic 152* (2), August, pp. 149–181.

Putman, John J. (1981), "A New Day for Ireland," *National Geographic 159* (4), April, pp. 442–469.

Putman, John J. (1986), "Madrid: The Change in Spain," *National Geographic 169* (2), February, pp. 142–181.

Pütz, Robert, Verena Schreiber, and Isabell Welpe (2007), "Ethnicity, Gender and Entrepreneurship: Turkish Entrepreneurs in Germany," in Léo-Paul Dana, Ed., *Handbook of Research on Ethnic Minority Entrepreneurship: A Co-evolutionary View on Resource Management,* Cheltenham, United Kingdom: Edward Elgar, pp. 488–510.

Pyke, Frank, Giacomo Becattini, and Werner Sengenberger (1992), *Industrial Districts and Inter-firm Co-operation in Italy,* Geneva: International Labour Organisation.

Rabellotti, Roberta (1995), "Is There an 'Industrial District Model'? Footwear Districts in Italy and Mexico Compared," *World Development 23*, pp. 29–41.

Raes, Stephan (2000), "Regionalization in a Globalizing World: The Emergence of Clothing Sweatshops in the European Union," in Jan Rath, Ed., *Immigrant Businesses: The Economic, Political and Social Environment,* Basingstoke, United Kingdom: Macmillan, pp. 20–36.

Rainnie, Al, and Michael Scott (1986), "Industrial Relations in the Small Firm," in James Curran, John Stanworth, and David Watkins, Eds., *The Survival of the Small Firm,* Aldershot, United Kingdom: Gower, pp. 42–60.

Rama, Ruth, and Ascension Calatrava (2002), "The Advantages of Clustering: The Case of Spanish Electronics Subcontractors," *International Journal of Technology Management 24* (7–8), pp. 764–791.

Rama, Ruth, Deron Ferguson, and Ana Melero (2003), "Subcontracting Networks in Industrial Districts: The Electronics Industries of Madrid," *Regional Studies 37* (1), pp. 71–88.

Range, Peter Ross (2003), "Corsica: France's Island Paradox," *National Geographic 203* (4), April, pp. 56–75.

Rath, Jan (2002), "Do Immigrant Entrepreneurs Play the Game of Ethnic Musical Stairs? A Critique of Waldinger's Model of Immigrant Incorporation," in Anthony M. Messina, Ed., *West European Immigration and Immigrant Policy in the New Century*, Westport, Connecticut: Praeger, pp. 141–159.

Rath, Jan (2003), "Undressing the Garment Industry: Immigrant Entrepreneurship in Seven Cities," in Jeffrey G. Reitz, Ed., *Host Societies and the Reception of Immigrants,* La Jolla, California: Centre for Comparative Immigration Studies, pp. 253–286.

Rath, Jan, and Robert Kloosterman (2003), "The Netherlands: A Dutch Treat," in Robert Kloosterman and Jan Rath, Eds., *Immigrant Entrepreneurs: Venturing Abroad in the Age of Globalization,* Oxford: Berg, pp. 123–146.

Rath, Jan, and Anna Swagerman (2011), *Promoting Ethnic Entrepreneurship in European Cities,* Luxembourg: Publications Office of the European Union.

Raton, Pierre (1969), *Liechtenstein: Staat und Geschichte*, Vaduz: Liechtenstein-Verlag.

Reid, James Macarthur (1938), *The History of the Clydesdale Bank 1838–1938*, Glasgow: Blackie and Son Limited.

Reynolds, Paul Davidson (1997), "New and Small Firms in Expanding Markets," *Small Business Economics 9* (1), pp. 79–84.

Rezaei, Shahamak, Marco Goli, and Léo-Paul Dana (2013a), "An Empirical Study of the Underground Economy in the Kingdom of Belgium," *International Journal of Business & Globalisation 11* (2), pp. 159–170.

Rezaei, Shahamak, Marco Goli, and Léo-Paul Dana (2013b), "Informal Opportunity among SMEs: an Empirical Study of Denmark's Underground Economy," *International Journal of Entrepreneurship and Small Business 19* (1), May, pp. 64–76.

Rezaei, Shahamak, Marco Goli, and Léo-Paul Dana (2014), "Beyond Legal Entrepreneurship: The Case of Austria," *International Journal of Entrepreneurship and Small Business 21* (2), February, pp. 202–215.

Ribéreau-Gayon, Pascal (2000), "Preface," in Pascal Ribéreau-Gayon, Denis Dubourdieu, Bernard Donèche, and Aline Lonvaud, *Handbook of Enology: The Microbiology of Wine and Vinifications*, Chicester: John Wiley & Sons.

Ribéreau-Gayon, Pascal, Denis Dubourdieu, Bernard Donèche, and Aline Lonvaud (2000), *Handbook of Enology: The Microbiology of Wine and Vinifications*, Chicester: John Wiley & Sons.

Rice, William Gorham (1925), "The Singing Towers of Holland and Belgium," *National Geographic 47* (3), March, pp. 357–376.

Rigtering, J. P. Coen, Sascha Kraus, Fabian Eggers, and Søren Henning Jensen (2014), "A Comparative Analysis of the Entrepreneurial Orientation/Growth Relationship in Service Firms and Manufacturing Firms," *The Service Industries Journal 34* (4), pp. 275–294.

Ring, Peter Smith, Gregory A. Bigley, Thomas D'Aunno, and Tarun Khanna (2005), "Perspectives on *How* Governments Matter," *Academy of Management Review 30* (2), April, pp. 308–320.

Riseth, Jan Åge (2003), "Sami Reindeer Management in Norway: Modernization Challenges and Conflicting Strategies. Reflections Upon the Co-management Alternative," in Svein Jentoft, Henry Minde, and Ragnar Nilsen, Eds., *Indigenous Peoples: Resource Management and Global Rights*, Delft, The Netherlands: Eburon Academic, pp. 229–247.

Rocha, Hector O. (2004), "Entrepreneurship and Development: The Role of Clusters. A Literature Review," *Small Business Economics 23* (5), pp. 363–400.

Rocha, Hector O., and Rolf Sternberg (2005), "Entrepreneurship: The Role of Clusters. Theoretical Perspectives and Empirical Evidence from Germany," *Small Business Economics 24* (3), pp. 267–292.

Roggeveen, Suzanne, and Masja van Meeteren (2013), "Beyond Community: An Analysis of Social Capital and the Social Networks of Brazilian Migrants in Amsterdam," *Current Sociology 61* (7), pp. 1078–1096.

Rosa, Peter, Sara Carter, and Daphne Hamilton (1996), "Gender as a Determinant of Small Business Performance: Insights from a British Study," *Small Business Economics 8* (6), pp. 463–478.

Rose, John Holland (1902), *The Life of Napoleon I including New Materials from the British Official Records,* London: George Bell and Sons.

Rotefoss, Beate, and Lars Kolvereid (2005), "Aspiring, Nascent and Fledging Entrepreneurs: An Investigation of the Business Start-up Process," *Entrepreneurship and Regional Development 17* (2), pp. 109–127.

Routamaa, Vesa, and Katri Mäki-Tarkka (2005), "The Case of Finland," in Anders Lundström, Ed., *Creating Opportunities for Young Entrepreneurship: Nordic Examples and Experiences,* Örebro: Swedish Foundation for Small Business Research, pp. 113–175.

Ruong, Israel (1937), *Geographica: Fjällapparna I Jukkasjärvi Socken,* Uppsala, Sweden: Appelbergs Boktryckeriaktiebolag.

Ruong, Israel (1956), "Types of Settlement and Types of Husbandry among the Lapps in Northern Sweden," *Studia Ethnographica Upsaliensia 2*, pp. 105–132.

Ruong, Israel (1967), *The Lapps in Sweden*, translated by Alan Blair, Stockholm: The Swedish Institute for Cultural Relations with Foreign Countries.

Sanford, George Allan (1929), "A Vacation in Holland," *National Geographic 56* (3), September, pp. 363–378.

Santayana, George (1905), *The Life of Reason,* New York: Charles Scribner's Sons.

Santini, Cristina, Samuel Rabino, and Lorenzo Zanni (2011), "Chinese Immigrants Socio-economic Enclave in an Italian Industrial District: The Case of Prato," *World Review of Entrepreneurship, Management and Sustainable Development 7* (1), pp. 30–51.

Savitt, Ronald (1998), "This Thing I Call Europe," *International Marketing Review 15* (6), pp. 444–447.

Say, Jean-Baptiste (1803), *Traite d'Economie Politique ou Simple Exposition de la Manière dont se Forment, se Distribuent, et se Consomment les Richesses*; revised (1819); translated (1830) by C. R. Prinsep, *A Treatise on Political Economy: On Familiar Conversations on the Manner in Which Wealth is Produced, Distributed and Consumed by Society*, Philadelphia: John Grigg & Elliot.

Say, Jean-Baptiste (1816), *Catechism of Political Economy: Or, Familiar Conversations of the Manner in Which Wealth is Produced, Distributed, and Consumed by Society*, London: Sherwood.

Scalero, Italo (2011), *I Grandi Imprenditori del XIX Secolo: Centocinquant'anni di Storia di Italia di Scoperte, di Invenzioni, di Impresa, di Lavoro,* Seggiano di Pioltello, Italy: Casa Editrice Dott. Antonio Milani (CEDAM).

Scase, Richard (1980), *The State in Western Europe*, London: Croom Helm.

Scase, Richard, and Robert Goffee (1987), *The Real World of the Small Business Owner*, London: Croom Helm.

Schäfer, Henry, and Rüdiger Goldschmidt (2010), "Corporate Social Responsibility of Large Family-owned Companies in Germany," *International Journal of Entrepreneurship and Small Business 11* (3), pp. 285–307.

Scheinberg, Sari, and Ian C. MacMillan (1988), "An 11 Country Study of Motivations to Start a Business," *Frontiers of Entrepreneurship Research*, Wellesley, Massachusetts: Babson College, pp. 669–687.

Schinzel, Ursula (2013), "Why Are People in Luxembourg Happy? An Exploratory Study of Happiness and Culture Measured by the Dimension of a Language as Identifier in the Grand Duchy," *Journal of Customer Behaviour 12* (3), pp. 315–340.

Schinzel, Ursula (2016), "Impact of National Culture on e-Recruitment Practices in Luxembourg," *World Review of Entrepreneurship, Management and Sustainable Development 12* (2–3), pp. 318–336.

Schinzel, Ursula (in press), "Three Official Languages in Multicultural Luxembourg," *World Review of Entrepreneurship, Management and Sustainable Development.*

Schmalzer, Thomas, Rene Wenzel, Lisa Mahajan, and Eva Penz (2015), *Global Entrepreneurship Monitor 2014: Bericht zur Lage des Unter nehmertums in Österreich*, Graz: FH Joanneum University of Applied Sciences.

Schmidt, Karl-Heinz (1992), *Internationalization, Subcontracting and Firm-Size*, Paderborn: Universität — Gesamthochschule Paderborn.

Schmidt, Karl-Heinz (1999), *State and Industrialization during the 19th Century*, Paderborn: Universität Paderborn, Fachbereich Wirtschaftswißenschaftn.

Schmude, Jürgen, Friederike Welter, and Stefan Heumann (2008), "Entrepreneurship Research in Germany," *Entrepreneurship: Theory & Practice 32* (2), pp. 289–311.

Schot, Johan W. (1998), "The Usefulness of Evolutionary Models for Explaining Innovation: The Case of the Netherlands in the Nineteenth Century," *History and Technology 14*, pp. 173–200.

Schuessler, Felix, Michael T. Schaper, and Sascha Kraus (2014), "Entrepreneurship in an Alpine Micro-nation: The Case of Liechtenstein," *International Journal of Entrepreneurship and Small Business 22* (1), pp. 106–114.

Schumpeter, Joseph A. (1912), *Theorie der wirtschaftlichen Entwicklung*, Munich and Leipzig: Dunker und Humblat.

Schumpeter, Joseph A. (1934), *The Theory of Economic Development: An Inquiry into Profits, Capital, Credit, Interest, and the Business Cycle*, translated by Redvers Opie, Cambridge, Massachusetts: Harvard University Press.

Schwarz, Erich J., and Eva Grieshuber (2003), *Vom Gründungs- zum Jungunternehmen*, Vienna and New York: Springer.

Schøtt, Thomas (2010a), *Social and Commercial Entrepreneurship in Denmark 2009*, Odense, Denmark: University of Southern Denmark.

Schøtt, Thomas (2010b), *Training and Network Organization in Entrepreneurship in Denmark 2010 — studied via Global Entrepreneurship Monitor*, Kolding, Denmark: University of Southern Denmark.

Scofield, John (1969), "The Friendly Irish," *National Geographic 136* (3), September, pp. 354–391.

Sear, Leigh, and Robert T. Hamilton (2004), "Business Support for Internationalization in England," in Léo-Paul Dana, Ed., *The Handbook of Research on International Entrepreneurship*, Cheltenham, United Kingdom: Edward Elgar, pp. 352–369.

Segarra, Pere, Eleni Papaoikonomou, and Xiaoni Li (2012), "The Entrepreneurial Experience of Small and Medium Sized Firms in Times of Crisis: Empirical Evidence from Catalonia, Spain," in Jean Bonnet, Marcud Dejardin and Antonia Madrid-Guijarro, Eds., *The Shift to the Entrepreneurial Society*, Cheltenham, United Kingdom: Edward Elgar, pp. 198–210.

Selin, Håkan (2009), "The Rise in Female Employment and the Role of Tax Incentives: An Empirical Analysis of the Swedish Individual Tax Reform of 1971," Working paper 2009:4, Uppsala: Department of Economics, Uppsala University.

Séraphin, Hughes (2016), "Northern and Western Europe" in Wayne Visser, Ed., *The World Guide to Sustainable Enterprise, Volume 3 Europe*, Sheffield, United Kingdom: Greenleaf, pp. 13–22.

Séraphin, Hugues, Anja Stoll and Jean-Christophe Carteron (2016), "France," in Wayne Visser, Ed., *The World Guide to Sustainable Enterprise, Volume 3 Europe*, Sheffield, United Kingdom: Greenleaf, pp. 92–98.

Servais, Per, Erik S. Rasmussen, Bo B. Nielsen, and Tage Koed Madsen (2008), "Internationalization of Danish SMEs," in Léo-Paul Dana, Isabell M. Welpe, Mary Han, and Vanessa Ratten, Eds., *Handbook of Research on European Business and Entrepreneurship: Towards a Theory of Internationalization*, Cheltenham, United Kingdom: Edward Elgar, pp. 171–184.

Severy, Merle (1989), "The Great Revolution," *National Geographic 176* (1), July, pp. 18–49.

Shaboian, Selena Lucien, and Michael Motala (2016), "Germany," in Wayne Vissser, ed., *The World Guide to Sustainable Enterprise, Volume 3 Europe*, Sheffield, United Kingdom: Greenleaf, pp. 105–111.

Shakespeare, William (1637), *The Most Excellent Historie of the Merchant of Venice*, London: Laurence Hayes.

Sheats, Dorothea (1951), "I Walked Some Irish Miles," *National Geographic 99* (5), May, pp. 653–678.

Shor, Franc (1968), "Lombardy's Lakes, Blue Jewels in Italy's Crown," *National Geographic 134* (1), July, pp. 58–99.

Shor, Jean, and Franc Shor (1954), "North with Finland's Lapps," *National Geographic 106* (2), August, pp. 249–280.

Shor, Jean, and Franc Shor (1955), "Spain's 'Fortunate Isles,' the Canaries," *National Geographic 107* (4), April, pp. 485–522.

Silva, Ana Paula, and Graham Hall (2005), "Influences on the Growth of Portuguese SMEs," in Alain Fayolle, Paula Kyrö, and Jan Ulijn, Eds., *Entrepreneurship Research in Europe,* Cheltenham, United Kingdom: Edward Elgar, pp. 331–350.

Silva, Maria José, and João Leitão (2009), "Cooperation in Innovation Practices among Firms in Portugal: Do External Partners Stimulate Innovative Advances?" *International Journal of Entrepreneurship and Small Business 7* (4), pp. 391–403.

Simões, Vitor Corado (2004), *Annual Innovation Policy for Portugal,* Brussels: European Commission, Enterprise Directorate-General.

Simpich, Frederick (1945), "Paris Freed," *National Geographic 87* (4), pp. 385–400.

Smallbone, David (2016), "Entrepreneurship Policy: Issues and Challenges," invited paper at Rencontres de Saint-Gall, August.

Smallbone, David, John Kitching, and Rosemary Athayde (2010), "Ethnic Diversity, Entrepreneurship and Competitiveness in a Global City," *International Small Business Journal 28* (2), pp. 174–190.

Smallbone, David, Monder Ram and David Deakins (2007), "Access to Finance by Ethnic Minority Entrepreneurs in the UK," in Léo-Paul Dana, Ed., *Handbook of Research on Ethnic Minority Entrepreneurship: A Co-evolutionary View on Resource Management,* Cheltenham, United Kingdom: Edward Elgar, pp. 390–404.

Smiles, Samuel (1860), *The Story of the Life of George Stephenson, Railway Engineer,* London: John Murray.

Smiley, Xan (2001), "A Survey of Italy," insert in *The Economist*, July 7.

Smith, Robert, and Gerard McElwee (2013), "Confronting Social Constructions of Rural Criminality: A Case Story on 'Illegal Pluriactivity' in the Farming Community," *Sociologia Ruralis 53* (1), pp. 112–134.

Sombart, Werner (1913), *The Jews and Modern Capitalism,* translated by M. Epstein, London and Leipsic: T. Fisher Unwin.

Sombart, Werner (1922), *Der moderne Kapitalismus: Historisch-systematische Darstellung des gesamteuropäischen Wirtschaftslebens von seinen Anfängen bis zur Gegenwart,* Munich and Leipsic: Duncker & Humblot.

Soulier, André (1993), *Le Languedoc Pour Heritage: les paysages du Bas-Langudoc de la fin de l'Ancien Régime aux années 1930*, Montpellier: Les Presses du Languedoc.

Span, Tommy, André van Stel and Roy van den Berg (2015), *Global Entrepreneurship Monitor: The Netherlands 2014,* Zoetermeer: Panteia.

Spence, Martine (2008), "Monaco's Forgotten Glitter: Industrial SMEs and Their Worldwide Appeal," in Léo-Paul Dana, Isabell M. Welpe, Mary Han, and Vanessa Ratten, Eds., *Handbook of Research on European Business and Entrepreneurship: Towards a Theory of Internationalization*, Cheltenham, United Kingdom: Edward Elgar, pp. 478–493.

Spencer, Jennifer W., Thomas P. Murtha, and Stefanie Ann Lenway (2005), "How Governments Matter to New Venture Creation," *Academy of Management Review 30* (2), April, pp. 321–337.

Spilling, Olav R. (1998), "On the Re-Emergence of Small Scale Production: The Norwegian Case in International Comparison," *Small Business Economics 10* (4), pp. 401–417.

Spilling, Olav R., and Nina Gunnerud Berg (2000), "Gender and Small Business Management: The Case of Norway in the 1990s," *International Small Business Journal 18* (2), pp. 38–59.

Spooner, W. C. (1874), *The History, Structure, Economy and Diseases of the Sheep,* 3rd edition, London: Lockwood & Co.

Staley, Eugene, and Richard Morse (1971), "Developing Entrepreneurship: Elements for a Program," in Peter Kilby, Ed., *Entrepreneurship and Economic Development,* New York: Free Press, pp. 374–384.

Stamp, L. Dudley (1939), *A Commercial Geography*, London: Longmans, Green and Co.

Stenholm, Pekka, Tommi Pukkinen, Jarna Heinonen, and Anne Kovalainen (2009), *Global Entrepreneurship Monitor: Finnish 2008 Report,* Turku: Turku School of Economics.

Stenholm, Pekka, Sanna Suomalainen, Anne Kovalainen, Jarna Heinonen, and Tommi Pukkinen (2015), *Global Entrepreneurship Monitor Finnish 2014 Report*, Turku: University of Turku.

Sternberg, Rolf (2003), "Das Konzept endogener Regionalentwicklung — Implikationen für Existenzgründungen und deren Förderung," in Rolf Sternberg, Ed., *Endogene Regionalentwicklung durch Existenzgründungen? Empirische Befunde aus Nordrhein-Westfalen,* Hannover: Akademie für Raumforschung und Landesplanung.

Sternberg, Rolf (2005), "Entrepreneurship in German Regions and the Policy Dimension," in David. B. Audretsch, Heike Grimm, and Charles W. Wessner, Eds., *Local Heroes in the Global Village,* New York: Springer, pp. 113–144.

Sternberg, Rolf, Heiko Bergmann, and Christine Tamásy (2001), *Global Entrepreneurship Monitor: Länderbericht Deutschland,* Cologne: Universität zu Köln.

Sternberg, Rolf, and Ingo Lückgen (2005), *Global Entrepreneurship Monitor (GEM). Länderbericht Deutschland 2004.* Cologne: Wirtschafts-und Sozialgeographisches Institut, Universität zu Köln.

Sternberg, Rolf, Claus Otten, and Christine Tamásy (2000), *Global Entrepreneurship Monitor: Germany 2000 Country Report,* Cologne: Universität zu Köln.

Sternberg, Rolf, Arne Vorderwülbecke, and Udo Brixy (2015), *Global Entrepreneurship Monitor Unternehmensgründungen im weltweiten Vergleich: Länderbericht Deutschland 2014,* Hannover: Global Entrepreneurship Research Association.

Sternberg, Rolf, and Joachim Wagner (2004), "The Decision to Start a New Firm: Personal and Regional Determinants: Empirical Evidence from the Regional Entrepreneurship Monitor (REM) Germany," in Michael Fritsch, and Michael Niese, Eds., *Gründungsprozess und Gründungserfolg: Interdisziplinäre Beiträge zum Entrepreneurship Research*, Heidelberg: Physica, pp. 19–38.

Storey, David (1994), *Understanding the Small Business Sector,* London: Routledge.

Strinati, Dominic (1982), *Capitalism: The State and Industrial Relations*, London: Croom Helm.

Stuetzer, Michael Martin Obschonka, Udo Brixy, Rolf Sternberg, and Uwe Cantner (2014), "Regional Characteristics, Opportunity Perception and Entrepreneurial Activities," *Small Business Economics 42* (2), pp. 221–244.

Suárez-Ortega, Sonia (2003), "Export Barriers: Insights from Small and Medium-sized Firms," *International Small Business Journal 21* (4), pp. 403–419.

Suárez-Villa, Luis, and Ruth Rama (1996), "Outsourcing, R&D and the Pattern of Intra-Metropolitan Location: The Electronics Industries of Madrid," *Urban Studies 33* (1), pp. 155–197.

Supple, Barry (1983), "States and Industrialization: Britain and Germany in the Nineteenth Century," in David Held *et al.*, Eds., *States and Societies,* Oxford: Martin Robertson, pp. 170–180.

Susiluoto, Klaus (2003), "The City of Oulu — A Quantum Leap into the Future," *Nordicum Scandinavian Business Magazine 2*, pp. 6–7.

Szyperski, Norbert, and Heinz Klandt (1981), "The Empirical Research on Entrepreneurship in the Federal Republic of Germany," in Karl H. Vesper, Ed., *Frontiers of Entrepreneurship Research,* Wellesley, Massachusetts: Babson Center for Entrepreneurial Studies, pp. 158–178.

Terjesen, Siri, and Ainsley Lloyd (2015), *The 2015 Female Entrepreneurship Index: Analyzing the Conditions that Foster High-potential Female Entrepreneurship in 77 Countries*, Washington, DC: Global Entrepreneurship and Development Institute.

Terry, Schuyler Baldwin (1914), *The Financing of the Hundred Years' War, 1337–1360*, London: London School of Economics.

Testarmata, Silvia, and Alessia Montecchia (2016), "Switzerland," in Wayne Visser, Ed., *The World Guide to Sustainable Enterprise, Volume 3 Europe,* Sheffield, United Kingdom: Greenleaf, pp. 236–245.

Thierstein, Alain, and Beate Wilhem (2001), "Incubator, Technology, and Innovation Centres in Switzerland: Features and Policy Implications," *Entrepreneurship & Regional Development* 13, pp. 315–331.

Thomas, Cameron (1991), "Remembering the Blitz," *National Geographic 180* (1), pp. 60–77.

Thomas, Peter David Garner (1987), *The Townshend Duties Crisis: The Second Phase of the American Revolution, 1767–1773,* Oxford: Clarendon.

Thompson, Faith (1948), Magna *Carta: Its Role in the Making of the English Constitution, 1300–1629,* Minneapolis: University of Minnesota Press.

Tillman, Anne-Marie, and Sara Palander (2016), "Sweden," in Wayne Visser, Ed., *The World Guide to Sustainable Enterprise, Volume 3 Europe,* Sheffield, United Kingdom: Greenleaf, pp. 230–235.

Tomel, Guy (1894), *Le Bas du Pavé Parisien,* Paris: G. Charpentier & E. Fasquelle.

Thurik, Roy (1993), "Exports and Small Business in the Netherlands: Presence, Potential and Performance," *Small Business Economics 11* (3), pp. 49–58.

Tudisca, Salvatore, Anna Maria Di Trapani, Enrica Donia, Filippo Sgroi, and Riccardo Testa (2014), "Entrepreneurial Strategies of Etna Wine Farms," *International Journal of Entrepreneurship and Small Business 21* (2), pp. 155–164.

Tudisca, Salvatore, Filippo Sgroi, and Riccardo Testa (2011), "Competitiveness and Sustainability of Extreme Viticulture in Pantelleria Island," *New Medit 10* (4), pp. 57–64.

Turi, Johan Mathis (2002), "The World Reindeer Livelihood — Current Situation, Threats and Possibilities," in Sakari Kankaanpää, Ludger Müller-Wille, Paulo Susiluoto, and Marja-Liisa Sutinen, Eds., *Northern Timberline Forests: Environmental and Socio-economic Issues and Concerns,* Kolari, Finland: The Finnish Forest Research Institute, pp. 70–75.

Tytler, Patrick Fraser (1853), *Life of Sir Walter Raleigh Founded on Authentic and Original Documents*, London & Edinburgh: T. Nelson and Sons.

Ulijn, Jan, and Terrence E. Brown (2004), "Innovation, Entrepreneurship and Culture, a Matter of Interaction between Technology, Process and Economic Growth? An Introduction," in Terence E. Brown, and Jan Ulijn, Eds., *Innovation, Entrepreneurship and Culture: The Interaction between Technology, Progress and Economic Growth,* Cheltenham, United Kingdom: Edward Elgar, pp. 1–38.

Ulijn, Jan, and Alain Fayolle (2004), "Towards Cooperation between European Start-ups: The Position of the French, German, and Dutch Entrepreneurial and Innovative Engineer," in Terence E. Brown, and Jan Ulijn, Eds., *Innovation, Entrepreneurship and Culture: The Interaction between Technology, Progress and Economic Growth,* Cheltenham, United Kingdom: Edward Elgar, pp. 204–232.

Ulijn, Jan, and Hans J. M. G. Heerkens (1999), "The Death of an Innovative Firm Fokker: Were There Cultural Reasons?" *Journal of Enterprising Culture 7* (3), pp. 269–298.

Ulijn, Jan, Arie P. Nagel, and Wee Liang Tan (2001), "The Impact of National, Corporate and Professional Cultures on Innovation: German and Dutch Firms Compared," *Journal of Enterprising Culture 9* (1), pp. 21–52.

Underwood, Eric (1943), "The British Commonwealth of Nations: 'Organized Freedom' around the World," *National Geographic 83* (4), pp. 485–524.

Urbano, David, Nuria Toledano, and Domingo Ribeiro-Soriano (2011), "Socio-cultural Factors and Transnational Entrepreneurship: A Multiple Case Study in Spain," *International Small Business Journal 29* (2), pp. 119–134.

Van Auken, Howard E., and Domingo Garcia Perez de Lema (2003), "Financial Strategies of Spanish Firms: A Comparative Analysis by Size of Firm," *Journal of Small Business and Entrepreneurship 17* (1), Fall, pp. 17–30.

Van Gils, Anita, and Peter S. Zwart (2009), "Alliance Motives in SMEs: An Explorative Conjoint Analysis Study," *International Small Business Journal 27* (1), pp. 5–37.

Van Stel, André (2005), *Entrepreneurship and Economic Growth: Some Empirical Studies*, Rotterdam: Tinbergen Institute.

van Teeffelen, Lex, Lorraine Uhlaner, and Martijn Driessen (2011), "The Importance of Specific Human Capital, Planning and Familiarity in Dutch Small Firm Ownership Transfers: A Seller's Perspective," *International Journal of Entrepreneurship and Small Business 14* (1), pp. 127–148.

Vesilind, Priit J. (1983), "Hunters of the Lost Spirit," *National Geographic 163* (2), February, pp. 151–197.

Vestergaard, Jakob (2014), "Preface," in Charles Goodhart, Daniela Gabor, Jakob Vestergaard, and Ismail Erturk, Eds., *Central Banking at a Crossroads: Europe and Beyond*, London: Anthem Press, pp. vii–viii.

Vidal, Jean-Philippe (1995), "PME-Hypermarchés," *Libre-Service Actualités 16*, March, pp. 28–34.

Vignali, Claudio, Neil Robinson, and Gianpaolo Vignali (2010), "Italian Catholics of Lancashire and the Jewish Community of Yorkshire," in Léo-Paul Dana, Ed., *Entrepreneurship & Religion*, Cheltenham, United Kingdom: Edward Elgar, pp. 418–432.

Vikström, Anna, and Mats Westerberg (2010), "Success with Succession: An Empirical Study of Small Swedish Family Firms," *International Journal of Entrepreneurship and Small Business 11* (3), pp. 223–241.

Villiers, Alan (1954), "Golden Beaches of Portugal," *National Geographic 106* (5), November, pp. 673–696.

Villiers, Alan (1968), "The Netherlands: Nation at War With the Sea," *National Geographic 133* (4), April, pp. 530–571.

Vindt, Gérard (2012), "1954: L'Invention de la TVA," *Alternatives Economiques 312*, April, pp. 96–97.

Vogel, Ezra F. (1987), "Conclusion," in George Lodge and Ezra F. Vogel, Eds., *Ideology and National Competitiveness: An Analysis of Nine Countries*, Boston, Massachusetts: Harvard Business School Press, pp. 301–323.

Volery, Thierry (2008), "Managing the Challenges of Globalization: Evidence from Swiss Small and Medium-sized Enterprises," in Léo-Paul Dana, Isabell M. Welpe, Mary Han, and Vanessa Ratten, Eds., *Handbook of Research on European*

Business and Entrepreneurship: Towards a Theory of Internationalization, Cheltenham, United Kingdom: Edward Elgar, pp. 636–646.

Volery, Thierry, and Isabelle Servais (2001), *Global Entrepreneurship Monitor Rapport 2000 sur l'Entrepreneuriat en France*, Lyon: EM Lyon.

von Düben, Gustaf (1873), *Om Lappland och Lapparne, Företrädesvis de Svenske*, Stockholm: P. A. Norstedt & Söners Förlag.

Wagner, Joachim (2004), "Are Young and Small Firms Hothouses for Nascent Entrepreneurs? Evidence from German Micro Data," *Applied Economics Quarterly 50* (4), pp. 379–391.

Wagner, Joachim (2005), "Nascent Entrepreneurs: Institute for the Study of Labor IZA Discussion Paper 1293," in Simon C. Parker, Ed., *The Life Cycle of Entrepreneurial Ventures*, New York: Springer.

Wagner, Joachim, and Rolf Sternberg (2004), "Start-up Activities, Individual Characteristics, and the Regional Milieu: Lessons for Entrepreneurship Support Policies from German Micro Data," *The Annals of Regional Science 38*, pp. 219–240.

Wagner, Joachim, and Rolf Sternberg (2005), "Personal and Regional Determinants of Entrepreneurial Activities: Empirical Evidence from the Regional Entrepreneurship Monitor (REM)," *Jahrbuch für Regionalwissenschaft 25* (1), pp. 91–105.

Wahlbeck, Östen (2007), "Turkish Immigrant Entrepreneurs in Finland," in Léo-Paul Dana, Ed., *Handbook of Research on Ethnic Minority Entrepreneurship: A Co-evolutionary View on Resource Management*, Cheltenham, United Kingdom: Edward Elgar, pp. 433–444.

Walker, Harrison Howell (1940), "France Farms as War Wages: An American Explores the Rich Rural Region of the Historic Paris Basin," *National Geographic 77* (2), February, pp. 201–238.

Walker, Howell (1958), "Belgium Welcomes the World: Millions of Visitors to the 1958 World's Fair in Brussels See an Atomic-age Exposition in a Time-mellowed Land," *National Geographic 113* (6), June, pp. 795–838.

Walker, Howell (1963), "Italian Riviera, Land That Winter Forgot," *National Geographic 123* (6), June, pp. 743–790.

Walker, Howell (1965), "France Meets the Sea in Brittany: Headland of Europe, the Province of the Bretons Retains its Medieval Look, its Sea-washed Air, and its Misty Light as it Harnesses the Tides and Talks with Space," *National Geographic 127* (4), April, pp. 470–503.

Walsh, James S., and Philip H. Anderson (1995), "Owner-Manager Adaptation/Innovation Preference and Employment Performance: A Comparison of Founders and Non-Founders in the Irish Small Firm Sector," *Journal of Small Business Management 33* (3), July, pp. 1–8.

Wanzenböck, Herta (1998), *Überleben und Wachstum junger Unternehmen*, Vienna and New York: Springer.

Ward, Robin, and Richard Jenkins (1984), *Ethnic Communities in Business: Strategies for Economic Survival,* Cambridge: Cambridge University Press.

Weaver, K. Mark, David Berkowitz, and Les Davies (1998), "Increasing the Efficiency of National Export Development Programs: The Case of Norwegian Exporters" *Journal of Small Business Management 36* (4), pp. 1–11.

Weber, Max (1930), *The Protestant Ethic and the Spirit of Capitalism,* translated by Talcott Parsons, New York: Charles Scribner's Sons.

Weitensfelder, Hubert (2001), *Industrie-Provinz: Vorarlberg in der Frühindustrialisierung* 1740–1870, Frankfurt: Campus Verlag.

Welter, Friederike (2004), "The Environment for Female Entrepreneurship in Germany," *Journal of Small Business and Enterprise Development 11* (2), pp. 212–221.

Welter, Friederike (2006), "Women Entrepreneurship in Germany: Progress in a Still Traditional Environment," in Candida Brush, Nancy Carter, Elizabeth B. Gatewood, Patricia C. Greene, and Myra Hart, Eds., *Growth Oriented Women Entrepreneurs and Their Businesses,* Cheltenham, United Kingdom: Edward Elgar.

Welter, Friederike (2007), "Entrepreneurship in East and West Germany," *International Journal of Entrepreneurship and Small Business 4.*

Wennekers, Sander, and Roy Thurik (2001), "Institutions, Entrepreneurship and Economic Performance," in Anders Lundström and Lois Stevenson, Eds., *Entrepreneurship Policy for the Future,* Stockholm: Swedish Foundation for Small Business Research, pp. 51–87.

Werbner, Pnina (2007), "South Asian Entrepreneurship in Britain: A Critique of the Ethnic Enclave Economy Debate," in Léo-Paul Dana, Ed., *Handbook of Research on Ethnic Minority Entrepreneurship: A Co-evolutionary View on Resource Management,* Cheltenham, United Kingdom: Edward Elgar, pp. 375–389.

Westhead, Paul, and Sue Birley (1995), "Employment Growth in New Independent Owner-managed Firms in Great Britain," *International Small Business Journal 13* (3), pp. 11–34.

Westhead, Paul, Mike Wright, and Deniz Ucbasaran (2001), "The Internationalization of New and Small Firms: A Resource-Based View," *Journal of Business Venturing 16*, pp. 333–358.

Wexler, Mark (1979), "They've Got a Piece of the Rock," *International Wildlife 9* (3), pp. 20–25.

Wheeler, Colin, Kevin Ibeh, and Pavlos Dimitratos (2008), "UK Export Performance Research: Review and Implications," *International Small Business Journal 26* (2), pp. 207–237.

Whitaker, Ian (1955), *Social Relations in a Nomadic Lappish Community,* Oslo: Utgitt av Norsk Folkemuseum.

Wiessner, Frank (2001), *Arbeitslose werden Unternehmer*, Nürnberg: Institut für Arbeitsmarkt- und Berufsforschung.

Williams, Colin C. (2006), *The Hidden Enterprise Culture: Entrepreneurship in the Underground Economy,* Cheltenham, United Kingdom: Edward Elgar.

Williams, Colin C. (2011), "Entrepreneurship, the Informal Economy and Rural Communities," *Journal of Enterprising Communities: People and Places in the Global Economy 5* (2), pp. 145–157.

Williams, Colin C., Rositsa Dzhekova, Josip Franic, and Lyubo Mishkov (2015), "Evaluating the Policy Approach Towards the Undeclared Economy in FYR Macedonia," *International Journal of Entrepreneurship and Small Business 24* (2), pp. 268–286.

Williams, Maynard Owen (1924), "The Grand Duchy of Luxembourg," *National Geographic 46* (5), November, pp. 501–528.

Williams, Maynard Owen (1927), "Round about Liechtenstein," *National Geographic 52* (5), November, pp. 611–634.

Williams, Maynard Owen (1930), "Paris in the Spring," *National Geographic 70* (4), October, pp. 501–534.

Williams, Maynard Owen (1946), "Paris Lives Again," *National Geographic 150* (6), December, pp. 767–790.

Williamson, Hugh (2004), "Subtle Divisions that Mark a Reunited City," *Financial Times,* Thursday, September 23, p. 11.

Willoweit, Dietmar (1987), *Liechtenstein — fürstliches Haus und Staatliche Ordnung: Geschichtliche Grundlagen und moderne Perspektiven*, Vaduz: Liechtensteinische Akademische Gesellschaft.

Wilpert, Czarina (2003), "Germany: From Workers to Entrepreneurs," in Robert Kloosterman and Jan Rath, Eds., *Immigrant Entrepreneurs: Venturing Abroad in the Age of Globalization,* Oxford: Berg, pp. 233–260.

Windebank, Jan (1991), *The Informal Economy in France,* Aldershot, United Kingdom: Avebury.

Wirtschaftskammern Österreichs (2003), *Zahlen, Daten, Fakten. Wirtschaftsgrafik 2003. Ein statistischer Rückblick* (Numbers, Data, Facts, Economic Graphic 2003: A statistical review), Vienna: Austrian Federal Economic Chamber.

Wirtschaftskammern Österreichs (2004), *Statistisches Jahrbuch 2004*, Vienna: Austrian Federal Economic Chamber.

Wirtschaftskammer Österreich (2005), "Unternehmensneugründungen in Österreich 1993–2004," accessed November 15, 2010 from: http://wko.at/statistik/Extranet/Neugr/ng2004v-gesamt.pdf.

Wolf, Patricia, Stephanie Kaudela-Baum, and Jens O. Meissner (2012), "Exploring Innovating Cultures in Small and Medium-sized Enterprises: Findings from Central Switzerland," *International Small Business Journal 30* (3), pp. 242–274.

Wolf-Knuts, Ulrika (2001), "The Finland Swedes: A Compensating Minority," paper presented at Migration, Minorities, Compensation: Issues of Cultural Identity in Europe conference, Certosa di Pontigniano, March, pp. 143–152.

World Bank (2015), *The Little Data Book,* Washington, DC: World Bank.

Worrall, Simon (2000), "London on a Roll," *National Geographic 197* (6), pp. 2–23.

Wright, Richard W., and Léo-Paul Dana (2003), "Changing Paradigms of International Entrepreneurship Strategy," *Journal of International Entrepreneurship 1* (1), pp. 135–152. Reprinted in Benjamin M. Oviatt and Patricia Phillips McDougall, Eds., *International Entrepreneurship,* Cheltenham, UK: Edward Elgar, 2007, pp. 131–148.

Wrightson, John (1905), *Sheep: Breeds and Management,* 5th edition, London: Vinton & Company.

Wyrwich, Michael, Michael Stuetzer and Rolf Sternberg (2016), "Entrepreneurial Role Models, Fear of Failure, and Institutional Approval of Entrepreneurship: A Tale of Two Regions," *Small Business Economics 46* (3), pp. 467–492.

Youatt, William (1866), *Sheep, Their Breeds, Management, and Diseases,* London: Simpkin, Marshall and Co.

Young, David (2013), *Growing Your Business: A Report on Growing Micro Businesses,* London: The National Archives.

Young, Gordon (1978), "Norway's Strategic Arctic Islands," *National Geographic 154* (2), August, pp. 267–283.

Zaharia, Rodica Milena, Dragos Tuta-Mihaylov, Alexandru Ardelean, and Ileana Magureanu (2016), "Eastern and Southern Europe," in Wayne Visser, Ed., *The World Guide to Sustainable Enterprise, Volume 3 Europe,* Sheffield, United Kingdom: Greenleaf, pp. 2–12.

Zwingle, Erla (1991), "Docklands: London's New Frontier," *National Geographic 180* (1), pp. 32–59.

Zwingle, Erla (1995), "Venice: More Than a Dream," *National Geographic 187* (2), February, pp. 73–99.

Index